# Next Generation Technologies for Sustainable Development

The *Proceedings of the International Conference on Next Generation Technologies for Sustainable Development (ICNGT-2025)* highlight cutting-edge research and innovative practices aimed at building a sustainable and resilient future. Organized by SVKM's NMIMS Deemed-to-be University, Shirpur Campus, the conference brought together global experts, scholars, and industry leaders to share knowledge across eight interdisciplinary tracks. The discussions spanned pharmaceutical sciences and healthcare technologies, sustainable water management and clean energy, advanced textile innovations, smart agricultural practices, engineering solutions for sustainability, and transformative digital technologies in education and society. This volume reflects the spirit of collaboration and innovation that defined ICNGT-2025, offering insights into how science, technology, and policy can work together to address pressing global challenges. It serves as a valuable reference for researchers, academicians, and practitioners committed to creating impactful solutions that balance progress with responsibility, ensuring sustainability for generations to come.

**Dr. Sunita R. Patil** is the Director of SVKM's NMIMS University, Shirpur Campus. A dynamic academic leader with a strong background in Engineering and institutional development, she has played a pivotal role in fostering research, innovation, and academic excellence. Her leadership emphasizes interdisciplinary collaboration and sustainable campus development.

**Dr. Shyam S. Pancholi** is Associate Dean at the School of Pharmacy and Technology Management, SVKM's NMIMS, Shirpur. With extensive experience in academic leadership, pharmaceutical education, and research, he has guided numerous scholarly initiatives. His interests include pharmaceutical technology, regulatory affairs, and academic innovation in pharmacy curriculum and skill development.

**Dr. G. L. Gupta** is Professor of Pharmacology at SVKM's NMIMS, Shirpur. With 19+ years of experience, he specializes in neuropharmacology and CNS disorders. A prolific researcher, he has authored numerous publications, guided Ph.D. scholars, secured national grants, and presented internationally. His work focuses on herbal therapeutics and CNS drug discovery.

**Dr. Preeti C. Sangave** is Associate Professor at School of Pharmacy & Technology Management Shirpur, SVKMs NMIMS Deemed-to-be University, Shirpur, with over 18 years of Research and Teaching experience. She has published her work in peer-reviewed journals of repute, guided Ph.D. scholars and presented at national & international conferences. Research interests include fermentation technology, nanotechnology, biomolecules.

# Next Generation Technologies for Sustainable Development

*Edited by*

**Sunita R. Patil**
[ORCID number: 0000-0003-1380-3331]

**Shyam S. Pancholi**
[ORCID number: 0000-0002-5718-706X]

**Girdhari Lal Gupta**
[ORCID number: 0000-0003-3282-7849]

**Preeti C. Sangave**
[ORCID number:0000-0002-5309-3365]

**CRC Press**
Taylor & Francis Group
Boca Raton London New York

CRC Press is an imprint of the
Taylor & Francis Group, an **informa** business

First edition published 2026
by CRC Press
4 Park Square, Milton Park, Abingdon, Oxon, OX14 4RN

and by CRC Press
2385 NW Executive Center Drive, Suite 320, Boca Raton FL 33431

CRC Press is an imprint of Informa UK Limited

*British Library Cataloguing-in-Publication Data*
A catalogue record for this book is available from the British Library

ISBN: 9781041204701 (pbk)
ISBN: 9781041204671 (hbk)
ISBN: 9781003716648 (ebk)

DOI: 10.1201/9781003716648

Typeset in Times New Roman
by HBK Digital

# Contents

# List of Figures

# List of Tables

# Preface

It is with great pride and academic enthusiasm, we present the Proceedings of the International Conference on Next Generation Technologies for Sustainable Development (ICNGT-2025), hosted by SVKM's NMIMS Deemed to be University, Shirpur Campus in March 2025. This international gathering provided a multidisciplinary platform for academicians, researchers, technocrats, and industry professionals to share their cutting-edge research, innovations, and insights in the domain of sustainable development. The conference was organized by the leadership team of Shirpur campus, Dr. Sunita R. Patil, Director of NMIMS Shirpur Campus, and Chairperson & Editor for conference proceedings, Dr. Shyam S. Pancholi, Associate Dean, SPTM and Convener & Co-Editor, Dr. G. L. Gupta, Dr. Preeti Sangave, Coordinators and Associate Editors and team of Shirpur campus, ensuring the creation of a dynamic platform that promoted interdisciplinary collaboration and meaningful dialogue on critical themes of sustainable development, with the meticulous management of the review process and demonstrating a strong commitment, upholding academic integrity throughout.

**Dr. Sunita R. Patil**
Chairperson & Editor
Director, SVKM's NMIMS Shirpur
Campus

**Dr. Shyam S. Pancholi**
Convener & Co-Editor
Associate Dean, SPTM, NMIMS
Shirpur

**Dr. G. L. Gupta**
Coordinator & Associate Editor
Professor, SPTM, NMIMS Shirpur

**Dr. Preeti C. Sangave**
Coordinator & Associate Editor
Associate Professor, SPTM, NMIMS
Shirpur

# 1 Nanoparticle-based interventions for dysbiosis prevention and colorectal cancer management

*Sankha Bhattacharya[a] and Preeti C. Sangave[b]*

School of Pharmacy and Technology Management, SVKM'S NMIMS Deemed-to-be University, Shirpur, Maharashtra, India

## Abstract

One of the major etiologic factors is dysbiosis, an imbalance in gut microbiota. In the world health perspective, and colorectal cancer (CRC) remains a grave concern. The exceptional targeting, microbiome adjustment, and precise delivery of therapeutic drugs that NPs have made them an attractive tool for improving CRC management and addressing dysbiosis. It has been shown in preclinical studies to encapsulate probiotics, modulate the immune system, and target antibiotics. These new developments may decrease inflammation from dysbiosis by up to 90%. The concept of multi-functional therapeutics development evolves with the introduction of stimuli-responsive nanoparticles and bioengineered nanoparticles. Restoration of microbial balance and targeted therapeutics will potentially revolutionize CRC prevention and therapy based on nanoparticle-based approaches. However, more work would be needed to overcome some of the restrictions that this will continue to put on clinical scalable applications. The future utilization of CRC care in safety and access will be what makes these cutting-edge nanotechnologies.

**Keywords:** Bioengineered nanoparticles, colorectal cancer, dysbiosis, gut microbiota, nanoparticle therapeutics, targeted drug delivery

## Introduction

Colorectal cancer (CRC) is among the most common causes of health disorders worldwide and also one of the top causes of cancer-related deaths. In 2020, there were about 1.9 million new cases and 935,000 deaths related to CRC [10]. Success so far of modern screening and therapy modalities has hence improved patient outcome, while the incidence rates and in particular the mortality are yet rising significantly. Indeed, with increasing evidence, gut microbiota, a dynamic polymicrobial system of microorganisms residing within the human intestinal tract, is found playing an important role in the genesis of CRC [1]. The imbalanced condition of diversed gut microbiota has been considered among the pathways to onset CRC like inflammation, oxidative stress, carcinogenic metabolite, and many more which have been described so there is a necessity of getting knowledge regarding complex relation to be built by researcher to health care professional with appropriate approach for the prevention and lowering risk of development of this disease. Figure 1.1a [13].

## Mechanisms of action of nanoparticles in dysbiosis prevention

Nanoparticles (NPs) offer new avenues to dysbiosis, the significant imbalance of gut microbiota, often associated with the development of CRC. Among them is the potential to design

[a]sankhabhatt@gmail.com, [b]preeti.sangave@nmims.edu

DOI: 10.1201/9781003716648-1

their size, surface chemistry, and biocompatibility for targeted therapies. An important one is the delivery of antibiotics and antimicrobials, through which NPs increase the drug absorption and decrease the side effects by administering drugs to those sites where they are actually needed in the gut. For example, polymeric nanoparticles have targeted antibiotics to the pathogenic bacteria, thereby lessening the harmful effect on the beneficial microbes. Apart from their antimicrobial action, NPs modulate immune responses that have excellent potential to reduce inflammation-linked carcinogenesis in CRC. Immunomodulator or anti-inflammatory drug-loaded NPs can target immune cells within GALT. Some NPs, such as metallic silver and zinc oxide nanoparticles, inherently have antimicrobial action and also disrupt microbial membranes and thus may further help in recovering the dysbiosis [5], It has been shown that these components increase the efficiency of regulatory T cells while reducing the levels of pro-inflammatory cytokines. Moreover, liposomal nanoparticles loaded with curcumin or dexamethasone have been shown to break immune pathways, thus making it easy for anti-inflammatory healing and the reconstitution of mucosal lining. The latest innovation is encapsulating prebiotics and probiotics in nanoparticles, thus making them more stable and potent. It helps encapsulate these advantageous agents that protects them from any deterioration in the gut with hostile intestinal conditions and permits it to have a controlled release into its area of colonization within the gut. Nanoparticles coming from an alginate or chitosan-based probiotics mixture improved dramatically the composition of the gut microbiota, whereas nanoparticle formulations based on either alginate or chitosan reversed CRC-associated dysbiosis. Likewise, nanoparticles loaded with prebiotics, such as inulin or oligosaccharides, encourage the growth of beneficial microbes, promoting a balanced microbial ecosystem [4]. These strategies aim at rejuvenating microbial homeostasis for preventing dysbiosis that triggers CRC. The nanoparticle can indirectly hamper the progression of CRC through restoration of healthy gut microbiota. Recent studies published as preclinical research have been proved that nanoparticles carrying both combinations of antimicrobials, probiotics, and immune modulators produced synergistic effects, providing an excellent balance in the microbiota level along with a significant decline in inflammatory markers over an extended period. Despite these advances, much is still to be done: optimization of stability in nanoparticles, accuracy of targeting, and toxicity are among the issues that have not yet been addressed. Adaptability, however, is another excellent feature that promises the integration of nanoparticles into holistic therapeutic strategies for further prevention of dysbiosis and treatment of CRC.

**Applications of nanoparticles in CRC treatment:** Nanoparticles or NPs are the novel entities toward treating CRC as such, supplying multifunctional targets through which desired treatments of chemotherapy happen along with the preventive methods against dysbiosis besides all the applications cut-off at bioengineering terms through which treatment results have had improvements. Chemotherapy deliveries were somehow freed from systemic toxicities and shortages of their bioavailability since one major application of the particles was found Figure 1.1b. For instance, clinically approved formulations such as Doxil® (doxorubicin liposomes) for cancer therapy are now being explored for CRC because these liposomal formulations can directly deliver drugs to the tumour sites through EPR effects [7]. Moreover, polymeric nanoparticles like paclitaxel-loaded poly (lactic-co-glycolic acid) NPs have exhibited immense inhibition of tumor in CRC models as they allow controlled and sustained drug release with decreased side effects at off-targets. Similarly, gold nanoparticles conjugated with 5-fluorouracil reduced systemic toxicity without compromising its therapeutic efficacy from the preclinical studies of 5-FU, one of the most widely used CRC medications.

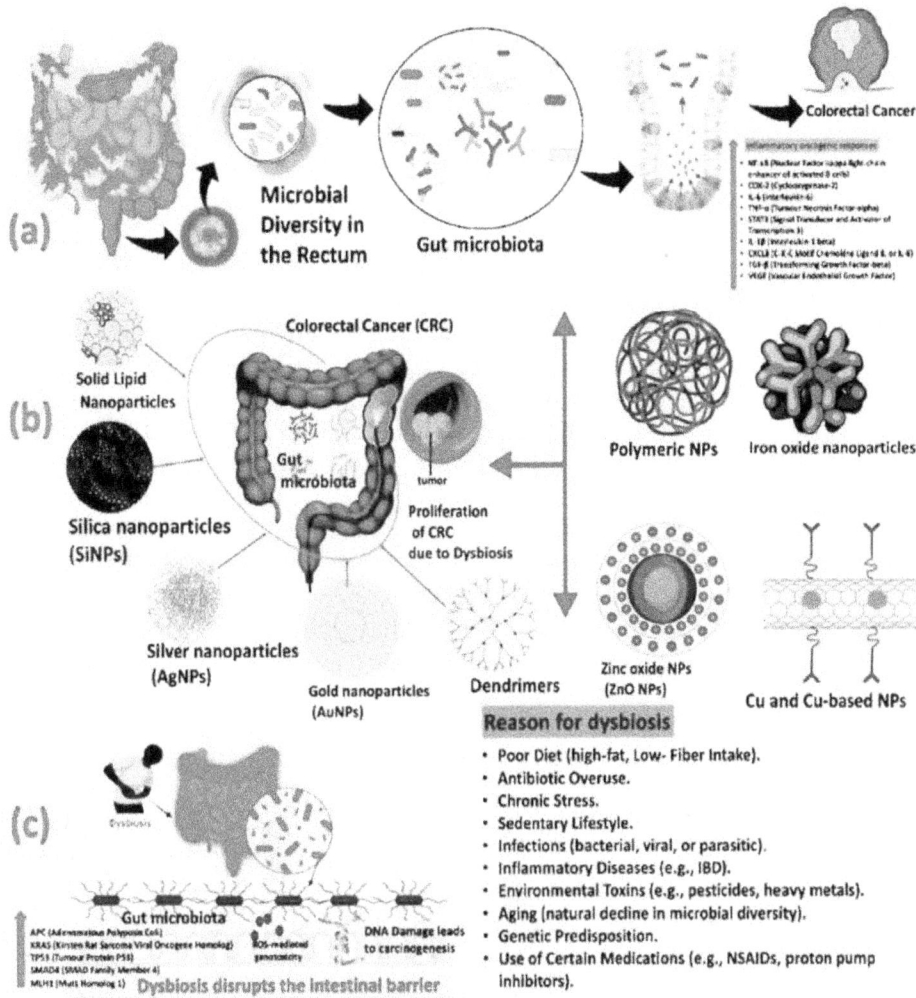

*Figure 1.1* (a) Microbial diversity and intestinal flora: this graph demonstrates why and how such a degree of diversity within the enteric flora of the intestinal gut supports healthful intestinal ecology while safeguarding protection from CRC development. (b) Nanoparticle-based interventions for colorectal cancer: This figure is a representation of the many types of nanoparticles used for the treatment of CRC focusing on their ability to selectively target cancer cells and their influence on gut microbiota to help mitigate CRC progression. (c) Dysbiosis and colorectal cancer: Figure, CRC dysbiosis factors and relationship to CRC, illustrates the elements which cause dysbiosis of the gut microbiome and its association with colorectal cancer

Source: Author

The NPs are essential within the prevention of dysbiosis-based cancer therapy; it is therefore evident and clear that huge involvement regarding gut microbiota is progressive. For example, nanocarriers of chitosan base containing probiotic *Lactobacillus rhamnosus* establish re-establishment of a microbial balance as well as upgrade the chemotherapy efficiency of the therapy, changing various immune responses. Anti-tumor effects could be enhanced through reduction in gut inflammation in mice with CRC from a recent study with the use of nanoparticles delivering both irinotecan and probiotics. Nano-carriers with curcumin, a bioactive molecule well-known for its anti-inflammatory and anti-cancer activities, have also proved to be promising candidates to treat CRC by targeting simultaneously tumor cells and correcting dysbiosis of the gut Figure 1.1c. Such products as Nanocurc™ reveal the practical applicability of such approaches that supply bioavailable formulations for clinical usage [3]. The innovations in bioengineered nanoparticles will revolutionize the treatment of CRC with unparalleled specificity and functionality. Bioengineered nanoparticles are engineered to carry ligands that specifically recognize forms specific to tumors, or carry EGFR-targeting peptides like folic acid, ensure selective binding and uptake by CRC cells, thereby expanding the scope for precision therapies. Recent developments include biogenic nanoparticles that are enrobed within red blood cell membranes to avoid innate immune system and enhance circulating half-lives. Another type of nano particles is covered with gut exosomes that direct release of their payload on intestinal epithelium. The most crucial one is theranostic nano particles, which involve a function of treatment and diagnosis combined in one nanoparticle are major tools in the management of CRC today. For instance, iron oxide nanoparticles that have been preconditioned with chemotherapeutical agents target the tumour and can also become a contrast agent to monitor MRI real-time treatment response. Novel hybrids of nanoparticles, such as mesoporous silica/metallic core hybrids, have been used in a multimodal fashion for chemotherapy and photothermal ablation together with the generation of ROS using preclinical models. Another promising tool to govern genetic regulation in CRC is lipid nanoparticles carrying gene-editing systems, CRISPR-Cas9 loaded, in which gene-editing systems knocked down oncogenes with an efficiency in CRC models [6]. Functionalized bioengineered nanoparticles decorated with specific ligands for tumor cells like folic acid or peptides targeting EGFR are absolutely certain to selectively bind and internalize into CRC cells, thereby making therapy much more precise. Some that have recently been developed are biomimetic nanoparticles covered with the membrane of a red blood cell to facilitate avoidance of immune detection and allow for a longer circulation period. There are nanoparticles covered with gut-derived exosomes that can directly target the payload to the intestinal epithelium. In addition to these, theranostic nanoparticles that can deliver both therapy and diagnostics are increasingly important in the CRC management process. For instance, iron oxide nanoparticles that provide direct delivery of chemotherapeutical agents to targeted tumours become MRI contrast agents that offer real-time imaging of the treatment outcome. There have also been preclinical demonstrations of novel hybrid nanoparticles that integrate mesoporous silica with metallic cores into multimodal therapies that have involved chemotherapy, photothermal ablation, and reactive oxygen species (ROS)-generating applications. Thirdly, CRISPR-Cas9-loaded nanoparticles, offering potential in the field of genetic modulation against CRC, have been demonstrated preclinically [9].

## Clinical studies and preclinical evidence

Much research has been done into NPs in preventing dysbiosis and treating CRC, with much support from abundant preclinical and clinical studies. In fact, preclinical models have been very instrumental in proving that NPs could restore the balance of the microbes and target cancer cells. For instance, a butyrate-containing short-chain fatty acid polymeric NPs have shown optimistic results in mice model by significantly reducing inflammation with at least p value less than 0.05 and reducing the size of a tumour. In addition, a LNP-encapsulated curcumin and resveratrol proved to enhance gut microbiomes through increased beneficial bacteria growth and were tested in mice models for CRC [2]. Metallic NPs, including gold and silver, demonstrate both antimicrobial and anti-tumour properties. A study indicated a 65% decrease in tumor size and diminished inflammation caused by dysbiosis when utilizing gold NPs in preclinical trials. Researchers are investigating nanoparticles for the treatment of CRC, with numerous formulations advancing through clinical trials. The Phase II CRACK report emphasizes focused medication distribution and microbiome alteration. Importantly, cetuximab combined with camrelizumab and liposomal irinotecan demonstrated a 25% objective response rate and a 75% disease control in RAS wild-type mCRC patients who had previously received anti-EGFR therapy. The median PFS and OS were 6.9 and 15.1 months, respectively, with tolerable toxicities (15.8% grade 3 adverse events), positioning it as a hopeful late-line mCRC treatment [11]. A combination of acoustic cavitation, gold nanoparticles, and intense pulsed light in a colon tumour model resulted in a more significant improvement in therapeutic outcome. The combined treatment group receiving intense pulsed light in addition to ultrasound and gold nanoparticles showed the maximum reduction in volume of the tumor as well as survival rate. The tumour doubling and five-folding times were highest in the groups treated with ultrasound plus gold nanoparticles, as well as in the groups that received intense pulsed light plus ultrasound plus gold nanoparticles. Based on this study, Sazgarnia et al claim that gold nanoparticles augment acoustic cavitation, which, in turn increases the effectiveness of ultrasonic and pulsed light therapy for cancer [12]. Preliminary results have shown that these encapsulated probiotics enhance microbial richness and reduce gastrointestinal side effects better than traditional probiotic products. Moreover, nanoparticle-based drugs that specifically interfere with cancer pathways such as EGFR or VEGF are at the advanced clinical trial stage. For example, SIR-Spheres (yttrium-90-labeled resin microspheres) are available in the market, which has shown promising efficacy for the direct delivery of radiation to liver metastases from CRC with response rates above 40% in combination therapy settings. Phase II trials of dendrimer-based NPs that carry chemotherapeutic agents, like paclitaxel [8], encouraging results indicate effective tumor infiltration and reduced side effects, yet obstacles persist. Variability in gut microbiota complicates standardization, and metallic nanoparticles present toxicity issues, particularly kidney impacts in rodents. Regulatory challenges continue, despite the existence of FDA-approved NPs such as abraxane. Researchers strive to create multifunctional nanoparticles that possess antimicrobial, immunomodulatory, and prebiotic properties. Hybrid NPs that deliver anti-inflammatory drugs and probiotics enhanced gut microbial diversity by 80% in CRC models. This promotes tailored nanoparticle treatments through precision medicine and AI-based predictions of microbiota interactions.

## Challenges and future perspectives

Nanoparticle therapies hold potential but encounter obstacles such as variable drug loading (40–70% targeting success), toxicity issues, and regulatory challenges. Although FDA-approved Abraxane emphasizes their cancer treatment potential, the modulation of microbiota is still insufficiently investigated. Metallic NPs exhibit robust antimicrobial properties but may compromise epithelial integrity. The absence of standardization in manufacturing and characterization makes clinical translation even more challenging. Just 25% of CRC nanoparticle studies focus on microbiota. Nonetheless, bioengineered nanoparticles, such as vesicles derived from exosomes, provide enhanced biocompatibility and lower chances of immune rejection, leading to safer applications.

## Conclusion

Recent studies have underlined the role of gut microbiota in the pathogenesis and progression of colorectal cancer (CRC). Most CRC patients are associated with an imbalance of the gut microbial community known as dysbiosis. Nanoparticles (NPs)-mediated modulation of gut microbiota could represent a promising strategy to potentially prevent CRC. Such NPs are capable of delivering therapeutic agents specifically to areas of the gut, targeting cancer cells, and restoring healthy balance to the microbial community. A lot has been done with nanomedicine, however, much more remains to be done, redesign NP. Delivery techniques should be improved, effectiveness should be evaluated in the long term. After all, using NPs can revolutionize the management of CRC, offering a targeted effective therapeutic strategy.

## References

[1] Ahmad, I., & Alqurashi, F. (2024). Early cancer detection using deep learning and medical imaging: a survey. *Critical Reviews in Oncology/Hematology*, 204, 104528. https://doi.org/10.1016/j.critrevonc.2024.104528.

[2] Alfutaimani, A. S., Alharbi, N. K., Alahmari, A., Alqabbani, A., & Aldayel, A. M. (2024). Exploring the landscape of lipid nanoparticles (LNPs): a comprehensive review of LNPs types and biological sources of lipids. *International Journal of Pharmaceutics: X*, 8, 100305. https://doi.org/10.1016/j.ijpx.2024.100305.

[3] Bisht, S., Khan, M. A., Bekhit, M., Bai, H., Cornish, T., Mizuma, M., et al. (2011). A polymeric nanoparticle formulation of curcumin (NanoCurc™) Ameliorates CCl₄-induced hepatic injury and fibrosis through reduction of pro-inflammatory cytokines and stellate cell activation. *Laboratory Investigation*, 91, 1383–1395. https://doi.org/10.1038/labinvest.2011.86.

[4] Dalbanjan, N. P., Eelager, M. P., & Narasagoudr, S. S. (2024). Microbial protein sources: a comprehensive review on the potential usage of fungi and cyanobacteria in sustainable food systems. *Food and Humanity*, 3, 100366. https://doi.org/10.1016/j.fooh.2024.100366.

[5] Garavaglia, B., Vallino, L., Amoruso, A., Pane, M., Ferraresi, A., & Isidoro, C. (2024). The role of gut microbiota, immune system, and autophagy in the pathogenesis of inflammatory bowel disease: molecular mechanisms and therapeutic approaches. *Aspects of Molecular Medicine*, 4, 100056. https://doi.org/10.1016/j.amolmed.2024.100056.

[6] Gonzalez, V. G., Grunenberger, A., Nicoud, O., Czuba, E., Vollaire, J., Josserand, V., et al. (2024). Enhanced CRISPR-Cas9 RNA system delivery using cell penetrating peptides-based

nanoparticles for efficient in vitro and in vivo applications. *Journal of Controlled Release*, 376, 1160–1175. https://doi.org/10.1016/j.jconrel.2023.12.011.

[7]   Haftcheshmeh, S. M., Jaafari, M. R., Mashreghi, M., Mehrabian, A., Alavizadeh, S. H., Zamani, P., et al. (2021). Liposomal doxorubicin targeting mitochondria: a novel formulation to enhance anti-tumor effects of Doxil® in vitro and in vivo. *Journal of Drug Delivery Science and Technology*, 62, 102351. https://doi.org/10.1016/j.jddst.2021.102351.

[8]   Li, H., Fang, Y., Gu, D., Du, M., Zhang, Z., Sun, L., et al. (2022). Paclitaxel and cisplatin combined with concurrent involved-field irradiation in definitive chemoradiotherapy for locally advanced esophageal squamous cell carcinoma: a phase ii clinical trial. *Radiation Oncology*, 17, 105. https://doi.org/10.1186/s13014-022-02036-9.

[9]   Li, X., Feng, Q., Han, Z., & Jiang, X. (2021). Enhancing gene editing efficiency for cells by CRISPR/Cas9 system-loaded multilayered nanoparticles assembled via microfluidics. *Chinese Journal of Chemical Engineering*, 38, 216–220. https://doi.org/10.1016/j.cjche.2021.06.005.

[10]  Liu, Z., Xu, H., You, W., Pan, K., & Li, W. (2024). Helicobacter pylori eradication for primary prevention of gastric cancer: progresses and challenges. *Journal of the National Cancer Center*. Volume 4, 299–310. https://doi.org/10.1016/j.jncc.2024.01.003.

[11]  Quan, M., Chen, J., Chen, Z., Hai, Y., Zhou, Y., Chao, Q., et al. (2023). China special issue on gastrointestinal tumors—cetuximab retreatment plus camrelizumab and liposomal irinotecan in patients with RAS wild-type metastatic colorectal cancer: cohort b of the phase II CRACK study. *International Journal of Cancer*, 153, 1877–1884. https://doi.org/10.1002/ijc.34589.

[12]  Sazgarnia, A., Shanei, A., Taheri, , Meibodi, , Eshghi, H., Attaran, N., et al. (2013). Therapeutic effects of acoustic cavitation in the presence of gold nanoparticles on a colon tumor model. *Journal of Ultrasound in Medicine*, 32, 475–483. https://doi.org/10.7863/ultra.32.3.475.

[13]  Venkatraman, G., Giribabu, N., Mohan, P. S., Muttiah, B., Govindarajan, V. K., & Alagiri, M., et al. (2024). Environmental impact and human health effects of polycyclic aromatic hydrocarbons and remedial strategies: a detailed review. *Chemosphere*, 351, 141227. https://doi.org/10.1016/j.chemosphere.2023.141227.

# 2 Synthesis and evaluation of novel quinazoline compounds as inhibitors of HIV-1 integrase

*Pankaj Wadhwa[1,2,a], Hemant R. Jadhav[1,b], Priti Jain[4] and Mahaveer Singh[3,c]*

[1]Birla Institute of Technology and Sciences Pilani, Pilani Campus, Vidya Vihar, Pilani, Rajasthan, India

[2]Department of Pharmaceutical Chemistry, Lovely School of Pharmaceutical Sciences, Lovely Professional University, Phagwara, Punjab, India

[3]School of Pharmacy and Technology Management, SVKM'S NMIMS University, Shirpur Campus, Maharastra, India

[4]School of Pharmaceutical Sciences, DPSR, University, Delhi, India

## Abstract

**Background:** The enzyme known as HIV-1 integrase (IN) has a pivotal role in process of replication of viruses by facilitating the incorporation of viral DNA within the genes of host cells, rendering it an essential target for anti HIV therapeutic strategies. The potential of tetrahydroquinazoline analogues as inhibitors of HIV-1 integrase are focused, prompting exploration of new analogues to improve antiviral potency.

**Objective:** The focus of research was to synthesize and analyse a collection of quinazoline derivatives for their inhibitory effects on the integrase enzyme associated with HIV-1. Moreover, the investigation aimed to clarify the relation of activity with structure (SAR) of these derivatives and assess binding interactions utilizing molecular docking techniques.

**Methodology:** A total of 14 analogues were prepared and were subsequently evaluated against wild-type HIV-1 integrase utilizing an ELISA-based colorimetric assay. The structure-activity relationships of the analogues were scrutinized to ascertain the influence of various substitutions on their inhibitory effectiveness and molecular modelling interaction were performed to clarify the orientations of the most potent compounds within the cavity of the HIV-1 integrase.

**Results and conclusion:** Among the fourteen synthesized molecules, three (9b, 9d, and 9m) demonstrated considerable inhibitory activity, with IC50 values recorded below 5.36 µM. This research successfully identified analogues exhibiting significant inhibition against the HIV-1 integrase enzyme. Future investigations may concentrate on refining the structural characteristics of these compounds to enhance their therapeutic potential.

**Keywords:** AIDS, HIV-1 integrase, integrase inhibitor, strand transfer

## Introduction

The discovery of involvement of HIV-1 for acquired immunodeficiency syndrome, (AIDS) enormous efforts are made to counter the disease [10]. However, excessive or improper use of anti-retroviral therapy (ART) leads to the progress of resistant viral strains [1]. HIV-1 integrase (IN) facilitates incorporation of DNA of virus into the host gene by 3′-processing

[a]pankajwadhwa88@gmail.com, [b]hemantrj@pilani.bits-pilani.ac.in, [c]mahaveer2singh@gmail.com

DOI: 10.1201/9781003716648-2

(3′-P) and with strand transfer (ST) reactions. The 3′-P catalyzes water-mediated enzymatic cleavage for the removal of the terminal dinucleotide followed by transference in nucleus of host cell. This is followed by insertion and covalent ligation of 3′ end of DNA of virus to the DNA of host takes place as a part of strand transfer [6, 2]. This process is dependent on N and C-terminal domains [11]. Interaction of catalytic triad (so-called DDE motif) of Integrase domain with $Mg^{2+}$ are essential for its catalytical activities [8]. The increasing popularity of HIV integrase (IN) as a validated target is due to lack of IN in mammalian cellular functions.

Taking into consideration the significant function of integrase in viral replication, various IN inhibitors were synthesized. These include raltegravir, (MK-0518, 1) [3]. Later, elvitegravir (EVG, GS-9137, 2) and dolutegravir (DTG, S/GSK1349572, 3) were also approved. Other candidates in clinical trials are viz. BI 224436, MK-2048, GS-9160, MK-0536, bictegravir and cabotegravir etc (Figure 2.1) [7, 9]. Keto-enol acid compounds resulted in hepatic effects [4], earlier derivatives were synthesized are thiazolothiazepines 4 [12], styrylquinazoline derivatives 5, furoyl pyrazolones 6, methyl chalcones 7, 1,3,4-oxa and thiadiazole showed metal chelation. Based on the information derived from these reports and the pharmacological significance of the quinazoline ring system, which encompasses properties such as anticancer, anti-HIV, anti-inflammatory, antimicrobial, anti-tubercular, and antiulcer activities [5, 13], as well as the druggability associated with the quinazolinone nucleus, we initiated the synthesis of quinazolinone derivatives (9a-9n) aimed at acting as of HIV-1 IN inhibitors. The effect of the quinazoline subunit on the inhibitory efficacy against HIV integrase was assessed, with the general structure illustrated in Figure 2.1. Docking studies reveal that the keto group located within the ring structure, and amidic carbonyl group of quinazolinones, plays a crucial role in binding with metal cofactors situated in active site, thereby facilitating hydrophobic interactions.

## Results and discussion

### Chemistry

A novel series of quinazoline derivatives (9a-9n) featuring a broad spectrum of substitutions at various positions of the phenyl ring were synthesized via a multi-step synthetic protocol as

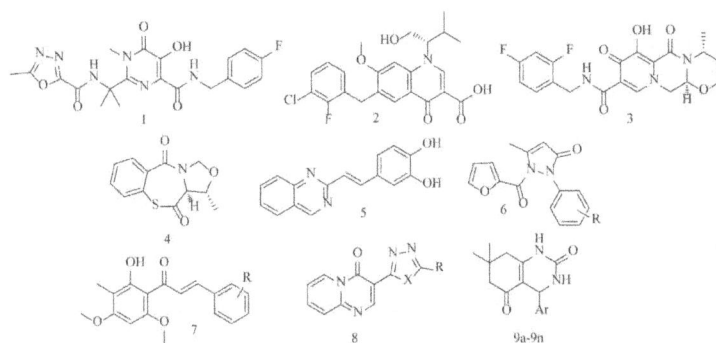

*Figure 2.1* Mentioned HIV-1 IN inhibitors (1-8) and structure of prepared molecules (9a-9n)
Source: Author

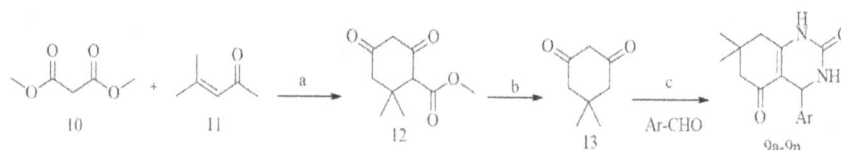

*Scheme 2.1* Reagents conditions applied: (a) NA2CO3, CH3OH, 5h, reflux (b) 4M NAOH, 6N HCL, 1.51 h, reflux (c) NH2CONH2, HCL, 2.5-4.5 h, and reflux
Source: Author

*Table 2.1* Docking scores and HIV-1 IN inhibition values.

| Molecules | Ar | Docking score | % Inhibition* (10μM) |
|---|---|---|---|
| Dolutegravir | ----- | −7.64 | 95.01 |
| 9a | Ph | −6.62 | 44.31 |
| 9b | 2-NO$_2$-Ph | −5.73 | 69.24 |
| 9c | 3-NO$_2$-Ph | −7.96 | 62.83 |
| 9d | 4-NO$_2$-Ph | −6.74 | 65.81 |
| 9e | 2-Cl-Ph | −5.82 | 45.27 |
| 9f | 4-Cl-Ph | −5.77 | 48.73 |
| 9g | 2,4-diCl-Ph | −5.58 | 46.43 |
| 9h | 2-OH-Ph | −6.16 | 52.26 |
| 9i | 4-OH-Ph | −6.27 | 54.36 |
| 9j | 3,4-diOMe-Ph | −6.18 | 46.34 |
| 9k | 2,5-diOMe-Ph | −6.28 | 49.71 |
| 9l | 4-OH-3-OMe-Ph | −5.356 | 46.68 |
| 9m | 1H-indol-3-yl | −5.71 | 67.84 |
| 9n | furan-2-yl | −5.62 | 46.63 |

Source: Author

depicted in Scheme-2.1. The initial step encompasses reaction of ester (dimethyl malonate) and 4-methyl-3-penten-2-one, which is subsequently hydrolyzed to get 5,5-dimethyl-1,3-cyclohexanedione. The final product is obtained through the condensation of dimedone, urea, and various substituted aromatic aldehydes.

*Discussion of HIV-1 inhibition with docking results*
Inhibition of HIV-1 integrase of compounds 9a-9n was evaluated with the use of HIV-1 Integrase assay kit procured from Xpressbio Life Science Products, USA as per given protocol by manufacturer. The percentage inhibition against HIV-1 IN was recorded at 10 μM and IC$_{50}$ was calculated. For docking studies with Glide (maestro version 9.3, Schrödinger suite) was performed. The results compared to dolutegravir considering it as standard, see Table 2.1. For cytotoxicity MTT assay with the use of HeLa cell line was done for both HIV-1 and HIV-2 using dolutegravir as reference drug. The results are shown in Table 2.2.

*Table 2.2* Results of anti-HIV activity.

| Compound code | EC501 (µM) | | $CC_{50}^{2}$ (µM) | HIV-2[3] SI |
|---|---|---|---|---|
| | HIV-1 (III$_{B}$) | HIV-2 | | |
| Dolutegravir | 0.000820 | 0.00230 | 1.440 | 619 |
| 9a | >82.3 | 113 | 82.3 | <1 |
| 9b | >116.65 | 112.14 | 116.65 | <1 |
| 9c | >29 | >50.8 | 29 | <1 |
| 9d | >71 | >77.3 | 71 | <1 |
| 9e | >60.18 | >60.18 | 60.18 | <1 |
| 9g | >4.49 | >4.49 | 4.49 | <1 |
| 9h | >55.1 | >55 | >55.1 | <1 |
| 9i | >108.90 | >108.90 | 108.90 | <1 |
| 9j | >92.1 | 109 | 92.1 | <1 |
| 9k | >25 | 9.98 | >25 | <1 |
| 9l | >11.4 | >11.5 | 11.4 | <1 |

Source: Author

Compound 9a (percentage inhibition 44.32, G Score -5.51) resulted in H bond with Cys 65 (by –C=O of C-2 position of quinazoline), Asp 116 (by –NH of C-1 position) and Asn 155 (by –C=O of C-5 position). Metal bond of Mg 1001 (by -C=O of C-2 position of quinazoline ring) was also present. Substitution with nitro group at position number 2, 3 and 4 (Compounds 9b-9d) showed good score and HIV-1 IN inhibitory activity. Compound 9b (percentage inhibition 69.25, G Score -7.349) formed H bond interactions with Cys 65 (by –C=O of C-2 position of quinazoline ring), Thr 66, His 67, Lys 159 (by 2-nitro group), Asp 116 (by –NH of C-1 position) and Lys 156 (by –C=O of C-5 position). Compounds 9c and 9d lacked H bond interactions with Cys 65, His 67, which resulted in reduced docking score and inhibitory activity compared to 9b. Additionally, compound 9d formed hydrogen bond with Asn 155 and metal bond with Mg 1001.

When compound 9a was substituted with chlorine group at 2-position (9e), it showed presence of similar interactions and HIV-1 IN inhibitory activity, but para chloro substituted (9f) showed better activity. It formed H bond with Cys 65 (by –C=O of C-5 position), Thr 66, His 67, Lys 156 (by carbonyl group of quinazoline ring), Glu 152 (by –NH of C-1 position) and chelation with Mg 1001. Chlorine at ortho and para positions (compound 9g) resulted in hydrogen bond, metal coordination and lipophillic interactions with Glutamate 152, Lysine 156 and Lysine 159.

Substitution of OH group at 2$^{nd}$ or 4$^{th}$ place (9h and 9i) resulted in more than 50 % HIV-1 IN inhibition. Visual analysis of docked pose showed that both compounds' forms hydrogen bonding and metal coordination with Asp 116 (by –NH group of C-1 position), Glu 152 (*via* –C=O of C-5 position) and Mg 1001, respectively. Additionally, compound 9h forms hydrogen bonding with Cys 65 (by –C=O of C-2 position) and Asn 155 (by 2-hydroxy group). The improved docking score with HIV-1 IN inhibition of compound 9i might be due to involvement of 4th hydroxy group in H bond with amino acids His 67, Thr 66, Glu 152 and Lys 156.

9j (3,4-dimethoxy) and 9k (2,5-dimethoxy) showed almost similar activity compared to 9i. Both compounds showed hydrogen bonding and metal coordination interactions with Lys 156 (by –C=O of C-5 position), Lys 159 (by methoxy groups) and Mg 1001, respectively. Compound 9j also showed H bond interactions with Thr 66, His 67, which are absent in compound 9k. 9k, displayed similar interactions with improved docking score and inhibition compared to 9j. It formed H bond interactions with amino acids Cys 65 (by–C=O of C-2 place of quinazoline ring) and Asp 116 (by NH of C-1 position of quinazoline). Further effect of substitution of methoxy group at 4 position of compound 9i was studied. Compound 9l (having *p*-hydroxy and *m*-methoxy group) showed H bond interactions with Cys 65 (by–C=O of C-2 of quinazoline), Thr 66 (by *m*-methoxy group), Asp 116 (by –NH group of C-1 position) and Glu 152 (*via* –C=O of C-5 position and p-hydroxy group, respectively). The metal coordination bond with Mg 1001 was also present but it lacks interactions with His 67. It might be a reason for the slight reduction in Gscore and integrase inhibitory activity. Conversely, the substitution of the smaller heterocyclic furan (9n) ring revealed H bond interactions with Cys 65 (through the C=O of the C-2 position of the quinazoline and the -NH of the C-3 position, respectively), Thr 66, and Asn 155 (via the furan ring and th C=O group at the C-5 position, respectively); additionally, hydrophobic interactions with Lys 156, Lys 159, and metal bond with Mg 1001 were noted. Nonetheless, the furan ring was predominantly solvent-exposed, which may account for the diminished docking score and IN inhibitory activity.

Compounds with 2-nitro (9b) Figure 2.2A, 4-nitro substitution (9d) Figure 2.2B, and the indole ring (9m) Figure 2.2C exhibited more than 65% inhibition, IC50 values are presented in Table 2.1. Both nitro-substituted compounds (9b-9d) yielded IC50 values of 1.20 µM, 5.36 µM and 9m had IC50 of 4.56 µM.

With the promising computational results and *in vitro* findings, entire set of molecules evaluated for anti-HIV efficacy against HIV-1 and HIV-2. However, none of the molecules exhibited any anti-HIV activity lower than cytotoxic concentrations (Table 2.2). While the molecules demonstrated substantial potential in vitro, their activity was not observed in cell culture assays. This necessitates further investigation, which will be conducted in due course. $IC_{50}$ values for three compounds 9b, 9d, and 9m were found 1.20±0.12, 5.36±0.83, 4.56±0.56 respectively.

## Experimental

*General*

The compounds were synthesized by Scheme-2.1 and were column purified. Melting points were determined by Buchi B530 apparatus (Flawil, Switzerland) are reported uncorrected and Infrared (IR) spectrum was recorded by FTIR, Prestige 21 form Shimadzu. The 1H and 13C NMR spectrum was obtained by BRUKER DPX-400 NMR spectrometer with 1H operating at 400 MHz and 13C spectrum at 125.77 MHz. Mass was recorded with ESI-MS using a MICROMASS Quattro-II LCMS, waters and reagents were procured from Merck, Spectrochem, Sigma and CDH.

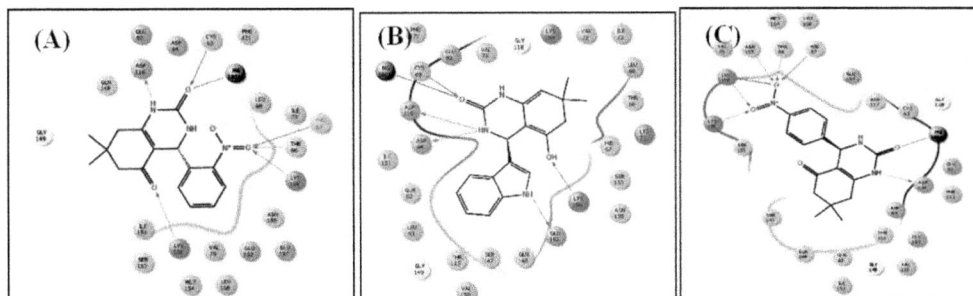

*Figure 2.2* 2D Images of molecules A: 9b; B: 9d; C: 9m
Source: Author

### Preparation of intermediate 12

To 1.5 g sodium methoxide taken in RBF in methanol (15 ml), 6 ml dimethyl malonate (10) was added. Mixture was reflux of 4hrs and allowed to cool and 3 ml of mesityl oxide (11) previously dissolved in methanol (5 ml) was added. The final mixture was refluxed for 45 minutes. Solvent removal was done under vacuum at 55°C.

### Preparation of intermediate 13

1g of intermediate (12) was dissolved in 10 ml of alcohol water mixture (1: 1) to this 15 ml of concentrated (4M) NaOH was added. Resultant mass was refluxed for 1.6 h and allowed to cool. After cooling mixture was acidified with 15 ml of HCl and solid was filtered later recrystallized with acetone obtained as yellow crystals (0.75 g).

### Preparation of compounds (9a-9n)

Intermediate 13 (0.75g) urea (0.5 g) and HCL 1 ml were taken in a RBF and refluxed for specified time as per Table 2.3. After cooling of mixture 16ml of ice cold water was added to get solid product which as further recrystallized from absolute ethanol to get derivatives (9a-9n). The spectral data and melting point of compound 9a-9n were in concordance with previously published values [14] have been provided as supplementary attachments.

### Integrase assay

The inhibition of HIV-1 integrase (IN) evaluated utilizing an in vitro HIV-1 Integrase Assay kit which was procured from Xpressbio Life Science Products, USA, in accordance with the established protocol. This experimental paradigm involves the deployment of strepta-vidin-coated 96-well plates, which are subsequently subjected to treatment with dou-ble-stranded HIV-1 long terminal repeat (LTR) U5 donor substrate (DS) oligonucleotide that has been end-labeled with biotin. Subsequently, full-length recombinant HIV-1 inte-grase protein was introduced onto the oligonucleotide used as substrate. All synthesized ole-cules were utilized at a concentration of 10 μM in duplicate, following which an alternative double-stranded target substrate (TS) oligonucleotide, incorporating modifications at the 3'-end, was added in the assay plate. The HIV-1 integrase facilitates the 3'-phosphorylation by cleaving the terminal two nucleotides from the exposed 3'-end of the HIV-1 LTR DS, thereby engaging in a strand-transfer reaction that permits integration of the DS into the TS.

*Table 2.3* Details of synthesized quinazoline derivatives using Biginelli condensation.

| Molecules | Time in hrs | % Yield | MP (°C) |
|-----------|-------------|---------|---------|
| 9a | 3.0 | 76 | 284-286 |
| 9b | 3.5 | 67 | 290-292 |
| 9c | 4.5 | 74 | 296-298 |
| 9d | 4 | 67 | > 300 |
| 9e | 5 | 45 | 295-297 |
| 9f | 4.5 | 48 | 203-205 |
| 9g | 3.0 | 54 | 228-230 |
| 9h | 3.5 | 58 | 212-214 |
| 9i | 4.0 | 55 | 205-207 |
| 9j | 4.0 | 47 | 284-286 |
| 9k | 4.0 | 52 | 268-270 |
| 9l | 4.5 | 56 | 271-273 |
| 9m | 2.5 | 62 | 219-221 |
| 9n | 2.5 | 64 | 249-250 |

Source: Author

Resulting products of this reaction were quantitatively analyzed calorimetrically utilizing an HRP-labeled antibody that specifically identifies the modification at the 3'-end of the TS. Dolutegravir was utilized as a positive control within this experimental framework.

## Conclusions

In summary, a total of fourteen quinazoline analogues (designated as 9a-9n) were prepared and subsequently evaluated for their anti-HIV efficacy through enzyme (IN) assays, in silico analyses, and cell culture assays targeting both HIV-1 and HIV-2. Importantly, three molecules, namely 9b, 9d, and 9m, exhibited noteworthy percent inhibition for HIV-1 IN, with IC50 values recorded below 5.36 μM. A satisfactory correlation was noted between the in vitro and in silico results. However, no derivatives displayed activity against HIV-1 or HIV-2 at concentrations beneath corresponding cytotoxic thresholds. This observation implies that such compounds may be regarded as unsuitable for further exploration within the realm of anti-HIV activity. Future research trajectories could encompass either modifications to the tetrahydroquinazoline ring or the incorporation of substitutions on the indole ring.

## References

[1]   Back, D. J., Khoo, S. H., Maher, B., & Gibbons, S. E. (2000). Current uses and future hopes for clinical pharmacology in the management of HIV infection. *HIV Medicine*, 1(s2), 12–17. doi: 10.1046/j.1468-1293.2000.00001.x.

[2] Dayam, R., Sanchez, T., & Neamati, N. (2005). Discovery and structure–activity relationship studies of a unique class of HIV-1 integrase inhibitors. *ChemMedChem: Chemistry Enabling Drug Discovery*, 1(2), 238–244. doi: 10.1002/cmdc.200500018.

[3] Evering, T. H., & Markowitz, M. (2007). Raltegravir (MK-0518): an integrase inhibitor for the treatment of HIV-1. *Drugs of Today*, 43(12), 865. doi: 10.1358/dot.2007.43.12.1146063.

[4] Hajimahdi, Z., Zarghi, A., Zabihollahi, R., & Aghasadeghi, M. R. (2012). Synthesis, biological evaluation, and molecular modeling studies of new 1,3,4-oxadiazole- and 1,3,4-thiadiazole-substituted 4-Oxo-4H-Pyrido[1,2-a]Pyrimidines as anti-HIV-1 agents. *Medicinal Chemistry Research*, 22(5), 2467–2475. doi: 10.1007/s00044-012-0241-5.

[5] Lee Y, Min CK, Kim TG, Song HK, Lim Y, Kim D, Shin K, Kang M, Kang JY, Youn HS, Lee JG, An JY, Park KR, Lim JJ, Kim JH, Kim JH, Park ZY, Kim YS, Wang J, Kim DH, Eom SH. Structure and function of the N-terminal domain of the human mitochondrial calcium uniporter. EMBO Rep. 2015 Oct;16(10):1318-33. https://doi.org/10.15252/embr.201540436

[6] Puras Lutzke, R., & Plasterk, R. (1997). HIV integrase: a target for drug discovery. *Genes and Function*, 1(5), 289–307. doi: 10.1046/j.1365-4624.1997.00026.x.

[7] Nair, V., & Chi, G. (2007). HIV integrase inhibitors as therapeutic agents in AIDS. *Reviews in Medical Virology*, 17(4), 277–295. doi: 10.1002/rmv.539.

[8] Singh, R., Yadav, P., Urvashi, & Tandon, V. (2016). Novel dioxolan derivatives of indole as HIV-1 integrase strand transfer inhibitors active against RAL resistant mutant virus. *ChemistrySelect*, 1(17), 5471–5478. doi: 10.1002/slct.201601024.

[9] Wadhwa, P., Jain, P., Rudrawar, S., & Jadhav, H. R. A. (2017). Quinoline, coumarin and other heterocyclic analogs based HIV-1 integrase inhibitors. *Current Drug Discovery Technologies*, 15(1), 2–19. doi: 10.2174/1570163814666170531115452.

[10] Weiss, R. A. (1993). How does HIV cause AIDS? *Science*, 260(5112), 1273–1279. doi: 10.1126/science.8493571.

[11] Lee Y, Min CK, Kim TG, Song HK, Lim Y, Kim D, Shin K, Kang M, Kang JY, Youn HS, Lee JG, An JY, Park KR, Lim JJ, Kim JH, Kim JH, Park ZY, Kim YS, Wang J, Kim DH, Eom SH. (2015). Structure and function of the N-terminal domain of the human mitochondrial calcium uniporter. EMBO Rep. 2015 Oct;16(10):1318–33. https://doi.org/10.15252/embr.201540436

[12] Jiwane, S., Singh, V., Namdeo, K., & Prajapati, S. (2010). Synthesis of Some Novel 2, 4-Thiazolidinedione Derivatives and Their Biological Screening as Antidiabetic Agents. *Asian Journal of Chemistry*, 21(7), 5068–5072.

[13] Ugwu DI, Ezema BE, Eze FU, Ugwuja DI. (2014). Synthesis and structural activity relationship study of antitubercular carboxamides. Int J Med Chem. 2014; 2014: 614808. doi: 10.1155/2014/614808

[14] Edilu, A., Adane, L. & Woyessa, D. (2015). In vitro antibacterial activities of compounds isolated from roots of Caylusea abyssinica. Ann Clin Microbiol Antimicrob 14, 15. https://doi.org/10.1186/s12941-015-0072-6

[15] Jiwane, S., Singh, V., Namdeo, K., & Prajapati, S. (2010). Synthesis of Some Novel 2,4-Thiazolidinedione Derivatives and Their Biological Screening as Antidiabetic Agents. Asian Journal of Chemistry, 21(7), 5068–5072

[16] Ugwu DI, Ezema BE, Eze FU, Ugwuja DI. Synthesis and structural activity relationship study of antitubercular carboxamides. Int J Med Chem. 2014;2014:614808. doi: 10.1155/2014/614808

# 3 Brij 58 ameliorates paracetamol-induced hepatotoxicity in rats by reducing the toxic metabolite formation through inhibition of CYP2E1-mediated metabolism

*Nagabhushanam Chunduru[1,a] and Ravindra Babu Pingili[2,b]*

[1]Department of Pharmacology, KVSR Siddhartha College of Pharmaceutical Sciences, Vijayawada, Andhra Pradesh, India

[2]Department of Pharmacology, SVKM's NMIMS School of Pharmacy and Technology Management, Babulde, Shirpur, Maharashtra, India

## Abstract

**Background:** One of the harmful byproducts of acetaminophen (paracetamol) is *N*-acetyl-*p*-benzoquinoneimine (NAPQI). When acetaminophen is administered acutely or in excess, it undergoes phase I metabolism via cytochrome P-450 2E1 (CYP2E1) resulting in the formation of NAPQI. Brij 58 is a non-ionic surfactant and has a reputation for being an effective CYP2E1 inhibitor.

**Objective:** The purpose of this investigation was to assess how Brij 58 affected the paracetamol metabolism mediated by CYP2E1 using isolated rat hepatocytes and rats.

**Methods:** *In vitro* investigations were conducted using rat hepatocytes that had been isolated. Collagenase perfusion was used to separate hepatocytes from rat liver. Krebs-Henseleit buffer was used to cultivate liver hepatocytes at 37°C in a rotating round-bottom flask at concentrations of $1 \times 10^6$ cells/mL. The concentrations of Brij58 used were 0.01,0.05,0.5,0.1, and 1% v/v. The concentration of NAPQI was determined by RP-HPLC after aliquots (0.1 mL) were taken from the incubation of the hepatocytes at 10, 20, 30, 40, 50, and 60 minutes. The addition of Brij 58 was shown to reduce NAPQI formation in *in vitro* tests. There were thirty male Wistar rats total, with six individuals in each of the five groups. As a control, Group I rats received SCMC at a concentration of 0.5%, Group II rats received paracetamol (300 mg/kg), Group III rats received propylene glycol (15 mg/kg) and paracetamol, Group IV rats received Brij 58 (5 mg/kg) and paracetamol and Group V rats received Brij 58 (10 mg/kg) and paracetamol for 21 consecutive days orally.

**Results:** When paracetamol was combined with propylene glycol and Brij 58, the $C_{max}$ and $AUC_{0-12}$ of the paracetamol were increased and the $C_{max}$ and $AUC_{0-12}$ of the NAPQI were decreased compared to the paracetamol group. The paracetamol group showed a substantial rise in liver enzymes and chemicals compared to the control group. In comparison to the paracetamol group, the levels of AST, ALT, ALP, TP, and TB were reduced in the groups of propylene glycol and Brij 58. The histopathological analysis revealed that propylene glycol and Brij 58 protected the liver.

**Conclusion:** Brij 58 significantly reduced the NAPQI production via inhibiting CYP2E1-mediated metabolism of paracetamol and ameliorated its hepatotoxicity in rats.

**Keywords:** Brij 58, hepatotoxicity, N-acetyl-p-benzoquinoneimine, paracetamol, propylene glycol

[a]chnb137@gmail.com, [b]ravindrapingili@gmail.com

DOI: 10.1201/9781003716648-3

## Introduction

As a safe analgesic at therapeutic levels, millions of people throughout the globe take paracetamol (acetaminophen), one of the most popular over-the-counter medications [1]. It is among the world's most popular pharmaceuticals and among the best-selling prescription medications in the US. Paracetamol is known to be toxic to the liver and kidneys in both humans and animals when taken in excess, whether intentionally or unintentionally. Metabolism plays a crucial role in paracetamol hepatotoxicity by turned into N-acetyl-p-benzoquinoneimine (NAPQI) by cytochrome P-450 2E1 (CYP2E1). When taken as directed, most of the paracetamol (about 90%) is broken down into its inactive components by sulfation and glucuronidation and less than 10% is transformed into NAPQI. In typical environments, glutathione (GSH) rapidly converts NAPQI into harmless metabolites. Nevertheless, NAPQI remains and causes liver injury in cases of GSH depletion, including paracetamol overdose, persistent alcohol use, and starvation [4]. The NAPQI binds to proteins in the mitochondria and triggers oxidative stress, mitochondrial malfunction, DNA damage, and necrotic hepatocyte death. Reduced NAPQI generation and subsequent liver damage would result from blocking CYP2E1 activity (Figure 3.1). Previous study results

*Figure 3.1* Mechanism involved in the paracetamol-induced hepatotoxicity
Source: Author

revealed that Brij58 (non-ionic surfactant) is an inhibitor of CYP2E1 [5, 6]. The question of whether Brij 58 blocks paracetamol's CYP2E1-mediated metabolism remains unanswered in scientific literature. This is why we set out to examine how Brij 58 affects the metabolism of paracetamol in the current study.

## Methodology

*Drugs and chemicals*
Sigma chemical company provided NAPQI, propylene glycol, and Brij 58.

*Experimental animals*
We obtained male Wistar rats (weighing 150-200 g) from Mahaveer Enterprises Hyderabad.

*Preparation and incubation of hepatocytes **in vitro***
Collagenase perfusion was used to separate hepatocytes from male Wistar rats livers, using a procedure that had been somewhat modified from that published before [2].

*In vivo studies on wistar rats*
Through a process of random selection, five sets of six animals were formed from the overall animal population. The sodium carboxymethyl cellulose (0.5%) suspension was used to suspend the paracetamol (PCM). The rats were given Brij 58 and paracetamol orally once day for 21 days. As a control, Group I rats received sodium carboxymethyl cellulose at a concentration of 0.5%, Group II rats received 300 mg/kg PCM, Group III rats received propylene glycol (15 mg/kg) and 300 mg/kg PCM, Group IV rats received Brij 58 (5 mg/kg) and 300 mg/kg PCM and Group V rats received Brij 58 (10 mg/kg) and 300 mg/kg PCM for 21 consecutive days orally. On the 21st day after treatment, 100 µL of blood was drawn from the retro-orbital plexus at 0.25, 0.5, 1.0, 1.5, 2.0, 4.0, 6.0, 8.0, and 12 hour intervals. Heparinized eppendorf tubes were used to collect blood samples, which were then maintained on ice for the duration of the experiment.

*Extraction of paracetamol and NAPQI from plasma*
Following Carmen's description, the paracetamol and NAPQI were extracted from the rat plasma using a one-step liquid-liquid extraction process Flores-Pérez et al. [3] and quantified using RP-HPLC (Figure 3.2).

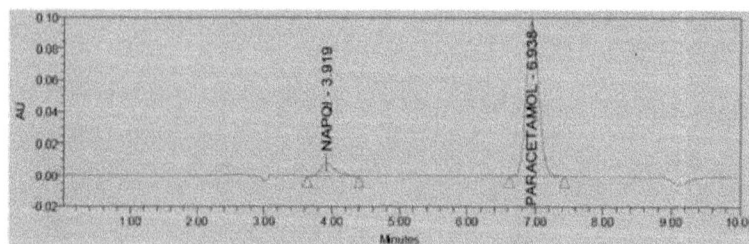

*Figure 3.2* Representative chromatograms at 205 nm
Source: Author

*Pharmacokinetic (PK) parameters*
Thermo kinetica software was used for calculating PK parameters.

*Biochemical analysis*
Pre- and post-treatment blood samples were taken for the purpose of biochemical parameter assessment.

*Histopathological studies*
Mansour et al. (2018) [6] provided the instructions for preparing the tissues and glass slides.

*Statistical analysis*
Graph Pad Prism 5.0 was used to compute all the statistics. Results were considered significant when the p-value was less than 0.05.

## Results

*Effect of Brij 58 on the pharmacokinetics of paracetamol*
Paracetamol plasma concentrations were substantially elevated when given in combination with propylene glycol and Brij 58, as compared to paracetamol control (Figure 3.3). The average paracetamol pharmacokinetic parameters were listed in Table 3.1. The paracetamol $C_{max}$ was found to be 12.768 ± 1.790 μg/mL when combined with 15 mg/kg of propylene glycol, 14.209 ± 1.025 μg/mL when combined with 5 mg/kg of Brij 58, and 16.433 ± 1.355 μg/mL when combined with 10 mg/kg of Brij 58. When rats were given propylene glycol and Brij 58, the $AUC_{0-12}$ for paracetamol rose from 69.610 ± 8.828 to 72.164 ± 33.132 μg/mL × h, 86.306 ± 8.273 μg/mL × h, and 93.086 ± 6.805 μ h. At doses of 10 and 20 mg/kg, respectively, the $AUC_{0-\alpha}$ of paracetamol rose from 62.058 ± 16.801 to 70.602 ± 9.004 and 78.963 ± 11.062 μg/mL × h by co-administration with Brij 58. The paracetamol $t_{max}$ was

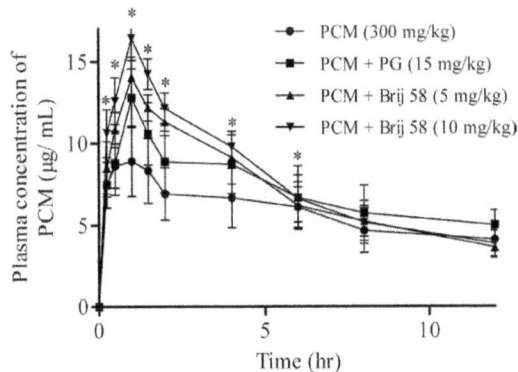

*Figure 3.3* Oral administration of paracetamol to rats with or without propylene glycol and Brij 58 (n = 6) yielded mean plasma concentration-time profiles of paracetamol. (•) Paracetamol alone; (■) as a control; (▲) in combination with Brij 58 (5 mg/kg); (▼) as a control with propylene glycol (15 mg/kg). This data is presented as Mean ± SD
Source: Author

*Table 3.1* Pharmacokinetic parameters of paracetamol in rats after treated with propylene glycol (15 mg/kg, p. o.) and Brij 58 (5 and 10 mg/kg, p. o.) on 21$^{st}$ day.

| PK Parameter | PCM (300 mg/kg) | PCM + PG (15 mg/kg) | PCM + Brij 58 (5 mg/kg) | PCM + Brij 58 (10 mg/kg) |
|---|---|---|---|---|
| $C_{max}$ (µg/mL) | 10.056 ± 1.154 | 12.768 ± 1.790* | 14.209 ± 1.025** | 16.433 ± 1.355** |
| $AUC_{0-12}$ (µg h/mL) | 69.610 ± 8.828 | 72.164 ± 33.132 | 86.306 ± 8.273** | 93.086 ± 6.805*** |
| $AUC_{0-\infty}$ (µg h/mL) | 156.270 ± 18.180 | 181.113 ± 41.948 | 123.618 ± 18.338 | 125.753 ± 12.855 |
| $t_{max}$ (h) | 1.250 ± 0.274 | 1 ± 0.0 | 1.083 ± 0.204 | 1 ± 0.0 |
| $t_{1/2}$ (h) | 10.270 ± 1.307 | 13.136 ± 3.289* | 15.070 ± 3.651** | 17.895 ± 1.355** |
| MRT (h) | 14.418 ± 2.989 | 15.268 ± 4.614 | 16.294 ± 4.389 | 18.636 ± 1.027* |
| CL/F (mL/h) | 0.123 ± 0.051 | 0.126 ± 0.290 | 0.111 ± 0.017 | 0.108 ± 0.013 |
| $V_z$/F (mL/kg) | 1.894 ± 0.258 | 1.442 ± 0.252* | 1.283 ± 0.427** | 1.083 ± 0.224** |
| Vss /F(mL/kg) | 1.927 ± 0.205 | 1.515 ± 0.256** | 1.300 ± 0.332** | 1.116 ± 0.130** |

Source: Author

somewhat lower, but not significantly so. Compared to the paracetamol control group, the $t_{1/2}$ of paracetamol following treatments with propylene glycol and Brij 58 was significantly longer ($P < 0.05$). With 15 mg/kg of propylene, the half-life rose from 10.270 ± 1.307 to 13.136 ± 3.289 hours, and with 5 mg/kg of Brij 58, it increased to 15.070 ± 3.651 hours. When given in conjunction with propylene glycol and Brij 58, paracetamol had a greater MRT.

The data are presented as the mean plus or minus the standard deviation. in comparison to the group given paracetamol alone (one-way ANOVA followed by Tukey's post-tests to compare each column to column), with ***p<0.001, **p<0.01, *p<0.05.

**Effect of Brij 58 on the pharmacokinetics of NAPQI** Figure 3.44 displays the plasma concentration-time profiles of NAPQI after oral treatment of paracetamol monotherapy, propylene glycol (15 mg/kg), and Brij 58 (5 mg/kg and 10 mg/kg). Plasma concentrations of NAPQI were lower in the group that received paracetamol in addition to propylene glycol and Brij 58, as compared to the group that received just paracetamol. Table 3.2 displays the mean pharmacokinetic characteristics of NAPQI after oral treatment of paracetamol to rats with or without Brij 58 (10 & 10 mg/kg). With propylene glycol (15 mg/kg), the $C_{max}$ of NAPQI was dramatically reduced from 0.579 ± 0.134 to 0.514 ± 0.056. With Brij 58 (5 mg/kg), it was reduced to 0.432 ± 0.071, and with Brij 58 (10 mg/kg), it was reduced to 0.335 ± 0.083 µg/mL.

All values are mean ± SD. *p<0.05 when compared to paracetamol alone group (one-way ANOVA followed by Tukeys post-tests to compare to each column to column).

## *Effect of Brij 58 on the formation of NAPQI in vitro*

Isolated rat hepatocytes were cultured *in vitro* to examine paracetamol's metabolism and harmful effects with and without Brij 58. Incubation conditions for hepatocytes included varying doses of Brij 58 and paracetamol alone. In order to isolate the harmful metabolite NAPQI, a rapid, simple, and quantitative HPLC technique was used. Paracetamol was

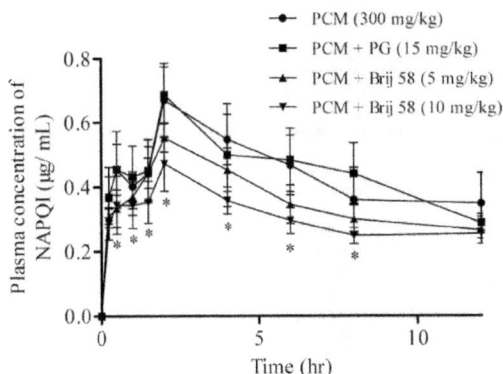

*Figure 3.4* Using Brij 58 and propylene glycol orally, we measured the mean plasma concentration-time profiles of NAPQI in 6 rats. (●) Paracetamol was used as a control; (■) 15 mg/kg of paracetamol with propylene glycol; (▲) 5 mg/kg of paracetamol with Brij 58; (▼) 10 mg/kg of paracetamol with Brij 58. This data is presented as Mean ± SD. Table 3.2. The pharmacokinetic characteristics of NAPQI after 21 days of treatment with propylene glycol (15 mg/kg, p. o.) and Brij 58 (5 and 10 mg/kg, p. o.)
Source: Author

*Table 3.2* The pharmacokinetic characteristics of NAPQI after 21 days of treatment with propylene glycol (15 mg/kg, p. o.) and Brij 58 (5 and 10 mg/kg, p. o.).

| PK Parameter | PCM (300 mg/ kg) | PCM + PG (15 mg/kg) | PCM + Brij 58 (5 mg/kg) | PCM + Brij 58 (10 mg/kg) |
|---|---|---|---|---|
| $C_{max}$ (μg/mL) | $0.671 \pm 0.117$ | $0.687 \pm 0.088$ | $0.553 \pm 0.044^*$ | $0.473 \pm 0.085^*$ |
| $AUC_{0-12}$ (μg h/ mL) | $5.295 \pm 0.471$ | $5.370 \pm 0.465$ | $4.317 \pm 0.248^*$ | $3.698 \pm 0.240^*$ |
| $AUC_{0-\infty}$ (μg h/mL) | $12.343 \pm 7.784$ | $8.591 \pm 1.083$ | $9.566 \pm 2.811^*$ | $8.916 \pm 2.404^*$ |
| $t_{max}$ (h) | $2.000 \pm 0.0$ | $2.000 \pm 0.0$ | $2.000 \pm 0.0$ | $2.000 \pm 0.0$ |
| $t_{1/2}$ (h) | $6.886 \pm 2.880$ | $7.578 \pm 1.838$ | $10.666 \pm 2.456^*$ | $14.008 \pm 6.377^*$ |

Source: Author

shown to be aggressively digested in hepatocytes, leading to the formation of NAPQI, a reactive hazardous metabolite. Figure 3.5 shows that compared to paracetamol alone, Brij 58 significantly decreased the generation of NAPQI, although the amount of reduction was dosage dependant.

### Effect of Brij 58 on the liver function tests and its structure

In this study, we looked at the effects of Brij 58 on liver function tests and its structure in rats that were given either paracetamol alone or a combination of the two. In Table 3.3, the findings are shown. Serum AST, ALT, ALP, TP, and TB levels were significantly elevated in rats given 300 mg/kg body weight of paracetamol orally compared to normal control rats by 206.83%, 139.511%, 146.00%, 110.89%, and 360.00%, respectively. In the group

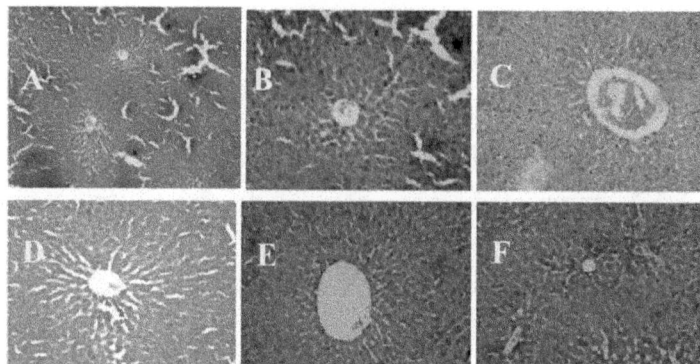

*Figure 3.5* All values are mean ± SD. ap<0.01 when compared to control group. bp<0.01 when compared to paracetamol group (one-way ANOVA followed by Tukeys post-tests to compare to each column to column)." PCM, Paracetamol. Figure 6. Rat livers were examined histopathologically. A and B, control group; C, paracetamol (300 mg/kg); D, propylene glycol 15 mg/kg and paracetamol (300 mg/kg); E, 5 mg/kg of Brij 58 and paracetamol (300 mg/kg); and F, 10 mg/kg of Brij 58 and paracetamol (300 mg/kg)
Source: Author

*Table 3.3* Effect of propylene glycol and Brij 58 on the liver function tests.

| Treatment | AST | ALT | ALP | TP | TB |
|---|---|---|---|---|---|
| Control | 154.833 ± 20.885 | 73.667 ± 9.606 | 178.667 ± 18.673 | 28.060 ± 1.066 | 20.475 ± 0.150 |
| PCM (300 mg/kg) | 345.667 ± 29.669[a] | 184.667 ± 12.580[a] | 410.333 ± 45.912[a] | 37.048 ± 2.976[a] | 22.312 ± 0.983[a] |
| PCM + PG (15 mg/kg) | 164.167 ± 20.331[b] | 86.333 ± 8.756[b] | 193.833 ± 26.491[b] | 34.532 ± 3.270[b] | 20.788 ± 0.133[b] |
| PCM + Brij 58 (5 mg/kg) | 272.5 ± 20.027[b] | 133.667 ± 14.855[b] | 230.333 ± 25.944[b] | 34.955 ± 4.834[b] | 21.097 ± 0.364[b] |
| PCM + Brij 58 (10 mg/kg) | 158.167 ± 15.829[b] | 104.833 ± 8.542[b] | 183.000 ± 24.747[b] | 31.162 ± 1.197[b] | 20.510 ± 0.183[b] |

Source: Author

that received paracetamol, these alterations were accompanied with steatosis, sinusoidal dilatation, severe necrosis, hemorrhage, and vascular congestion (Figure 3.6). Interestingly, when paracetamol was added to rats treated with Brij 58 (10 mg/kg), serum AST, ALT, ALP, TP, and TB levels dropped significantly (94.48%, 136.91%, 6.74%, 52.74%, and 333.60% respectively). This was accompanied by a protective effect on hepatic cells, as shown in Figure 3.6, and there was only scattered cytoplasmic vacuolization. The effects of propylene glycol were similar to those of Brij 58. Paracetamol had hepatotoxic effects, whereas Brij 58 therapy (5 mg/kg and 10 mg/kg) undid such effects.

## Discussion

In the present study, the groups that received both Brij 58 and paracetamol had higher plasma paracetamol concentrations and lower NAPQI concentrations. The current study results are supported by the previous scientific findings. "Oliver and Shih [5] conducted an *In vitro* studies on human and rat liver microsomes and have shown that certain substances can inhibit the CYP2E1-mediated metabolism of chlorzoxazone. These substances include Microcrystalline cellulose, Sucralose, Brij 58, Dicalcium Phosphate dehydrate, Brij 76, Mannitol, Brij 35, Tween 20, 40, 80, PEG 400, 2000, 4000, Pluornic F68, Saccharin, Cremophor RH40, Crospovidone, Croscarmellose Sodium, Pregelatinized starch, Sorbic acid, Citric acid, Myrj 52, Cremophor EL, Span 60, Sorbitol, and Lactose monohydrate. Propylene glycol (PG) was also reported as CYP2E1 inhibitor in both animal and human studies. In the present study Brij 58 inhibited the CYP2E1-mediated metabolism of paracetamol thereby increased its concentrations and decreased the concentrations of NAPQI. The functions of CYP2E1 and CYP3A4 in drug metabolism have been well documented, with CYP2E1 being linked to the formation of harmful byproducts. In their study, Martin et al. (2013) [7] used baculosome derived CYP enzymes to examine the effects of thirteen surfactants on seven different CYP isoforms at different doses (10000, 1000, 250, 500, 100, 10, 1, 0.1, 0.01 or 0µM). "The selected thirteen surfactants are sodium deoxycholate (SDC), sodium caprylate (SCP), α-tocopherol poly(ethylene glycol) succinate (TPS), Sucrose stearate, Sucrose palmitate, sodium 1,4-bis(2-ethylhexoxy)-1,4-dioxobutane-2-sulfonate (AOT), poly(ethyleneoxide) modified castor oil (cremophor EL), polyethylene glycol-hydroxystearate (solutol HS 15), poly(ethyleneoxide) sorbitan monolaurate (Tween 20), poly(ethyleneoxide) sorbitan monooleate (Tween 80), poly(ethylene glycol) hexadecyl ether (Brij 58), Alkyl (C12-16) dimethylbenzylammonium chloride (Hyamine) and Cetyl trimethylammonium bromide (CTAB). Hyamine, Tween 80, and CTAB all act as CYP3A4 and CYP2E1 inhibitors." Polymer polyethylene glycol, or PEG, is another CYP2E1 inhibitor. This opens up a new line of inquiry into the possibility of developing excipients to prolong the half-life and ultimate destiny of pharmaceuticals [8].

## Conclusion

The findings showed that Brij 58 greatly increased paracetamol plasma concentrations and drastically decreased *N*-acetyl-*p*-benzoquinoneimine plasma concentrations due to its inhibitory effect on cytochrome P-450 2E1. The histology of the rat's liver treated with Brij 58 showed considerable improvement when compared to the paracetamol group. The histology findings are being backed up by biochemical data as well.

## References

[1] Bastiaan, V., Daniel, J., & James, W. (2015). Target biomarker profile for the clinical management of paracetamol overdose. *British Journal of Clinical Pharmacology*, 80(3), 351–362. https://doi.org/10.1111/bcp.12699.

[2]  Carol, E., Jack, E., & Charles, A. (1984). Metabolism and cytotoxicity of acetaminophen in hepatocytes isolated from resistant and susceptible species. *Toxicology and Applied Pharmacology*, 76, 139–149. https://doi.org/10.1016/0041-008X(84)90037-1.

[3]  Flores-Pérez, C., Chávez-Pacheco, J., & Ramírez-Mendiola, B. (2011). A reliable method of liquid chromatography for the quantification of acetaminophen and identification of its toxic metabolite N-Acetyl-p-benzoquinoneimine for application in pediatric studies. *Biomedical Chromatography*, 25, 760–766. https://doi.org/10.1002/bmc.1511.

[4]  Jaeschke, H., Williams, C., Ramachandran, A., & Bajt, M. (2012). Acetaminophen hepatotoxicity and repair: the role of sterile inflammation and innate immunity. *Liver International*, 32(1), 8–20. https://doi.org/10.1111/j.1478-3231.2011.02501.x.

[5]  Dragostin, I., Dragostin, O. M., Samal, S. K., Dash, S., Tatia, R., Dragan, M., Confederat, L., Ghiciuc, C. M., Diculencu, D., Lupuşoru, C. E., & Zamfir, C. L. (2019). New isoniazid derivatives with improved pharmaco-toxicological profile: Obtaining, characterization and biological evaluation. *European journal of pharmaceutical sciences : official journal of the European Federation for Pharmaceutical Sciences, 137*, 104974. https://doi.org/10.1016/j.ejps.2019.104974

[6]  Mansour AA, Gonçalves JT, Bloyd CW, Li H, Fernandes S, Quang D, Johnston S, Parylak SL, Jin X, Gage FH. An in vivo model of functional and vascularized human brain organoids. Nat Biotechnol. 2018 Jun;36(5):432-441. doi: 10.1038/nbt.4127

[7]  Martin, P., Giardiello, M., McDonald, T. O., Rannard, S. P., & Owen, A. (2013). Mediation of in vitro cytochrome p450 activity by common pharmaceutical excipients. *Molecular pharmaceutics*, 10(7), 2739–2748 DOI: 10.1021/mp400175n

[8]  Ren, X., Mao, X., & Cao, L. (2009). Nonionic surfactants are strong inhibitors of cytochrome P450 3A biotransformation activity in vitro and in vivo. *European Journal of Pharmaceutical Sciences*, 36, 401–411. https://doi.org/10.1016/j.ejps.2008.11.002.

# 4 Box behnken design assisted with greenness and blueness assessment of a stability indicating RP-HPLC method for estimation of levosulpiride and pantaprazole sodium in capsule formulation

Hemant Kumar, Tatapudi[1,a], Vijay Srinivas, Pothula[2],
David Blessing Rani, Jakkala[3,b], Sambasiva Rao, Tummala[4],
Jami, Durgaganesh[2,c], Narasimharao, C. V.[5,d] and
Naveena, Gorrepati[6]

[1]School of Pharmacy and Technology Management. Shirpur, NMIMS University

[2]Stira Pharma, New Jersy, USA

[3]School of Pharmaceutical Sciences, Centurion University of Technology and Management, Vizianagaram, Andhra Pradesh, India

[4]Regulatory Affairs Stira Pharma, Hyderabad, India

[5]Shantiniketan College of Pharmacy, Maharashtra, India

[6]Lifecare pharmacy, Sanantonio, Texas, USA

## Abstract

An RP-HPLC technique that indicates stability was established and validated for the synchronous measurement of levosulpiride (LSP) and pantoprazolesodium (PAN) in a combination capsule formulation. Optimization with box-behnken design paired the green and blue assessment. This investigation involved the degradation of LSP and pantoprazole sodium under various stress test settings as prescribed by ICH. The two drugs were separated from their degradation products using a reversed phase (C18) analytical column with optimization done by Box-Behnken design consist mobile phase of 15 mM pottasium hydrogen orthophosphate: ethanol (70:30, v/v) buffer (pH 5). The retention times recorded for LSP and PAN were approximately 3.167 minutes and 5.999 minutes, respectively. The most environmentally friendly results were found when the level of environmental sustainability was evaluated using two advanced metrics: GAPI and AGREE. The practical applicability of the method was proven from BAGI. The proposed method was appropriate for assessing the stability of LSP and PAN prescription drugsand was effectively utilized in the qualitycontrol of bulk production and in formulations.

**Keywords:** Blueness, box behnken, greenness, levosulpiride, pantaprazole sodium, RP-HPLC, stability indicating

## Introduction

Levosulpiride (LSP) is the (S)-(-)-enatiomer of sulprde. Compared to the racemic and dextro forms, the levo form of sulpiride exhibits better antidopaminergic action, anti-emetic and antidyspeptic effects, and reduced acute toxicity [9]. LSP has a molecular formula

[a]hemkar_pharma@yahoo.co.in, [b]davidrani(at)rediffmail.com, [c]amidurgaganesh@gmail.com, [d]knarasimharao24@gmail.com, [d]naveengorrepati@gmail.com

DOI: 10.1201/9781003716648-4

C15H23N3O4S. It is an unconventional neuroleptic and a prokinetic agent [5]. LSP is also claimed to have mood elevating properties [4, 17, 19]. Pantaprazole sodium (PAN) chemically (Figure 4.1) has the molecular formula C16H14F2N3NaO4 S .1.5 H2O. PAN, a substituted benzimidazole derivative, is utilized for the short-term management of GERD (Rossi and Forgione, 1995). Literature survey reveals the availability of few methods for estimation of both pantaprazole sodium and Levosulpiride includes ultraviolet (UV) [6] HPLC as alone or in combination with other drugs ([15, 10] Poornima et al., 2014; Surve et al., 2013; Yoganand et al., 2013; Sirisha and Kumar, 2012; [1, 16, 20]; Thummala, 2014; [3, 18, 13]). There are some reported HPLC methods [12, 11, 14, 2] available for quantification of LSP and PAN in dosage form. Kothapalli et al. [13] and (Shivaraju et al., 2019) reported one stability indicating RP-HPLC method for estimation of LSP and PAN in combined dosage form. Unfortunately, both the methods have the drawbacks of long retention time of analytes and are not very sensitive. Moreover, the aforementioned approaches lack cost-effectiveness regarding solvent utilization and overall analysis duration. Consequently, the current investigation was undertaken. Given further contemplations, the objective of the study was to construct a novel framework that would enable the simultaneous application of GAC, BAGI and AQbD principles. The first-ever implementation of this integrated framework was used to design a green and reliable HPLC analysis of the two medications in their bulk and commercial formulations.

## Materials and Methods

Analysis and separation were conducted using a nucleosil ODS C8 column (250 mm × 4.6mm × 5 μm) at 250 nm in a temperature-controlled laboratory, with the column oven temperature consistently anchored at 30°C for all chromatographic runs. The mobile phase comprised a potassium hydrogen orthophosphate buffer (15 mM, pH 5) and ethanol in a 70:30 (v/v) ratio. The flowrate was established at 1 ml/min in isocratic mode, with an inject volume of 20 μL for all samples.

## Results and Discussions

### AQbD assisted method development

During initial experiments, the quantity of ethanol and buffer pH had an impact on the retention period. The Ishikawadiagram was used to choose the critical components for further analysis. For multivariate optimization, the BBD response surface design comprises of replicates at the centre and a set of points situated midway to the edge of a three-dimensional cube. Considering the influence of many factors, such as the % of ethanol (A), concentration of the phosphate buffer (B) and pH of buffer(C), on the time it takes for LSP to be retained (R1), and resolution factor of PAN (R2). BBD was utilized to enhance chromatographic parameters. The duration of LSP retention (R1) and the resolution of PAN (R2) were selected as the responses. Table 4.1 illustrates the impact of these three variables on the responses or critical quality attributes (CQAs).

The model was validated using design expert software, and its accuracy was further confirmed by analysis of variance (ANOVA), as presented in Table 4.2. The quadratic models were selected basedon the PRESSvalue, theresolution of PAN (R2), the retention period of

*Table 4.1* BBD for each run with responses.

| Run | Factors | | | Responses | |
|---|---|---|---|---|---|
| | A:% of ethanol(%v/v) | B:buffer concentration (mM) | C:buffer pH | retention time of levosulpride (min) | Resolution factor |
| 1 | 45 | 15 | 5.5 | 4.234 | 1.893 |
| 2 | 30 | 15 | 5 | 3.132 | 6.346 |
| 3 | 45 | 10 | 6 | 2.213 | 2.678 |
| 4 | 60 | 15 | 5 | 3.883 | 3.109 |
| 5 | 45 | 20 | 5 | 6.991 | 2.011 |
| 6 | 60 | 10 | 5.5 | 5.881 | 3.891 |
| 7 | 45 | 15 | 5.5 | 4.234 | 1.893 |
| 8 | 45 | 20 | 6 | 6.991 | 3.991 |
| 9 | 45 | 15 | 5.5 | 4.234 | 1.893 |
| 10 | 60 | 15 | 6 | 4.253 | 3.991 |
| 11 | 45 | 15 | 5.5 | 4.234 | 1.893 |
| 12 | 30 | 20 | 5.5 | 6.302 | 6.234 |
| 13 | 45 | 15 | 5.5 | 4.234 | 1.893 |
| 14 | 30 | 15 | 6 | 3.104 | 5.619 |
| 15 | 60 | 20 | 5.5 | 6.901 | 2.919 |
| 16 | 30 | 10 | 5.5 | 4.109 | 5.981 |
| 17 | 45 | 10 | 5 | 5.012 | 2.234 |

Source: Author

*Table 4.2* ANOVA, regression analysis of models and responses.

| Response | Standard deviation | Mean | % C.V. | PRESS | Adjusted R-square | Predicted R-square | Adequate precision | p value |
|---|---|---|---|---|---|---|---|---|
| Retention time of LSP (min) R1 | 0.0839 | 4.80 | 11.94 | 0.5531 | 0.9849 | 0.9843 | 19.94 | <0.0001 |
| Resolution factor for PAN R2 | 0.4277 | 3.44 | 9.26 | 14.67 | 0.9804 | 0.9832 | 6.37 | 0.0255 |

Source: Author

LSP (R1). Significant effects were observed with p-values below 0.05. The achieved signal-to-noiseratios for each response demonstrated appropriate signal intensity, as shown in Table 4.2.

The volume of ethanol and morality of buffer showed the most prominent effect on resolution of PAN and retentiontime for LSP. 2D and 3D RSM diagrams are generated in accordance with the significant variables, as depicted in Figure 4.1(a-d) the third variable remains constant at a predetermined level, which is typically the optimal value. The response typical graphs are illustrated in Figure 4.1(a-d), which clearly demonstrates the interdependence and interaction between the variables (factors A and B), with factor C remaining constant. As shown in Figures 4.1(a) and (b), the volume of ethanol significantly affected the retention duration of LSP and the resolution of PAN. The LSP exhibited an increase in resolution as the volume of ethanol and buffer concentration was elevated. The desirabilityplot for theresponses was shown in Figure 4.2. The optimized condition: molarity of buffer (15 mM), the volume of ethanol (30 % v/v) and pH of buffer (5.0) resulted in the retentiontime of LSP and PAN at 3.123 and 5.230 min, respectively. The optimized chromatogram was shown in Figure 4.3.

*The proposed method's validation*
`The linearity was examined utilizing., 18.5, 37.5, 56.25, 75, 93.75 and 112.5 μg mL$^{-1}$, of LSP and 10,20,30,40,50 and 60 μg mL$^{-1}$ of PAN. Table 4.3 displays a summary of the parameters. The linearity was confirmed by the elevated correlation coefficient and the minimal intercept value. The recovery percentages for LSP and PAN were recorded between 97.28% and 100.48%, and 99.53% to 100.51%, respectively. the recovery values (%) and %RSD, which show how accurate the suggested approach is. The "intra-day precision" of the method varied from 0.81% to 1.72% RSD for LSP and PAN. The "inter-day precision" of themethod ranged from 0.88 to 1.86 %RSD for LSP and PAN, indicating that the developed method demonstrates precision. The low RSD (%) values suggest that the proposed method demonstrates repeatability. The (LODs) for LSP and PAN medicines were 0.07

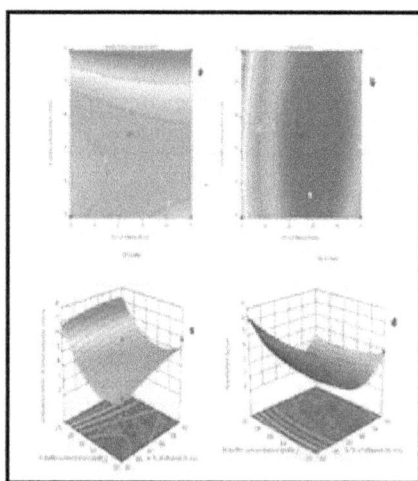

*Figure 4.1.* 2D plot response curve (a and b) and 3D RSM plot (c and d)
Source: Author

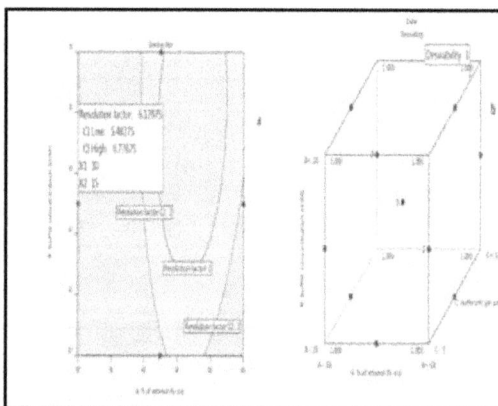

*Figure 4.2.* Overlay plot (a) and Desirability plot (b)
Source: Author

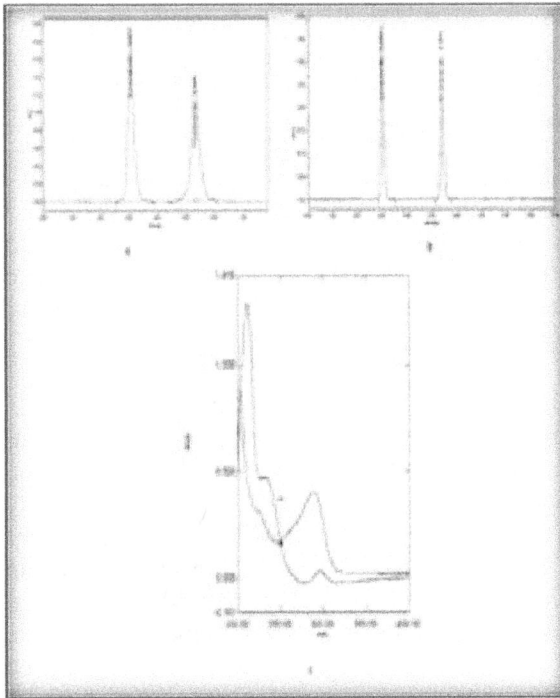

*Figure 4.3*. Chromatogram from standard solution (a), Sample solution (b) and UV spectra of analytes (c)
Source: Author

*Table 4.3* Linear regression analysis of calibration curves (n = 6).

| Drug | Linearity range (µg mL−1) | Intercept | Slope | Correlation coefficient (r2) | LOD (µg/mL) | LOQ (µg/mL) |
|------|---------------------------|-----------|-------|-------------------------------|-------------|-------------|
| LSP | 18.5-112.5 | 4697. | 40048 | 0.9999 | 0.07 | 0.22 |
| PAN | 10-60 | 7761.8 | 50662 | 0.9998 | 0.05 | 0.15 |

Source: Author

and 0.05 µg/mL, while the (LOQs) were 0.22 and 0.15 µg/mL, respectively (Table 4.3). Intentional modifications to the methodology, such as alterations in the mobile phase composition, flowrate, and pH of the phosphate buffer, did not have a significant impact on peak tailing, theoretical plates, or the percentas says of LSP and PAN. The results are presented. To assess the robustness of the proposed approach, six samples were produced and analyzed under various settings, including differentanalysts, days, columns, and systems. The RSD for LSP and PAN pharmaceuticals was shown to be under 2%. Thecomparison of findings obtained from two separate analysts, on differentdays and using various columnswith the sameHPLC equipment, demonstrated that the approach was robust across analysts, days, and columns. The RSD of LSP and PAN pharmaceuticals from the sixsample preparations must not exceed 2.0%.

*Stability indicating*

In the degradation investigation, LSP exhibited more deterioration than PAN under all stress levels. Despite the observation of unidentified degradant peaks in all degradation conditions, no degradant peaks were detected at the retention times of LSP or PAN. Consequently, LSP and PAN exhibit stability for a designated duration (4 hours) when the proposed approach is employed; otherwise, they are vulnerable to acids, alkalis, heat, hydrogen peroxide, and photolytic stress. This also signifies the method's specificity. The degradation profile was shown in Figure 4.4.

*Eco-friendly method assessment and applicability of the method*

Figure 4.5 illustrates the resulting complex GAPI results, showcasing the long-term viability and expansive scope of the procedure. AGREE metrics, the most recent green evaluation tool, incorporates all twelve green analytical concepts. The sum of the scores assigned to the different principles was computed to produce the provided result of 1. An indicator of the method's greenness is a value that approaches one. The overall outcome, as seen in Figure 4.5, demonstrates that the method has a significantly positive and enduring effect on the environment, particularly when the specific details of the method are inputted into the software. BAGI tools were used to evaluate the suggested HPLC method, which got a good score of 72.5, which means it can be used in a lot of situations. They got such high scores because they used reagents and instruments that are standard in all research labs. LSP and PAN were determined using the suggested approach for commercially sold formulations using Entracid L CAPSULES. For LSP and PAN respectively, the % recovery turned out to be 100.08±0.18 and 100.25±0.45.

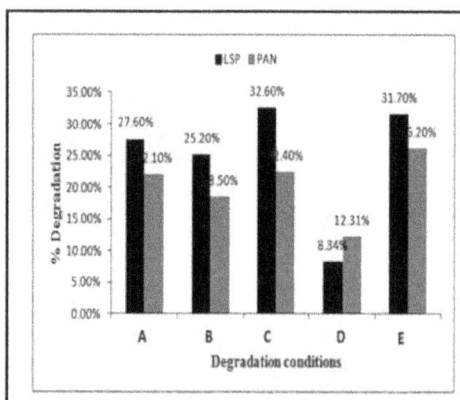

*Figure 4.4* Degradation data of both drugs in acid (A) base (B) oxidative (D) thermal (D) and photolytic (E)
Source: Author

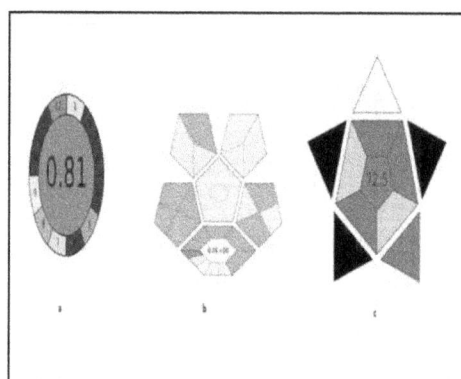

*Figure 4.5* AGREE plot (a) GAPI plot (b) and BAGI plot (c) from proposed method
Source: Author

## Conclusion

An analytical technique using HPLC based on AQbD-GAC principles has been developed for thesimultaneous measurement of LSP and PAN in capsule dosageform. This technique is characterized by its environmentally friendly nature, simplicity, high sensitivity, accuracy, reliability, and cost-effectiveness. The results of the greenevaluation tools also indicated that the technique was the most ecologically conscious and easily adjustable forindustrial and quality control purposes. According to the BAGI evaluation, the suggested approach provides notable advantages in terms of time and cost economy, hazard reduction, and general efficiency.

## References

[1] Agarwal, N., & Jagadeesh, B. (2012). Development and validation of stability indicating RP-HPLC for the simultaneous estimation of levosulpiride and rabeprazole sodium. International Journal of Pharma Bio Sciences, 3, 718–726.

[2] Arige, S. S., Arige, S. D., & Rao, A. L. (2017). Method development and validation of simultaneous estimation of pantoprazole sodium and levosulpiride in combined dosage form by RP-HPLC Method. World Journal of Pharmacy and Pharmaceutical Sciences, 6(7), 913–923.

[3] Battu, P. R., & Reddy, N. K. K. (2009). Development and validation of RP-HPLC for the pantoprazole sodium sesquihydrate in pharmaceutical dosage forms and human plasma. International Journal of ChemTech Research, 1(2), 195–198.

[4] Distrutti, E., Fiorucci, S., Hauer, S. K., Pensi, M. O., Vanaisa, M., & Morelli, A. (2002). Effect of acute and chronic levosulpiride administration on gastric tone and perception in functional dyspepsia alimentation. Pharmacology and Therapeutics, 16, 613–622.

[5] Fitton, A., & Wiseman, L. (1996). Pantoprazole: a review of its pharmacological properties and therapeutic use in acid related disorders. Drugs, 51(3), 460–482.

[6] Guslandi, M. (1993). The clinical use of levosulpiride. Current Therapeutic Research, 53(5), 484–501.

[7] Rossi, F., & Forgione, A. (1995). Pharmacotoxicological aspects of levosulpiride. *Pharmacological research*, 31(2), 81–94. DOI: 10.1016/1043-6618(95)80052-2

[8] Thummala, V. R., Seshadri, R. K., Tharlapu, S. S., Ivaturi, M. R., & Nittala, S. R. (2014). Development and Validation of a UPLC Method by the QbD-Approach for the Estimation of Rabeprazole and Levosulpiride from Capsules. *Scientia pharmaceutica*, 82(2), 307–326 DOI: 10.3797/scipharm.1310-17

[9] Singh J. International conference on harmonization of technical requirements for registration of pharmaceuticals for human use. J Pharmacol Pharmacother. 2015 Jul-Sep;6(3):185–7. doi: 10.4103/0976-500X.162004

[10] *Indian Pharmacopoeia* (2010). Vols. I, II, III. Government of India, Ministry of Health & Family Welfare. Delhi, India: The Controller & Publication.

[11] Jin, S. E., Ban, E., Kim, Y. B., & Kim, C. K. (2007). Development of HPLC method for the determination of levosulpiride in human plasma. Journal of Pharmaceutical and Biomedical Analysis, 35(4), 929–936.

[12] De Baere, S., Eeckhaut, V., Steppe, M., De Maesschalck, C., De Backer, P., Van Immerseel, F., & Croubels, S. (2013). Development of a HPLC-UV method for the quantitative determination of four short-chain fatty acids and lactic acid produced by intestinal bacteria during in vitro fermentation. *Journal of pharmaceutical and biomedical analysis*, 80, 107–115. DOI: 10.1016/j.jpba.2013.02.032

[13] Sirisha T, Gurupadayya B, Siddiraju S. Optimized and Validated RP-UPLC Method for the Determination of Losartan Potassium and Chlorthalidone in Pharmaceutical Formulations. Adv Pharm Bull. 2015 Mar;5(1):133-6. doi: 10.5681/apb.2015.019

[14] Kalaiselvi, P., & Lalitha, K. G. (2014). Analytical method development and validation of levosulpiride and pantoprazole in tablets by RP-HPLC method. *Journal of Biomedical and Pharmaceutical Research*, 3, 75–80.

[15] Khanage, S. G., Shinde, R. C., Mohite, P. B., & Deshmukh, V. K. (2013). Simultaneous estimation of levosulpiride and pantoprazole sodium in capsule dosage form by RP-HPLC method. *Annals of West University of Timisoara, Series Chemistry*, 22, 23–34.

[16] Kothapalli, L. C., Inamdar, A. A., Nanda, R. K., & Thomas, A. B. (2014). Development and validation of a stability-indicating HPLC method for simultaneous estimation of pantoprazole sodium sesquihydrate and levosulpiride in a combined dosage form. *International Journal of Research in Pharmaceutical Sciences*, 4, 32–38.

[17] Le THH, Phung TH, Le DC. Development and Validation of an HPLC Method for Simultaneous Assay of Potassium Guaiacolsulfonate and Sodium Benzoate in Pediatric Oral Powder. J Anal Methods Chem. 2019 Mar 7;2019:6143061. doi: 10.1155/2019/6143061

[18] Mamatha, K., Prasad, V. V. L. N., Haque, M. A., & Bakshi, V. (2014). Development and validation of RP-HPLC method for simultaneous estimation of levosulpiride and pantoprazole in combined pharmaceutical dosage form. *International Journal of Pharmaceutical Research and Health Sciences*, 2(6), 514–518.

[19] Manjunath, S., Chouhan, V., & Sandeep, S. (2011). Spectrophotometric estimation of levosulpiride in bulk drug and formulations. *International Journal of Pharmacy and Pharmaceutical Sciences*, 3, 135–137.

[20] Mullapudi, A., S. Pingali, and T. Santosh. 2013. Development and Validation of a Stability-Indicating Method for the Simultaneous Determination of Levosulpiride and Rabeprazole by High-Performance Liquid Chromatography. *International Journal of Pharmacy and Drug Analysis*. 1: 25–36.

[21] Mucci, A., Nolfe, G., & Maj, M. (1995). Levosulpiride: a review of its clinical use in psychiatry. *Pharmacological Research*, 31(2), 95–101.

[22] Patel, R., Kakadiya, J., Patel, P., & Shah, N. (2014). Development and validation of high-performance thin-layer chromatographic method for simultaneous estimation of levosulpiride and esomeprazole in combined pharmaceutical formulation. *World Journal of Pharmacy and Pharmaceutical Sciences*, 3, 1621–1636.

[23] Paul, W., and Jungnickel. 2000. Pantoprazole: A New Proton Pump Inhibitor. *Clinical Therapeutics*. 22(11): 1268–1293.

[24] Pawar, P. D., Gabhe, S. Y., Potawale, S. E., & Mahadik, K. R. (2014). Validated normal phase HPTLC method for the simultaneous quantification of levosulpiride and esomeprazole in capsule dosage form. *International Journal of Pharmacy and Pharmaceutical Sciences*, 6, 347–350.

# 5 Diagnosing Alzheimer's disease through hippocampal MRI analysis using artificial intelligence

*Meghna B. Jayakar[a], Aaryan Bhagat, Shubhangi Ojha[b] and Rashmi Patel[c]*

Department of Data Science, NMIMS MPSTME, Mumbai, Maharashtra, India

## Abstract

Alzheimer's disease (AD) is a progressive neurodegenerative disorder characterized by synapse loss and neuronal atrophy particularly throughout the hippocampus and cerebral cortex. Hippocampal atrophy serves as a critical biomarker for early diagnosis. In this study, we build upon the DenseCNN2 model, a lightweight 3D deep convolutional neural network designed for AD classification using hippocampus magnetic resonance imaging (MRI) segments. Using T1- weighted structural MRI data from the Alzheimer's disease neuroimaging initiative (ADNI), we focused on the hippocampus and applied a variety of machine learning techniques to classify AD versus cognitively normal (CN) subjects. Logistic Regression, Random Forest, 3D convolution neural networks (CNN) and our proposed model, HippocampusNet2D could predict AD patients with a high accuracy of over 90%. HippocampusNet2D uses a 2D CNN architecture to predict the presence of the disease. This multi-faceted approach aims to enhance the reliability of hippocampal-based diagnostic models.

Keywords: Alzheimer's disease, classification, deep convolutional neural network, DenseCNN2, hippocampal atrophy, machine learning, magnetic resonance imaging

## Introduction

Alzheimer's disease (AD) is the most common neurodegenerative disorder, accounting for 60–70% of dementia cases globally [1, 9]. The Alzheimer's Disease International reports that someone in the world develops dementia every 3 seconds, over 55 million people worldwide had dementia in 2020 (ADI-Dementia Statistics). By 2050, this number is projected to exceed 150 million [3]. The incidence of AD doubles every five years after age 60, and the prevalence increases sharply in those aged 85 and older. Despite this growing burden, current treatments primarily address late-stage symptoms. Neurodegeneration in AD likely begins 10 to 30 years before the symptoms manifest, emphasizing the need for early intervention [1]. During this preclinical phase, amyloid plaques and neurofibrillary tangles accumulate leading to cognitive decline, particularly episodic memory loss. Hippocampal atrophy, a key feature of AD, correlates with cognitive impairment and is one of the earliest brain changes observed (Reisberg, 2019).

Hippocampal atrophy: *Condition characterized by degeneration of the hippocampus; neurons atrophy causing memory loss and spatial disorientation (PainAssist, 2018).*

[a]jayakarmeghna@gmail.com, [b]aaryan10bhagat@gmail.com, [c]rashmipatel.in@gmail.com

DOI: 10.1201/9781003716648-5

*Hippocampus helps with information and retention of memories, and cognitive mapping. Presently, no known cure for hippocampal atrophy exists.*

Reliable biomarkers for early diagnosis and understanding of AD pathogenesis are crucial. While cerebrospinal fluid, blood and neuroimaging biomarkers show promise, there remains a need for more accessible and non-invasive diagnostic methods. This study addresses this gap by exploring the use of artificial intelligence (AI) techniques as a diagnostic aid for healthcare professionals.

## Medical Diagnostic Techniques and Challenges

The pathological indicators for AD can be viewed under a microscope as neurotic plaques generating A-42, amyloid beta peptide and neurofibrillary tangles composed of hyperphosphorylated tau [3]. Apolipoprotein E (APOE) alleles show the strongest link to AD among known genetic factors. Age, genetics, and environment significantly influence disease. Current treatments include combination therapy, NMDA receptor antagonists and cholinesterase inhibitors. However, factors like oxygen deprivation, hypoglycemia, vascular dysfunction, neuroinflammation, abnormal proteins, misfolded proteins and metal dyshomeostasis contribute to AD progression. Hence, new diagnostic and treatment approaches are essential. Traditional methods for diagnosis face considerable limitations due to AD's complexity and the inadequacies of existing approaches. Diagnosis historically relied on post-mortem analysis, while current methods depend heavily on clinical symptoms and cognitive assessments, risking misdiagnosis or delay [5]. Standard diagnostic criteria, such as those by the National Institute on Aging and Alzheimer's Association Flavell et al. [4], fail to account for all disease stages, overlooking cases with biomarkers but no cognitive symptoms. Limited access to biomarker testing, variability in disease presentation, symptom overlap with other dementias, and inconsistent integration of comprehensive assessments further complicate accurate and timely diagnosis. In this study, we are using diagnostic biomarkers found in neuro-images, specifically in MRI scans. Figure 5.1 highlights the differences in MRI scans of patients from normal to AD.

## Literature Review

AD diagnosis has benefited from AI techniques, particularly those utilizing MRI-based method- ologies. Deep learning (DL) models such as artificial neural networks and

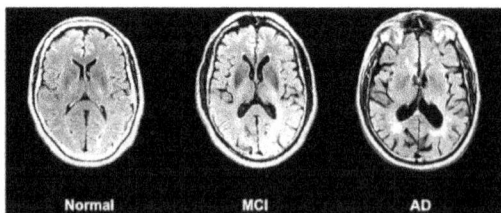

*Figure 5.1* Neurodegeneration in individuals - cognitively normal (CN), mild cognitive impairment (MCI) and AD [2]
Source: Author

convolution neural networks (CNN) have demonstrated high accuracy in analyzing structural brain changes in MRI scans. Integrating hippocampal segmentation and visual shape analysis allows CNN-based models to achieve over 90% accuracy. Apart from Random Forest (RF) and SVM, DL architectures-DenseCNN2 and 3D-CNN have been used to improve feature extraction from MRIs; PCA, k-NN for dimensionality reduction and classification have enhanced diagnostic accuracy. Integration of multi-modal data sources - PET scans, cognitive assessments further enhances diagnostic accuracy. Future advancements should focus on refining longitudinal data analysis. The model proposed in this study is inspired by DenseCNN2's architecture, however, it uses 2D data as input to optimize computational efficiency while maintaining high diagnostic accuracy.

## Materials and Methods

This section describes the methodology as shown in Figure 5.2.

## Data Collection

We obtained the AD and cognitive normal (CN) scans from Alzheimer's disease neuroimaging initiative (ADNI). Table 5.1. Both AD and CN scans were T1-weighted structural MRIs in DICOM and NIFTI formats.

CN and AD patients scans were labeled with 0's and 1's to signal the absence/presence of the condition as a requirement for our baseline models target binary input Neuroimaging libraries–NiBabel (NiBabel), Table 5.2. Nilearn (Nipy) were used for accessing and visualizing the scans, pydicom (PyPI) handled DICOM files, dcm2niix (PyPI) converted them to NIFTI.

## Data Preprocessing and Splitting

All DICOM files were converted to NIFTI for compatibility with ML pipelines. Scans were resized to a standard resolution, ensuring uniformity, reducing computational complexity, allowing batch processing during model training. Binary labeling allows us to frame the problem as a classification task, the models could learn to differentiate between normal and AD scans. Normalization techniques were not applied, this study focuses on evaluating

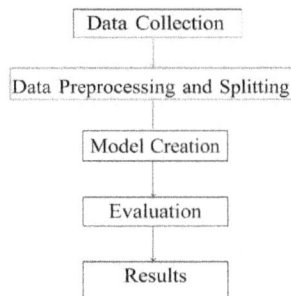

*Figure 5.2* Methodology
Source: Author

*Table 5.1*  Scan type and number.

| Scan type | Number of scans |
|---|---|
| Diagnosed Alzheimer's individuals | 304 |
| Cognitive normal individuals | 162 |
| Total scans | 466 |

Source: Author

*Table 5.2*  Scan labels.

| Scan type | Label |
|---|---|
| CN Subjects | 0 |
| AD Diagnosed subjects | 1 |

Source: Author

ML/DL models on raw neuroimaging data, aligning with real-world diagnostic workflows, ensuring that models learn directly from original scan distribution without preprocessing-induced biases. No augmentation techniques were applied however future work could explore these strategies to enhance model generalization. All ADNI scans were pre-screened for quality and relevance per protocol. The 466 scans were split 80/20 for training and validation, following ML standards.

## Model Creation

The first part of this study focuses on creating a baseline using classical ML models for AD Classification, the next on utilizing DL models, allowing for a comprehensive comparison of their performance, and insights into their strengths/limitations in clinical workflows. ML Models logistic regression (LR): Simple yet powerful ML algorithm used for classification. Models the probability of a given input belonging to a class label, selected for simplicity and interpretability [6]. Decision Tree (DT): Supervised ML algorithm utilized for classification and regression. This algorithm could aid in medical research for identifying AD by breaking down choices in a tree-like structure (Tarekegn et al., 2020). Random Forest (RF): Ensemble learning algorithm works by constructing multiple DTs while it trains and aggregates their results for improved accuracy (Cutler et al., 2007). SVM: Supervised ML algorithms - excels in high-dimensional spaces. Used to identify the ideal hyperplane between classes, handles non-linear correlations between features through kernel functions, making it ideal for classification in medical studies (Cortes and Vapnik, 1995). AdaBoost: Ensemble learning technique—strengthens classification by integrating multiple weak classifiers. Focuses on difficult-to-classify examples in following rounds by repeatedly adjusting the weights of mistaken instances (Freund and Schapire, 1997). XGBoost: Trains DTs sequentially—each new tree attempts to correct the errors made by the previous tree. The first DL model is a simple 3D-CNN, Figure 5.3 a class of DL models created to handle volumetric data [8], (Ji et al., 2013). Makes them efficient at analyzing medical MRI images - they can record spatial connections in three dimensions (Tran et al., 2015).

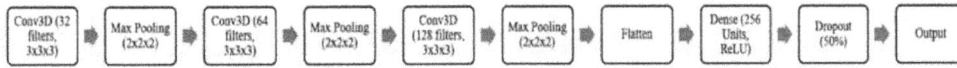

*Figure 5.3* 3D-CNN model architecture
Source: Author

*Figure 5.4* HippocampusNet2D model architecture
Source: Author

**Convolutional layers:** The model includes three 3D convolutional layers with 32, 64, and 128 filters, each using a (3, 3, 3) kernel and ReLU to capture increasingly complex features.

**Pooling layers:** Each Conv layer is followed by a 3D max pooling layer with a (2, 2, 2) kernel to downsample spatial dimensions.

**Flattening and dense layers:** The pooled output is flattened into a 1D vector, passed through a dense layer with 256 units and ReLU, and regularized with a 50% dropout layer.

**Output layer:** Single sigmoid-activated unit provides class probabilities (AD or CN). The model uses the Adam optimizer, binary cross-entropy loss, and accuracy as the performance metric. In this study, we use a 2D CNN – HippocampusNet2D, inspired by the DenseCNN2 architecture proposed by the authors of Katabathula et al. [7]. The HippocampusNet2D architecture is a 2D convolutional neural network designed to classify hippocampal MRI slices and distinguish between images associated with AD and CN conditions, unlike DenseCNN2 which utilizes 3D segments of the hippocampus.

The HippocampusNet2D model, depicted in Figure 5.4, handles 1-channel MRI slices via a 2D convolutional block featuring filters with double the growth rate, a kernel size of 3, followed by Batch Normalization (BN) and ReLU activation, and incorporates 2 × 2 max pooling for reducing dimensions. Dense Block 1 consists of four layers with a growth rate of 16, each featuring BN, ReLU, and a 3 × 3 convolution. Transition layer 1 diminishes feature maps and spatial dimensions using BN, ReLU, 1 × 1 convolutions, and 2 × 2 average pooling. Dense Block 2, like the first one, consists of four densely connected layers that merge features from earlier layers. A concluding BN and ReLU layer come before global average pooling, which compresses feature maps into individual values. A dense layer with 50% dropout converts these features into a single logit that forecasts the probability of AD. The model is trained utilizing binary cross entropy with logits loss and optimized with Adam for effectiveness and reliability.

## Results and inference

Support represents the actual occurrences of each class label in the dataset and varies across models, as shown in Table 5.3.

*Table 5.3* Support for each model.

| Model | CN (0) Scans | AD (1) Scans |
| --- | --- | --- |
| ML and ensemble models | 24 | 70 |
| 3D-CNN | 33 | 61 |
| HippocampusNet2D | 74 | 51 |

Source: Author

*Table 5.4* Model accuracy scores.

| Model | Accuracy score |
| --- | --- |
| Logistic Regression | 100% |
| Support Vector Machine | 74.47% |
| Decision Tree Classifier | 98.94% |
| Random Forest Classifier | 100% |
| AdaBoost Classifier | 98.94% |
| XGBoost Classifier | 74.47% |
| Simple 3D CNN | 100% |
| HippocampusNet2D | 99.20% |

Source: Author

## Accuracy

Table 5.4 shows the accuracy scores of each model used.

The models showed varying accuracy: LR, RFC, and 3D-CNN reached 100%, suggesting overfitting or strong spatial feature capture. HippocampusNet2D performed nearly perfectly, learning complex AD patterns. DT and AdaBoost scored 98.94%, indicating solid performance but potential generalization issues. SVM and XGBoost underperformed, needing further tuning. High accuracy suggests highly separable features, but accuracy alone isn't the best metric.

## Classification Report and Confusion Matrix

Table 5.5 shows the performance for predicting AD - Class 1. The performance metrics for each model varies, with some models such as LR and RFC achieving perfect scores across all metrics, while others such as SVM and XGBoost show lower precision.

LR, RFC, and 3D-CNN all achieved perfect performance with metrics of 1.00, indicating their strong ability to distinguish between CN and AD. SVM and XGBoost had a Recall of 1.00, correctly identifying all AD cases, but their Precision was lower (0.74), suggesting a tendency to over-predict AD with false positives. DT and AdaBoost classifiers performed well, with high Precision and Recall, though there was a slight trade-off: Decision Tree had fewer FNs, while AdaBoost leaned toward FPs. HippocampusNet2D closely matched the top models, with 0.98 Precision and 1.00 Recall, effectively identifying AD with minimal

*Table 5.5* Precision, recall, F1-scores.

| Model | Precision | Recall | F1-score |
|---|---|---|---|
| Logistic Regression | 1.00 | 1.00 | 1.00 |
| Support Vector Machine | 0.74 | 1.00 | 0.85 |
| Decision Tree classifier | 1.00 | 0.99 | 0.99 |
| Random Forest classifier | 1.00 | 1.00 | 1.00 |
| AdaBoost classifier | 0.99 | 1.00 | 0.99 |
| XGBoost classifier | 0.74 | 1.00 | 0.85 |
| 3D CNN for classification | 1.00 | 1.00 | 1.00 |
| HippocampusNet2D | 0.98 | 1.00 | 0.99 |

Source: Author

*Table 5.6* Confusion matrices.

| Model | TP | FP | FN | TN |
|---|---|---|---|---|
| Logistic Regression | 70 | 0 | 0 | 24 |
| SVM | 70 | 24 | 0 | 0 |
| Decision Tree classifier | 69 | 0 | 1 | 24 |
| Random Forest classifier | 70 | 0 | 0 | 24 |
| AdaBoost classifier | 70 | 0 | 0 | 24 |
| XGBoost | 70 | 24 | 0 | 0 |
| 3D CNN | 61 | 0 | 0 | 33 |
| HippocampusNet2D | 51 | 1 | 0 | 73 |

Source: Author

FPs. Overall, LR, RF, 3D-CNN performed excellently, and HippocampusNet2D performed well, while SVM and XGBoost need further tuning for improved performance.

Table 5.6 shows LR, RFC, AdaBoost, and 3D-CNN achieved perfect classification, with no FPs or FNs.SVM, XGBoost had no FNs but predicted 24 FPs. DT had one FN but no FPs. HippocampusNet2D achieved near-perfect classification - 51 TPs and one FP. While ROC curves are useful for assessing model discrimination, they were excluded to focus on the most relevant metrics. Future work could incorporate ROC-AUC for more detailed performance comparison.

## Limitations

The quality of data significantly impacts the effectiveness of AI models, as scarce training data may lead to overfitting and achieve flawless accuracy. Limited sample sizes can also restrict the applicability of findings. The intricate nature of deep learning models creates difficulties in understanding them, hindering their adoption in clinical settings. Moreover, creating these models demands significant computational power and specialized knowledge, which might not be available in every healthcare environment. Ethical issues such as patient confidentiality, data protection, and biases in algorithms need to be resolved prior to the broad deployment of AI models.

## Conclusion and Future Scope

The suggested convolution neural networks (CNN) architecture, HippocampusNet2D, achieved impressive results, coming close to the precision of models with flawless scores, showing that DL methods can efficiently evaluate MRI scans for diagnosing Alzheimer's disease (AD). Achieving high precision in MRI-based AD diagnosis has significant clinical ramifications, encompassing better diagnostic accuracy, early identification, non-invasive assessment, tailored medicine, and improved research potential. Although the model attained notable accuracy, issues such as overfitting and generalization remain. Future studies should concentrate on broadening datasets, improving models, and incorporating biomarkers like cerebrospinal fluid and genetic information for thorough diagnostics. Integrating MRI scans, blood tests, and cognitive evaluations could enhance precision even more. Tackling ethical issues such as bias, privacy, and transparency is crucial for the responsible deployment of AI. Moreover, longitudinal studies may assess the effectiveness of models in tracking disease progression, thereby aiding clinical trials and drug development.

## References

[1] Borroni, B. (2006). Predicting Alzheimer dementia in mild cognitive impairment patients. *European Journal of Pharmacology, * 545(1), 73–80. https://www.academia.edu/12830532/Predicting_Alzheimer_dementia_in_mild_cognitive_impairment_patients.

[2] Chandra, A., Dervenoulas, G., & Politis, M. (2019). Magnetic resonance imaging in Alzheimer's Disease and mild cognitive impairment. *Journal of Neurology, * 266, 1293–1302. https://doi.org/10.1007/s00415-018-9016-3.

[3] Dafre, R., & Wasnik Sr, P. (2023). Current diagnostic and treatment methods of Alzheimer's Disease: a narrative review. *Cureus, * 15(9), e45649. https://doi.org/10.7759/cureus.45649.

[4] Flavell, J., Ahern, E. G. M., Logan, B., Shaw, T. B., Adam, R. J., McElligott, C. A., et al. (2025). Factors associated with true-positive and false-positive diagnoses of behavioural variant frontotemporal dementia in 100 consecutive referrals from specialist physicians. *European Journal of Neurology, * 32(1), e70036. https://doi.org/10.1111/ene.70036.

[5] Hooper, C., Lovestone, S., & Sainz-Fuertes, R. (2008). Alzheimer's Disease, diagnosis and the need for biomarkers. *Biomarker Insights, * 3(May 27), 317–323. https://doi.org/10.4137/bmi.s682.

[6] Hosmer, D. W., Lemeshow, S., & Sturdivant, R. X. (2013). *Applied Logistic Regression.* (Vol. 398). Hoboken, NJ: John Wiley & Sons. https://doi.org/10.1002/9781118548387.

[7] Tarekegn, A., Ricceri, F., Costa, G., Ferracin, E., & Giacobini, M. (2020). Predictive Modeling for Frailty Conditions in Elderly People: Machine Learning Approaches. *JMIR medical informatics, * 8(6), e16678 DOI: 10.2196/16678

[8] Cutler, D. R., Edwards, T. C., Jr, Beard, K. H., Cutler, A., Hess, K. T., Gibson, J., & Lawler, J. J. (2007). Random forests for classification in ecology. *Ecology, * 88(11), 2783–2792. DOI: 10.1890/07-0539.1

[9] Cortes, C., Vapnik, V. Support-vector networks. *Mach Learn* 20, 273–297 (1995). https://doi.org/10.1007/BF00994018

[10] Freund, Y., Schapire, R.E. (1995). A desicion-theoretic generalization of on-line learning and an application to boosting. In: Vitányi, P. (eds) Computational Learning Theory. EuroCOLT 1995. Lecture Notes in Computer Science, vol 904. Springer, Berlin, Heidelberg. https://doi.org/10.1007/3-540-59119-2_166

[11] Katabathula, S., et al. (2021). Alzheimer's research & therapy. *Alzheimer's Research and Therapy,* 13, 104. https://doi.org/10.1186/s13195-021-00837-0.

[12] Litjens, G., T. Kooi, B. E. Bejnordi, A.A.Adiyoso Setio, F. Ciompi, M. Ghafoorian, et al. (2017). A Survey on Deep Learning in Medical Image Analysis. *Medical Image Analysis.* 42: 60–88. https://doi.org/10.1016/j.media.2017.07.005.

[13] Sharman, E. H. (2016). Reactive Oxygen Species and Protein Oxidation in Neurodegenerative Disease. *In Inflammation, Aging, and Oxidative Stress*, edited by S. Bondy and A. Campbell, 213–235. Cham: Springer. https://doi.org/10.1007/978-3-319-33486-8_11.

# 6 A comprehensive approach to brain tumor detection and classification

*Bhushan Nandwalkar[a], Ashish Awate[b], Mohit Desal,*
*Ayush Kakaria[c], Nishita Shah[d] and Pooja Mali*

SVKM's Institute of Technology, Dhule, Maharashtra, India

## Abstract

Brain tumors pose a significant healthcare challenge due to rising incidence rates, particularly among adults. Early and precise diagnosis is critical to improving survival outcomes. This study presents a deep learning-based system for automated brain tumor detection from magnetic resonance imaging (MRI) scans. The proposed approach employs advanced preprocessing techniques to enhance image clarity, coupled with data augmentation for improved model generalization. Using convolutional neural networks (CNNs) such as Inception-V3 and AlexNet, the system achieves robust feature extraction, classification, and prediction. To address the increasing brain tumor prevalence in India, the system is implemented using a wide dataset ensuring adaptability for any other demographics and classification of the tumor. Real-time analysis allows a user-friendly interface, thus easier integration into clinical workflows. Reduced errors in diagnosis and accelerating treatment decisions with an automated analysis of MRI results help radiologists to work more effectively in their diagnostic performances. This system provides the scale and accessibility for further cases of brain tumors and broader clinical applications.

**Keywords:** Brain tumors, classification, convolutional neural networks, deep learning, diagnosis, magnetic resonance imaging

## Introduction

Brain tumors pose a significant healthcare challenge due to their increasing prevalence and high mortality rates, making early and accurate diagnosis crucial for enhancing patient survival rates. Traditional MRI-based diagnosis relies heavily on radiologists, a method that is time-consuming and susceptible to human error. This has spurred the development of automated detection systems that utilize deep learning techniques. Recent progress in convolutional neural networks—like AlexNet, Inception-V3, ResNet, and U-Net variants—and hybrid methods combining CNN-FCN architectures, transfer learning, and attention mechanisms has greatly enhanced tumor classification and segmentation. However, many current studies fail to provide a thorough performance comparison among these CNN architectures and do not adequately tackle the challenges of real-world clinical implementation. The need for reliable diagnostic tools is especially high in India, a country where the annual incidence of brain tumours is between 3-10 per 100,000 according to the Indian Council of Medical Research (ICMR or Ministry of Health & Family Welfare), which constitutes only 2% of all cancers. To tackle these problems, our work provides an automatic deep learning-based

[a]bhushan.nandwalkar@svkm.ac.in, [b]Ashish.Awate@svkm.ac.in, [c]ayushkakaria1234@gmail.com, [d]shah@nmims.edu

DOI: 10.1201/9781003716648-6

brain tumor detection system with unique preprocessing, data augmentation, AlexNet and Inception-V3 architecture CNN classification as well, emphasising on how the comparison of CNN architectures can bring in real-time evaluation and improves on its clinical importance.

## Literature Review

Glan and Kumar [1] proposed a better algorithm for tumor segmentation from T2 and FLAIR multimodality MRI images. Genetic algorithms (GA)/support vector machines (SVM) for quality improvement in segmentation were used in the current study. A powerful way to detect the edges of tumors outside, in a robust manner, is the most valuable solution we can obtain for MRI segmentation quality. This led to a better genetic algorithm optimization for SVM classification, which in turn picked out the regions (i.e., tumor) more accurately. Kiran et al. [2] used the SVM algorithm for brain tumor diagnosis in MRI Siamese contrast enhancement and noise reduction-improved pre-processing methods while they undertook their research tasks. The result of this work proved that SVM can be used in the classification of tumor versus non-tumor tissue with sufficient resources, and it can be a tucked away option for deep architecture (Li et al. (2019). This paper has taken a giant step in improving the classification and segmentation of brain tumor through deep learning. A model for attention mechanism to brain tumor segmentation on multi-modal MRI scans. It achieved great performance with a deep learning model, armed by feature extraction and enhancing the segmentation. The intent-detection attention mechanism pays attention only to the tumor regions, so less random misclassification and higher predictability of predictions.

Nadeem et al. [4] explored tumor analysis using deep learning via CNNs. Feature extraction from MRI images was made to distinguish between different kinds of tumors. The study revealed both the benefits of deep learning on handling large data and that classification accuracy is much better in deep models than classical ML. Sun et al. [6] also proposed an end-to-end model that consolidated 3D CNNs and radiomic feature extractions for tumor segmentation and survival prediction on all multimodal MRI information was taken as inputs to be preprocessed by histogram equalization, ensuring input image quality and making accurate deep radiomic analysis survival prediction. Paul et al. [5] developed an automatic deep convolutional neural network (CNN) brain tumor detector. It was highly accurate for tumor detection and identification after a few tuning of CNN architecture. The paper proved that CNNs beat plain approaches in classification and feature learning, making perfect for real-world application to medical high. The studies highlight advancements in brain tumor detection and segmentation using deep learning. Glan and Kumar [1] designed an improved genetic algorithm SCA-based SVM for better select features and accurate tumour segmentation in addition, multimodal MRI helped with superiority. Kiran et al. [2] tuned SVM using preprocessing methods that can be used in resource-limited environments, while an attention mechanism for feature augmentation was proposed by Li et al. [3] to lower misclassification rates. CNNs were employed for tumor classification by Nadeem et al. [4], with a focus on big annotated datasets. Paul et al. [5] demonstrated the value of deep learning in the clinical context by developing a real-time CNN-based detection system. The results validate deep learning's superiority in accuracy and automation, but they also highlight computational burdens and data scarcity.

## Proposed Methodology

Advanced pre-processing techniques would be in place with deep learning models from which the detection and classification process of brain tumors would utilize AlexNet and Inception-V3. The methods of pre-processing include noise reduction, normalization, and augmentation to ensure that any image quality is maximized, and the models are sufficiently sound. AlexNet achieves 80% accuracy, while Inception-V3 performs slightly better at 82%. The results will establish the effectiveness of the system in the classification of tumors into four categories. With such accurate and timely predictions, the system is expected to minimize diagnostic errors, speed up treatment planning, and support radiologists, thus bringing out the potential for scalable and significant clinical applications.

### Data set description/database schema description
1. **Name:** Brain MRI tumor classification dataset
2. **Total images:** 3,459
3. **Number of classes:** 4

- **No tumor (Normal brain):** 395 images
- **Meningioma:** 708 images
- **Glioma:** 1426 images
- **Pituitary tumor:** 930 images

### Architecture overview
**User input:** The process begins with user input, which is usually images of the brain taken through MRI for use in tumor detection.

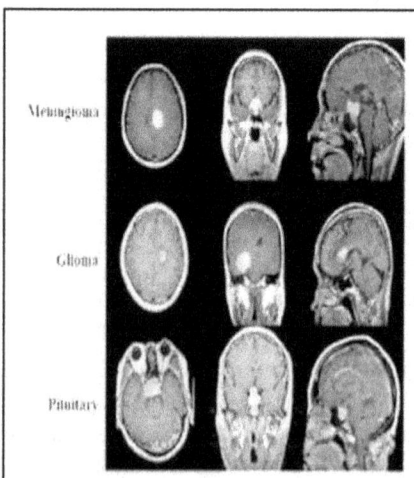

*Figure 6.1* Dataset
Source: Author

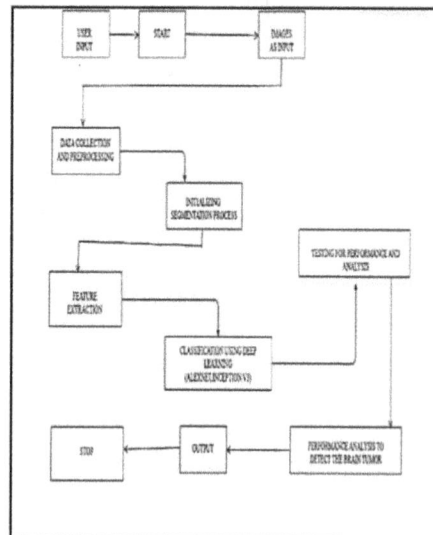

*Figure 6.2* Architecture
Source: Author

**Start:** This first step initiates the process, ensuring that the system is well-prepared to handle the input.

**Images as input:** The MRI images that have been provided serve as input to the system, constituting the dataset for subsequent analysis. Figure 6.2.

**Data collection and preprocessing:** Preprocessing techniques:

MRI images were gathered and classified into four categories of tumors: No tumor, meningioma, glioma, and pituitary tumor. The dataset was shuffled to avoid biases related to order, guaranteeing an equitable and varied data distribution that improves model dependability. Figure 6.1. It was divided into training (56%), validation (14%), and testing (30%) subsets utilizing stratified sampling to tackle class imbalance and maintain uniform model performance. Pixel intensity values were adjusted to a [0,1] range (by applying a factor of 1/255), enhancing model training stability and accelerating convergence. To improve data quality, Gaussian filtering was utilized to diminish high-frequency noise while maintaining structural details, and histogram equalization was used to boost contrast, enhancing the visibility of tumor regions for efficient feature extraction. Class distributions were evaluated using count plots to guarantee equitable representation in all subsets, reducing learning bias and enhancing balanced training. To enhance model adaptability and reduce overfitting, several augmentation methods were dynamically implemented during training, such as rescaling (1/255), rotation (±15°), width shift (±10%), zoom (1%), shear (1%), brightness modification (0.3–1.5), and flipping both horizontally and vertically. These methods added variability in orientation, position, size, and brightness, improving the model's robustness and generalization. The enhancement methods significantly boosted the model's accuracy and dependability in evaluating new MRI images, aiding in steady tumor identification and categorization.

**Initializing segmentation process:** Segmentation divides the region of interest, like the potential tumor areas, from the rest of the MRI image. It makes sure that the system concentrates on the most relevant parts for feature extraction.

**Feature extraction:** This is the extraction of texture, shape, and intensity from the segmented images. These characteristics are essential to classify normal and abnormal regions of the brain.

**Classification using deep learning (AlexNet, Inception V3):** The features that are extracted are classified through deep learning models, that is, AlexNet and Inception V3. This is used to classify as a tumor or not; if it is a tumor, then what type of tumor, that is, glioma, meningioma, pituitary tumor, or any other.

**Inception-V3:** An efficient and highly accurate architecture of CNN is identified. The architecture uses Inception modules, which run multiple convolutions with different kernel sizes in parallel, so the network can recognize a large range of features at different scales. Besides that, it uses additional classifiers for training stability and avoidance of overfitting, with the use of batch normalization that enables faster convergence. Such improvements make Inception-V3 very useful in such complex tasks as detection in medical images, in which accuracy and computational power play important roles.

**Convolution layers:** Each convolutional layer applies a kernel to extract features:

$$y_{ij}^{(l)} = \text{ReLU} \left( \sum_{m=1}^{M} \sum_{n=1}^{N} w_{mn}^{(l)} x_{(i+m)(j+n)}^{(l-1)} + b^{(l)} \right)$$

where:
- $\chi^{(l-1)}$ is the input to the layer l,
- $w_{mn}^{(l)}$ is the kernel weight of size M×N,
- $^{(l)}$ is the bias term.
- ReLU is the activation function, ReLU(z)=max (0, z)

## 2. Loss function (categorical cross-entropy):
Measures classification error:

$$\mathcal{L} = -\frac{1}{N} \sum_{i=1}^{N} \sum_{j=1}^{C} y_{ij} \log(\hat{y}_{ij}).$$

**AlexNet**: AlexNet is an influential model for deep learning that remarkably accelerated the process of image recognition and won the 2012 ImageNet competition. The model includes several layers of convolution followed by fully connected layers, making use of ReLU activation to help accelerate training speed and avoid vanishing gradients. Additional techniques applied in the model include data augmentation and dropout to prevent overfitting. Newer architectures have outperformed this, but AlexNet stands as a major milestone for deep learning to be achieved for image classification.

*Convolution layers*
Each convolutional layer applies a kernel to extract features:

$$y_{ij}^{(l)} = \text{ReLU} \left( \sum_{m=1}^{M} \sum_{n=1}^{N} w_{mn}^{(l)} x_{(i-m)(j+n)}^{(l-1)} + b^{(l)} \right)$$

where:
- $\chi^{(l-1)}$ is the input to the layer l,
- $w_{mn}^{(l)}$ is the kernel weight of size M×N,
- $^{(l)}$ is the bias term.
- ReLU is the activation function, ReLU(z) = max (0, z)

Layers in the code:
- **Conv2D-1**: 96 filters, kernel size 11 × 11, stride 4.
- Conv2D-2: 256 filters, kernel size 5 × 5, padding = 'same'.
- Conv2D-3, Conv2D-4, Conv2D-5: 384 and 256 filters, kernel size 3 × 3, padding = 'same'.

## 2. Loss Function (Categorical Cross-Entropy):
Measures classification error:

$$\mathcal{L} = -\frac{1}{N} \sum_{i=1}^{N} \sum_{j=1}^{C} y_{ij} \log(\hat{y}_{ij}).$$

where $y_{ij}$ is the ground truth $\hat{y}_{ij}$ is the predicted probability.

By implementing these preprocessing and augmentation techniques with cutting-edge deep learning models, our system improves accuracy, reduces classification errors, and boosts reliability in detecting and classifying brain tumors.

**Testing for performance and analysis:** This one is used to verify the performance of classification models with tools such as accuracy, precision, and other metrics. At this step, we need to evaluate whether the models are performing stably and accurately for brain tumor detection or not. We then do a thorough analysis to validate tumor detection and classification, model predictions vs. the ground truth.

**Output:** This gives final output (Tumor detection is there or not and if detected what type of tumor)

**Stop:** The process concludes after providing the output, marking the end of the procedure.

## Conclusion

*Inception V3 matrix*

The confusion matrix for Inception-V3 indicates robust classification performance, especially in identifying glioma. However, there are some misclassifications, particularly between meningioma and no-tumor, as well as between pituitary tumor and glioma. Despite these inaccuracies, the model shows improved overall accuracy and superior feature extraction abilities when compared to AlexNet.

*Alexnet CNN matrix*

The confusion matrix for AlexNet indicates a significant misclassification rate, especially between glioma and pituitary tumor, as well as meningioma and no-tumor. This implies that the model has difficulty differentiating between specific tumor types because of shared characteristics. Although it remains effective, AlexNet demonstrates lower accuracy when compared to Inception-V3.

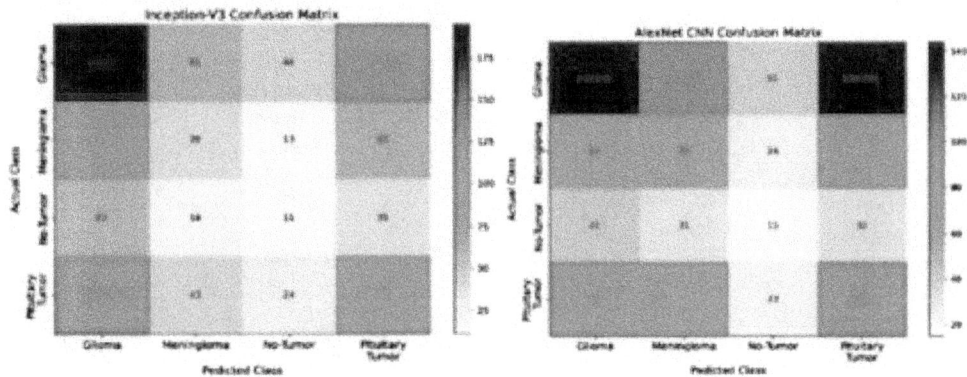

Using advanced techniques in image processing and artificial intelligence, the system is keen on early detection. This may become imperative in the determination of prompt medical interventions and better chances of survival. It helps in validating the results from radiologists. The system can scale with adaptability across diverse demographics of patients and healthcare settings. Finally, this research strives to eradicate diagnostic errors to optimize clinical workflows and speedy, accessible, and accurate solutions, hence continuing for better patient outcomes and significant developments in medical diagnostic techniques.

*Future scope*

This is a wide domain with much potential. More advanced classification models can be developed wherein, besides detecting the presence of tumors, they can differentiate among various types of brain tumor, including benign and malignant forms, as well as some specific subtypes of tumors. Such systems using multi-modal data such as genetics, clinical history, and other imaging modalities, including CT or PET scans, may increase diagnostic precision and provide an overall view of the disease. These models can be implemented in medical service organizations to assist radiologists to triage urgent cases and prepare individualized treatments. Future systems with continuous advancements in AI can incorporate federated learning for patient data privacy and federated model training across many institutions. Ultimately, these advancements will make tumor classification systems more precise, scalable, and accessible, supporting better patient care and outcomes in various healthcare settings.

# References

[1]  Glan, D. G., & Kumar, S. S. (2018). An Improved tumor segmentation algorithm from T2 and FLAIR multimodality MRI brain images by support vector machine and genetic algorithm. *Cogent Engineering, 5*(1), 1470915. https://doi.org/10.1080/23311916.2018.1470915.

[2]  Kiran, B. D., Parameshachari, D., & Sunil Kumar, D. S. (2022). SVM-based brain tumor detection and classification system. In *2022 IEEE 2nd Mysore Sub Section International Conference (MysuruCon),* Mysuru, India, (pp. 1–4). https://doi.org/10.1109/MysuruCon55714.2022.9972652.

[3]  Li, Z., X. Wang, and X. Li. (2021). Brain Tumor Segmentation Based on Deep Learning and an Attention Mechanism Using MRI Multi-Modalities Brain Images. *Scientific Reports.* 11: 90428. https://doi.org/10.1038/s41598-021-90428-8.

[4]  Nadeem, M. W., M. A. Al Ghamdi, M. Hussain, M. A. Khan, K.M.Khan, S.H. Almotiri, S.A.Butt, et al. (2020). Brain Tumor Analysis with Deep Learning. *Brain Sciences.* 10(2): 118. https://doi.org/10.3390/brainsci10020118.

[5]  Paul, A., Sahu, P. K., Das, P. K., & Meher, S. (2023). Deep convolutional neural network-based automatic detection of brain tumor. In 2023 2nd International Conference for Innovation in Technology (INOCON), (pp. 1–6). IEEE. https://doi.org/10.1109/INOCON57975.2023.10101238.

[6]  Sun, L., Zhang, S., Chen, H., & Luo, L. (2019). Brain tumor segmentation and survival prediction using multimodal MRI scans with deep learning. *Frontiers in Neuroscience, 13,* 810. https://doi.org/10.3389/fnins.2019.00810.

# 7 Leveraging free and open access resources for designing new oral hypoglycemic agents

*Aastha Shrivastava, Kshitij Doshi and Piyush Ghode*[a]

Department of Pharmaceutical Chemistry, SVKM's NMIMS School of Pharmacy and Technology Management, Shirpur, India

## Abstract

Antidiabetic drug therapy has witnessed new paradigms in the past two decades with the emergence of the drugs exhibiting novel mechanisms; and inhibition of sodium glucose cotransporter-2 (SGLT2) is one of them. The present work undertakes computational *de-novo* design of the novel SGLT2 inhibitors through incremental construction approach using free and open-source software. Of the top ranked compounds, the azabicyclo[3.2.0]heptan-7-one derivative (compound 5) emerged as the most significant candidate for further hit and lead optimization on the basis of favorable drug and lead likeliness parameters. The study exhibits putative application of free and open-source programs for hit and lead identification, and further wet lab studies can be undertaken to corroborate the results.

Keywords: de-novo, free and open source, SGLT2, T2DM

## Introduction

Among the three major types of disease, type-2-diabetes mellitus (T2DM) is a major concern owing to the modern lifestyle. According to the International Diabetes Federation (IDF), diabetes mellitus (DM) affects 463 million people around the world with claims of an astounding 9.3% of adults aged 20–79 years being affected. India ranks second just after China with 77 million affected adults (aged 20–79) which is estimated to increase to 101 million in 2030 and ~134 million by 2045. This calls for severe measures for prevention and management of the disease [4]. Although healthy routine along with refraining from overeating and sedentary lifestyle is recommended for controlling the blood glucose levels, use of antidiabetic medications is required for management of T2DM in a majority of population. SGLT2 inhibitors block the SGLT2 action in the kidneys and thereby reducing the glucose reabsorption from the urine and reintroducing it into the bloodstream. By inhibiting this process, the concentration of glucose in the urine increases, and the blood sugar levels are lowered. SGLT2 inhibitors do not affect the secretion of insulin from the pancreas [1]. They are a newer antidiabetic class with the first drug dapagliflozin being launched in 2012 in Europe. The drug was subsequently approved by FDA in 2014. Since then, different SGLT2 inhibitors have been approved and are available in market, such as canagliflozin, empagliflozin and ertugliflozin [12]. Discovery of phlorizin paved the way for identification of the role of SGLTs in the renal absorption of glucose and a direct effect on the glycaemic index. But owing to its non-selectivity and poor pharmacokinetic profile it was considered inappropriate for clinical use. None-the-less, it provided a good starting point for designing selective SGLT2 inhibitors. In addition to the abovementioned agents, other drugs have

[a]piyushghode@gmail.com

DOI: 10.1201/9781003716648-7

also been approved to be used in certain countries e.g. janagliflozin (China), enavogliflozin (DWP-16001) (South Korea) and tofogliflozin (Japan) along with one compound, rongliflozin as investigational drug.Chemically, SGLT2 inhibitors can be classified based on the basis of glycosidic linkage between the sugar moiety and other functional groups or ring systems *e.g.* O-glucoside SGLT2 inhibitors, C-glucoside SGLT2 inhibitors, N-glucoside SGLT2 inhibitors, S-glucoside SGLT2 inhibitors, non-glucoside SGLT2 inhibitors and naturally occurring SGLT2 inhibitors [6, 3]. A very small portion of organic chemical space ($\sim 10^{60}$ molecules) has been explored for drug development which can be one of the limiting factors in the discovery of new agents through high throughput screening. Therefore, *de-novo* generation of new molecules can be a crucial strategy to come up with new scaffolds against different targets. It is a promising strategy for generation of new hits and leads. This process typically involves a combination of computational modelling and experimental validation [8]. This study encompasses the generation of new SGLT2 inhibitors through fragment connection approach. The generated molecules following Lipinski criteria were docked in the active site of SGLT2 and the most significant molecule was chosen based on the binding affinity.

## Materials and Methods

The 2D structure drawing was done through MarvinSketch from ChemAxon("ChemAxon," n.d.). UCSF Chimera [11] was used for 3D visualization of ligands, proteins and docked complexes. The e-Lea3D de-novo design pipeline Douguet, [2] was used to generate the molecules *de-novo* in the active site of SGLT2 (through fragment connection utilizing genetic algorithm) and the generated molecules were docked through the program protein ligand ant system (PLANTS) [5]. The crystallographic structure of SGLT2 was downloaded from the protein data bank (PDB; ID: 7VSI [9]) containing empagliflozin as the bound ligand.

## Results and Discussion

Some novel SGLT2 inhibitor structures were obtained through computational *de-novo* design approach by "growing" the compounds inside the active site by combination of fragments of some FDA approved drugs. The obtained compounds were subjected to Lipinski filtration in order to obtain the prospective orally bioavailable compounds. Finally, the docking scores of these compounds were compared along with required interactions with the active site residues to infer the most significant compounds which can be considered as potential hits and that can be utilized to develop the "lead compounds" with enhanced SGLT2 inhibition. In all, six such runs were performed to obtain 104 unique molecules. Visual inspection of ligand receptor interactions and comparing the docking scores of respective compounds gave the most important compound.

The best five molecules among these are reported in Table 7.1.

Among the generated compounds, compound 1 and 2 show interactions with important active site amino acids. The amino acids responsible for activity as well as stabilization of protein-ligand complex of SGLT2 are (SER 287, ASN 75, GLN 457, PHE 98, THR 87 and LYS 321) [10], whereas other interactions within the active site may stabilize the protein

*Table 7.1* Most significant compounds with their respective docking scores.

| Generation number | Structure | PLANTS score | Interactions (Bond length) |
|---|---|---|---|
| 1. | | -111.960 | PHE 98, LYS 321, HIS 80 SER 287, TRP 291, THR 153 |
| 2. | | -104.120 | TRP 291, LYS 321, ASN 75, THR 87, THR 153 |
| 3. | | -103.780 | TRP 291, LYS 321, ASN 75, THR 87 |
| 4. | | -102.160 | SER 287, LYS 321, PHE 98, TYR 290 |
| 5. | | -102.050 | SER 287, TRP 291, LYS 321, ASN 75, PHE 98 |

Source: Author

ligand complex. Thus, compound 1 has polar interactions with PHE 98, LYS 321, HIS 80, SER 287, TRP 291 and THR 153; Compound 2 has polar interactions with TRP 291, LYS 321, ASN 75, THR 87 and THR 153; Compound 3 has interactions with TRP 291, LYS 321, ASN 75 and THR 87. Compound 4 shows interactions with SER 287, LYS 321, PHE 98 and TYR 290, whereas Compound 5 interacts with SER 287, TRP 291, LYS 321, ASN 75 and PHE 98. Therefore, it can be inferred that all these compounds can serve as good "hits" for the identification of new "leads".

Figure 7.1 illustrates the interactions of the compounds to SGLT2 active site Following the docking study, all the compounds were subjected to prediction of various ADMET properties. **Table 7.2** provides the major physicochemical properties, lipophilicity, pharmacokinetics

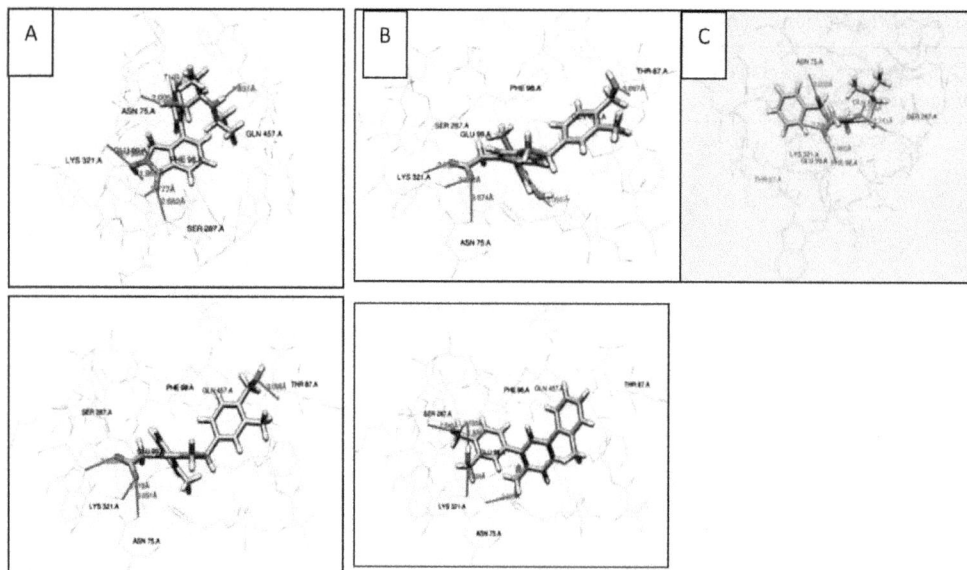

*Figure 7.1* Interaction of the Docked Compounds in the SGLT2 active site A: Compound 1;
B: Compound 2; C: Compound 3; D: Compound 4; E: Compound 5
Source: Author

along with drug and lead likeliness data for all the compounds. In addition, synthetic accessibility gives an idea about the ease or difficulty in synthesizing the compounds (Score between 1 and 10, where 1 suggests very easy and 10 suggests very difficult). According to Table 7.2, all the compounds show good predictions for the GI absorption. A comparison of the molecular weights of all the compounds also shows that they are following Lipinski's criteria for drug likeliness. Compounds 2 and 4 are predicted to not cross the blood brain barrier (BBB) and thus are less likely to produce CNS side effects. The p-gp substrates may not be good lead or drug candidates as it can result in efflux of drugs from cells. Among our compounds, 1-3 are predicted as p-gp substrates and therefore compounds 4 and 5 can be considered as superior to them on this parameter. The compounds which do not exhibit the inhibition of CYP2D6 and CYP3A4 should be preferred over the ones which inhibit them in order to avoid drug-drug interactions due to modified metabolism of some drugs. Only compound 5 is predicted as the non-inhibitor of both these enzymes. Thus, compound 5 emerges as the most significant compound obtained from this study. Further, it shows facile synthetic accessibility than compounds 1, 2 and 3 and a moderate bioavailability, it presents more versatility in modification of functional group and resulting in a better compound through these modulations.

## Summary and Conclusion

This work encompasses the generation of new molecules through fragment connection approach which may serve as prospective lead candidates against T2DM. The incremental construction method through adjoining the fragments of FDA approved drugs was applied

*Table 7.2* The physicochemical and pharmacokinetic parameters for the generated compounds.

| Comp. No. | Formula | #H-bond acceptors | #H-bond donors | MW | MR | TPSA | Consensus Log P | GI absorption | BBB permeant | Pgp substrate | CYP2D6 inhibitor | CYP3A4 inhibitor | Lipinski violations | Lead likeness | Bioavailability Score | Synthetic Accessibility |
|---|---|---|---|---|---|---|---|---|---|---|---|---|---|---|---|---|
| | $C_{22}H_{28}N_2O_2$ | 3 | 2 | 352.47 | 109.51 | 52.57 | 3.17 | High | Yes | Yes | Yes | No | No | No (MW>350) | 0.55 | 3.66 |
| | $C_{25}H_{24}O_4$ | 4 | 3 | 388.46 | 113.81 | 77.76 | 3.90 | High | No | Yes | Yes | No | No | No (MW>350) | 0.56 | 3.88 |
| | $C_{25}H_{24}O_3$ | 3 | 2 | 372.46 | 111.79 | 57.53 | 4.30 | High | Yes | Yes | Yes | No | Yes | No (MW>350) | 0.85 | 3.85 |
| | $C_{23}H_{22}O_4$ | 4 | 3 | 362.42 | 106.08 | 77.76 | 3.53 | High | Yes | No | Yes | Yes | No | No (MW>350) | 0.56 | 2.91 |
| | $C_{18}H_{24}N_2O_3$ | 4 | 1 | 316.39 | 91.33 | 60.85 | 1.46 | High | No | No | No | No | No | Yes | 0.55 | 3.49 |

Source: Author

for generation of these new molecules. Further, the newly generated molecules were screened on the basis of Lipinski's filters in order to get candidates with acceptable oral bioavailability. Considering all the parameters required for drug/lead likeliness, compound 5 may be considered as the most significant molecule of lead generation, which can be utilized for lead optimization.

**Acknowledgment**

The authors wish to thank SVKM's NMIMS Deemed to be University for making the necessary facilities available in order to perform this study.

## References

[1]   Cowie, M. R., & Fisher, M. (2020). SGLT2 Inhibitors: mechanisms of cardiovascular benefit beyond glycaemic control. *Nature Reviews Cardiology,* 17(12), 761–772. https://doi.org/10.1038/s41569-020-0406-8.

[2]   Douguet, D. (2010). E-LEA3D: a computational-aided drug design web server. *Nucleic Acids Research,* 38(suppl_2), W615–621. https://doi.org/10.1093/nar/gkq322.

[3]   Du, X., Lizarzaburu, M., Turcotte, S., Lee, T., Greenberg, J., Shan, B., et al. (2011). Optimization of triazoles as novel and potent nonphlorizin SGLT2 Inhibitors. *Bioorganic and Medicinal Chemistry Letters,* 21(12), 3774–3779. https://doi.org/10.1016/J.BMCL.2011.04.053.

[4]   A Cross-Sectional Retrospective Study Assessing Potentially Inappropriate Medications for Elderly Diabetic Patients in a Tertiary Care Hospital in Saudi Arabia. Risk Management and Healthcare Policy, 2024 DOI: https://doi.org/10.2147/RMHP.S484334

[5]   Korb, O., Stutzle, T., & Exner, T. E. (2009). Empirical scoring functions for advanced protein-ligand docking with PLANTS. *Journal of Chemical Information and Modeling,* 49(1), 84–96. https://doi.org/10.1021/ci800298z.

[6]   Li, A. R., Zhang, J., Greenberg, J., Lee, T., & Liu, J. (2011). Discovery of non-glucoside SGLT2 inhibitors. *Bioorganic and Medicinal Chemistry Letters,* 21(8), 2472–2475. https://doi.org/10.1016/J.BMCL.2011.02.056.

[7]   Foxwell, H.J., Menascé, D.A. MARVIN: A Web-Based System for Representing, Retrieving, and Visualizing Analogies. World Wide Web 7, 385–419 (2004). https://doi.org/10.1023/B:WWWJ.0000040802.02242.e9

[8]   Mouchlis, V. D., Afantitis, A., Serra, A., Fratello, M., Papadiamantis, A. G., Aidinis, V., et al. (2021). Advances in de novo drug design: from conventional to machine learning methods. *International Journal of Molecular Sciences,* 22(4), 1676. https://doi.org/10.3390/IJMS22041676.

[9]   Niu, Y., Liu, R., Guan, C., Zhang, Y., Chen, Z., Hoerer, S., et al. (2021). Structural basis of inhibition of the human SGLT2–MAP17 glucose transporter. *Nature,* 601(7892), 280–284. https://doi.org/10.1038/s41586-021-04212-9.

[10]   Ohkura, K., & Tabata, A. (2023). Molecular aspects of C-glycosides: interactive analysis of C-linked compounds with the SGLT2 molecular model. *Anticancer Research,* 43(8), 3747–3754. https://doi.org/10.21873/ANTICANRES.16559.

[11]   Pettersen, E. F., Goddard, T. D., Huang, C. C., Couch, G. S., Greenblatt, D. M., Meng, E. C., et al. (2004). UCSF chimera—a visualization system for exploratory research and analysis. *Journal of Computational Chemistry,* 25(13), 1605–1612. https://doi.org/10.1002/jcc.20084.

[12]   Xu, L., Wu, Y., Li, J., Ding, Y., Chow, J., Li, L., et al. (2025). Efficacy and safety of 11 sodium-glucose cotransporter-2 inhibitors at different dosages in type 2 diabetes mellitus patients inadequately controlled with metformin: a bayesian network meta-analysis. *BMJ Open,* 15(2), e088687. https://doi.org/10.1136/BMJOPEN-2024-088687.

# 8 Quantitative assessment of medical device recall: a three-year perspective on cause and consequences

*Ramesh Kolluru[1,a], Pankaj Nerkar[2,b], Rahul Raut[2],*
*Satyajeet Jadhwar[2] and Atul Patil[2]*

[1]School of Agricultural Sciences and Technology, Narsee Monjee Institute of Management Studies, Shirpur, Maharashtra, India

[2]R.C. Patel Institute of Pharmaceutical Education and Research, Shirpur, Maharashtra, India

## Abstract

This paper presents a quantitative analysis of recalls of medical devices (MD) events conducted by the US Food and Drug Administration (USFDA) during the period of 2021–2023. The objective is to evaluate the frequency, cause and impact of recalls, with consideration to systemic problems and proposed recommendations for future initiatives. All statistics about medical device recall from the year 2021 to 2023 were obtained from the USFDA official website with a particular dive into the medical device safety and recall section. Using this, we have collected information that covers why MD are recalled, the types of recalls that exist, who may be affected, and what happens after the recall.

Throughout the study period, 178 MD were recalled, with an annual increase of 57 in 2021, 60 in 2022, and 61 in 2023. The majority of recalls (mostly Class I recall) involved high-risk issues with severe health consequences and were primarily due to device malfunctions, leakage, software errors, mislabelling, and battery issues. Other notable causes included unauthorized distribution, equipment malfunctions, and contamination. With 46% of patients and 45% of healthcare workers impacted.

The study emphasizes the critical need for stringent regulatory oversight, robust quality control measures, and effective communication strategies to mitigate risks and ensure patient safety. Recommendations include issuing prompt recall and correction notifications to stakeholders and implementing targeted strategies to address specific risks. Collaborative efforts among regulatory agencies, manufacturers, and healthcare providers are essential for improving the effectiveness and safety of MD.

**Keywords:** Device malfunctions, equipment malfunction, healthcare professionals, medical devices, patient, recall, United States Food And Drug Administration

## Introduction

The IMDRF defines a medical device (MD) as any instrument, machine, implant, software, or material intended for use on humans, either alone or with other devices. These devices serve purposes such as diagnosing, treating, preventing, or monitoring diseases, supporting physiological functions, sustaining life, or analysing human specimens, without achieving their primary function through chemical, immunological, or metabolic means [6, 5]. In the U.S., the Federal Food, Drug, and Cosmetic Act (FFDCA) governs MD, with the FDA's

[a]ramesh.kolluru@nmims.edu, [b]nerkarpankaj@gmail.com

DOI: 10.1201/9781003716648-8

CDRH overseeing regulation before and after market entry. To sell a device, FDA approval requires a marketing application [5]. FFDCA Section 201(h) defines medical devices as those used to treat, diagnose, or prevent disease without relying on chemical or metabolic action. Examples include thermometers and tongue depressors [18]. The USFDA classifies medical devices into three categories (I, II, III) based on risk and safety requirements, with Class I being low-risk and Class III high-risk [13, 15].

## Medical device Classification: (Figure 8.1)

*Class I medical devices*
Class I devices have low to moderate risk and require general controls with minimal regulatory oversight. Most do not need FDA premarket review, relying instead on self-assessment. Examples include tongue depressors, bandages, hospital beds, and oxygen masks.[5, 2].

*Class II medical devices*
Class II devices require FDA general and specific controls and a 510(k) premarket notification before sale. Examples include blood pressure cuffs, catheters, pregnancy tests, and surgical gloves [20, 10, 8].

*Class III medical devices*
Class III devices require FDA premarket approval and oversight due to high risk. They support or sustain life, with examples including pacemakers, defibrillators, and cochlear implants [5, 2].

*USFDA regulations for medical devices*
The USFDA's CDRH regulates medical devices under 21 CFR, covering registration (Part 807), premarket review (510k, PMA - Part 814), investigational exemptions (IDE), quality standards (Part 820), and labeling/reporting (Parts 801, 803) to ensure safety and accountability [11, 21].

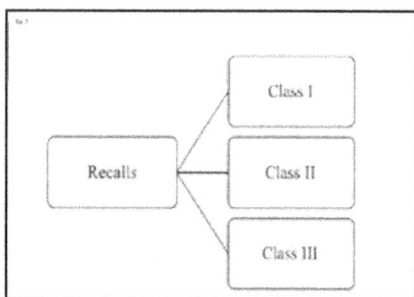

*Figure 8.1* Classification of MD
Source: Author

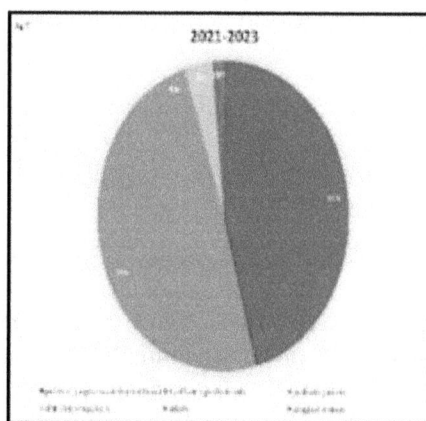

*Figure 8.2* Medical device recall classification
Source: Author

*Approaches for healthcare device marketing in the USA: 510k*
A premarket application (510k) must be proposed to the USFDA to demonstrate that the product proposed for sale is fundamentally identical to an existing lawfully marketed product in terms of safety and efficacy. Submitters must justify their claims of substantial equivalence by comparing their product to one or more similar, authorized commercial items.

**Pre-market approval (PMA)**
Pre-market approval is necessary for devices that are life-sustaining or could pose health risks, primarily Class III devices. Manufacturers must obtain PMA approval before they can market these devices [12, 19].

*Recall*
A recall occurs when a company removes or corrects a product violating USFDA regulations. Manufacturers may voluntarily withdraw defective products to protect public health [9, 16].

**Medical device recall**
A medical device recall removes or corrects faulty equipment that violates FDA rules due to malfunction, safety risks, or health concerns [1, 7].

*Who initiates medical device recall?*
A medical device recall is typically initiated by the organization responsible for the device, such as the producer or distributor, when they identify a violation of regulations. It involves: initiating the recall and notifying the FDA [1].

*Regulations for medical device recalls*
The recall process involves notifying the FDA, which oversees recalls under 21 CFR Part 806. It aligns with Part 7 for voluntary recalls and Part 810 for mandatory recalls of high-risk devices [4].

## Classification of Medical Device Recalls

The USFDA groups recalls on the rank of health risk the product poses to users or patients, categorizing them into Class I, II, and III recalls (Figure 8.2).

**Class I**
Class I recalls involve items that might cause major health problems, harm, or death. If there is a risk that using or being displayed to a product that breaks the law might result in serious health repercussions, a Class I recall is required.

*Class II*
Class II recalls cover items that might cause significant injury or brief sickness to consumers. This categorization applies when exposure to or usage of a non-compliant product may cause transient health problems that can be reversed with medical care.

*Class III*
Class III recalls are initiated for products or devices that are unlikely to cause serious health risks [7, 17, 14].

**Potential reasons for medical device recalls**
Medical device recalls often occur owed to various issues, including overheating, battery failures, leaks, distribution of devices lacking FDA authorization, software glitches, and high rates of false positives. These problems highlight the critical need for rigorous quality control to make sure the safety with reliability of MD.

**People affected owing to medical device failure**
The impact of medical device failures extends to a diverse group of individuals and organizations, including patients receiving care, healthcare providers, caregivers, and all personnel involved in patient treatment. Clinicians, healthcare administrators, and distributors are also affected, as they depend on the reliability of these devices for safe and effective care and operations [3].

## Methodology

This quantitative study analyzes USFDA medical device recalls from 2021–2023, focusing on affected users and recall causes. Data from the FDA's website includes recall reasons, classifications, impacted individuals, and recommended actions, organized in Excel by year. Statistical analysis identified recall trends, categorizing reasons, recall class, actions, and affected groups. Pie charts and bar graphs illustrate recall distribution and frequency.

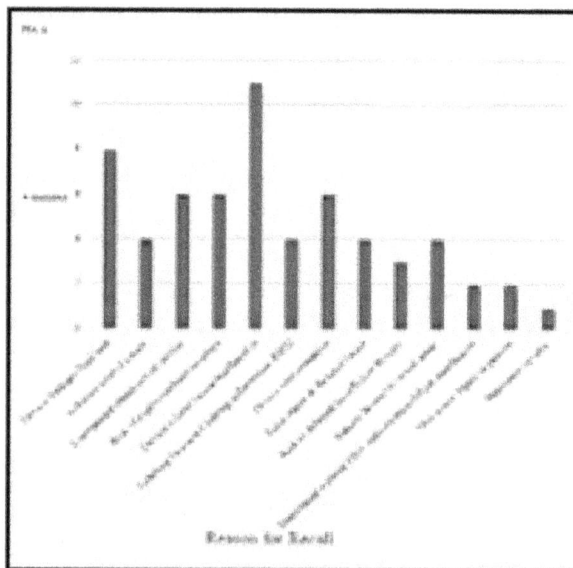

*Figure 8.3*  Total number of medical device recalls between 2021to 2023
Source: Author

# Result

*Total number of medical devices recalls from 2021 to 2023*

The Figure 8.3 illustrates the analysis of medical device recalls, focusing on incidents that occurred between 2021 and 2023. The US FDA issued recalls for 178 MD during these three years. The number of recalls in 2021, 2022, and 2023 were 57, 60, and 61, respectively, indicating a rising trend in recalls each year. All recalled MD during this period fall under class I recalls.

*Reasons for medical device recalls & their numbers in 2021*

The Figure 8.4 represents the medical devices recalled in the year 2021, a total of 57 medical devices were recalled by the US FDA. Out of those, six were recalled due to the reason of fluid leakage or device leakage; 22 medical devices were recalled due to the reason of device failure or malfunction; four were recalled due to software malfunction; four were recalled due to mislabeled or label-related issues; six medical devices were recalled due to the risk of false or inaccurate results; six due to the presence of a bezel component crack; five for the reason of a device battery issue; and 4 due to the reason of device contamination.

*Reasons for medical device recalls & their numbers in 2022*

The Figure 8.5 shows the MD recalled in 2022, with a total of 60 devices recalled by the US FDA. The majority of these recalls were due to two main reasons: approximately 14 devices were recalled because of equipment malfunctions, hardware issues, or other related problems. Additionally, 12 devices were recalled for being distributed without proper FDA authorization or illegally. Other notable reasons included battery issues and inaccurate results, which accounted for 4 and 5 recalls, respectively. Other causes involved skin

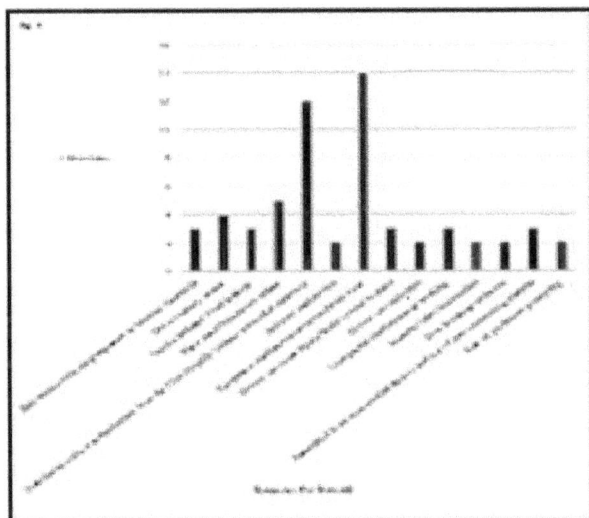

*Figure 8.4* Reasons for medical device recalls and their numbers in 2021
Source: Author

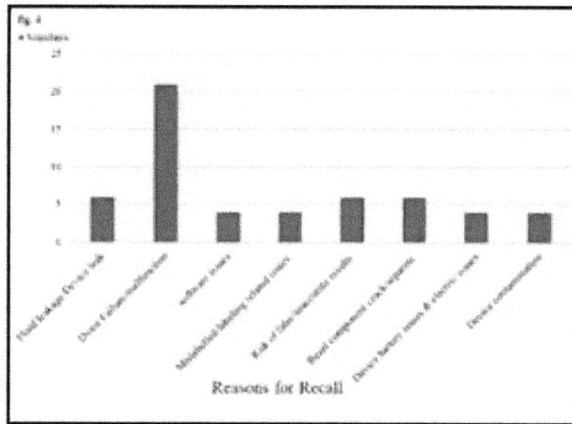

*Figure 8.5* Reasons for medical device recalls and their numbers in 2022
Source: Author

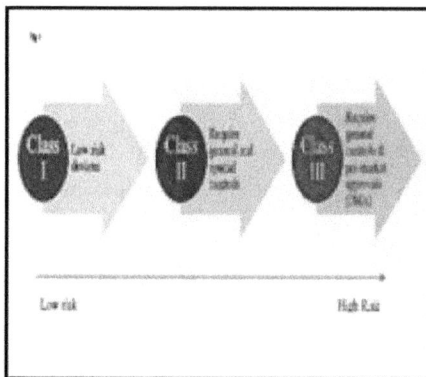

*Figure 8.6* Reasons for medical device recalls and their numbers in 2023
Source: Author

exposure to harmful chemicals, device contamination, unexpected shutdowns, and incorrect labeling, each resulting in 3 incidents. Less frequently, issues such as device contamination, filter breakage, assembly in uncontrolled facilities, and the risk of guidewire prolapsing were noted, with 2 recalls each.

*Excuses for medical device recalls and their numbers in 2023*
The Figure 8.6 illustrates the MD recalled in 2023, where the US FDA recalled nearly 61 devices. The recalls were mainly due to various issues impacting device functionality, safety, and accuracy. The leading cause was device-related malfunctions, which accounted for 11 recalls. Additionally, fluid leaks and risks of explosion, burns, or overheating led to 8 and 6 recalls, respectively. Unexpected shutdowns and device contamination were also significant contributors, each resulting in 6 recalls. Software issues, labelling problems, false

alarms, and battery or electrical issues were cited in 4 recalls each. Furthermore, concerns regarding delayed or insufficient therapy led to 3 recalls. There were 2 recalls due to devices being distributed without FDA authorization or illegally, and another 2 related to potential patient injuries; one recall was issued for devices that provided inaccurate results.

### *People's or stakeholders affected due to medical device recall (2021–2023)*

The medical device recall from 2021 to 2023 had significant effects on various stakeholders, as illustrated in the Figure 8.7. Approximately 46% of patients who underwent treatment were affected by the recall. Similarly, over 45% of healthcare professionals experienced repercussions. Pediatric patients represented about 4% of those impacted. Distributors or suppliers faced around 3% of their operations being affected by the recall. Furthermore, adult patients and pregnant women each saw a 1% impact due to the medical device recall.

When a medical device exhibits adverse effects or events, the following actions should be taken:

• Send an urgent medical device recall letter.
• **Send an urgent medical device repair or notification letter.**

These communications typically provide guidance for medical device users, including patients and healthcare professionals. Recommendations may include quarantining the product, ceasing its use, refraining from purchasing, monitoring its use, disposing of all unused products, returning specific lots, examining inventory, and checking functionality, among others [17] (Brown, 2022 )

### Discussion

Every year, the FDA receives a extensive number of safety-related reports concerning injuries, malfunctions, deaths, and other adverse incidents linked to MD from various sources, including manufacturers, hospitals, clinicians, and patients. Investigations conducted after a product is on the market, whether by manufacturers, independent researchers, or the FDA, may uncover additional safety issues. Manufacturers and distributors of MD are responsible for protecting public health with safety from substandard, misleading, or dangerous

*Figure 8.7* People's or stakeholders affected due to medical device recall (2021–2023)
Source: Author

products. When difficulties with a device occur, organizations must respond swiftly to assess whether a recall is warranted, develop alternative solutions, and ensure transparency throughout the recall process. While the FDA oversees most regulatory aspects, the manufacturer is typically the first entity involved in medical device recalls. Contrary to what the term suggests, recalls do not always mean that a product is immediately removed from use. Instead, they can involve various other "corrections," such as inspections, adjustments, minor repairs, updated labelling, and informing patients. An analysis of US FDA medical device recalls from 2021–2023 shows a relating trend, with a total 178 Class I recalls, which pose significant health risks. The annual increase—57 recalls in 2021, 60 in 2022, and 61 in 2023—underscores the urgent need for enhanced regulatory oversight and quality control. The percentage of failure of medical devices was calculated. In 2021, the main reasons for recalls were device malfunctions (21 recalls), fluid leaks, and software problems. This pattern continued into 2022, with equipment malfunctions and unauthorized distributions being significant issues. By 2023, device malfunctions still topped the list, alongside concerns about leakage and safety risks like overheating. Around 46% of patients and 45% of healthcare professionals were affected by these recalls, highlighting the extensive impact. Vulnerable groups, such as paediatric and pregnant patients, were also included. Taking prompt action is vital; sending urgent recall and correction letters can help reduce risks, guiding users on necessary measures like isolating affected products and stopping their use.

## Conclusion

The review of medical device recalls from 2021–2023 shows considerable systemic challenges in the industry, with the US FDA recalling 178 MD, pointing to serious health risks. The recalls were mainly due to device malfunctions, fluid leaks, software issues, mislabelling, and battery failures, impacting a broad range of stakeholders, including healthcare professionals, paediatric and pregnant patients, and distributors. This stresses the requirement for focused policies to manage risks and address specific demographic issues. Quick actions, such as sending recall and correction letters, are crucial for reducing harm and ensuring patient safety. The findings stress the importance of strict regulatory oversight, strong quality control, and effective communication to maintain safety and efficacy standards in MD.

## Conflict of Interest

According to the authors, none of their known financial conflicts or personal connections could have influenced the research presented in this study.

## References

[1]   Avchar, P., Kashid, G., Chormale, R., Dayma, A., & Mankar, K. (2024). USFDA regulatory oversight of medical device recalls. *Journal of Chemical Health Risks,* 14(3), 603–610.

[2]   Bhaskar, R., Ola, M., Saharan, S., & Nikam, V. (2023). Regulatory requirements for medical device registration in Kingdom of Saudi Arabia, US and European union. *International Journal of Drug Regulatory Affairs,* 11(2), 75–85.

[3] Carr, P. J., Higgins, N. S., Cooke, M. L., Mihala, G., & Rickard, C. M. (2018). Vascular access specialist teams for device insertion and prevention of failure. *Cochrane Database of Systematic Reviews, 20*(3), CD011429. https://doi.org/10.1002/14651858.

[4] Everhart, A. O., Sen, S., Stern, A. D., Zhu, Y., & Karaca-Mandic, P. (2023). Association between regulatory submission characteristics and recalls of medical devices receiving 510(k) clearance. *Journal of the American Medical Association, 329*(2), 144–156. https://doi.org/10.1001/jama.2022.22974.

[5] Gupta, S. (2016). Medical device regulations: a current perspective. *Journal of Young Pharmacists, 8*, 6–11.

[6] Sun, J., Wu, K., Liu, B., & Zhang, S. (2021). *Zhongguo yi liao qi xie za zhi = Chinese journal of medical instrumentation, 45*(1), 62–66.. DOI: 10.3969/j.issn.1671-7104,2021.01.013

[7] Kamisetti, R. R. (2022). Regulatory control on medical devices – a case study on device recalls by USFDA. *Journal of Intellectual Property Right, 27*, 190–201.

[8] Brown JS, Mendelsohn AB, Nam YH, Maro JC, Cocoros NM, Rodriguez-Watson C, Lockhart CM, Platt R, Ball R, Dal Pan GJ, Toh S. The US Food and Drug Administration Sentinel System: a national resource for a learning health system. J Am Med Inform Assoc. 2022 Nov 14;29(12):2191-2200 doi: 10.1093/jamia/ocac153

[9] Curtis, K. M., Nguyen, A. T., Tepper, N. K., & Whiteman, M. K. (2025). Using updated clinical recommendations to support contraceptive decision-making: U.S. Medical Eligibility Criteria for Contraceptive Use, 2024. *Contraception*, 111015. Advance online publication.. DOI: 10.1016/j.contraception.2025.111015

[10] Mooghali, M., Ross, J. S., Kadakia, K. T., & Dhruva, S. S. (2023). Characterization of US food and drug administration class I recalls from 2018 to 2022 for moderate- and high-risk medical devices: a cross-sectional study. *Medical Devices (Auckl), 16*, 111–122. https://doi.org/10.2147/MDER.S412802.

[11] Darrow, J. J., Avorn, J., & Kesselheim, A. S. (2021). FDA Regulation and Approval of Medical Devices: 1976-2020. JAMA, 326(5), 420–432.. DOI: 10.1001/jama.2021.11171

[12] Ratna, J. V., Parimalambica, M., & Murthy, K. V. R. (2018). Requirements for introducing medical devices in India and US market – a comparative study of regulations. *International Journal of Drug Regulatory Affairs, 6*(4), 9–20.

[13] Sagar, D., & Gupta, P. (2022). A comparative study of medical device regulation in US and India. *International Journal of Drug Regulatory Affairs, 10*(1), 83–87.

[14] Mooghali M, Rathi VK, Kadakia KT, Ross JS, Dhruva SS. Medical device risk (re)classification: lessons from the FDA's 515 Program Initiative. BMJ Surg Interv Health Technol. 2023 Sep 28;5(1):e000186.. doi: 10.1136/bmjsit-2023-000186

[15] Everhart AO, Sen S, Stern AD, Zhu Y, Karaca-Mandic P. Association Between Regulatory Submission Characteristics and Recalls of Medical Devices Receiving 510(k) Clearance. JAMA. 2023 Jan 10;329(2):144-156.. doi: 10.1001/jama.2022.22974

[16] Smy L, Ledeboer NA, Wood MG. At-home testing for respiratory viruses: a minireview of the current landscape. J Clin Microbiol. 2024 May 8;62(5):e0031223U.S. Food and Drug Administration. 2020b. Recalls, Corrections and Removals (Devices). doi: 10.1128/jcm.00312-23

# 9 Automatic segmentation and classification of tumor from 3D volumetric CT scan images

*Suraj Patil[1,a], Suyog Pande[2,b], Varsha Nemade[1,c] and Bhushan Inje[1,d]*

[1]Computer Science Department, MPSTME, Shirpur, Maharashtra, India

[2]AIML Department, MPSTME, Shirpur, Maharashtra, India

## Abstract

The manual detection of cancerous tissue is challenging and time-intensive. To overcome this, computer-aided diagnosis (CAD) systems are used to enhance decision-making and ensure precise detection, facilitating effective therapy. The main objective of this paper is to accurately detect liver cancer through an automated approach. A novel contribution involves using an optimized U-Net model to segment the liver from CT scan images, while an optimized fuzzy centroid region-growing algorithm is employed to extract the tumor from the segmented liver. Further the classification of tumor as cancerous or non-cancerous is done through optimized convolutional neural network model. The experimental analysis reveals that the suggested model outperforms the latest results from previous studies and offers significant support to radiologists in diagnosing tumors from CT scan images.

**Keywords**: Computer aided diagnosis, computer tomography images, deep learning, liver tumor

## Introduction

The liver is a vital metabolic organ and responsible for functions such as detoxification and digestion. It is susceptible to some diseases like hepatitis and hepatic steatosis, which leads to liver tumor and hepatic sclerosis, and it is the one of the major causes that leads to death [1]. The tumor region must be targeted for eliminating the tumor tissues and preserving the healthy tissues. For assessing and treating liver tumor, CT is one of the significant techniques that employ imaging models [4]. By using manual delineation, the segmentations of liver tumor are acquired from the radiologist experts. Though, the volumetric CT images are traced manually using slice-by-slice procedure that leads to labour-intensive and poor reproduction. Further due to heterogenous shape and size of liver, the training of deep learning model for liver extraction from 3D volumetric scan is complex [15]. The significant contribution of this research lies in implementing novel liver tumor segmentation and classification using CT images, combining an improved U-Net and MF-SSA algorithm. A hybrid U-Net model is proposed for liver segmentation, while an optimized fuzzy centroid-based region growing algorithm is used for tumor segmentation [16]. The NN+CNN hybrid classifier, optimized with MF-SSA, enhances accuracy by adjusting hidden layer neurons

## Related Work

For liver and tumor segmentation, several sophisticated approaches are introduced from CT images for overcoming the constraints [6]. Automated, interactive, and semi-automatic

---

[a]suraj.patil@nmims.edu, [b]suyog.pande@nmims.edu, [c]varsha.nemade@nmims.edu, [d]Bhushan.inj@nmims.edu

DOI: 10.1201/9781003716648-9

approaches are sophisticated algorithms. In general, both the semi-automatic and interactive models need many user directions, which leads to the inefficiency of treatment and an increase in computational cost [2]. For enhancing the accuracy and decreasing the computational cost and time, fully automatic models are needed. For registration, segmentation, and classification, DNN is the novel approach in image processing that has many variations, which consists of DBN, GAN, auto-encoder networks, RNN, and convolutional neural network (CNN). In many research contributions, CNN is used for liver and tumor segmentation [7]. The finest liver segmentation algorithm is CNN as its architecture learns more information that incorporates the liver shapes [17]. During hepatic tumor segmentation, CNNs doesn't acquire the best results because it is very complex for learning the unpredictable tumor texture and shape with less amount of training data. Thus, for attaining best results in tumor segmentation and classification using fully automated models, new deep learning algorithms need to be used. Lee et al. [5] implemented an improved mask R-CNN model for accurately detecting liver lesions from CT images. The performance of the mask R-CNN model is validated experimentally, and results show that the R-CNN model outperforms other fundamental models, such as the ResNet-50 model, by exhibiting excellent accuracy. However, the problem with this approach is that it is very time-consuming. Jin et al. [10] designed a hybrid deep attention network to extract liver and tumor from CT scan images. The proposed architecture employs the U-Net Model (RA-U-Net), a 3D hybrid residual-aware segmentation approach, to extract contextual information by integrating low-level and high-level feature maps [3]. The attention modules are arranged in a layered manner to accommodate the growth of the network. This allows for the modification of attention-aware characteristics for extraction of liver and tumor from medical image. The proposed approach yields a dice score accuracy of 96%. The issue with this strategy lies in the fact that the residual mechanism lacks the capability to identify several lesions of different sizes [8].

## Proposed Architectural Model

The model is designed using LiTS dataset which contains 3D volumetric CT scan images. The image preprocessing involves three techniques: histogram equalization to enhance contrast, and median filtering along with anisotropic diffusion filtering to remove noise [9]. The proposed model works in three stages. First a novel hybrid U-Net model is designed to segment the liver from 3D volumetric scan. This is a very important step because the CT scan images contain overlapping of multiple organs in the abdomen and correct delineation of liver from surrounding tissue is critical task. This is achieved by U-Net model designed using ResNet-34 and ResNet-50. The combination of these two architectures overcomes the problem of information loss during encoding and decoding of input image and also solves problem of vanishing gradient as network becomes deep. A region-growing algorithm is employed for tumor segmentation within the segmented liver, with the seed point optimized using the mean fitness-based salp swarm algorithm (MF-SSA) [11]. The main objective of this algorithm is to maximize entropy while minimizing pixel variance, thereby ensuring accurate tumor segmentation. Features such as LDP and GLCM are extracted from the tumor-segmented image and processed using a neural network (NN). At the same time, the tumor-segmented binary image is analyzed using a CNN. The results of both operations are

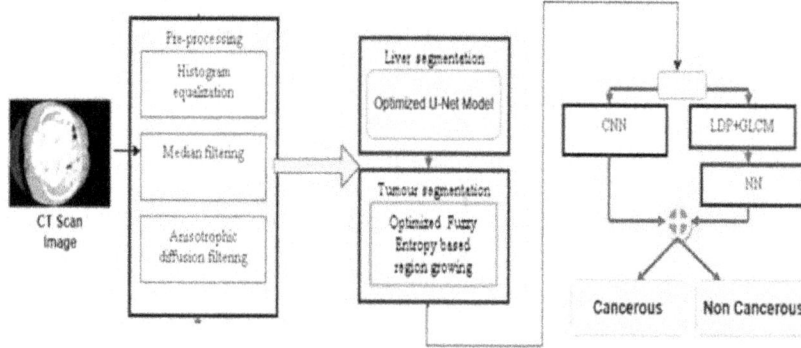

*Figure 9.1* Proposed model of automatic liver tumor detection and classification
Source: Author

then combined, and an AND bit operation is applied to classify the CT images as healthy or unhealthy [12]. Since the number of hidden neurons affects the final classification accuracy, the hidden neuron counts in both NN and CNN is optimized using the mean fitness-based salp swarm algorithm (MF-SSA). The proposed architecture for fully automatic liver tumor segmentation and classification is illustrated in Figure 9.1.

## Salp swarm optimization algorithm for liver and tumor segmentation

The salp swarm optimization (SSA) technique optimizes the number of hidden layer neurons in a hybrid U-Net model for liver segmentation from CT scans, resolving vanishing gradient issues during convolution [13, 14]. After liver segmentation, mean fitness SSA is applied for tumor segmentation. Inspired by salps' swarming behavior, SSA employs a leader-follower strategy in a search space to locate the optimal solution for tumor segmentation. The mathematical representation to update the leader's position is given by Eq. (9.1).

$$ps_y^1 = \begin{cases} Fs_y + b_1\left((Ub_y - Lb_y)b_2 + Lb_y\right) & b_3 \geq 0 \\ Fs_y - b_1\left((Ub_y - Lb_y)b_2 + Lb_y\right) & b_3 < 0 \end{cases} \tag{9.1}$$

In the above equation, the position of first salp $y$ in dimension is given by $ps_y^1$, the position of food source in $y^{th}$ dimension is denoted as $Fs_y$, the upper and lower limits of $y^{th}$ dimension is indicated by $Ub_y$ and $Lb_y$. The random numbers are represented as $b_1$, $b_2$ and $b_3$. The term $b_1$ is the significant parameter in SSA as it balances exploration and exploitation defined in Eq. (9.2). The present iteration is given by $it$ and the maximum count of iterations is denoted as $it_{max}$. The other two random numbers $b_2$ and $b_3$ are generated in between 0 and 1.

$$b_1 = 2e^{\left(\frac{4it}{it_{max}}\right)^2} \tag{9.2}$$

## Experimental Setup

The experimental setup utilizes the LiTS17 dataset, which consists of 131 CT scan images, each containing one or two tumors of varying sizes (ranging from 5 to 121 mm) and different contrast levels. Each 2D volumetric slice has a resolution of 512 × 512 pixels, with a height variation between 0.56 and 0.87 mm. The model is trained on an A100 GPU with 25 GB of RAM, supported by the Colab Pro+ cloud platform.

## Result and Discussion

For experiment, maximum count of iterations was considered as 25, and the population size was initialized as 10. The accuracy, precision and false negative rate (FNR) was analyzed to measure the performance of proposed system. The accuracy of the developed MF-SSA-NN+CNN was compared over existing meta-heuristic algorithms and results were analyzed for different learning percentage rates as shown in Figure 9.2. When compared to other heuristic methods, the enhanced MF-SSA-NN+CNN has the best accuracy around 95.87%.

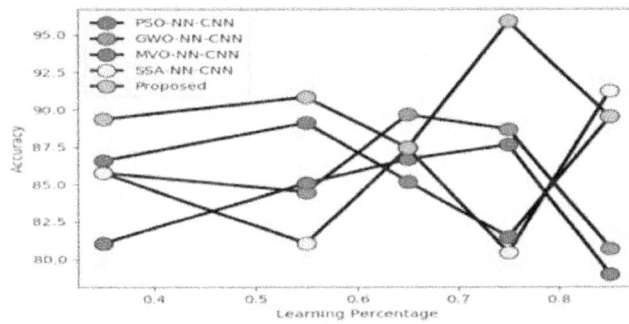

*Figure 9.2* Accuracy of proposed MF-SSA algorithm for tumor segmentation
Source: Author

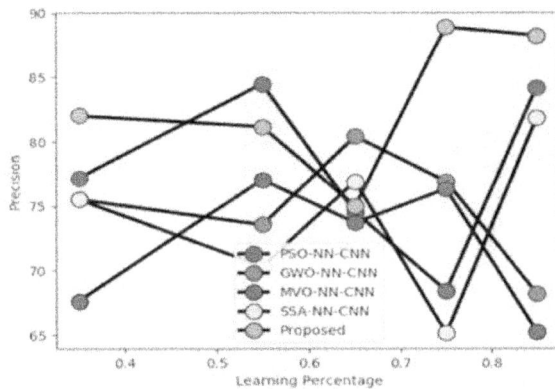

*Figure 9.3* Precision of proposed MF-SSA algorithm for tumor segmentation
Source: Author

The implemented MF-SSA-NN+CNN outperforms PSO-NN+CNN, GWO-NN+CNN, SSA-NN+CNN, MVO-NN+CNN.

The precision and FNR of the developed MF-SSA-NN+CNN was compared to existing meta-heuristic algorithms and results were analysed for different learning percentage rate as shown in Figures 9.3 and 9.4 respectively.

The accuracy of tumor classification using different classifiers with proposed algorithm for different learning percentages is shown in Figure 9.5.

The overall analysis of the proposed MF-SSA-NN+CNN and the hybrid classifier named NN+CNN, which is the combination of NN and CNN and is shown in Table 9.1. The improved MF-SSA-NN+CNN achieves superior accuracy in liver tumor segmentation compared to other machine learning algorithms. It outperforms NN by 12%, CNN by 32.8%, and NN+CNN by 2.1%. Additionally, the precision and false negative rate (FNR) of the

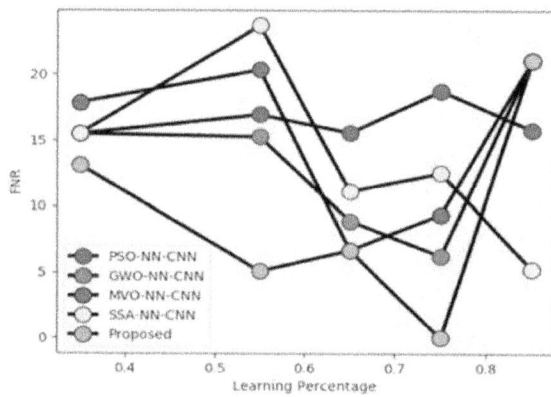

*Figure 9.4* False negative rate of proposed MF-SSA algorithm for tumor segmentation
Source: Author

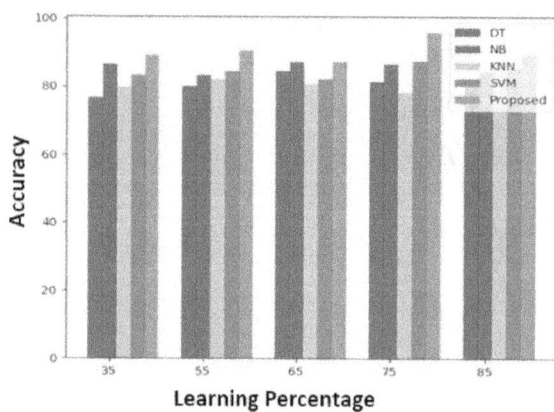

*Figure 9.5* Performance of proposed algorithm for tumor classification
Source: Author

*Table 9.1* Overall analysis regarding influence of optimized learning with respect to deep learning framework.

| Performance measures | Accuracy (%) | Precision (%) | FNR (%) |
| --- | --- | --- | --- |
| NN [11] | 85.56 | 76.47 | 18.75 |
| CNN [12] | 72.16 | 56.09 | 28.12 |
| NN+CNN | 93.81 | 86.11 | 31.25 |
| MF-SSA- NN+CNN | 95.87 | 88.88 | 0 |

Source: Author

proposed MF-SSA-NN+CNN demonstrates high performance in effectively detecting and segmenting liver tumors

## Conclusion

In this paper, a new approach for segmenting and classifying tumor is proposed. We have used LiTs17 benchmark dataset to develop the proposed model. The segmentation of liver is done by new variant of hybrid model and segmentation of tumor and classification is designed by fuzzy centroid region growing algorithm and deep learning convolutional neural network (CNN) model optimized by salp swarm technique. The suggested MF-SSA-NN+CNN was shown to be 12% improvement than NN, 32.8% improvement than CNN, and 2.1 percent better than NN+CNN based on the results of the trial. Hence, it is confirmed that the developed MF-SSA-NN+CNN achieved promising result in liver tumor segmentation and classification.

## References

[1]  American Cancer Society (2024). Cancer Facts & Figures 2024. *American Cancer Society.* https://www.cancer.org/research/cancer-facts-statistics/all-cancer-facts-figures/2024-cancer-facts-figures.html.

[2]  Bakas, S., Chatzimichail, K., Hunter, G., Labbé, B., Sidhu, P. S., & Makris, D. (2017). Fast semi-automatic segmentation of focal liver lesions in contrast-enhanced ultrasound, based on a probabilistic model. *Computer Methods in Biomechanics and Biomedical Engineering: Imaging & Visualization,* 5(5), 329–338.

[3]  Bilic, P., Christ, P., Li, H. B., Vorontsov, E., Ben-Cohen, A., Kaissis, G., et al. (2023). The liver tumor segmentation benchmark (LiTs). *Medical Image Analysis,* 84, 102680. https://doi.org/10.1016/j.media.2022.102680.

[4]  Chartrand, G., Cresson, T., Chav, R., Gotra, A., Tang, A., & De Guise, J. A. (2016). Liver segmentation on CT and MR using laplacian mesh optimization. *IEEE Transactions on Biomedical Engineering,* 64(9), 2110–2121. https://doi.org/10.1109/TBME.2016.2634024.

[5]  Lee, C., Yiwamoto, Y., Lin, L., Hu, H., Chen, YW. (2022). Improved Mask R-CNN with Deformable Convolutions for Accurate Liver Lesion Detection in Multiphase CT Images. In: Chen, YW., Tanaka, S., Howlett, R.J., Jain, L.C. (eds) Innovation in Medicine and Healthcare. Smart Innovation, Systems and Technologies, vol 308. Springer, Singapore. DOI https://doi.org/10.1007/978-981-19-3440-7_13

[6]   Chlebus, G., Meine, H., Moltz, J. H., & Schenk, A. (2017). Neural network-based automatic liver tumor segmentation with random forest-based candidate filtering. *arXiv preprint* arXiv:1706.00842. https://arxiv.org/abs/1706.00842.

[7]   Christ, P. F., Ettlinger, F., Grün, F., Elshaera, M. E. A., Lipkova, J., Schlecht, S., et al. (2017). Automatic liver and tumor segmentation of CT and MRI volumes using cascaded fully convolutional neural networks. *arXiv preprint* arXiv:1702.05970. https://arxiv.org/abs/1702.05970.

[8]   Fernández-Navarro, F., Carbonero-Ruz, M., Alonso, D. B., & Torres-Jiménez, M. (2016). Global sensitivity estimates for neural network classifiers. *IEEE Transactions on Neural Networks and Learning Systems,* 28(11), 2592–2604. https://doi.org/10.1109/TNNLS.2016.2580501.

[9]   Gotra, A., Sivakumaran, L., Chartrand, G., Vu, K. N., Vandenbroucke-Menu, F., & Kauffmann, C. (2017). Liver segmentation: indications, techniques and future directions. *Insights into Imaging,* 8, 377–392. https://doi.org/10.1007/s13244-017-0542-0.

[10]  Jin, Q., Meng, Z., Sun, C., Cui, H., & Su, R. (2020). RA-UNet: a hybrid deep attention-aware network to extract liver and tumor in CT scans. *Frontiers in Bioengineering and Biotechnology,* 8, 605132. https://doi.org/10.3389/fbioe.2020.605132.

[11]  Kirimtat, A., Krejcar, O., & Selamat, A. (2020). Brain MRI modality understanding: a guide for image processing and segmentation. In *Bioinformatics and Biomedical Engineering: 8th International Work-Conference, IWBBIO 2020, Granada, Spain, May 6–8, 2020, Proceedings,* (pp. 705–715). Springer International Publishing.

[12]  Liao, M., Zhao, Y. Q., Liu, X. Y., Zeng, Y. Z., Zou, B. J., Wang, X.-F., et al. (2017). Automatic liver segmentation from abdominal ct volumes using graph cuts and border marching. *Computer Methods and Programs in Biomedicine,* 143, 1–12. https://doi.org/10.1016/j.cmpb.2017.02.012.

[13]  Mirjalili, S., Gandomi, A. H., Mirjalili, S. Z., Saremi, S., Faris, H., & Mirjalili, S. M. (2017). Salp swarm algorithm: a bio-inspired optimizer for engineering design problems. *Advances in Engineering Software,* 114, 163–191. https://doi.org/10.1016/j.advengsoft.2017.07.002.

[14]  Mirjalili, S., Mirjalili, S. M., & Lewis, A. (2014). Grey wolf optimizer. *Advances in Engineering Software,* 69, 46–61. https://doi.org/10.1016/j.advengsoft.2013.12.007.

[15]  Nemade, V., Pathak, S., & Dubey, A. K. (2024). Deep learning-based ensemble model for classification of breast cancer. *Microsystem Technologies,* 30(5), 513–527. https://doi.org/10.1007/s00542-023-06539-2.

[16]  Patil, S., & Kirange, D. K. (2023). A novel hybrid u-net with custom triplet flatten loss function for liver lesion detection. *International Journal of Computer Theory and Engineering,* 15(2), , 82–89.

[17]  Pedersen, M. E. H., & Chipperfield, A. J. (2010). Simplifying particle swarm optimization. *Applied Soft Computing,* 10(2), 618–628. https://doi.org/10.1016/j.asoc.2009.08.004.

# 10 Machine learning-based prediction of adrenergic agonists using structural alerts

*Ranajit N. Shinde[a] and Shashikant B. Bagade[b]*

Department of Pharmaceutical Chemistry, School of Pharmacy and Technology Management, SVKM'S NMIMS Deemed to-be University, Shirpur, Maharashtra, India

## Abstract

Adrenergic drugs are a class of agents that bind to adrenergic receptors α and β and are used in the treatment of wide variety of diseases. Naturally, these receptors are activated by the two neurotransmitters, adrenaline and noradrenalin. Adrenoceptors are present in various organs and tissues as well as in peripheral and central nervous system (CNS). Adrenergic receptors are classified into α- and β-adrenoreceptor classes and further sub classification of α- and β-receptors into the α1 and α2 subtypes of α-receptors and the β1, β2, and β3 subtypes of β-adrenoceptors. In general, aliphatic amine separated by two carbons from a catechol is minimally required for adrenergic agonist activity. Most adrenergic drugs fit into this defined SAR, but a few adrenergic drugs do not permit such straightforward structural definition of their activity. Therefore, in this study, we collected 71 direct acting adrenergic agonists and subjected to the predictive substructure analysis. It generated 8 structural alerts identifying adrenergic agonists with an accuracy of 94 % on a training dataset of 158 molecules and 96 % accuracy on test set dataset of 105 molecules. Most structural alerts provided high accuracy in distinguishing active and inactive molecules. One of the alert [N=C(N)] however provided weak prediction accuracy. This predictive model is very helpful in screening large chemical libraries for the identification of adrenergic agonist as well to identify off target effects of leads developed for other indications.

Keywords: Adrenergic receptors, α- and β-receptors, Central nervous system (CNS), Peripheral nervous system

## Introduction

Adrenergic agonists target adrenergic receptors (α- and β-receptors) and are especially crucial in the management of cardiovascular diseases and respiratory disorders including asthma, chronic obstructive pulmonary disease (COPD), and hypertension. These compounds can produce a wide range of effects that mimic the action of naturally occurring catecholamines (such as epinephrine and norepinephrine) in the body [12]. Based on their therapeutic importance, the development of new adrenergic agonists has been a prominent area of research within a drug discovery. Several classes of drugs have been identified as adrenergic agonist. Catecholamines are the primary endogenous adrenergic agonists and include epinephrine, norepinephrine, and dopamine. Structurally, these compounds possess a catechol moiety (benzene ring with two hydroxyl groups at positions 3 and 4) and an amine group [10]. Synthetic derivatives, such as isoproterenol, are widely used in clinical settings for their adrenergic activity. These compounds act primarily by binding to

[a]ranajit.shinde@nmims.edu, [b]shashikant.bagade@nmims.edu

DOI: 10.1201/9781003716648-10

α and β adrenergic receptors. Phenylethanolamines class includes drugs such as phenylephrine and metaraminol. Unlike catecholamines, they lack one or both catechol hydroxyl groups, resulting in selectivity for α1-adrenergic receptors, enhancing oral bioavailability and resistance to COMT metabolism [2]. Clonidine and oxymetazoline fall into the imidazoline class. They possess an imidazoline ring and demonstrate selective activity at α2-adrenergic receptors. The imidazoline ring confers high receptor affinity and prolonged action due to resistance to metabolic degradation [11]. Beta phenylethanolamines selective β-adrenergic agonists, such as albuterol and salmeterol, belong to this group. These compounds feature increased lipophilicity and extended side chains, enhancing β2-receptor selectivity and duration of action [1]. Non-catecholamines such as ephedrine, pseudoephedrine, and amphetamines function primarily by indirectly increasing synaptic norepinephrine release. These compounds also exhibit direct agonist activity at adrenergic receptors. Their non-catechol structure enhances stability, resistance to COMT and MAO degradation [13]. Identification of novel adrenergic agonists involve experimental methods such as the use of drug receptors, cellular assays, and preclinical models. However, these methodologies are usually dispersive, costly and require a lot of resources [8]. New theories based on the molecular descriptors, molecular docking, quantitative structure activity relationship, as well as molecular modelling simulations have appeared as suitable methods for identifying potential adrenergic modulators [15]. These models allow the easy finding of compounds which are active thus less resources are required for their experimental isolation and investigation. A few computational studies were focused on predicting the regulatory activity of certain compounds on adrenergic receptors, using computational methods. For example, ligands' 3D structure and lipophilicity has been used to predict the duration of action at β2 adrenergic receptors [4]. Luca Chiesa along with Esther Kellenberger have used molecular dynamics simulations of the agonist/receptor complex to identify β2 agonist and antagonists [3]. Wankhade and others have developed prediction models based on various molecular descriptors using machine learning and deep learning algorithms for the adrenergic α2a antagonists [14]. These efforts have illustrated the ability that computer approaches hold with regards to improving drug discovery workflows especially by extracting information form large chemical datasets. However, creating a predictive model with a high accuracy and high generalization ability over alpha (α1, α2) and beta (β1, β2) is still a very difficult. Accordingly, it is common that existing models either have a small dataset for trained or do not understand the receptor-ligand complexity fully. Additionally, they extend the modelling complexities due to the multiplicity of adrenergic receptor subtypes and selectivity. This research seeks to construct a high-performance model applicable for the prediction of adrenergic agonists that can utilize information from a wide range of known compound structures. Here we describe the constructed and trained model for adrenergic agonist prediction for alpha (α1, α2) and beta (β1, β2) receptors using 158 drugs as a training set and 105 molecules set aside to test the model. The accuracy of the model has achieved 94% for the training set and 96% for the test set. It indicates robustness of the model for the rapid screening of possible adrenergic agonist compounds. There are considerable improvements with respect to time and resource savings that the model presents as compared to complex testing measures and is a real asset in drug discovery activities.

## Methodology

Drugs that have been approved as adrenergic agonists were collected from the literature sources such as such as books, research articles, pharmacopoeia, chemical libraries and dataset maintained at government departments such as Food and Drug Administration. Collectively, 71 adrenergic drugs and 192 non-adrenergic drugs were collected. They were provided with binary classification as 1 (active, adrenergic) and 0 (inactive, non-adrenergic). This dataset of 263 drugs was then divided into training set and test set. The training set included 60 active and 98 inactive, while the test set included 11 active and 94 inactive drug molecules. The smiles notation of all molecules was then collected from the Pubchem database and stored as excel sheets. These excel sheet were then used as input file for the creation of binary (adrenergic/non-adrenergic predictive models). SARpy software was then used to develop prediction model for adrenergic drugs [5, 6]. SARpy selects the essential structural fragments for the adrenergic activity after converting chemical structures of the compounds in the training set into fragments of a desired size. The system uses SMILES in canonical form.

## Results

The training dataset present in the form of SMILES was provided to the SARpy. The model was trained on dataset of 60 adrenergic drug and 98 non-adrenergic drugs. Models were built by varying minimum and maximum number of atoms that can be present in the sub-structures, identified as structural alerts. A confusion matrix was used to assess the performance of classification models. In the context of SARpy, the confusion matrix was a table that compares the actual class versus predicted class. The table was represented using False Positives (FP), False Negatives (FN), True Positives (TP) and True Negatives (TN) elements. These elements were then used to estimate model's performance parameters such as accuracy, sensitivity and specificity. Table 10.1 shows prediction statistics of the final model. The model identified as the best model contained 8 structural alerts. The confusion metrics of this model are shown in Table 10.1.

Table 10.1 shows that the best model predicted 55 adrenergic and 93 non-adrenergic drugs correctly out of 60 and 98 respectively. However, it wrongly predicted 5 adrenergic drugs and non-adrenergic and 5 non-adrenergic drugs and adrenergic. In order to validate the model, we prepared test set containing 11 adrenergic drugs and 94 non-adrenergic drugs. These molecules were unknown to the model i.e. they were not part of the training set. It was observed that the developed model performed better on the test set also. Confusion matrix for the test set is shown in Table 10.2.

*Table 10.1* Confusion matrix for training set.

| | **Predicted as** | |
| --- | --- | --- |
| | **Adrenergic** | **Non-adrenergic** |
| Adrenergic (60) | 55 | 05 |
| Non-adrenergic (98) | 05 | 93 |

Source: Author

*Table 10.2* Confusion matrix for test set.

| | Predicted as | |
|---|---|---|
| | Adrenergic | **Non-adrenergic** |
| Adrenergic (11) | 10 | 01 |
| Non-adrenergic (94) | 03 | 91 |

Source: Author

*Table 10.3* Statistical parameters for the prdictivity of the model on the training set and test set.

| | **Training set** | **Test set** |
|---|---|---|
| % Accuracy[a] | 94 | 96 |
| % Sensitivity[b] | 92 | 91 |
| % Specificity[c] | 95 | 97 |

[a]Accuracy: (True Positives + True Negatives) / (Total Instances), [b]Sensitivity: True Positives/(True Positives + False Negative), [c]Specificity: True Negatives/(True Negatives + False Positives)

Source: Author

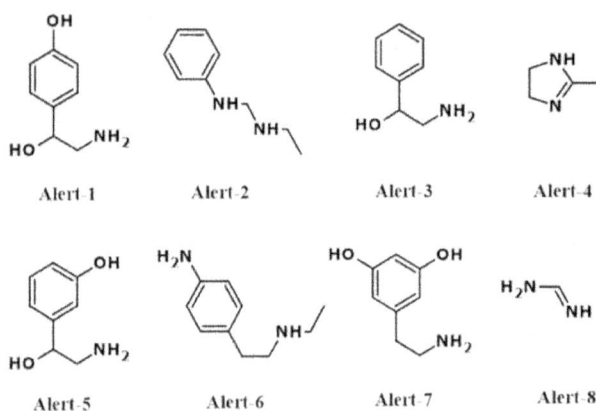

*Figure 10.1* Eight alerts (Sub-structures) obtained as independent variables in the predictive model of adrenergic and non-adrenergic drugs
Source: Author

Table 10.3 provides the statistical figures for the predictivity on the training set and test set. It shows that the built model was having overall predictive accuracy of 94% and 96% on the training set and test set respectively. In addition, its ability to predict true positive (adrenergic) and true negative (non-adrenergic) in both the set was found to be more that 90 %.

The eight alerts are listed in Figure 10.1. If one of the alerts is present in a drug molecule, then that molecule is predicted as active molecules (adrenergic agonist). Collectively from training set and test set six adrenergic drugs were predicted as false negative i.e. non-adrenergic drugs. These five false negatives are: Pirbuterol, Prenalterol, Doxofylline, Dexmedetomidine and Mivazerol from the training set and Xamoterol from the test set. Equally, eight non-adrenergic drugs were predicted as false positive i.e. adrenergic. Cepharanthine, Sulfaguanidine, Verapamil, Epinastine and Florfenicol were found to be part of the training set and Benzthiazide, Pinacidil and Aminoguanidine were part of the test set. It was observed that among eight false positive compounds, five compounds contained NCN substructure. Two drugs Sulfaguanidine and Epinastine belonged to the training set and 3 drugs Benzthiazide, Pinacidil and Aminoguanidine belonged to the test set. This put for them that this alert found to have low predictivity compared to the others.

## Discussion

The predictive model developed for adrenergic agonists demonstrated high accuracy and reliability in distinguishing adrenergic and non-adrenergic drugs. With an overall predictive accuracy of 94% in the training set and 96% in the test set, the model exhibited robust generalizability. The high sensitivity (92% for training and 91% for test) and specificity (95% for training and 97% for test) further validate the model's ability to correctly identify true adrenergic agonists while minimizing false positives. The model's effectiveness is attributed to the identification of eight structural alerts, which played a key role in classification. However, the presence of false negatives and false positives suggests certain limitations in the structural alerts used for prediction. The six false negatives, pirbuterol, prenalterol, xamoterol, dexmedetomidine, mivazerol, and doxofylline, indicate that some adrenergic agonists were misclassified as non-adrenergic, potentially due to structural variations that did not align with the identified alerts. Pirbuterol can be matched by the Alert-1. However, Pirbuterol contains a pyridine ring instead of a phenyl ring. Prenalterol, and xamoterol, both β-adrenergic partial agonists contain hydroxyphenoxy group, different from that of catecholamine present in Alert-1. Dexmedetomidine and mivazerol could have identified with Alert-4, however, these drugs contain the imidazole group instead of imidazoline, which is present in alpha agonists such as naphazoline, oxymetazoline and xylometazoline. Interestingly, Doxofylline is not like any of the structural alerts. Insufficient representation of these molecular patterns in the training set may have led to their misclassification. Similarly, among eight false positives, cepharanthine, sulfaguanidine, verapamil, epinastine, florfenicol, benzthiazide, pinacidil and aminoguanidine, five drugs found to have NCN alert. These are sulfaguanidine, epinastine, benzthiazide, pinacidil and aminoguanidine. all of these found to contain Alert-8 i.e. NCN. The model has trained using only five drugs having NCN substructure i.e. epinastine, guanabenz, guanfacine, moxonidine, and sulfaguanidine contain NCN alert. Insufficient training with drugs containing guanidine group may have resulted in poor prediction. Remaining three false positive predictions: cepharanthine, verapamil, and florfenicol are used clinically for the treatment of leukopenia, hypertension, and bacterial infection respectively. Cepharanthine is a big alkaloid containing bisbenzylisoquinoline while Florfenicol is a sulfone, a secondary alcohol, an organofluorine compound. Verapamil is a phenylalkylamine and has shown adrenergic blocking activity [7, 9]. This finding highlights the need for refinement in the structural alerts, either through additional feature selection techniques or a more detailed substructure analysis. Future work will focus on improving the model's discriminatory power by integrating more datasets and considering alternative molecular descriptors to enhance predictive reliability.

## Conclusion

The predictive computational model developed in this study demonstrates high accuracy and reliability in distinguishing adrenergic agonists from non-adrenergic drugs, with 94% and 96% accuracy on the training and test datasets, respectively. The identification of eight key structural alerts significantly enhances the screening process for adrenergic agonists, providing a robust tool for rapid evaluation of chemical libraries. Despite some limitations, such as the relatively low predictive power of the NCN Alert, the model offers valuable insights into the structural determinants of adrenergic activity, streamlining the discovery of potential therapeutics targeting $\alpha$ and $\beta$ adrenergic receptors. This work underscores the potential of computational approaches to complement experimental methods in drug discovery, saving time and resources while expanding the scope of receptor-ligand interaction analysis. Future efforts could focus on refining predictive capabilities for challenging substructures and extending the model to include diverse adrenergic receptor subtypes. The findings of this research pave the way for more efficient identification of adrenergic agonists and exploration of their off-target effects, furthering advancements in pharmacological and medicinal chemistry.

## References

[1]   Nocentini, A., & Supuran, C. T. (2019). Adrenergic agonists and antagonists as antiglaucoma agents: a literature and patent review (2013-2019). *Expert opinion on therapeutic patents*, 29(10), 805–815. doi: 10.1080/13543776.2019.1665023

[2]   Brunton, L. L., Dandan-Hilal, R., & Knollmann, B. C. (2018). Goodman & Gilman's the Pharmacological Basis of Therapeutics, (13th edn). *McGraw-Hill Education.*

[3]   Chiesa, L., & Kellenberger, E. (2022). One class classification for the detection of B2 adrenergic receptor agonists using single-ligand dynamic interaction data. *Journal of Cheminformatics,* 14(1), 74. https://doi.org/10.1186/s13321-022-00654-z.

[4]   Chiesa, L., Sick, E., & Kellenberger, E. (2023). Predicting the duration of action of B2-adrenergic receptor agonists: ligand and structure-based approaches. *Molecular Informatics,* 42(12), e202300141. https://doi.org/10.1002/minf.202300141.

[5]   Ferrari, T., Gini, G., Bakhtyari, N. G., & Benfenati, E. (2011). Mining toxicity structural alerts from SMILES: a new way to derive structure activity relationships. In *2011 IEEE Symposium on Computational Intelligence and Data Mining (CIDM)*, (pp. 120–127). https://doi.org/10.1109/CIDM.2011.5949444.

[6]   Golbamaki, A., Benfenati, E., Golbamaki, N., Manganaro, A., Merdivan, E., Roncaglioni, A., et al. (2016). New clues on carcinogenicity-related substructures derived from mining two large datasets of chemical compounds. *Journal of Environmental Science and Health. Part C, Environmental Carcinogenesis and Ecotoxicology Reviews,* 34(2), 97–113. https://doi.org/10.1080/10590501.2016.1166879.

[7]   Hansen, J., Xiong, Y., Siddiq, M. M., Dhanan, P., Hu, B., Shewale, B., et al. (2024). Multiscale mapping of transcriptomic signatures for cardiotoxic drugs. *Nature Communications,* 15(1), 7968. https://doi.org/10.1038/s41467-024-52145-4.

[8] Jacobson, K. A., Tosh, D. K., Jain, S., & Gao, Z. G. (2019). Historical and current adenosine receptor agonists in preclinical and clinical development. *Frontiers in Cellular Neuroscience,* 13, 124. https://doi.org/10.3389/fncel.2019.00124.

[9] Karliner, J. S., Motulsky, H. J., Dunlap, J., Brown, J. H., & Insel, P. A. (1982). Verapamil competitively inhibits alpha 1-adrenergic and muscarinic but not beta-adrenergic receptors in rat myocardium. *Journal of Cardiovascular Pharmacology,* 4(3), 515–520. https://doi.org/10.1097/00005344-198205000-00025.

[10] Lemke, T., Zito, W., Roche, V., & Williams, D. (2017). *Essentials of Foye's Principles of Medicinal Chemistry.* (7th edn.), Wolters Kluwer.

[11] Lemke KA. Perioperative use of selective alpha-2 agonists and antagonists in small animals. Can Vet J. 2004 Jun;45(6):475-80. PMID: 15283516 .

[12] Rang, H. P., Ritter, J. M., Flower, R. J., & Henderson, G. (2007). *Rang and Dale's Pharmacology,* (10th edn.), Elsevier Churchill Livingstone.

[13] Andrade C. Stahl's Essential Psychopharmacology: Neuroscientific Basis and Practical Applications. Mens Sana Monogr. 2010 Jan-Dec;8(1):146–50. doi: 10.4103/0973-1229.58825.

[14] Wankhade, N., Dayasagar, U., Sharma, A., Kamble, P., Varma, T., & Garg, P. (2024). DeepADRA2A: predicting adrenergic α2a inhibitors using deep learning. *Journal of Biomolecular Structure and Dynamics,* 42(22), 12353–1264. https://doi.org/10.1080/07391102.2023.2270056.

[15] Zhu, S., Wu, M., Huang, Z., & An, J. (2021). Trends in application of advancing computational approaches in GPCR ligand discovery. *Experimental Biology and Medicine (Maywood, N.J.),* 246(9), 1011–1024. https://doi.org/10.1177/1535370221993422.

# 11 Crystal engineering and formulation development of albendazole

*Snehal N. Pawar*[a]*, Vishakha R. Shelke*[b]*, Kanchan D. Nikam*[c] *and Vinod J. Mokale*[d]

University Department of Pharmaceutical Sciences, MGM University, Chhatrapati Sambhajinagar (Aurangabad), Maharashtra, India

## Abstract

For parasitic worm infections, the Food and Drug Administration has approved the use of albendazole, an anthelmintic. It has poor bioavailability and water solubility because it is a BCS class II medicine. In this case, the delayed commencement of action is due to the fact that its oral absorption is rate-limited. The pharmaceutical co crystals of Albendazole with GRAS (generally regarded as safe) molecules were created using crystal engineering, a novel approach in the field of solubility enhancement. The Albendazole pharmaceutical co crystals were made with 09 conformers in a 1:1 ratio. Via the use of a neat grinding technique. Among them, gallat co crystal produces the best outcome. Researchers studied the co-crystal formulations by measuring their saturation solubility, in-vitro dissolution, and stability. In addition, analytical characteristics such as differential scanning calorimetry, powder X-ray diffraction, and Fourier transform infrared spectroscopy (FTIR) were used to describe the Co crystal (DSC). When compared to the ordinary medication, the optimizedco crystal formulation dissolved faster and had higher equilibrium solubility.

**Keywords:** Albendazole, bioavailability, co crystals, crystallization, dissolution

## Introduction

The word "crystal engineering" was first introduced by the physicist Pepinsky [4]. At the meeting of American Physical Society in Mexico City in August 1955 in an abstract entitled *Crystal Engineering: A New Concept in Crystallography*. The modern definition according to Gautam Desiraju, it is "the understanding of intermolecular interactions in the context of crystal packing and the utilization of such understanding in the design of new solids with desired physical and chemical properties [11]. The challenges of low aqueous solubility provide an ideal situation for the application of crystal engineering techniques for improving bioavailability [1]. Co-crystals are crystalline materials formed by two or more stable compounds. The components that are assembled in co-crystals can be in the neutral state, thus forming molecular co-crystals, or bear charges, such as in ionic co-crystals, and can be metal complexes, whether neutral or charged, thus forming hybrid co-crystals [2]. Van der Waals and hydrogen bonding are the two primary intermolecular interactions in crystal engineering, however more recent applications have made use of C-H···π and halogen bonding [6]. Albendazole is an FDA-approved medication for treating a variety of parasitic worm infections. It is an anthelminthic medication with numerous indications such as cystic

[a]srathod@mgmu.ac.in, [b]vishakhashelke21@gmail.com, [c]mandlikkanchan24@gmail.com, [d]mokalevinod@gmail.com

DOI: 10.1201/9781003716648-11

hydatid disease of the liver, lung, and peritoneum resulting from the larval form of the dog tapeworm, Echinococcus granulosus (Furukawa et al., 2013). This activity will discuss the role of the interprofessional team in the use of this medication. Albendazole is a benimidazol drug which is used in anthelmintic remedy belongs to BCS class II [3]. Albendazole was selected as it has poor solubility, compressibility, and flow properties which might be set with the help of co-crystallization. The objective of this present study was to check crystal stars with maximum solubility were selected and evaluated by DSC, FTIR, and PXRD.

*Materials & methods*
A complimentary sample of albendazole was sent to me by Navketan pharma Aurangabad. This study made use of solvents and other chemical substances that were purchased from Loba Chemise Pvt. Ltd., Mumbai, and were of analytical quality.

*Preparation of co-crystals*
In a 1:1 stoichiometric ratio, albendazole was co crystallized with various co-crystals formers that were mentioned on the GRAS list. Preparation methods are depicted in Table 11.1

## Characterization of Co-Crystals

*Melting point determination*
Using a digital melting point instrument, we found out what the melting point of Co crystals was (lab-tronics ltd) [13].

*FT-IR spectroscopy*
Identifying the produced compounds' unique peaks in the fingerprint area using infrared spectroscopy is a crucial step in structural elucidation and verification.

*Differential scanning calorimetry (DSC)*
A differential scanning calorimeter DSC-60A from Shimadzu was used to conduct thermal investigation of the co-crystals [7].

*Table 11.1* Preparation of co-crystal.

| Sr. No. | Coding of co-crystal Alb + Co-former | Alb + Co-former | Qty taken of Co-former (gm) |
|---|---|---|---|
| 1 | NF1 | Alb+ Salicylic acid | 0.138 |
| 2 | NF2 | Alb+ Benzoic acid | 0.122 |
| 3 | NF3 | Alb+Mandelic acid | 0.152 |
| 4 | NF4 | Alb+Cinnamic acid | 0.148 |
| 5 | NF5 | Alb+ tartaric Acid | 0.150 |
| 6 | NF6 | Alb+sacharine | 0.183 |
| 7 | NF7 | Alb+oxallic acid | 0.126 |
| 8 | NF8 | Alb+Ferulic acid | 0.194 |
| 9 | NF9 | Alb+ Gallic acid | 0.170 |

Source: Author

### Drug content analysis
The UV spectrophotometric approach was used to determine the drug content in the co-crystals [8].

### Solubility determination
Following the protocol laid out by Higuchi and Connors, experiments measuring saturation solubility were carried out in triplicate [9].

### Formula for formulation
Table 11.2 summarizes the quantity per tablet. Following the gallate crystal's preparation by neat grinding, the crystal was compressed into a tablet using the direct compression method.

### Drug content (Assay)
In a 100 ml volumetric flask, 10 mg of Albendazole powder was taken and dissolved in 0.1N HCl. After being filled to the brim, the volume was filtered using Whatman filter paper. The absorbance at 308 nm was used to assess the concentration of Albendazole.

### In vitro disintegration time
The disintegration time is measured by placing one tablet in each tube and placing the basket arch in a one-liter beaker of water maintained at $37°C \pm 2°C$. The basket assembly is raised and lowered using a conventional motor-driven system (Esai et al., 2016).

### In vitro dissolution test
The USP tablet dissolving equipment Veego VDA-6DR USP standards, a USP type 2 apparatus, was used to conduct the in vitro dissolution investigation at a speed of 75 rpm (Rockville, 2003).

### Stability study
The Albendazole intravenous tablet were sealed in aluminum foil and kept for one month according to the conditions specified by the ICH for both the long term and expedited investigations [5].

*Table 11.2* Formula for formulation.

| Ingredients | Quantity |
| --- | --- |
| SSG | 35 mg |
| Povidone | 19.5 mg |
| Starch | 70 mg |
| Magnesium stearate | 7 mg |
| Colloidal silicon dioxide | 3.5 mg |
| Saccharine sodium | 7 mg |
| MCC PH 101 | 9 mg |
| Gallate co-crystals | 615 mg |
| Total | 750 mg |

Source: Author

## Result and Discussion

### *Determination of solubility of drug and co-crystals*

The solubility data of all four co-crystals was used to narrow the selection down to one, the Gallate co-crystal. Oxalate, ferulic acid, and urea were the other three with wavelength problems; they were stony in character. Gallate co-crystals are more soluble than Albendazole and have a shorter wavelength (Remenar, J. F.,et al 2004).

### *Preformulation characteristics of co-crystals*

Preformulation Characteristics of Drug and Co-Crystals given in Table 11.3.

*Table 11.3* Preformulation characteristics of drug and co-crystals.

| Parameter | Albendazole-GA | Albendazole |
|---|---|---|
| Bulk density | 0.311gm/cm$^3$ | 0.45 |
| Tapped density | 0.401gm/cm$^3$ | 0.55 |
| Compressibilty index | 33.33% | 18.18% |
| Hausners ratio | 1.51 | 1.22 |
| Angle of repose | 28.26 | 45.56 |

Source: Author

### *Formulation study*

In terms of solubility, medication content, and powder flow characteristics, gallate co crystals (Albendazole gallic acid) emerged as the clear leader after examining all of these metrics.

### *Evaluation of co-crystal*

#### *Melting point and solubility determination*

Using a digital melting point device, the drug, CCF, and co-crystal melting temperatures were initially calculated in a laboratory setting (LAB-TRONICS Ltd). Table 11.4 summarize the M.P, solubility of co crystals prepared by Neat Grinding.

*Table 11.4* M.P, solubility of co crystals prepared by neat grinding.

| Drug/Conformer | M.P. of co-former (°C) | M.P. of co-crystal (°C) | Solubility (mg/ml) | Std Deviation |
|---|---|---|---|---|
| Albendazole | 208-209 | 197-200 | 0.079 | 0.006 |
| Alb-Salicylic acid | 157-159 | 147-150 | 0.858 | 0.061 |
| Alb-Benzoic acid | 122 | 145-149 | 0.048 | 0.045 |
| Alb-Mandelicacid | 134-136 | 159-160 | 0.2683 | 0.078 |
| Alb-Cinnamic acid | 132-134 | 162-164 | 0.191 | 0.089 |
| Alb-tartaric acid | 204-206 | 159-161 | 0.0633 | 0.068 |
| Alb-sacharine | 228-229 | 199-200 | 0.129 | 0.0654 |
| Alb-oxallic acid | 11-102 | 12-121 | 0.858 | 0.125 |
| Alb-Ferulic acid | 174 | 163-165 | 10.98 | 0.158 |
| Alb-Gallic acid | 258-265 | 173-175 | 0.62 | |

Source: Author

### *Differential scanning calorimetry (DSC)*

Direct scanning calorimetry (DSC) discovered co-crystals had a melting point higher than Albendazole's, it was not greater than 233 degrees Celsius (213) as shown in Figure 11.1 and Table 11.5.

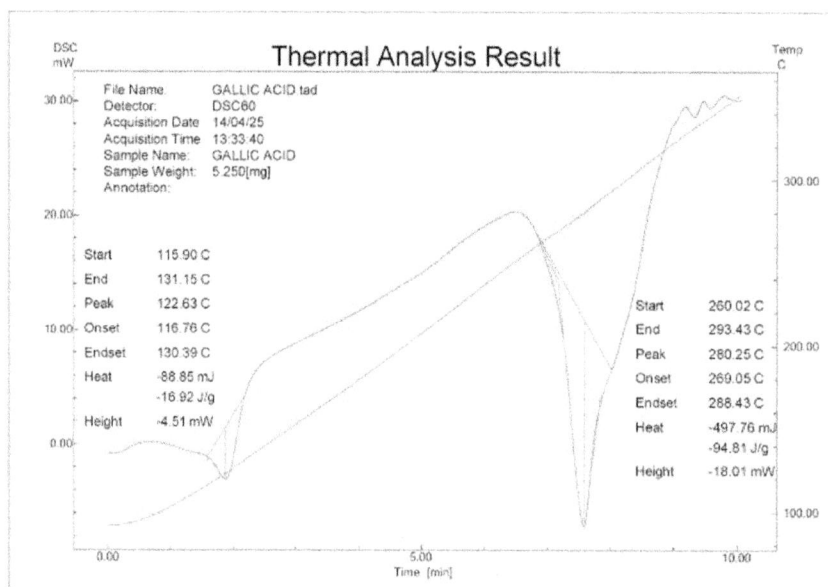

*Figure 11.1* DSC Thermogram of albendazole
Source: Author

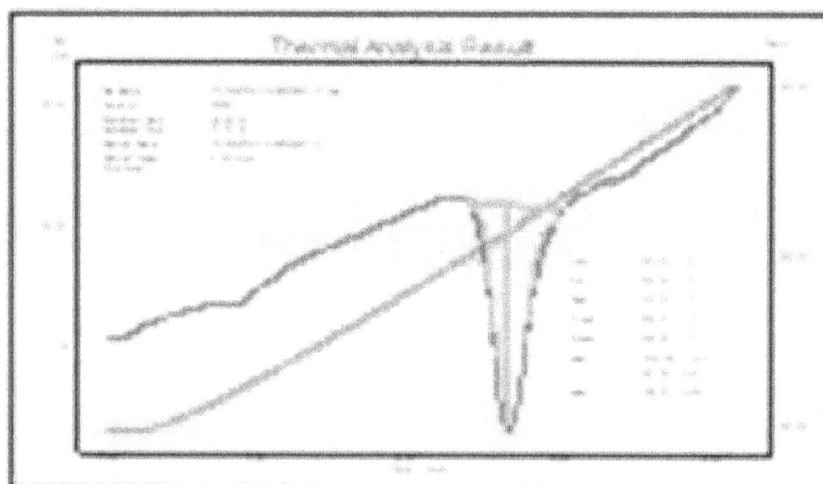

*Figure 11.2* DSC thermogram of gallic acid
Source: Author

*Table 11.5* DSC data for Alb co-crystals.

| Sr. No. | Name | Theoretical Melting Point | Melting Point by DSC |
|---|---|---|---|
| 1 | Albendazole | 208-209°C | 280°C |
| 2 | Gallic acid | 258-265°C | 213°C |
| 3 | Gallateco-crystal | - | 233°C |

Source: Author

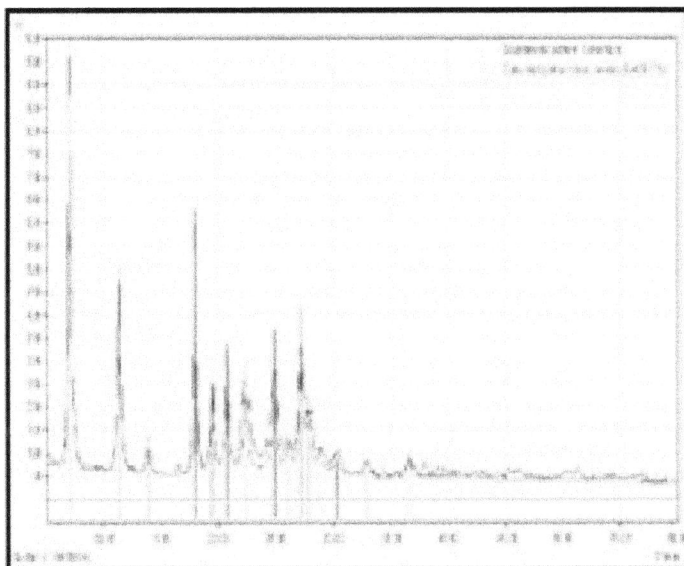

*Figure 11.3* XRD of pure Alb
Source: Author

### XRD data for drug and co-crystals

Determining whether a medication is crystalline or amorphous is the primary use of XRD analysis. By definition, a crystalline chemical will have distinct peaks, whereas an amorphous medication will have less defined peaks. Here, XRD graphs (Figures 11.3 and 11.4) reveal that all of the formulations exhibit crystalline character.

Figures 11.5–11.7 display PXRD patterns of gallic acid and Albendazoleco-crystals, respectively, whereas Figures 11.6 and 11.7 exhibit PXRD patterns of pure Albendazole. It appears from these PXRD patterns that the co-crystals are crystalline.

This drug's identity is confirmed by the IR spectra, which displays distinct stretching peaks at 2248 cm−1 for C-N, 1820 cm−1 for C=O, 1191 cm−1 for C-C, and 1639 cm−1 for C=N. Table 11.6. This indicates that all main groups are present in the structure. Figure 11.6 illustrates this point.

As demonstrated in Figure 11.7, the retention of all drug-corresponding peaks in the infrared spectra of albendazole and gallic acid verifies the development of co-crystals.

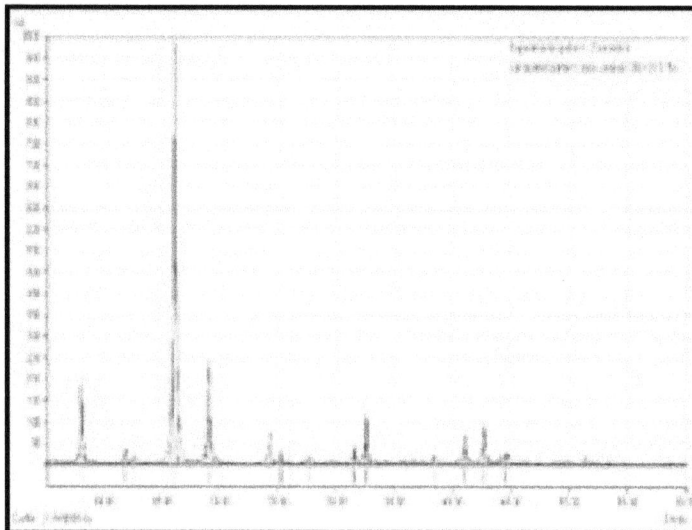

*Figure 11.4* XRD of Gallic acid
Source: Author

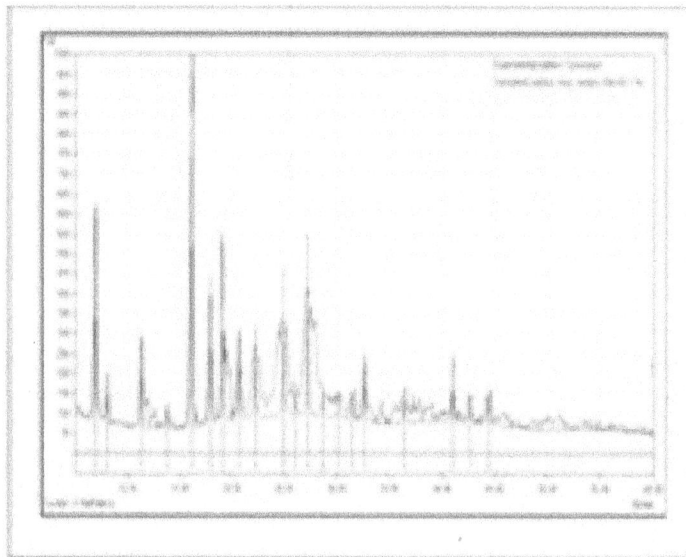

*Figure 11.5* XRD of Co-crystal
Source: Author

## Powder dissolution of drug and co crystals

Powder dissolution of pure drug and co crystals is summarized in Table 11.7 and Figure 11.8.

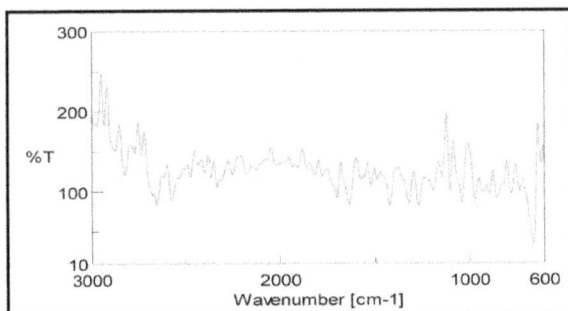

*Figure 11.6* FT-IR spectrum of Alb
Source: Author

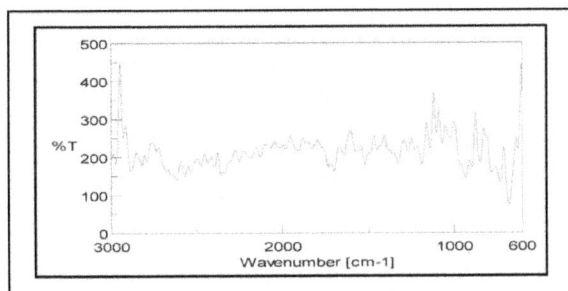

*Figure 11.7* FT-IR spectrum of – gallat co-crystal
Source: Author

*Table 11.6* FTIR data of drug.

| Sr. No. | Wavelength | Group | Reported |
|---|---|---|---|
| 1 | 2248 | C-N | 2100-2400 |
| 2 | 1820 | C=O | 1840-1750 |
| 3 | 1191 | C-C | 700-1200 |
| 4 | 1639 | C=N | 1615-1700 |

Source: Author

*Table 11.7* Powder dissolution of drug and co-crystal.

| Time (Min) | % DR of Drug | Std Deviation | % DR of co-crystal | Std Deviation |
|---|---|---|---|---|
| 10 | 36.6 | 0.34 | 48.5 | 0.78 |
| 15 | 58.4 | 0.36 | 65.4 | 0.89 |
| 20 | 67.5 | 0.77 | 65.9 | 0.91 |
| 25 | 71.3 | 0.89 | 84.2 | 0.96 |
| 30 | 86.7 | 0.123 | 98.4 | 0.98 |

Source: Author

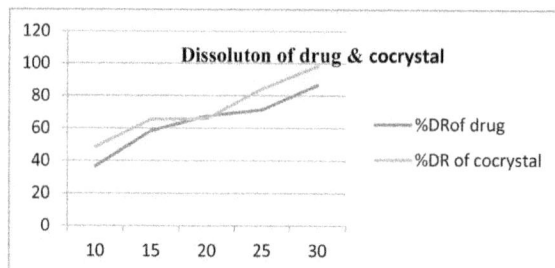

*Figure 11.8* Dissolution of drug & co-crystal
Source: Author

*Table 11.8* Drug content of co-crystals.

| Sr. No. | Sample Name | Drug content per 100 mg co-crystals | Weight (mg) of co-crystal equivalent to 400 mg Albendazole |
|---|---|---|---|
| 1 | Albendazole | 99.8 | - |
| 2 | Gallate co-crystal | 92.0 | 615 |

Source: Author

*Table 11.9* In vitro dissolution data of marketed preparation (Albenza) and formulated preparation.

| Time (Min) | % DR of Marketed Preparation | % DR of Formulated Preparation |
|---|---|---|
| 10 | 75.2 | 70.1 |
| 15 | 77.4 | 72.3 |
| 20 | 86.6 | 80 |
| 25 | 91.1 | 90 |
| 30 | 93.7 | 97.2 |

Source: Author

### Drug content analysis of co-crystals

The homogeneity of the contents was determined by conducting drug content analysis on co-crystals. The data on the drug content of the co-crystals is reported in Table 11.8.

### Solubility determination

The gallate co-crystals had the highest increase in solubility compared to Albendazole, whose solubility was 0.079 mg/ml.

### In vitro dissolution data for formulation

The *in vitro* dissolution data for formulation was studied and summarized in Table 11.9 and shown in Figure 11.9.

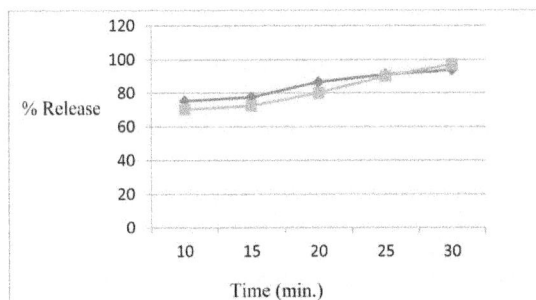

*Figure 11.9* Dissolution graph of marketed (Albenza) & formulated preparation
Source: Author

*Table 11.10* Stability data.

| Time period | Color Change | Drug Content (%) | In vitro Disintegration Time (Min) |
|---|---|---|---|
| Initials | White | 98.2 | 52 |
| **15 days** | | | |
| 40°C ± 2⁰C/ RH 75% ± 5% | No change | 97.8 | 51 |
| 25°C± 2°C/ RH 60% ± 5% | No change | 98.6 | 54 |
| **30 days** | | | |
| 40°C ± 2°C/ RH 75% ± 5% | No change | 96.9 | 54 |
| 25°C ± 2°C/ RH 60%± 5% | No change | 98.10 | 52 |

Source: Author

From dissolution study it was observed that formulation show comparatively faster drug dissolution.

### Stability study
Following the guidelines laid out by the ICH the Albendazole I.R. tablet Table 11.10 showed the results for stability studies in given conditions

## Conclusion

Co-crystals are new aspect for pharmaceutical industries and provides new ideas to deal with poorly soluble drugs. Co-crystals have the potential to be much more useful in pharmaceutical product than solvates or hydrates. Future research also focused on the scale-up of co-crystal system and implement manufacturing of final dosage form on commercial scale. Studies regarding polymorphism of co-crystals provide stringent in order to accelerate the development of new pharmaceuticals. A future challenging aspect is related to the development of efficient co-crystals screening technologies. This can be achieved by Albendazole an anthelmintic drug used for the treatment of helmintis was successfully co-crystallized by crystal engineering approach by neat grinding.

## References

[1]   Aakeröy, C. B., & Salmon, D. J. (2005). Building co-crystals with molecular sense and supra-molecular sensibility. *CrystEngComm*, 7(2), 439–448.

[2]   Braga, D., Grepioni, F., Maini, L., Prosperi, S., Gobetto, R., & Chierotti, M. (2010). From unexpected reactions to a new family of ionic co-crystals: the case of barbituric acid with alkali bromides and caesium iodide. *Chemical Communications*, 46, 7715–7717.

[3]   Childs, S. L., Stahly, A., Stahly, D., Remenar, J. F., & Zaworotko, W. (2004). Crystal engineering approach to forming co-crystals of amine hydrochlorides with organic acids. molecular complexes of fluoxetine hydrochloride with benzoic, succinic and fumaric acids. *Journal of the American Chemical Society*, 126, 13335–13342.

[4]   Desiraju, G. R. (1989). Crystal Engineering: The Design of Organic Solids. Amsterdam: Elsevier.

[5]   Gaur, A., Mariappan, T. T., Bhutani, H., & Singh, S. (2005). A possible reason for the generation of out-of-trend stability results: variable air velocity at different locations within the stability chamber. *Pharmaceutical Technology*, 29, 46–49.

[6]   Grepioni, F., Casali, L., Fiore, C., Mazzei, L., Sun, R., Shemchuk, O., et al. (2022). Steps towards a nature-inspired inorganic crystal engineering. *Dalton Transactions*, 19, 7390–7400.

[7]   Parasakthi, N., Rajadhas, G., & Thirupathi, A. T. (2011). Formulation and evaluation of albendazole fast dissolving tablets. *Research Journal of Pharmacy and Technology*, 4, 1717–1720.

[8]   Panzade, P., Shendarkar, G., Shaikh, S., & Rathi, P. (2017). Pharmaceutical co-crystal of piroxicam: design, formulation and evaluation. *Advanced Pharmaceutical Bulletin*, 7, 399–408.

[9]   Penjuri, S. C. B., Ravouru, N., Damineni, S., Bns, S., & Poreddy, S. R. (2016). Formulation and evaluation of lansoprazole loaded nanosponges. *Turkish Journal of Pharmaceutical Sciences*, 13, 304–310.

[10]  Remenar, J. F., Casali, L., Fiore, C., Mazzei, L., Sun, R., Shemchuk, O., et al. (2004). Crystal engineering of novel co-crystals of a triazole drug with 1,4-dicarboxylic acids. *Journal of the American Chemical Society*, 28, 8456–8457.

[11]  Subramanian, S., & Zaworotko, M. J. (1995). Manifestations of noncovalent bonding in the solid-state. 6. H-4(Cyclam)(4+) (Cyclam = 1,4,8,11-tetraazacyclotetra-decane) as a template for crystal engineering of network hydrogen-bonded solids. *Canadian Journal of Chemistry*, 73, 414–424.

[12]  Institute of Medicine (US) Council on Health Care Technology; Goodman C, editor. Medical Technology Assessment Directory: A Pilot Reference To Organizations, Assessments, and Information Resources. Washington (DC): National Academies Press (US); 1988.

[13]  Zong, S., Wang, J., Xiao, Y., Wu, H., Zhou, Y., Guo, Y., et al. (2017). Solubility and dissolution thermodynamic properties of lansoprazole in pure solvents. *Journal of Molecular Liquids*, 241, 399–406.

# 12 TLC-densitometric estimation of roxadustat from bulk and pharmaceutical formulation

*Shashikant B. Bagade[a], Akshada Sanap and Ranajit N. Shinde[b]*

SVKM's NMIMS School of Pharmacy and Technology Management, Shirpur, Dhule, Maharashtra, India

## Abstract

A novel, rapid, cost-effective thin-layer chromatography (TLC) densito metric method for estimation of roxadustat (RXT) was established for the quantitative estimation of this drug as API and dosage form. The best possible separation of RXT was obtained through high-performance thin-layer chromatography under these specific conditions. The drug was spotted with an automatic TLC-sample applicator on solid support made of aluminum silica gel coated TLC plates with fluorosilicate 254. The dimension of this plant was 10 cm × 10 cm with 250 μ thick layer. The drug RXT was separated using a toluene:ethyl acetate:methanol:formic acid mobile phase (2.0:5.0:2.5:0.1 v/v/v) and detected at 268 nm, showing a compact spot (Rf 0.57 ± 0.02). The method was linear ($r^2 = 0.9994$) from 200 to 600 ppm/band and validated per ICH Q2 (R2) guidelines. A new, simple TLC-densitometry method for analyzing RXT in bulk and pharmaceutical samples has been developed and the method allows both identification and quantification.

**Keywords:** Analytical method, densitometry, high-performance thin-layer chromatography, linearity, roxadustat

## Introduction

Roxadustat (RXT) or FG-4592, received approval in China in 2018 for treating patients with chronic kidney disease, both those requiring dialysis and those who do not. Initially, it was approved for dialysis-dependent patients and further additional approval for non-dialysis-dependent patients was there in August 2019. RXT is a hypoxia-inducible prolyl hydroxylase inhibitor with a proven promising erythropoiesis-stimulating ability [2, 12]. For patients with chronic kidney disease and anemia, this drug increases oxygen-carrying capacity in the blood by employing hypoxia-inducible factor prolyl hydroxylase inhibitors (HIF-PHIs). The chemical name of RDT is 2-(4 hydroxy-1-methyl-7- phenoxy isoquinoline-3-carboxamide) acetic acid [4, 1, 7]. The drug Roxadustat Figure 12.1 soluble in various organic solvent like dimethyl sulphoxide (DMSO), water, dimethyl dimethyl formamide (DMF), and ethanol. The drug shows the therapeutic effects by addressing the problem that arises when damaged kidneys fail to produce enough erythropoietin, a vital hormone for red blood cell production. It can result in anemia, the kidneys are not working as well as they should in chronic kidney disease and the drug RXT stabilizes the hypoxia-inducible intracellular transcription factor [3, 13, 11, 14]. There are different instrumental methods reported for the quantitative and qualitative estimation of RXT from different sample matrix. However, many analytical methods are reported for RXT presence in biological sample. There are

[a]shashikant.bagade@nmims.edu, [b]ranajit.shinde@nmims.edu

DOI: 10.1201/9781003716648-12

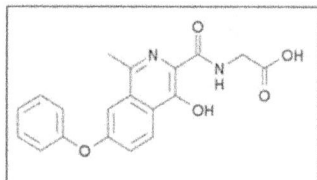

*Figure 12.1* Chemical structure of roxadustat
Source: Author

some qualitative and quantitative estimation procedures available for the determination of RXT, using HPLC, NMR, UV spectrophotometric GC-MS and UHPLC-MS [15, 8, 9]. In this study we proposed development and simple, accurate HPTLC method for estimation of RXT with validation [5] of developed method. The method employing the separation power of thin-layer chromatography (TLC) and high-performance thin-layer chromatography (HPTLC), along with densitometry for determination, allows for the isolation of the analyte from complex mixtures. HPTLC is a widely used technique because it uses semi-automated instrumentation and high-performance adsorbent plates for sample application, chromatographic development, derivatization, and chromatogram interpretation [10, 6].

## Materials and Methods

The chemicals and reagents employed were of analytical reagent (AR) or high-performance liquid chromatography (HPLC) grade. The pure drug sample was generously provided by Artis Biotech, India. The adsorbent layer includes the aluminum TLC plates coated with silica gel-coated dia) and HPLC-grade methanol, toluene, ethyl acetate, and formic acid.

## Preparation of solutions

### *Preparation of standard and sample solution*
The standard solution using pure form of RXT was prepared with methanol as solvent. The weighed amount of drug used was ~20 mg and dissolved in 10 ml of solvent to get 2000 µg/ml solution. Subsequently, this solution was further diluted to get 400µg/ml solution. The optimal mobile phase for spot development was a mixture of toluene, ethyl acetate, methanol, and Formic acid, with a volumetric ratio of 2.0:5.0:2.5:0.1(v/v/v/v). To determine the RXT concentration, both pure RXT and 20 mg RXT tablets were used. A stock solution of 2000 µg/ml was produced by dissolving one unit tablet equivalent powder in 10 ml of methanol. This stock solution was then diluted by taking 2 ml and adding methanol to a final volume of 10 ml, resulting in a 400 µg/ml solution. The prepared solution was then sonicated for 15 minutes at 25±0.2°C

### *Method for densitometry estimation of RXT*
### **Chromatography**
The estimation of RXT was performed using 200 × 100 mm dimension of TLC silica gel with 60 F$_{254}$ TLC plates having aluminum support. Initially all the plates are prewashed and conditioned with methanol and activated to suitable temperature i.e. 105°C before use. The

Camag Linomat-V sample applicator, utilizing nitrogen flow, was used to apply closely spaced bands of the drug solution on the TLC plates. It was facilitated with 100-μL syringe (Hamilton, Reno, Nevada, USA). The sample application rate 150 nl/s. The ascending mode of plate development was finalized for the solvent to run, and the migration distance was set up to 11 mm. The optimized mixture of solvents for mobile phase was used, containing Ethyl acetate, Methanol, Toulene and Formic with 5.0:2.5:2.0:0.1 (v/v). The chamber for the development with twin-trough arrangement was utilized in clean and dry condition to run the mobile phase with 10 minute time for chamber saturation. After heating the plates were dried using hot air and TLC-densitometric scanning was performed on selected wavelength i.e. 268 nm. Th TLC Scanner-3 machine was used with vision cats' software at absorbance and reflectance mode. The bead slit with dimention 6.0 mm × 0.45 mm was set for scanning of tracks on TLC plate.

### *Validation of developed method*

The suitability of the TLC-densitometric method for RXT quantification was confirmed with validation study. It was validated using linearity, precision, accuracy/recovery, and repeatability tests, aligning with the current ICH Q2(R2) standards (Bokser AD et al 2022) Table 12.1.

### *Linearity of method*

For linearity five standard solutions were prepared at different concentrations: 50%, 75%, 100%, 125%, and 150% levels of the standard solution. The working standard solution comprises data points with volumes of 2 μL at the 50% level, 3 μL at the 75% level, 4 μL at the 100% level, 5 μL at the 125% level, and 6 μL at the 150% level. The calibration curve was plotted each consisting of three data points, was constructed with a series of pure drug solutions with 200–600 ng per band as concentration. The results were recorded with peak

*Table 12.1* Results of validation of method.

| Parameters | Results |
|---|---|
| Linearity range (ng/spot) (50–150% levels) | 200–600 ng/spot |
| Correlation coefficient | 0.9994 |
| Regression equation | (y=mx+c) |
| Slope (m) | 0.0018 |
| Intercept (c) | 0.0083 |
| Limit of detection (LOD) | 50 ng/spot |
| Limit of quantitation (LOQ) | 200 ng/spot |
| **Method Precision (%RSD)** | |
| Repeatability of application (n = 3) | 1.79 |
| Repeatability of measurement (n = 3) | 0.69 |

Source: Author

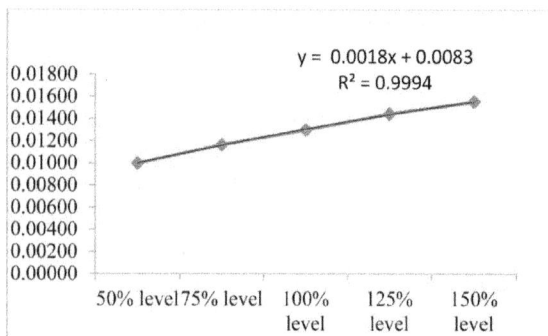

*Figure 12.2*  Linearity of RXT at different levels of % concentration
Source: Author

area and peak height. A calibration curve was drawn by plotted as concentration in nanogram per band verses peak area. The recovery of the drug was ascertained by the results were expressed as % recovery and standard deviation Figure 12.2.

### *Precision*
The validation of method includes estimation for inter and intra day precision which is a measure of reliability of analytical procedure. The samples of within day and between days refers to result variation at different concentrations. However, the inter day precision study refers to variation in results calculated from different measurements at different days. See Table 12.1. The precision of the TLC-densitometry plates of RXT sample spots were determined by replicate analysis. The standard and the with a volume of 4 μL each. To calculate the relative standard deviation (RSD), we analyzed both standard and sample solutions at five varying concentrations, performing each analysis five times within a single day. The value for % RSD was below 2% showing precision of the method.

### *Recovery*
The method's accuracy was confirmed through recovery studies, which employed the standard addition technique and were performed at three levels. The results obtained were highly accurate, closely aligning with the known values.

   (Standard drug, that is, 0.2 mg, 0.4 mg, and 0.6 mg representing 80%, 100%, and 120% respectively). The average recovery of RXT standard from spiked samples ranges from 99% to 101%. RSD% of spiked level ranges from 0.17% to 1.24%. These values met the acceptance criteria of 95–105% for recovery and <5% for RSD (Table 12.2).

## Results and Discussion

### *Mobile phase selection*
The major objective of this study was to quantify RXT in tablet dosage form for that a specific HPTLC method was established. The diluent for the drug was methanol which was the chosen solvent due to its solubility. The most effective mobile phase was developed after optimization of the different blends of solvents showing good separation of

*Table 12.2* Recovery studies of RXT.

| Spike level (n = 3) | Amount added (mg) of RXT STD | Mean area of RXT STD in Sample | Amount found (mg) of RXT STD in Sample | Mean % recovery of RXT STD in Sample | RSD % |
|---|---|---|---|---|---|
| 100 % Base level | 0 | 0.0177 | 0.00 | 99.20 | 0.76 |
| 10% Spike (80%) | 0.2 | 0.0182 | 0.202 | 101.07 | 0.74 |
| 20% Spike (100%) | 0.4 | 0.0183 | 0.402 | 100.39 | 1.24 |
| 30% Spike (120%) | 0.6 | 0.0185 | 0.605 | 100.90 | 0.77 |

Source: Author

*Table 12.3* % Estimation results of RXT from bulk and tablet sample.

| Sample area of RXT STD | Assay of bulk RXT sample | Assay of RXT tablet sample |
|---|---|---|
| 0.01451 | 98.57 | 97.76 |
| 0.01463 | 99.39 | 98.85 |
| 0.01487 | 101.02 | 102.68 |
| 0.01486 | 100.95 | 100.34 |
| 0.01461 | 99.25 | 98.78 |
| 0.01458 | 99.05 | 98.11 |
| Mean | 99.71 | 99.42 |
| SD | 1.02909 | 1.82520 |
| % RSD | 1.03 | 1.84 |

Source: Author

the analyte. The optimized mobile phase was a toluene:ethyl acetate:methanol:formic acid mixture (2.0:5.0:2.5:0.1 v/v/v/v), yielding an RF of 0.57±0.02. Optimal separation was achieved with a 20-minute chamber saturation and a solvent migration distance of 11mm.After development using set chromatographic parameters, the acceptable value of Rf value for RXT was found to be 0.57±0.02. The typical densitogram of RXT is shown in Figure 12.3.

*Selection of detection wavelength and absorbance peak intensity*
The HPTLC method's sensitivity, when using UV detection, is influenced by the choice of absorbance or reflectance mode and the scanning at specific wavelength. The plate was scanned across the UV-visible spectrum (200-800 nm) to determine the optimal detection wavelength, which was found to be 268 nm based on significant light absorption (Figure 12.2).

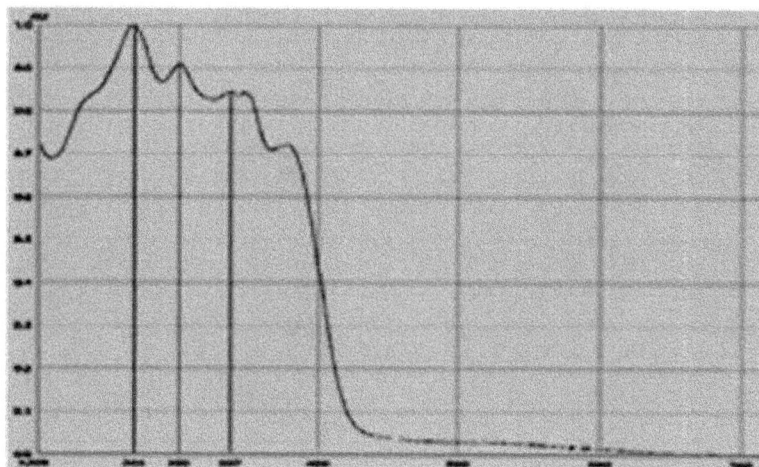

*Figure 12.3* *In situ* spectrum of RXT
Source: Author

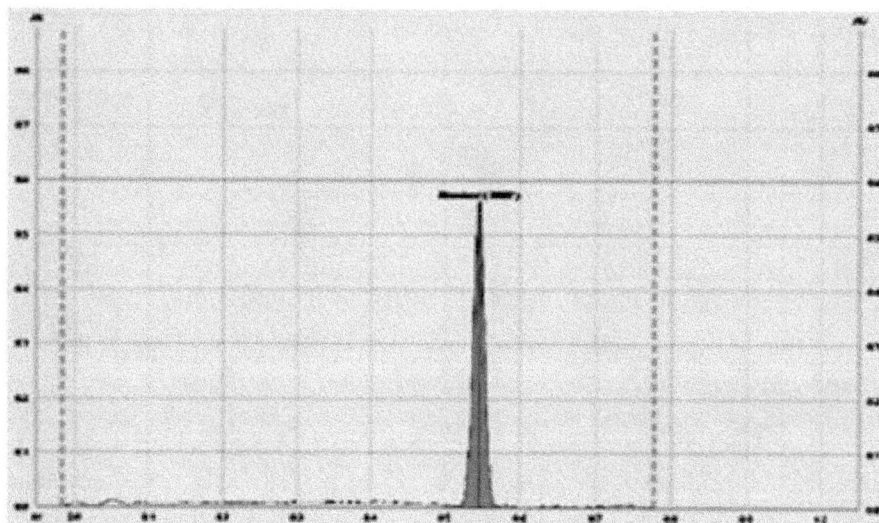

*Figure 12.4* The typical chromatogram of RXT
Source: Author

## Chromatographic Results

The solvent system was optimized using a mobile phase of toluene, ethyl acetate, methanol, and formic acid (2.0: 5.0: 2.5: 0.1 v/v/v/v). The resulting HPTLC analysis delivered enhanced retention and precise detection, making it ideal for RXT identification in different pharmaceutical dosage forms. Figure 12.4.

## Method Validation

The proposed analytical method was validated for the different method validation parameters.

### Linearity

The linearity of analytical method linearity refers to its capacity to produce results that increase consistently with the analyte's concentration within a specific range. This was confirmed by using least squares linear regression to analyze the calibration curve, which showed linearity for RXT between 50% and 150% of the target concentration per spot.

### Accuracy/recovery

To confirm the method's accuracy, recovery tests were conducted. This involved adding known quantities of RXT to sample solutions and then measuring the amount present using the developed method. The results showed that the measured amounts were very close to the expected amounts, with recovery rates consistently between 99% and 101%, demonstrating strong accuracy.

### Precision

The method's precision, or its ability to produce consistent results, was evaluated by analyzing multiple samples. To assess intra-day precision (consistency within a single day), five replicates of five different RXT concentrations were measured. To evaluate inter-day precision (consistency over multiple days), the same set of concentrations was measured over five consecutive days. The %RSD for all measurements was less than 5%, indicating excellent precision and minimal variability in the results. Table 12.3.

## Conclusion

The research successfully established and validated a simple, economical, and highly selective TLC-densitometric method for precisely measuring roxadustat (RXT) in both tablet formulations and pure drug samples. Adhering to International Council for Harmonisation (ICH) guidelines, the method demonstrated exceptional linearity, precision, and accuracy. Strong linear relationships were evidenced by high correlation coefficients, while low relative standard deviation (%RSD) values confirmed high reproducibility. Recovery studies consistently yielded results near 100%, validating the method's accuracy. Notably, the method exhibited excellent selectivity, effectively separationg RXT. When compared to techniques like HPLC, this method offers substantial cost advantages due to simplified sample preparation, reduced reagent consumption, and lower equipment expenses. This validated method provides a reliable and efficient tool for quality control analysis of RXT in pharmaceutical formulations, facilitating quality assessment of raw materials, finished products, and stability studies.

## References

[1]   Becker, K., & Saad, M. (2017). A new approach to the management of anemia in CKD patients: a review on oxadustat. *Advances in Therapy,* 34, 848–853. DOI: 10.1007/s12325-017-0508-9.

[2]  Chen, N., Hao, C., Peng, X., Lin, H., Yin, A., Hao, L., et al. (2019). Roxadustat for anemia in patients with kidney disease not receiving dialysis. *New England Journal of Medicine,* 381(11), 1001–1010. DOI: 10.1056/NEJMoa1813599.

[3]  Chen, N., Hao, C., Liu, B. C., Lin, H., Wang, C., Xing, C., et al. (2019). Roxadustat treatment for anemia in patients undergoing long-term dialysis. *New England Journal of Medicine,* 381(11), 1011–1022. DOI: 10.1056/NEJMoa1901713.

[4]  Dhillon, S. (2019). Roxadustat: first global approval. *Drugs,* 79, 563–572. DOI: 10.1007/s40265-019-01077.

[5]  Bokser AD, Adegbenle YH, Stoisavljevic V, Norton JC. In Vitro Stability and Recovery Studies of Pimavanserin in Water and in Different Vehicles Orally Administered. Drugs R D. 2022 Mar;22(1):95–104. doi: 10.1007/s40268-022-00381-8

[6]  Kovesdy, C. P. (2022). Epidemiology of chronic kidney disease: an update. *Kidney International Supplements,* 12(1), 7–11. DOI: 10.1016/j.kisu.2021.11.003.

[7]  Meloun, M., Pilařová, L., Javůrek, M., & Pekárek, T. (2018). Multiwavelength UV-metric and pH-metric determination of the dissociation constants of the hypoxia-inducible factor prolyl hydroxylase inhibitor Roxadustat. *Journal of Molecular Liquids,* 268, 386–402. DOI: 10.1016/j.molliq.2018.07.076.

[8]  Mazzarino, M., Perretti, I., Stacchini, C., Comunità, F., de la Torre, X., & Botrè, F. (2021). UPLC–MS-based procedures to detect prolyl-hydroxylase inhibitors of HIF in urine. *Journal of Analytical Toxicology,* 45(2), 184–194. DOI: 10.1093/jat/bkaa055.

[9]  Nethra, K., Mohammed, S. Z., Kavitha, J., Seetharaman, R., Kokilambigai, K. S., & Lakshmi, K. S. (2022). Development and validation of stability indicating HPTLC method for the simultaneous estimation of tinidazole and fluconazole and its applicability in marketed dosage form. *International Journal of Applied Pharmaceutics,* 14(5), 153–160. DOI: 10.22159/ijap.2022v14i5.44460.

[10]  Portolés, J., Martín, L., Broseta, J. J., & Cases, A. (2021). Anemia in chronic kidney disease: from pathophysiology and current treatments, to future agents. *Frontiers in Medicine,* 8, 642296. DOI: 10.3389/fmed.2021.642296.

[11]  Provenzano, R., Besarab, A., Sun, C. H., Diamond, S. A., Durham, J. H., Cangiano, J. L., et al. (2016). Oral hypoxia–inducible factor prolyl hydroxylase inhibitor Roxadustat (FG-4592) for the treatment of anemia in patients with CKD. *Clinical Journal of the American Society of Nephrology,* 11(6), 982–991. DOI: 10.2215/CJN.06890615.

[12]  Thomas, R., Kanso, A., & Sedor, J. R. (2008). Chronic kidney disease and its complications. *Primary Care: Clinics in Office Practice,* 35(2), 329–344. DOI: 10.1016/j.pop.2008.01.008.

[13]  Yan, Z., & Xu, G. (2020). A novel choice to correct inflammation-induced anemia in CKD: oral hypoxia-inducible factor prolyl hydroxylase inhibitor Roxadustat. *Frontiers in Medicine,* 7, 393. DOI: 10.3389/fmed.2020.00393.

[14]  Zheng, X., Chen, X., Liu, T., Jiang, J., Cui, X., Zhao, Q., et al. (2022). Liquid chromatography-tandem mass spectrometry methods for quantification of Roxadustat (FG-4592) in human plasma and urine and the applications in two clinical pharmacokinetic studies. *Journal of Chromatography B,* 1203, 123274. DOI: 10.1016/j.jchromb.2022.123274.

# 13 Empowering textile & apparel sector by Dint of artificial intelligence

*Tushar C. Patil[a] and Vijay S. Shivankar[b]*

Centre for Textile Functions, SVKM's NMIMS, Shirpur, Maharashtra, India

## Abstract

The textile and apparel sector is not only fulfilling the clothing needs of human beings but also playing a vital role in customization of specialized engineering applications. It globally stands at the 5th position in the largest employment generating industrial segment. Textile value chain viz. production processes as well as source raw materials facilities connected globally through supply chain management to create various textile products and specialized smart textiles. For getting the at most potentiality, textile and apparel industry require to adopt the new emerging technologies based on artificial intelligence (AI). With embedding the Industry 4.0 concept AI tools are now being adopted and commercially used for fault detection, production and quality assessment, logistics and distribution as well as fashion forecasting sectors of textiles, however some of these are at the lab stage. AI technology is getting attention from entire textile value chain including technical segments like agro-textiles, medical and healthcare textiles, automotive and defense textiles etc. This comprehensive review paper explores the scope and role of AI in textiles and apparel industry. It will ignite entire value chain of textile through bringing the innovative applications empowered by new dimensions based on high processing power tools, which will enhance the quality of production, and provides a range of smart textile applications.

**Keywords:** Fashion forecasting, Industry 4.0, technical textiles

## Introduction

Textile and apparel industry comprises production processes like spinning, weaving and knitting, apparel manufacturing along with technical textiles line-up. Entire textile value chain connected globally through supply chain management [6]. To integrate with current qualitative scenario textile and apparel industry require to adopt the new advance technologies powered by artificial intelligence (AI) tools. AI is now discovering the various operational methods based on the lacunas of the existing production and quality management processes of the textile sector. These advanced methods formulated through innovative intelligence advancement and will boost the pace of various manufacturing and data based operations of the textiles segment [9]. Advanced technological innovations are influencing current global scenario as well as engraving the manufacturing sectors to lay down the research which incorporate e-gazettes equipped with sensors and data processing devices. To improve the functional properties of clothing, new innovations are taking shapes in the form of smart textiles.

Furthermore, sustainability and recycling parameters are also getting increasing demand from the consumers. Researchers and manufacturers conduct evolutionary work in the area

---

[a]tushar.patil@nmims.edu, [b]vijay.shivankar@nmims.edu

DOI: 10.1201/9781003716648-13

concerned to come up with new. Textile operations and product quality aspects are highly influenced by that are raw material, technology adopted for processing and skilled manpower. Entire supply chain including operational processes, production and quality aspects are driven by these parameters. In the current scenario of automation, textile industry is moving through various challenges like bottle necks in demand & supply, higher energy charges, higher wages, international policies in case of export certification standards and technological limitations. These challenges influencing capacity utilization as well as expansion of the processes [6].

To overcome these operational process requirements, it needed to reform towards automated technology powered by advanced innovative AI tools, which also includes the use of sensors, data processing and simulation techniques. These tools will enhance the entire textile value chain by assessment and optimization of production parameters, Use of AI concept based tools are now improvising the quality aspects through color matching and design development and fashion prophesy [11]. This review explores the role of AI in empowering the textiles and apparel sector by improving the quality of production and providing e-solutions to improve supply chain management.

## Overview on the Textile and Apparel Sector Processes

*Operational sequences of textiles*
Textile and apparel manufacturing processes includes designing and distribution of clothing including technical textile products and their related accessories. Entire textile value chain is indented by stages like product design and development, raw material sourcing, manufacturing processes, quality assurance. Textile sector includes the manufacturing of synthetic fibers, yarns and fabrics, whereas these materials are directly or indirectly used in the end product. Textile industry includes various operational line-ups, which also involves cultivation of natural fibers like cotton, wool, silk followed by yarn manufacturing operations known as spinning. Whereas advanced spinning techniques incorporates manufacturing of man-made synthetic fibers like polyester, nylon and aramid, etc.

Further weaving and knitting are the operations where fabrics have been manufactured by the interlacement and interloping methods respectively. Chemical processing and finishing operation involves the improving the aesthetic, functional as well as technical properties of the fabrics, whereas stitching involves in the final garment and apparel manufacturing operation [7]. These four manufacturing segments are depending on each other to meet the quality and aesthetic demands of the consumer. Figure 13.1 shows operational flow of the textile and apparel industry.

*Versatile applications of textiles*
Apparel and home textile are the most consumable domain of textiles. Home textile encompasses products like bed sheets, curtains, carpets etc. Additionally, textiles play a vital role in advancing technical performance and are also used for specialized applications in health care and medical, industrial processes, defense, agriculture, automotive, civil, and aerospace sectors. This specialized segment is known as technical textiles and accelerating the scope by synchronizing with sensors and electronic gadgets will start to evolve in smart

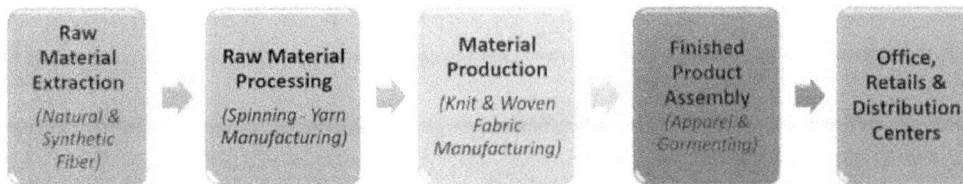

*Figure 13.1* Textile value chain operations
Source: Author

textiles. Smart textile sector is anticipating for technical advances to meet demands of new transpiring interdisciplinary innovative textile applications [6].

Depending on the ease of need, textile material can be used directly or indirectly in the end product. In the case of Technical textile applications, where technical as well as functional properties are concerned, fiber, yarn, and fabrics are used directly or indirectly to manufacture the end product, such as face masks and sanitary pads in medical textiles are made from the non-woven fleece of the fibers.

## Need of AI Based Transformation in Textiles

*Scope of AI in textile sector*
Electronic gadgets, sensors, data processors are the key drives of the Industry 4.0 concept and has vital role in automation of the technology. In textile operations, mechanical processing of the material influences the quality of the product. The very first operation of the textiles is begun with fiber processing followed by yarn and fabric manufacturing, this will lead the keen process optimization throughout the operational sequence. On other hand technological advancements accelerated highly, but lacuna remains in forecasting the relation between raw material, machinery settings and expected product properties. This laid the condition where the technical cadre has to depend on their intuition to control the process.

Quality assurance and testing of the raw material and end product properties is also influencing the entire operational parameters. Going for process optimization in this case will found very critical where it is required to execute immediately while processing the material [5]. Transforming from existing situation, textile industry has stared adopting the innovative and advanced technology equipped with electronic gadgets, sensors and microprocessors along with IT based solutions their use in the manufacturing operations. The role of microelectronics in concern with advance technology like AI is now becoming more remarkable in case of accelerating the entire textile value chain [4].

*Working principle of AI*
Artificial intelligence is a branch of computer science that is capable of performing tasks traditionally associated with human intelligence. AI consists of systems for processing massive amounts of data and looking for patterns to model in their decision-making. AI systems are based on a primary approach through machine learning (ML), where computers learn from large datasets by identifying patterns and relationships within the data [3]. Figure 13.2 shows the working model of A.I.

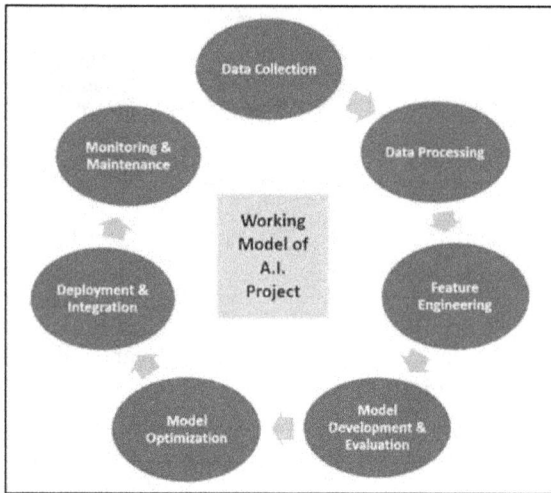

*Figure 13.2* A.I. working model
Source: Author

## AI Powered tools in textiles and apparel sector

### Conceptual AI powered tools

The AI tools helps to create design patterns, precise optimization of manufacturing processes with waste reduction, and also accelerates the supply chains. In fibre quality grading, prediction of yarn quality as well as diagnosis of fabric defects and predictions for coloring recipe. Artificial neural network (ANN) is based on backward integration with a variable learning and linear regressions [1]. This will be applicable in the entire value chain of textile and apparel industry, right from raw material to fabrication of finished textile products [8, 4].

Whereas adaptive neuro-fuzzy inference system (ANFIS) is now recently used to assess yarn properties. Now ANN has also involved in anticipating utility aspects like moisture and heat transfer ratio as well as air permeability of the fabrics [10].

### A.I. Powered healthcare smart textiles

Dormant lifestyles have led to an increase in several diseases, which are intensified by physical immobility and loss of function. Through health monitoring, rehabilitation, and training assessment, smart electronic textiles (e-textiles) have emerged as a promising solution to address the diseases probably led by immobile lifestyle [2]. These interactive textiles, embedded with sensors and electronics, allow for real-time data collection and processing regarding human body motion. Individual and personalized remote health care monitoring can possible by use of smart apparel powered by AI. Seamless garment engraved with sensory applications puts an additional feature of real time data monitoring of an individual and can prove the care potentiality beyond the current state of art techniques. The AI powered health care wearable textiles can bring the enhanced life quality to the human being. Smart wearable textiles can monitor or analyse the real time data of breathing, body temperature

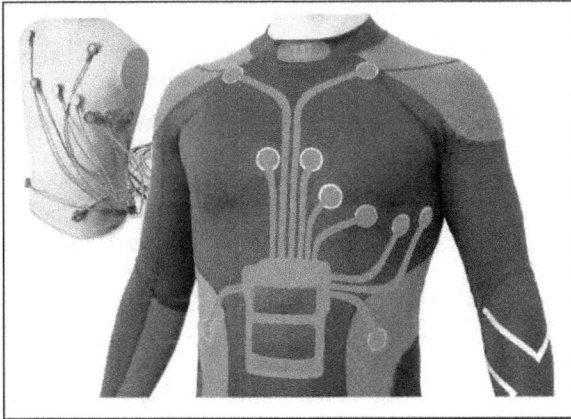

*Figure 13.3* Health care smart textiles
Source: https://acmemills.com/industry-news-blog/application-of-smart-textiles-in-medical-and-healthcare/

which may leads to abnormalities or early symptoms. This allows person to respond in an efficient manner and saves the life [4, 10].

Figure 13.3 illustrates health care smart textile with sensor monitoring.

*AI powered process optimization and quality control*
AI can be used to analyze the previous database of the production units to optimize the process parameters as well as production schedules. Like as automobile industry, AI-powered robots can be used to automate the operations which are conducted manually. This will give the accuracy and efficient process results with higher productivity. Raw material and end product quality parameters can be monitored by using AI equipped sensors and cameras which will improves the accuracy and efficiency of quality control processes. It can help to rectify the defects right from yarn to garment stage and will help to reduce the waste percentage [3].

*AI tools for supply chain management*
By using AI powered tools based on the analytics and prediction techniques textile and apparel sector can overcome through supply chain risk which affects the production schedule and delivery of the assignments. This can also reduce stock out risk as well as overstocking of the inventory [6].

*AI in textile color and design*
Based on the data analysis for color and design ambits, customer choices, AI can develop textile and apparel design patterns which further align and meets the market demands. Designers integrate AI based tools to innovate aesthetic designs which were complex and time consuming if done manually. This merging of technology and creativity fosters the rapid innovative technique to develop designs in the apparel industry. Such application of AI in textile design is the utilization of generative adversarial networks (GANs). It has ability to create innovative designs by learning from huge database of existing textile designs [9].

This leads to generate diverse design styles and motifs by providing textile designers with advanced technological tool. AI powered tools can also use to optimize the tailoring patterns with specific requirements of the consumers. Before initiating the bulk production in process, manufacturers need to ensure the color specification to be matched with the original requirements of the customer. Data Color developed the fabric color matching tool based on the AI technique which improves the accuracy and efficiency of the test results and helps to rectify the tolerance level followed This application may help manufacturers and customers to accelerate the inspection process of color matching in the textile dyeing and printing sector [4].

## Conclusion

Over the past few years artificial intelligence (AI) technologies have started to influence the entire operational globe and nearly 54% respondents from manufacturing segment have found significant growth through it. Now its time for textile and apparel sector to gear-up with such innovative advancements, in order to implant new innovative research based innovations to transform in e-textiles domain. Based on the lacunas of the existing production and quality management processes of the textile sector, AI is now discovering the various operational methods such as yarn and fabric defect detection, color matching etc. These methods formulated through innovative intelligence advancement and will boost the pace of various manufacturing and data based operations of the textiles segment. It will ignite entire value chain of textile through bringing the innovative applications empowered by new dimensions based on high processing power tools, which will enhance the quality of production, and provides a range of smart textile applications.

## References

[1] Chattopadhyay, R. (2004). Artificial neural networks: applications to textiles. *Textile Progress*, 35(1), 1–46.
[2] Cleary, F., Srisa-An, W., Henshall, D. C., & Balasubramaniam, S. (2023). Emerging AI technologies inspiring the next generation of E-textiles. *IEEE Access*, 11, 56494–56508.
[3] Machado, J., Soares, F., Trojanowska, J., & Yildirim, S. (Eds.), (2021). Innovations in Mechatronics Engineering. Springer Nature.
[4] Meena, J. S., Choi, S. B., Jung, S. B., & Kim, J. W. (2023). Electronic textiles: new age of wearable technology for healthcare and fitness solutions. *Materials Today Bio*, 19, 100565.
[5] Nair, G., & Trivedi, V. (2024). Application of AI & ML in quality control department of textile and apparel industry. In Proceedings of International Conference on Sustainable Design Practices, NIFT (HP) India, ISSN: 2583-5262.
[6] Patil, T., Chaudhari, B., Patale, Y., Shinde, T., Parsi, R., Gulhane, S., et al. (2021). Development of techno-feasible mobile app for process optimization in textile industry. In Advances in Systems Engineering: Select Proceedings of NSC 2019, (pp. 281–292). Singapore: Springer Singapore.
[7] Patil, T. C., & Basak, S. (2018). Role of preparatory process for improving loom performance. *Journal of Textile Association*, 79(3), 180–184.
[8] Pereira, F., Carvalho, V., Vasconcelos, R., & Soares, F. (2022). A review in the use of artificial intelligence in textile industry. In Innovations in Mechatronics Engineering, (pp. 377–392). Springer International Publishing.

[9] Sikka, M. P., Sarkar, A., & Garg, S. (2024). Artificial intelligence (AI) in textile industry operational modernization. *Research Journal of Textile and Apparel*, 28(1), 67–83.

[10] Wilson, A. (2023). Smart textiles for personal protection equipment (PPE). In Smart Clothes and Wearable Technology, (pp. 583–597). Woodhead Publishing.

[11] Pereira, F., Carvalho, V., Vasconcelos, R., Soares, F. 2022. A Review in the Use of Artificial Intelligence in Textile Industry. Springer, Cham. 377–392.

# 14 Mechanical behavior of tissue cultured variety banana fiber reinforced polypropylene composite

*Prafull P. Kolte[a]*

SVKM's NMIMS MPSTME, Centre for Textile Functions, Shirpur, Maharashtra, India

## Abstract

Banana crop (*Musa sepientum*) is an imperative and popular fiber producing crops all over the world. Every component of Banana plant has multiple uses. Due to the rising availability of low-cost synthetic fibre, fibre crops, especially banana fibre, fell behind as the commercialisation of agriculture accelerated the growth of main food crops and cash crops. In this research, the tissue-cultured variety of banana plant (Graint Naine G-9) is used for fiber extraction. The extracted fibers were arranged in the crisscross arrangements for composite preparation with polypropylene resin. The composite specimens were fabricated using the traditional hand lay-up method, which was followed by the hot compression moulding method. The prepared composite samples tested for the tensile, flexural and impact behavior of banana fiber composite. The research recommended that banana fibre composites were advantageous for a wide range of possible uses that didn't call for exceptionally high load-bearing capacities. These investigated composites can be regarded as very dependable materials for the production of lightweight materials used in the packaging, automotive, and medical industries, among other fields.

**Keywords:** Banana fiber composite, compression molding, hand lay-up technique, mechanical behavior of composite, polypropylene resin

## Introduction

Tissue cultured G9 variety of banana fiber is the popular and most commonly grown variety of Cavendish bananas [1]. These are the highest yielding plantain among all banana kinds imported to India from Israel. It is an economically lucrative, solid green fruit with a high export value that yields 16 hands and 16 fingers, with 225–250 fruits per plant. This cultivar has great landscaping potential and is wind resistant. The G9 is 6 to 8 feet tall when fully grown. The ideal size for export is 41 mm, which is the typical size of G9 fruit. The fruit is 10.5 to 11 inches in length and 5.5 to 6 inches in length. Its natural fibre is quite strong and may be readily combined with cotton or other synthetic fibres to create blended fabrics and textiles [12, 14].

The banana plant's pseudo-stem produces banana fibre, a lignocellulosic fibre with relatively good mechanical properties. Sclerenchymatous cells with highly lignified cell walls and a small lumen in cross section make up plant fibres. Fibre cells act as support tissue and are dead when they reach maturity [6]. Compared to synthetic fibres, natural fibres have several advantages, including low density, suitable mechanical and stiffness qualities. They are biodegradable and recyclable as well [8].

In addition to producing delicious fruit, the banana or plantain plant also yields banana fibre, which is used in textiles. Natural fibre found in the bast of banana plant. Natural

---

[a]prafullkolte@gmail.com

DOI: 10.1201/9781003716648-14

fibres offer significant advantages, such as low mass per unit volume, resistance to deformation, and easy decomposable and ecofriendly in nature. Additionally, natural fibres are biodegradable and recyclable. Numerous studies have been conducted on the application of natural fibres as reinforcement [3, 4, 9–11]. Banana fibre is a bast fibre which ligno-cellulosic in nature. The stem of banana plant is a rich source of banana fibre, used to extract the fibres. The banana fibre extracted with relatively high mechanical properties. Its height ranges from 300 to 1220 centimeters and is surrounded by 8 to 12 big leaves. The leaves of the banana plant are about 270 cm long and 60 cm wider in size [5, 13].

In this study, the banana fibers extracted from the G variety of banana plant stem used for the fibre reinforced composite material. The tensile strength, impact strength and flexural strength of the banana fibre reinforced composite material tested.

## Material and Method

The tissue cultured G variety banana plant cultivated locally collected. The banana fibers extracted from the banana stem (Figure 14.1) with the help of banana fiber extraction machine shown in Figure 14.2. The extracted banana dries in sunlight for a day as shown in Figure 14.3. The dried banana fibers (Figure 14.4) stored at standard atmospheric condition in the box. The chemical composition and properties of the banana fiber mentioned in the Tables 14.1 and 14.2. The polypropylene thermoplastic resin chips (Figure 14.5) used for the study purchased from the market. The characteristic properties of the polypropylene resin shown in Table 14.3.

Fiber hand layup technique is commonly used for composite manufacturing on the hot compression molding machine (Figure 14.6). The close mold of size 15 × 15 × 0.5 cm is used for composite sample preparation. The stacking of fibre with PP chips granules in the close mold manually.The variables for the composite sample's preparation is as follows:

Sample 1) Plain resin (PP)
Sample 2) Banana fiber volume: - (10 gm, 20 gm, 30 gm, 40 gm, 50 gm)

*Figure 14.1* G9 variety banana plant stem
Source: Author

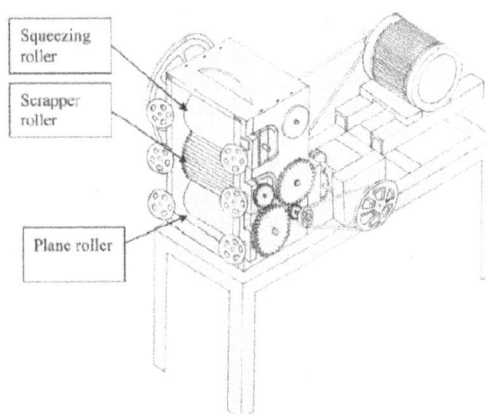

*Figure 14.2* Banana fibre extraction machine
Source: Author

*Figure 14.3* Banana fiber plant
Source: Author

*Figure 14.4* Banana fibre
Source: Author

*Table 14.1* Chemical composition of banana fiber.

| Major constituents (%) | | Minor constituent (%) | |
| --- | --- | --- | --- |
| Cellulose | 69.5 | Fat and wax | 1.5 |
| Hemicellulose | 15 | Alco-ben extractive | 1.70 |
| Pectin | 3.46 | Ash | 1.5 |
| Alpha cellulose | 61.50 | | |
| Lignin content | 5.4 | | |

Source: Author

*Table 14.2* Properties of banana fiber.

| Sr. No. | Properties | Measurement |
| --- | --- | --- |
| 1 | Diameter ($\mu$m) | 0.08 – 0.250 ($\mu$m) |
| 2 | Density (gm/cm$^3$) | 1350 (gm/cm$^{3)}$ |
| 3 | Tensile strength (MPa) | 56 (MPa) |
| 4 | Tensile modulus (GPa) | 3.5 (GPa) |
| 5 | Elongation at break (%) | 2.60% |

Source: Author

*Figure 14.5* Polypropylene chips
Source: Author

*Table 14.3* Properties of polypropylene resin.

| Sr. No. | Properties | Measurement |
|---------|-----------|-------------|
| 1 | Density (gm/cm³) | 0.91–0.94 |
| 2 | Tensile strength (Pound/sq.in) | 3200–5000 |
| 3 | Water absorption, 24hr (%) | 0.01 |
| 4 | Elongation (%) | 3–700 |
| 5 | Softening point (°C) | 140-150 |
| 6 | Melting point (°C) | 160–166 |

Source: Author

*Figure 14.6* Compression molding machine
Source: Author

Banana fiber length: - (30 mm)
Sample 3) Banana fiber length: - (10 mm, 20 mm, 30 mm)
Banana fiber volume: - (30 gm, 20 gm, 10 gm)
Sample 4) MAgPP binder volume: - (5%, 10%, 15%)
Banana fiber volume: - (30 gm)
Banana fiber length: - (30 mm)
Cutting of the samples for testing (As per the ASTM standards of testing).

**Preparation of sample:**
1. Cut the fibers into 1 inch length.
2. Weight the fiber and polypropylene chips as per the fiber friction volume.
3. Prepare a sample by alternate layers of fiber and resin.
4. Take the prepared sample into the machine and apply pressure on it.

**Conditions:**
Temperature: 200°C, Time: 45-50 min, Pressure: 125 Pascal

## Result and Discussion

*Tensile behavior*

ASTM designation D 638-03, which describes the standard testing procedure for the tensile properties of plastics, was followed in the fabrication of tensile test specimens. As shown in Figure 14.7, the composite specimens were prepared for tensile testing. The tensile testing instrument TINIUS OLSEN (H5KS) of 5kN loading capacity was used for testing. The tensile strength of the specimen premeditated from the load-elongation curve. Five replicate specimens were evaluated for the tensile tests conducted at standard testing condition [2, 7].

Figure 14.8 shows the banana fiber reinforced composite tensile strength increases initially with fibre proportion, later it will decrease. A total of 30 gm proportion of the fiber in composite shows maximum tensile strength.

Figures 14.9 and 14.10 show the banana fiber reinforced composite tensile strength increases with fibre length and MAgPP binder proportion.

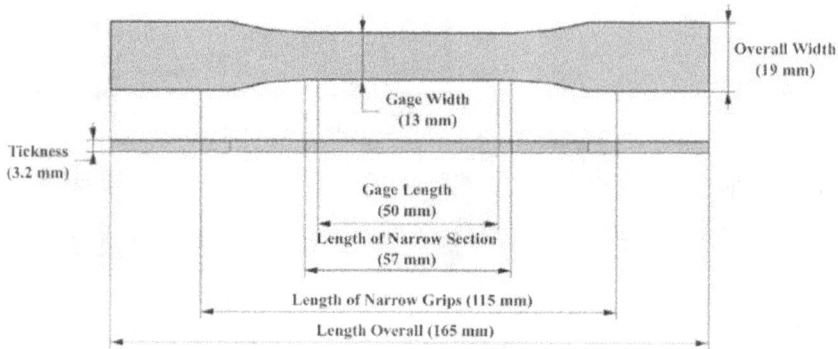

*Figure 14.7* Tensile test specimen template
Source: Author

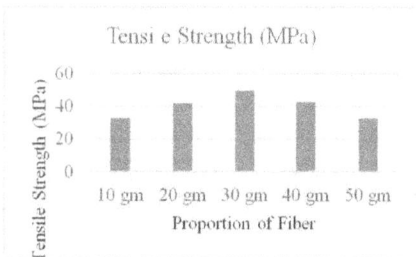

*Figure 14.8* Effect of fiber proportion on tensile strength
Source: Author

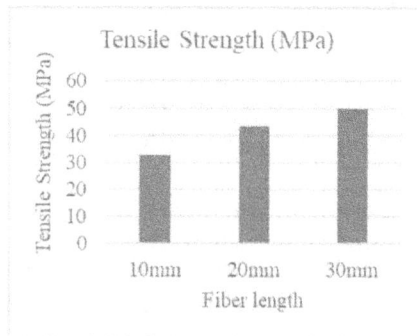

*Figure 14.9* Effect of fibre length on tensile strength
Source: Author

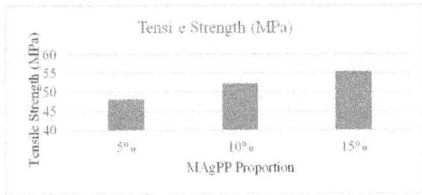

*Figure 14.10* Effect of binder proportion on tensile strength
Source: Author

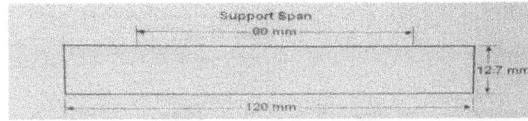

*Figure 14.11* Flexural Test specimen template
Source: Author

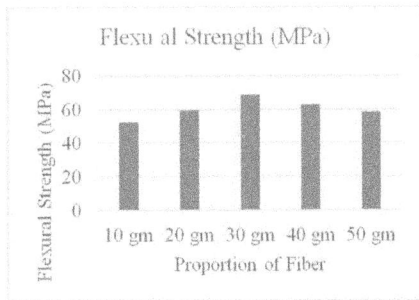

*Figure 14.12* Effect of fibre proportion on flexural strength
Source: Author

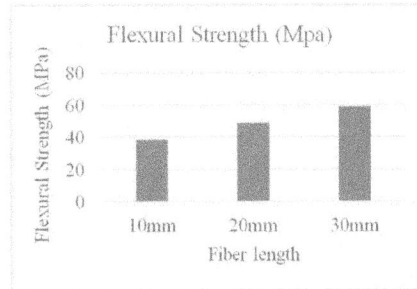

*Figure 14.13* Effect of fibre length on flexural strength
Source: Author

*Flexural Behavior*

Flexural test samples were created with the reference of ASTM D 790-07, which specifies the standard testing methodology for the flexural strength of samples. Flexural testing instrument TINIUS OLSEN (H5KS) of 5kN loading capacity was used for testing. The testing followed the 3-point bending method. The specimens used had nominal dimensions of 120 mm by 12.7 mm by 4 mm, an 80 mm span, and a cross-head speed of 2 mm per minute. The specimen dimensions were shown in Figure 14.11. Five replicate specimens were evaluated for the flexural tests conducted at standard testing condition [2, 7].

Figure 14.12 shows banana fiber reinforced composite flexural strength increases initially with fibre proportion, later it will decrease. 30 gm proportion of the fiber in composite shows maximum flexural strength.

Figures 14.13 and 14.14 shows banana fiber reinforced composite flexural strength increases with fibre length and MAgPP binder proportion.

*Impact behavior*

The izod impact strength was assessed using specimens measuring standanred dimensions shown in Figure 14.15, which outlines the typical testing procedures for evaluating the impact strength. The testing was conducted with an avery-denison impacto meter, utilizing a striker with an energy of 2.7 J. Five replicate specimens were evaluated for the impact tests conducted at standard testing condition [2, 7].

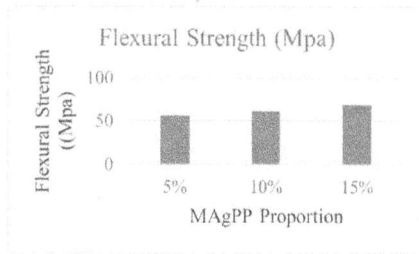

*Figure 14.14* Effect of binder proportion on flexural strength
Source: Author

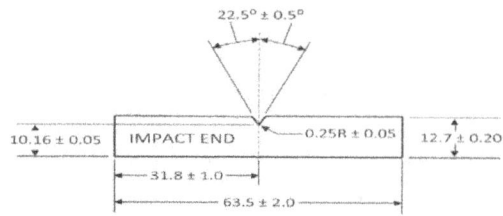

All dimensions shown in millimeters.

*Figure 14.15* Impact test specimen template
Source: Author

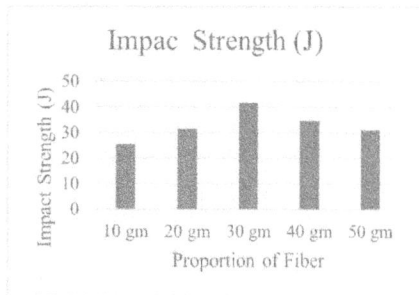

*Figure 14.16* Effect of fibre proportion on impact strength
Source: Author

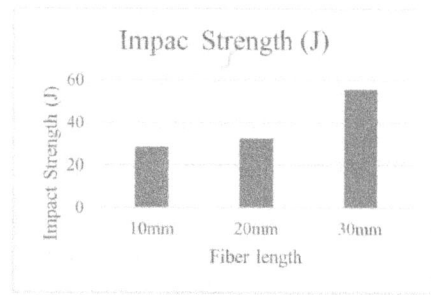

*Figure 14.17* Effect of fibre length on impact strength
Source: Author

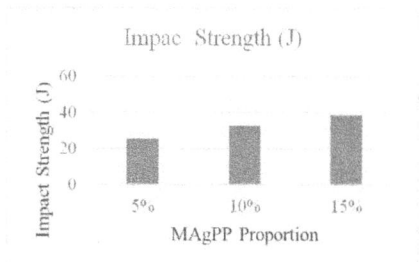

*Figure 14.18* Effect of binder proportion on impact
Source: Author

Figure 14.16 shows the banana fiber reinforced composite impact strength increases initially with fibre proportion, later it will decrease. 30 gm proportion of the fiber in composite shows maximum flexural strength.

Figures 14.17 and 14.18 show the banana fiber reinforced composite impact strength increases with fibre length and MAgPP binder proportion.

## Conclusion

Tensile, flexural and impact behavior of tissue cultures (Graint Naine G-9) banana fibre/PP/MAgPP composites with different reinforcement configurations were evaluated in this paper. This paper demonstrates that fibre length, fibre proportion and binder proportion play an important role in obtaining mechanical strength. It was discovered that PP/Banana composites had the highest tensile strength, flexural strength, and impact strength compared to unreinforced PP. Based on these experimental results, it is possible to readily construct low-cost, environmentally friendly, high-strength polymer matrix composites for both the automotive and domestic markets. In the future, it may be used in automotive applications.

## References

[1] Amir, N., Abidin, K. A. Z., & Shiri, F. B. M. (2017). Effects of fibre configuration on mechanical properties of banana fibre/PP/MAPP natural fibre reinforced polymer composite. *Procedia Engineering*, 184, 573–580. https://doi.org/10.1016/j.proeng.2017.04.140.

[2] Chaudhary, S. N., Borkar, S. P., & Mantha, S. S. (2010). Sunnhemp fiber-reinforced waste polyethylene bag composites. *Journal of Reinforced Plastics and Composites*, 29(15), 2241–2252. https://doi.org/10.1177/0731684409345615.

[3] Islam, M. S., Pickering, K. L., & Foreman, N. J. (2011). Influence of alkali fiber treatment and fiber processing on the mechanical properties of hemp/epoxy composites. *Journal of Applied Polymer Science*, 119(6), 3696–3707. https://doi.org/10.1002/app.31335.

[4] Kolte, P. P., & Shivankar, V. S. (2023). The potential of abelmoschus esculentus fiber. *Journal of the Textile Association*, 83(6), 420–423. https://doi.org/10.56716/4/1489.

[5] Kumar, M., & Channabasappa, G. (2008). A study of short areca fiber reinforced PF composites. *Lecture Notes in Engineering and Computer Science*, 2171(1), 2–4.

[6] Mahesh, D., Kowshigha, K. R., Raju, N. V., & Aggarwal, P. K. (2020). Characterization of banana fiber-reinforced polypropylene composites. *Journal of the Indian Academy of Wood Science*, 17(1), 1–8. https://doi.org/10.1007/s13196-019-00244-x.

[7] Turukmane, R. N. (2016). A review – nano technology in textile composites. *International Journal on Textile Engineering and Processes*, 2(3), 19–22.

[8] Sai Krishnan, G., Shanmugasundar, G., Vanitha, M., & Sivashanmugam, N. (2020). Mechanical properties of chemically treated banana and ramie fibre reinforced polypropylene composites. IOP Conference Series: Materials Science and Engineering, (Vol. 961, no.1). https://doi.org/10.1088/1757-899X/961/1/012013.

[9] Sengupta, S., Debnath, S., Ghosh, P., & Mustafa, I. (2020). Development of unconventional fabric from banana (musa acuminata) fibre for industrial uses. *Journal of Natural Fibers*, 17(8), 1212–1224. https://doi.org/10.1080/15440478.2018.1558153.

[10] Srinivasa, C. V., & Bharath, K. N. (2011). Impact and hardness properties of areca fiber-epoxy reinforced composites. *Journal of Materials and Environmental Science*, 2(4), 351–356.

[11] Venkateshappa, S. C., Jayadevappa, S. Y., & Puttiah, P. K. W. (2012). Mechanical behavior of areca fiber reinforced epoxy composites. *Advances in Polymer Technology*, 31(4), 319–330. https://doi.org/10.1002/adv.20255.

[12] Vishnu Vardhini, K. J., Murugan, R., & Surjit, R. (2018). Effect of alkali and enzymatic treatments of banana fibre on properties of banana/polypropylene composites. *Journal of Industrial Textiles*, 47(7), 1849–1864. https://doi.org/10.1177/1528083717714479.

[13] Yusriah, L., Sapuan, S. M., Zainudin, E. S., & Mariatti, M. (2012). Exploring the potential of betel nut husk fiber as reinforcement in polymer composites: effect of fiber maturity. *Procedia Chemistry*, 4, 87–94. https://doi.org/10.1016/j.proche.2012.06.013.

[14] Zaman, H. U., Khan, M. A., & Khan, R. A. (2013). Banana fiber-reinforced polypropylene composites: a study of the physico-mechanical properties. *Fibers and Polymers*, 14(1), 121–126. https://doi.org/10.1007/s12221-013-0121-8.

# 15 Review of nonconventional natural fibres: okra fibre, Caryota urens fibre, and saccharum munja fibre

*Turukmane Ranjit[a] and Shivankar Vijay[b]*

Centre for Textile Functions, SVKM'S, Narsee Monjee Institute of Management Studies, Mukesh Patel School of Technology Management & Engineering (MPSTME), Shirpur, Dhule, Maharashtra, India

## Abstract

The textile industry is constantly searching for novel natural and synthetic fibres. However, many natural fibres have already been used in various textile industries. There are certain issues with synthetic fibres, which mostly affect the environmental eco-balance, hence, we have come across some sustainable fibres, which are widely available in certain parts of Maharashtra and are used for a numerous range of applications in the composite manufacturing industry. Few novel natural fibres available in India have been the focus of research scientists for manufacturing new textile, woven, nonwoven, and polymer composites. Fibres from jute, sugar cane, flax, okra, typha, munja, and spadix are used for the production of textile composites.

**Keywords:** Munja, natural fibres, okra, spadix, typha

## Introduction

Novel natural fibres presently have distinct advantages over synthetic alternatives, leading researchers to prioritise the development of materials based on these fibres. Wide exploration of various plants, such as jute, coir, banana, sisal, cereal straw, maize stalks, kenaf, and rice husk, has demonstrated the potential of natural fibres for diverse textile applications [4]. Whereas some natural fibres were traditionally confined to producing hardboard and particleboard, a significant shift has occurred. Researchers have made groundbreaking advancements in integrating natural fibres into polymer composites. This transformation is set to revolutionize the field, capitalizing on the opportunities that polymers have brought since their emergence in the nineteenth century. Due to exceptional dimensions and properties, natural fibres have been gradually substituted for synthetic fibres in various applications [22]

It has been studied that due to the ample use of synthetic fibres in vivid applications, societal problems enormously increased, causing degradation issues like generating high pollution levels throughout the manufacturing and recycling processes of synthetic fibre-made polymeric composites [1]. Novel natural fibres are available, affordable, lightweight, and environmentally friendly, which makes them highly useful. these fibres can be easily obtained in various regions of India and can be used as a replacement for synthetic fibres in reinforcing materials. However, natural bast fibres are commonly employed in producing

[a]turukmane.aryan@gmail.com, [b]vijay.shivankar@nmims.edu

DOI: 10.1201/9781003716648-15

furniture and automotive components, such as panels, seat backings, car liners, dashboards, and other interior elements [6].

## Okra Fibres (Abelmoschus esculentus)

Okra fibres are derived from the stalk of the *Abelmoschus esculentus* plant (commonly known as okra) and belong to the bast fibre *Malvaceae* family. Okra fibre has gained significant interest from researchers and industries due to its biodegradable and eco-friendly nature and excellent properties. Okra fibres are primarily composed of cellulose (60–70%), hemicellulose (15–20%), lignin (5–10%), pectins (3.4%), fats and waxes (3.9%), with water-soluble compounds (2.7%), [23]. These fibres are bright, shiny, and strong, with a fibre that resembles that of hardwood fibres. The structure of okra fibres includes elementary fibres enveloped in non-cellulosic compounds [5]

The extraction of okra fibres involves various retting processes, including water retting and chemical retting. During water retting, the bark of the Okra plant is soaked for several days to break down the pectin skin, facilitating the extraction of the fibres [26]. The water retting process results in the extraction of fibres with high cellulose content. It was stated that the primary benefits of lignin and pectin components are helping to add strength and resistance features to the okra fibre [18].

However, the high mechanical strength of okra fibres makes it suitable for manufacturing biocomposites and textiles. The high specific strength and low density of okra fibre make it even more appealing for a variety of industrial applications. It is a perfect material for manufacturing lightweight, long-lasting items and provides ecological solutions; hence, okra fibres developed a special interest in industry and researchers. The sustainability of okra fits perfectly with the rising demand for materials that are for industrial applications.

The author underlined the potential of okra fibres and emphasized their mechanical strength, low density, and biodegradability as critical characteristics for driving their industrial importance [8]. Okra fibres proved to be a major component of sustainable materials of the future due to their continuous improvements in extraction methods and applications. Hossen et al. [9] studied that the cross-section of okra fibre shows a multilateral shape that varies from irregular profiles to reasonably spherical. Whereas cells of okra fibre are

*Figure 15.1* Abelmoschus esculentus plant [5]
Source: Author

unevenly polygonal with a central lumen or hole. The author states that the major difference lies between the diameters of the individual fibre and the lumen, along with their rough shapes. Substantially, it impacts on the mechanical and dimensional properties of okra bast fibres (OBFs). This natural fibre was derived with an exceptional arrangement and contributes to the fibre's strength and flexibility.

## Caryota Urens Fibre

The medium-sized palm Caryota plant can grow up to 20 meters in height with extended internodes on stems, whereas the plant prefers wet, gloomy, chilly conditions, whereas it grows best in monsoon and peri-humid regions [14]. It was described that the fibrous part of the caryota urens fibre is extricated using a water-retting technique. While extracting the fibres, the central side of the Caryota urens was manually taken out from the outer sheath using a serrated needle set on a wooden board to extract the fibres. Afterwards, these fibres are washed and rinsed with fresh water and later allowed to dry for two to four hours at room temperature (27°C) in the shadow to ensure dryness for better quality.

After extraction, the dried fibres would be conditioned in a hot air oven set at 105°C ± 2°C until they reach a specific weight to remove the moisture [7]. The conditioning procedure guarantees the proper moisture content. The presence of cellulose in Caryota urens is attributed to strength and durability, which makes them suitable for a range of applications, [17].

The eco-friendly and biodegradable nature of Caryota fibres and their exceptional qualities have been used in composites where Caryota uren's fibres are identified as a rich source of cellulose (it consists of about 42% cellulose by weight); it has a remarkable tensile strength [15]. The authors Devi and Annapoorani [25] emphasized the strength and resistance of the caryota fibre with minimal environmental effect and highlighted the potential of sustainability of the same fibre in various applications.

The microscopy analysis of Caryota uren's fibre indicates that it possesses a clean and smooth surface, characterised by a thick layer of uniform deposits along its length [24]. The fibre's polygonal cross-section with a central lumen significantly enhances its mechanical strength and flexibility. The cellulosic content of the Caryota fibre improves its bonding

*Figure 15.2* Caryota urens tree [14]
Source: Author

properties with polymer matrices, making it highly suitable for composite applications. Scanning electron microscopic images further reveal a consistent diameter and surface texture, denoting the fibre's high quality and uniformity. Consequently, these attributes render Caryota uren's fibre an excellent candidate for use as a reinforcement material in bio-composites [2].

## Saccharum Munja fibre

*Saccharum munja* fibre, abundantly found in India, holds significant potential beyond rope-making and these fibres are utilized to craft various handmade products, such as fans, purses, brooms, mats, shelters, and crop protection coverings [19].

Many researchers have proven that munja fibre plays a crucial role in supporting the livelihoods of rural communities. The robust and resilient nature of munja fibre makes it highly suitable for a range of applications, providing a steady source of income for many people. Munja fibre's strength and versatility make it an ideal material for numerous uses, including construction, crafts, and textiles. Outside its economic benefits, fibre plants contribute significantly to environmental conservation efforts as they are particularly effective in stabilizing rough slopes that are prone to erosion, helping to maintain the integrity of the landscape, whereas it helps prevent soil erosion and protect valuable topsoil, ensuring the continued fertility of agricultural land. In some regions with challenging terrain and high levels of rainfall, the erosion control properties of munja plants are especially beneficial. Sometimes, munja fibre's ability to anchor soil and prevent landslides is crucial for preserving the natural landscape and safeguarding human settlements. However, the environmental benefits of munja plants extend to improving water quality by reducing sediment runoff into waterways, thus supporting aquatic ecosystems.

As per the investigation of Devnani and Sinha [3], utilizing munja plants offers significant benefits to both the economy and the environment. These plants allow communities to harness their unique properties to create various products, support their livelihoods, and promote environmental conservation. The microscopic properties of Munja fibre are closely linked to its structural and chemical behavior, similar to other lignocellulosic fibres. However, in addition to cellulose, munja fibres contain hemicellulose and lignin, which contribute to their overall characteristics.

*Figure 15.3* Saccharum munja grass [19]
Source: Author

The arrangement and size of the fibre cells play a vital role in determining the mechanical and physical properties of munja fibre. Those properties make munja fibres suitable for diverse applications, including construction, crafts, and textiles. The structural integrity provided by the unique cell arrangement enhances the fibre's strength and durability, making it a valuable material for various industries. However, munja plants offer a multifaceted solution to economic and environmental challenges, making them indispensable resources for rural communities and ecological conservation [10].

## Properties of non-conventional fibres

### Source, Region, cost and structural details of non-conventional fibres

1. Okra fibre [16]

- Okra (*Abelmoschus esculentus*) is found in tropical and subtropical regions like Africa, India, and Southeast Asia.
- Prefers warm climates, well-drained loamy soil, and moderate rainfall.
- Typically, the cost of fibre per kg would be $5–$20.
- Strong, lightweight bast fibre used in textiles and biodegradable products. Fine and smooth texture.

2. Caryota urens fibre [21]

- Caryota urens are native to Southeast Asia, India, and the Pacific Islands.
- Requires humid tropical climates, well-drained soil, and regular watering.
- Typically, the cost of fibre per kg would be $10–$30.
- Coarse, durable fibre used for ropes, mats, and brushes. Dense, woody texture.

3. Munja fibre [12]

- Munja (Saccharum munja), found mainly in India and South Asia.
- Grows in tropical climates require fertile soil and moderate watering.
- Typically, the cost of fibre per kg would be $3–$8.
- Coarse, fibrous texture used for ropes, mats, and crafts. Strong and durable.

*Table 15.1* Non-conventional natural fibres properties [3, 8, 15].

| Sr. No | Properties | Okra fibre | Caryota urens fibre | Saccharum munja fibre |
|--------|------------|------------|---------------------|------------------------|
| 1 | Diameter($\mu$m) | 100-300 | 320.47 | 354 |
| 2 | Density (g/cm³) | 1.37 | 1.3 | 1.423 |
| 3 | Tensile strength (MPa) | 170-300 | 150-250 | 337 |
| 4 | Tensile modulus (GPa) | 8-20 | 470 | 8.91 |
| 5 | Elongation at Break (%) | 2-5 | 3.8 | 2.14% |

Source: Author

## Applications of okra fibre

It is used in making fabrics, ropes, and mats, reinforcement in polymer composites for lightweight structural applications, and also used in eco-friendly packaging materials and materials for absorbing oils and liquids [20].

## Applications of Caryota urens fibre

Caryota urens fibres are used as reinforcement in polymer composites for structural applications, automobile, aerospace and domestic applications [11].

## Applications of Saccharum munja fibre

Brooms and brushes, ropes and baskets, stuffing cushions and fodder, the leaves contain crude protein and fiber, used as fodder [13].

## Conclusions

*Saccharum munja*, okra, and Caryota fibres offer significant potential for applications in construction, packaging, industry, and textiles. India is the leading producer of *Saccharum munja* and okra fibres, while Caryota fibres are gaining popularity because of their exceptional mechanical properties and sustainability. Textile research institutions are developing innovative, cost-effective, durable, and biocompatible composites using these natural fibres. Utilizing okra stems for value-added products helps reduce greenhouse gas emissions from burning waste and provides farmers with additional income opportunities. This practice encourages the cultivation of okra plants and related fibres. Further developments highlight natural fibres' potential to contribute to economic growth and environmental sustainability. Through these efforts, natural fibres can become crucial in promoting a greener and more sustainable future.

## References

[1]   Azwa, Z. N., Yousif, B. F., Manalo, A. C., & Karunasena, W. (2013). A review on the degradability of polymeric composites based on natural fibres. *Materials and Design*, 47, 424–442. https://doi.org/10.1016/j.matdes.2012.11.025.

[2]   Dewi, S. P., Ridla, M., Laconi, E. B., & Jayanegara, A. (2018). Increasing the quality of agricultural and plantation residues using combination of fiber cracking technology and urea for ruminant feeds. *Tropical Animal Science Journal*, 41(2), 137–146. https://doi.org/10.5398/tasj.2018.41.2.137.

[3]   Devnani, G. L., & Sinha, S. (2019). Extraction, characterization and thermal degradation kinetics with activation energy of untreated and alkali treated saccharum spontaneum (kans grass) fiber. *Composites Part B: Engineering*, 166, 436–445. https://doi.org/10.1016/j.compositesb.2019.02.042.

[4]   Dunne, R., Desai, D., Sadiku, R., & Jayaramudu, J. (2016). A review of natural fibres, their sustainability and automotive applications. *Journal of Reinforced Plastics and Composites*, 35(13), 1041–1050. https://doi.org/10.1177/0731684416633898.

[5]   Fatima, M., Rakha, A., Altemimi, A. B., Van Bocktaele, F., Khan, A. I., Ayyub, M., et al. (2024). Okra: mucilage extraction, composition, applications, and potential health benefits. *European Polymer Journal*, 215: 113193. https://doi.org/10.1016/j.eurpolymj.2024.113193.

[6] Fangueiro, R., & Rana, S. R. M. E. (Eds.), (2016). Natural Fibres: Advances in Science and Technology Towards Industrial Applications. Springer XI, (p. 456). https://doi.org/10.1007/978-94-017-7515-1.

[7] Gairola, S., Sinha, S., & Singh, I. (2022). Novel millet husk crop-residue based thermoplastic composites: waste to value creation. *Industrial Crops and Products*, 182, 114891. https://doi.org/10.1016/j.indcrop.2022.114891.

[8] Gupta, P. K., Patra, S., & Samanta, K. K. (2019). Potential of okra for application in textiles: a review. *Journal of Natural Fibers*, 18(11), 1788–1800. doi:10.1080/15440478.2019.1697997.

[9] Hossen, M. T., Islam, T., Mahee, E. I., Reza, Z. T., Rahman, M., & Mahmud, M. S. (2021). A comprehensive study on physico-mechanical characteristics of okra fibre (abelmoschus esculentus) for textile applications. *Indian Journal of Science and Technology*, 14(9), 765–775. https://d oi.org/10.17485/IJST/v14i9.2268.

[10] Iqbal, T., Iqbal, S., & Batool, F. (2022). Saccharum munja derived biochar loaded with hematite nanomaterial for remediation of chromium (III) from aqueous environment: isothermal, error analysis, kinetic and thermodynamic studies. *European Journal of Materials Science and Engineering*, 7(1), 49–71. DOI: 10.36868/ejmse.2022.07.01.049.

[11] Kumara, E. A. D. S. N., Ranasinghe, P., & Abeysekera, W. K. S. M. (2023). Extraction and characterization of fibers from caryota urens L. (kithul) leaves. 1–4 .

[12] Kumar, S. A. S. (2012). Environment friendly removal of silica from wheat straw saccharum munja. *IPPTA*, 24(3), 165–168.

[13] Lila, M. K., Komal, U. K., Singh, Y., & Singh, I. (2020). Extraction and characterization of munja fibers and its potential in the biocomposites. *Journal of Natural Fibers*, 19(7), 2675–2693. doi:10.1080/15440478.2020.1821287.

[14] Ranawake, A. L., & Pathirana, R. (2024). Indigenous knowledge in the kithul (caryota urens l.) industry of Sri Lanka and its scientific basis. *Genetic Resources and Crop Evolution*, 71, 3997–4016. https://doi.org/10.1007/s10722-023-01847-7.

[15] Ramalingam, V., Sameer, M., & Ramalingam, G. (2022). Comparative study on the performance of caryota urens fiber reinforced concrete of different grades along with digital image processing techniques. *ITECKNE*, 19(2), 120–131. DOI: 10.15332/iteckne.v19i2.2827.

[16] Rai, S., Hossain, M., & Hossain, F. (2012). Evaluation of okra (abelmoschus esculentus (moench) l.) as bast fibre crop. *Journal of Crop and Weed*, 8(1), 101–104.

[17] Sakthivel, J. C., Sivaraman, S. S., Sathish, J., & Venkatesh, D. (2021). Extraction and characterization of fibre from musa plant bract. *Indian Journal of Fibre and Textile Research*, 46(June), 191–194. https://doi.org/10.56042/ijftr.v46i2.36575.

[18] Stawski, D., Çalişkan, E., Yilmaz, N. D., & Krucińska, I. (2020). Thermal and mechanical characteristics of okra (abelmoschus esculentus) fibers obtained via water- and dew-retting. *Applied Sciences*, 10(15), 5113. https://doi.org/10.3390/app10155113.

[19] Singh, G. P., Madiwale, P. V., Jagtap, R. N., & Adivarekar, R. V. (2014). Extraction of fibers from saccharum munja grass and its application in composites. *Journal of Applied Polymer Science*, 131(19): 1–8. https://doi.org/10.1002/app.40829.

[20] Santulli, C., Sarasini, F., Fortunati, E., Puglia, D., & Kenny, J. M. (2014). Okra fibres as potential reinforcement in biocomposites. *Biomass and Bioenergy: Processing and Properties*, 175–190 . DOI 10.1007/978-3-319-07641-6_11.

[21] TG, L., VK., K., Gopalan, V., & Hasan, S. B. A. (2024). Ensuring the potential of caryota urens fruit stem fibre as biodegradable reinforcement for polymer composite structural applications. *Biomass Conversion and Biorefinery*, 1–16 . https://doi.org/10.1007/s13399-024-06111-1.

[22] Thomas, S., Paul, S. A., Pothan, L. A., & Deepa, B. (2011). Natural fibres: structure, properties and applications. In Cellulose Fibers: Bio- and Nano-Polymer Composites: Green Chemistry

and Technology, (pp. 3–42). Berlin, Heidelberg: Springer Berlin Heidelberg. 15: 12915–12930. https://doi.org/10.1007/s13399-024-06111-1.

[23] Ullah, S., Kilpeläinen, P., Ilvesniemi, H., Pakkanen, H., & Alén, R. (2018). Chemical characterization of okra stalk (abelmoschus esculentus) as potential raw material for biorefinery utilization. *Cellulose Chemistry and Technology*, 52(3-4), 155–162.

[24] Vijayalakshmi, R., Vaishnavi, M., & Geetha, R. (2022). Study on the workability, mechanical properties of fish tail palm fibre reinforced concrete-emphasis on fibre content and fibre length. *European Journal of Environmental and Civil Engineering*, 27(4), 1484–1502. doi:10.1080/19 648189.2022.2086178.

[25] Yamuna Devi, S., & Grace Annapoorani, S. (2019). Physical and thermal characterization of natural fibre extracted from caryota urens spadix fibre. *Indian Journal of Fibre & Textile Research (IJFTR)*, 44(2), 193–198. DOI: 10.56042/ijftr.v44i2.18638.

[26] Zimniewska, M., Frydrych, I., Mankowski, J., & Trywianska, W. (2013). Process and quality control in cultivating natural textile fibres. In Process Control in Textile Manufacturing, (pp. 81–108). Woodhead Publishing. https://doi.org/10.1533/9780857095633.2.81.

# 16 Development of an in-house instrument for acoustic property evaluation of fabrics

*Sujit S. Gulhane[a] and Vijay S. Shivankar[b]*

Centre for Textile Functions, MPSTME, NMIMS, Shirpur Campus, Maharashtra, India

## Abstract

This paper describes the creation of an in-house tool to measure the acoustic performance of fabrics, focusing on noise absorption and transmission loss. The tool employs the impedance tube method according to the ASTM C384-04 and ASTM E2611-09 standards to ensure precise and dependable testing. Various needle-punched nonwoven fabric samples made from polypropylene (PP) and polyethylene terephthalate (PET) were tested to examine how key structural parameters, such as thickness and mass per unit area (GSM), affect their acoustic behavior. These findings indicate that thicker and higher GSM fabrics exhibit superior sound absorption and insulation properties. The PET fabrics performed better in the higher-frequency range. This tool offers a reliable and rapid solution for routine testing and enhancement of acoustic fabric properties, supporting noise-reduction technologies for diverse industrial applications.

**Keywords:** Acoustic fabrics, acoustic insulation, impedance tube, noise reduction, sound absorption, sound transmission loss

## Introduction

Noise is a major problem in industry, transportation, and everyday life, affecting human health, workplace efficiency, and comfort. Arenas [1] mentioned the need for quieter car interiors so there is a demand for advanced acoustic materials. Textiles are the solution, in this case, lightweight, design flexibility, affordability, and dual function in sound absorption and insulation.

Among textile materials, nonwoven fabrics are recognized for their good acoustic properties which can be attributed to their high surface area, unique fiber arrangement and porosity [9]. They manage sound waves through reflection, absorption, and transmission mechanisms and are thus suitable for noise mitigation. However, Samuel et al. [11] said that precise measurement of acoustic parameters like sound absorption and transmission loss is necessary to refine fabric structure to meet the requirements of automotive and industrial sectors. Standard testing methods, such as impedance tubes and sound-barrier pipes, are widely used to test the acoustic properties of textiles. Whereas Setunge and Gamage [12] mentioned that these methods require specialized instruments and have challenges, such as sample preparation, calibration and following standard testing protocol. To address these limitations, this study designed and developed an in-house instrument and testing method for testing fabrics used in automotive applications. This study investigated the relationship between fabric properties and their effect on sound quality. It emphasizes crucial elements, such as layer arrangement, porosity, weight per unit area, thickness, and fiber type. Using

---

[a]sujit.gulhane@nmims.edu, [b]vijay.shivankar@nmims.edu

DOI: 10.1201/9781003716648-16

accepted testing techniques, the goal was to present a thorough understanding of how textile structures absorb sound and minimize transmission loss. The development of high-performance, reasonably priced acoustic materials, specifically for automobile interiors, depends on this study.

## Objectives of the Study

The study aims to develop a proprietary instrument and testing protocol to evaluate the acoustic properties of textiles, focusing on automotive applications. It compares the performance of nonwoven, woven, and composite fabrics in noise reduction. Developing an internal testing instrument offers key benefits:

Cost-effectiveness: Reduces reliance on external labs, cutting costs and increasing testing frequency, which improves product quality control.

Enhanced R&D: Enables on-site evaluation of acoustic properties, aiding in R&D and ensuring consistent sound absorption, insulation, and reflection.

## Evaluation of acoustic properties of fabrics: methods and key parameters

Assessing acoustic properties is crucial in industries like automotive, where noise reduction enhances passenger comfort. Lightweight, affordable, and flexible fabrics are widely used in components such as headliners, door panels, carpets, and trunk liners to improve sound absorption, reduce reflection, and minimize noise transmission [13]. Acoustic evaluation focuses on understanding sound-material interactions to enhance noise control and sound management [10]. Below are methods used by acoustic materials to reduce noise.

Optimizing sound absorption: Sound absorption is a key property of acoustic fabrics, where sound wave energy is absorbed and transformed into very small amount of heat.

Minimizing reflection: The acoustic material has very low reflection of sound wave, instead it absorbs or scatter the sound wave.

Enhancing insulation: The sound insulation is the important property of the acoustic fabrics; it avoids transmission of noise from one side to other side. The factors of acoustic material such as Low-porosity, high-density materials are imparting noise insulation property of the fabrics.

## Methods of evaluating acoustic properties

*Impedance tube method*

The impedance tube is used as ASTM C384-04 and ASTM E2611-09, which is a reliable technique for evaluating acoustic properties. Sound waves generated by a loudspeaker travel through a cylindrical impedance tube and interact with the acoustic material sample, reducing sound energy upon contact. Sound meters measure this energy change to determine the material's acoustic performance. Parameters like sound reflection, absorption, and transmission are calculated based on these measurements [3, 7].

Standing wave ratio method: It is used to evaluate a material's sound absorption. Sound meter measure pressure maxima (antinodes) and minima (nodes), and the SWR is calculated as the ratio of maxima to minima. The sound absorption coefficient is derived from the SWR value [5].

Transfer matrix method: The transfer matrix method uses a four-microphone setup to analyze sound wave transmission and reflection in materials. Two sound detector microphone are attached on the sound source side and two on the transmission side, enabling a comprehensive assessment of sound absorption, reflection, and transmission. Its wider frequency range and fixed microphone setup allow for faster data acquisition and analysis of various material properties [14].

*Key parameters of acoustic properties*
Sound absorption coefficient ($\alpha$): It refers to proportion of incident sound energy that is absorbed by a material. This is the most important parameter of the acoustic material indicates the effectiveness in reducing sound energy, by converting it into heat [8].

Noise reduction coefficient (NRC): It is the mathematical term calculated as the mean noise absorption coefficient four standardized frequencies: 250 Hz, 500 Hz, 1000 Hz, and 2000 Hz. The NRC value ranges from 0 to 1, 0 indicating no absorption and total reflection, while 1 indicates perfect absorption [9].

Sound transmission loss (TL): It occurs when sound passes through the material and its change in energy from source side to transfer side used to measure the TL. Typically, TL is measured in decibels (dB) [4].

## Materials and Methods
*Construction of the in-house instrument for measuring acoustic properties*
The Figure 16.1 is the image of in-house instrument developed to determine the acoustic properties of fabrics. The in-house instrument is made with impedance tube, test sample holder with gaskets, a sound source, and microphones.

Impedance Tube: A 100 mm diameter tube directs sound waves towards the test sample. It is divided into two sections by the sample holder—one for sound generation and the other for transmitted sound. Two holes, 100 mm apart on either side of the flange, measure sound pressure.

Test Sample Holder & Gasket: The holder secures the sample using flanges tightened with wing nuts and bolts, ensuring no sound leaks from the edges.

Sound source: A Philips BT50B/00 speaker generates sound waves at required frequencies for testing NRC and TL. It is silicon sealed at the opening of the tube.

*Figure 16.1* In-house instrument for measuring acoustic properties
Source: Author

Microphones: Two omnidirectional 1352-EN-00 microphones, with a 30–130 dB range and ±1.5 dB accuracy, measure sound. They are tightly sealed with silicon in the holes of the tubes which cover frequencies ranging from 31 Hz to 8000 Hz.

## Fabric Samples and Specifications

Table 16.1 presents the specifications of 14 different types of nonwoven needle-punched samples of polypropylene (PP) and polyethylene terephthalate (PET) fibres. The products have a broad selection in thickness and GSM values to evaluate the performance of instrument which are often used for acoustic purposes Bhat and Messiry [2] and used in various applications. The table below shows the detailed specifications of sample.

## Steps for acoustic measurements

The in-house acoustic test equipment for measuring fabric sound absorption coefficient ($\alpha$), the noise reduction coefficient (NRC), and the sound transmission loss (TL) are discussed below.

**Sound absorption coefficient ($\alpha$):** It is determined as the ratio of incident and absorbed sound energy by the material by the standing wave ratio (SWR) method. The fabric sample is held in place in the holder at the end of the impedance tube, edges sealed by a rubber gasket and a rigid backing plate to avoid transmission of sound. Sound waves are produced at 250 Hz, 500 Hz, 1000 Hz, and 2000 Hz. Sound energy is absorbed by the sample, and sound pressure is sensed by the microphone at each of these frequencies, which are recorded as pressure minimum (Pmin). Pressure maximum (Pmax) is determined when the sample

*Table 16.1* Specifications of needle punched nonwoven fabric samples.

| Sr. No. | Sample ID | Fiber type | Sample thickness In mm | Sample weight in GSM |
|---|---|---|---|---|
| 1 | N1 | Polypropylene | 5 | 600 |
| 2 | N2 | Polypropylene | 3.2 | 500 |
| 3 | N3 | Polypropylene | 3 | 400 |
| 4 | N4 | Polypropylene | 2.7 | 300 |
| 5 | N5 | Polypropylene | 2.1 | 200 |
| 6 | N6 | Polypropylene | 1.1 | 160 |
| 7 | N7 | Polypropylene | 1.5 | 150 |
| 8 | N8 | Polypropylene | 2.5 | 150 |
| 9 | N9 | PET | 4.2 | 1000 |
| 10 | N10 | PET | 3.8 | 800 |
| 11 | N11 | PET | 2 | 700 |
| 12 | N12 | PET | 3 | 600 |
| 13 | N13 | PET | 1.3 | 250 |
| 14 | N14 | PET | 1 | 180 |

Source: Author

is taken out and the peak sound pressure is measured. SWR and α are computed using the below equations.

**Calculation of SWR and α:**

SWR=Pmax/Pmin

Use the SWR to calculate the sound absorption coefficient (α):

α=1–[(SWR-1)]^2/[(SWR+1)]^2

**Measurement of noise reduction coefficient (NRC):** The NRC measures the average sound absorption performance of a material across standard frequencies: 250 Hz, 500 Hz, 1000 Hz, and 2000 Hz [6].

- Perform sound absorption tests: Repeat the steps mentioned for measuring the sound absorption coefficient (α) at the specified frequencies (250 Hz, 500 Hz, 1000 Hz, and 2000 Hz).
- Calculate NRC: Compute the average of the sound absorption coefficients (α) measured at the four standard frequencies:

NRC=(α250+α500+α1000+α20004)/4

**Measurement of sound transmission loss (TL):** Transmission loss measures the reduction in sound energy as it passes through the material and is calculated using the Transfer Matrix Method ASTM E2611-09 [9]. Place the sample at the center of tube, sealing the edges with petroleum jelly. Position microphones 1 and 2 at 100 mm from both sides of the sample, as shown in Figure 16.1. Activate the speaker to generate broadband sound waves. Measure sound pressures (P1 and P2 without the sample, P3 and P4 with the sample) using microphones in side of the source and receiver tubes. Finally, calculate the transmission coefficient (τ) using the measured pressures.

τ=((P1-P2))/((P3-P4))

## Results and Discussion

*Sound absorption coefficient (α) and the noise reduction coefficient (NRC)*
Table 16.2 summarizes the α and NRC values for each sample at specified frequencies. The results show how each material absorbs sound at various frequencies, with the NRC offering an overall measure of sound absorption performance. The effect of fabric structure on acoustic behavior is analyzed based on these test results.

*Effect of material type*
The NRC values for polypropylene ranged from 0.66 (N8) to 0.80 (N1), showing improved sound absorption with increased thickness and GSM. However, polypropylene samples were not as effective at damping sound, particularly at higher frequencies. On the contrary,

*Table 16.2* Sound absorption coefficient (α) and noise reduction coefficient (NRC).

| Sample ID | Sound absorption coef. (250 Hz) | Sound absorption coef. (500 Hz) | Sound absorption coef. (1000 Hz) | Sound absorption coef. (2000 Hz) | Noise reduction coef. (NRC) |
|---|---|---|---|---|---|
| N1 | 0.65 | 0.78 | 0.85 | 0.90 | 0.80 |
| N2 | 0.62 | 0.75 | 0.82 | 0.88 | 0.77 |
| N3 | 0.60 | 0.70 | 0.78 | 0.85 | 0.73 |
| N4 | 0.58 | 0.68 | 0.75 | 0.80 | 0.70 |
| N5 | 0.55 | 0.65 | 0.70 | 0.78 | 0.67 |
| N6 | 0.50 | 0.62 | 0.68 | 0.75 | 0.64 |
| N7 | 0.48 | 0.60 | 0.65 | 0.72 | 0.61 |
| N8 | 0.52 | 0.63 | 0.72 | 0.78 | 0.66 |
| N9 | 0.70 | 0.82 | 0.88 | 0.95 | 0.84 |
| N10 | 0.68 | 0.80 | 0.85 | 0.92 | 0.81 |
| N11 | 0.64 | 0.75 | 0.80 | 0.85 | 0.76 |
| N12 | 0.62 | 0.72 | 0.78 | 0.83 | 0.74 |
| N13 | 0.50 | 0.60 | 0.68 | 0.75 | 0.63 |
| N14 | 0.45 | 0.58 | 0.65 | 0.70 | 0.60 |

Source: Author

PET samples (N9 to N14) performed better in sound absorption with the NRC value of 0.60 (N14) to 0.84 (N9). PET outperformed the other materials owing to its high density and strength, which helps in better interaction of sound with the material. The higher the GSM of fabric, the more acoustically absorptive it is across all frequencies. For instance, PP sample N1 (600 GSM) and PET sample N9 (1000 GSM) have NRCs of 0.80 and 0.84, whereas lower GSM fabrics, PP N6 (160 GSM) and PET N14 (180 GSM), achieved lower NRCs of 0.64 and 0.60, respectively. Thicker fabrics like PP N1 (5 mm) and PET N9 (4.2 mm) better absorbed sound at lower frequencies than thinner samples like N7 (1.5 mm) and N14 (1 mm). Thicker samples were more consistent across the frequencies while thinner fabrics were the opposite as they absorbed lower frequencies poorly while higher frequencies well.

*Sound transmission loss (STL)*
Table 16.3 presents the detail of the STL results from each of the samples organized by frequency (125 Hz, 250 Hz, 500 Hz, 1000 Hz, 2000 Hz, and 4000 Hz frequencies.). STL, in the context of noise control, is an important measure for the purpose of specifying how fabric impedes sound energy as a function of frequencies tested. The findings indicate that STL outcomes are sensitive to many variables: the density of fibers, the material's thickness, and the head GSM. The way to analyze these variables also assists in establishing a fabric's characteristics with respect to these qualities as an important part of sound barrier attributes.

**Impact of material composition:** The findings show that STL values of polypropylene fabrics at 125 Hz are less than those of PET fabrics but the difference is less at 4000 Hz.

*Table 16.3* Sound transmission loss (STL).

| Sample ID | STL at 125 Hz | STL at 250 Hz | STL at 500 Hz | STL at 1000 Hz | STL at 2000 Hz | STL at 4000 Hz |
|---|---|---|---|---|---|---|
| N1 | 15.2 | 22.5 | 26.5 | 30.0 | 34.5 | 38.0 |
| N2 | 14.0 | 21.0 | 25.0 | 28.0 | 33.0 | 36.5 |
| N3 | 13.5 | 20.0 | 24.0 | 27.5 | 31.5 | 35.0 |
| N4 | 12.5 | 18.5 | 23.0 | 26.0 | 30.0 | 33.5 |
| N5 | 11.0 | 17.0 | 22.0 | 25.0 | 28.5 | 32.0 |
| N6 | 10.5 | 15.0 | 20.5 | 23.5 | 27.0 | 30.5 |
| N7 | 10.0 | 14.5 | 19.5 | 22.0 | 25.5 | 29.0 |
| N8 | 11.5 | 16.0 | 21.5 | 24.0 | 28.0 | 31.5 |
| N9 | 18.0 | 25.0 | 29.0 | 32.0 | 36.0 | 39.5 |
| N10 | 17.5 | 24.5 | 28.5 | 31.5 | 35.0 | 38.0 |
| N11 | 16.0 | 23.0 | 27.0 | 30.0 | 33.5 | 37.0 |
| N12 | 15.0 | 22.0 | 26.0 | 29.0 | 32.0 | 36.0 |
| N13 | 13.0 | 19.5 | 24.5 | 27.0 | 31.0 | 34.0 |
| N14 | 12.0 | 18.0 | 23.0 | 25.5 | 29.0 | 33.0 |

Source: Author

Lower GSM and thickness polypropylene fabrics possess greater STL, especially at higher frequencies. PET fabrics are stiffer in nature and are sound blocking in nature and hence are more suitable to be used in sound insulation. STL increases with fabric thickness and GSM. Sample N1 (5 mm, 600 GSM) possesses the highest STL, especially at higher frequencies, whereas thinner ones like Sample N6 (1.1 mm, 160 GSM) possess lower STL. Higher GSM fabrics, i.e., N9 (1000 GSM) and N10 (800 GSM), offer better soundproofing since there is greater density, which is sound penetration resistant.

## Conclusion

This research created an in-house tool to evaluate acoustic characteristics such as α, NRC, and Sound Transmission Loss at different frequencies. The objective was to develop a tool that would assist acoustic textile producers in optimizing fabric performance. Results showed strong correlation between fabric properties like thickness and GSM with acoustic performance, confirming the instrument's effectiveness. The developed tool is cost-effective and practical for routine evaluation, enabling manufacturers to monitor and improve sound-proofing efficiency during production.

## References

[1]   Arenas, J.P. (2016). Applications of Acoustic Textiles in Automotive/Transportation, In: Pad-hye, R., Nayak, R. (eds) Acoustic Textiles. Textile Science and Clothing Technology. Springer, Singapore, 143–163. https://doi.org/10.1007/978-981-10-1476-5_7.

[2]  Bhat, G., & Messiry, M. E. (2020). Effect of microfiber layers on acoustical absorptive properties of nonwoven fabrics. *Journal of Industrial Textiles*, 50(3), 312–332. https://doi.org/10.1177/1528083719830146.

[3]  Bhattacharya, S. S., & Bihola, D. V. (2019). Development of impedance tube to measure sound absorption coefficient. *International Journal of Engineering and Advanced Technology*, 8(6), 3218–3222. https://doi.org/10.35940/ijeat.F8818.088619.

[4]  Dogra, S., & Gupta, A. (2021). Test method to determine the acoustic properties of building materials by using four microphone impedance tube. *Akustika*, 40, 35–42. https://doi.org/10.36336/akustika20214036.

[5]  Fackler, C., Pitney, T. S., & Xiang, N. (2013). Acoustic determination of impedance tube microphone locations. *The Journal of the Acoustical Society of America*, 134(5_Supplement), 4004. https://doi.org/10.1121/1.4830608.

[6]  Kim, B. S., Seong, Y., & Park, J. (2019). Modified two-thickness method for measurement of the acoustic properties of porous materials. *Applied Acoustics*, 146, 184–189. https://doi.org/10.1016/j.apacoust.2018.10.033.

[7]  Lan, Y., Merkel, T., & Sarradj, E. (2023). Modified two-microphone method: determination of acoustic properties in upper audible and lower ultrasonic range using impedance tube based on two MEMS microphones. *Applied Acoustics*, 211, 109509. https://doi.org/10.1016/j.apacoust.2023.109509.

[8]  Muralidharan, V. (2022). Sound absorption behaviour of hybrid multilayer coir structure. In AIP Conference Proceedings. (Vol. 2446). https://doi.org/10.1063/5.0110175.

[9]  Paul, P., Mishra, R., & Behera, B. K. (2021). Acoustic behaviour of textile structures. *Textile Progress*, 53(1), 1–64. https://doi.org/10.1080/00405167.2021.1986325.

[10]  Heng, R. B. W. (1988). Acoustic absorption properties of materials. *Construction and Building Materials*, 2(2), 85–91. https://doi.org/10.1016/0950-0618(88)90020-7.

[11]  Samuel, B. T., Barburski, M., Witczak, E., & Puszkarz, A. K. (2023). Enhancement of low and medium frequency sound absorption using fabrics and air gaps. *Textile Research Journal*, 93(21-22), 5112–5123. https://doi.org/10.1177/00405175231186176.

[12]  Setunge, S., Gamage, N. (2016). Application of Acoustic Materials in Civil Engineering, In: Padhye, R., Nayak, R. (eds) Acoustic Textiles. Textile Science and Clothing Technology. Springer, Singapore, 165–183. https://doi.org/10.1007/978-981-10-1476-5_8.

[13]  Tang, X., & Yan, X. (2017). Acoustic energy absorption properties of fibrous materials: a review. *Composites Part A: Applied Science and Manufacturing*, 101, 360–380. https://doi.org/10.1016/j.compositesa.2017.07.002.

[14]  Witczak, E., Jasińska, I., Lao, M., Krawczyńska, I., & Kamińska, I. (2021). The influence of structural parameters of acoustic panels textile fronts on their sound absorption properties. *Applied Acoustics*, 178, 107964. https://doi.org/10.1016/j.apacoust.2021.107964

# 17 A review on the importance of multi-functional finishes on fabric

*Amarjeet Daberao[a] and Vijay Shivankar[b]*
CTF, SVKM, MPSTME, NMIMS, Shirpur, Dhule, Maharashtra, India

## Abstract

Today various finishes are taking place on the fabric to get feel, comfort, and aesthetic value which are prime necessity to human beings. These finishes are changing their values in every sense covering all areas from yarn to fabrics. Much research is being carried out to prove the importance of that finish depending on its application and end use. Finishing applied on the fabric is one task and making it to stay on the fabric for longer duration of washing is another important task, so efforts have been taken in this direction to preserve the finish applied on the fabric for longer period. Implementing various methodology towards the application of the finish can be achieved by many trials and method and the one which shows more durability can be practiced sharpening the harness of the specialty finish. Formation of recipe with involvement of working methodology decides the number of washings cycle the particular finish will last. Antimicrobial, electromagnetic shielding and flame retardant are some finishes which are required to stay on the fabric for longer time. Many electronic equipment's are generating electromagnetic radiation in our household and surrounding, finish will absorb all the radiation thus providing healthier environment. In this research work methodology are discussed which can enhance the effect of finishing along with its durability.

**Keywords:** Anti-microbial, dyeability, electromagnetic force, fastness, flame-retardant

## Introduction

Many new finishes are taking place to facilitate the comfort and aesthetic value to the user. so now many researchers are trying to enhance the quality and application of the fabrics in various ways. It is observed that when any fabricsurroundings, longer time it generates foul smell due to growth of micro-organism on the fabric, so the main cause of the growth of the bacterial is due to condition created by the nature, so there are many natural and artificial antimicrobial agent present in our surrounding which if we apply on the fabric during the finishing we can get a long lasting effect allowing us to store the fabric for longer time. It is found that carcinogenic waves are created in our surrounding when a combination of electronic and magnetic field takes place in any equipment's so this electromagnetic radiation created causes many diseases which is harmful to humans.so after generating a chemical finish on the fabric by using conductive coating will absorb the electromagnetic waves generated and this will dissipate in the earthing.

It has been observed that many five-star hotels and fire brigade places require a fabric which will not burn immediately when it comes in the contact of the fire, it is required to prolong the time required to burn the fabric and this cab be achieved if we take the material for manufacturing of this particular type of fabric which will not burn easily, but taking such

[a]amarjeet.daberao@nmims.edu.in, [b]Vijay.shivankar@nmims.edu

DOI: 10.1201/9781003716648-17

material will be costlier. Chemical finishes are another alternative which can reduce the cost. Blending is carried out to bring more homogeneity in the fibre properties even in 100 % single fibre stock. Such homogeneity or intimacy of blending is essential for the consistency of yarn quality. In a blend of different fibres, this aspect acquires even greater importance. The objective of blending two or more fibres includes functional and aesthetic fabrics, process performance, economy and incorporation of fancy effects in yarns and fabrics.

In this review paper the author Cloud et al. [3] discussed the effect of finishes which are seen on the human defining about thermal and sensorial comfort. Many products are produced that they require to protect humans during hazardous situations like flame proof, liquid barrier, antimicrobial and ultraviolet protection. Phase change materials are also developed which change their colour and behavioral properties along with the change in climatic conditions. The author had discussed the nano technology approach for getting smart finish so as the enhance the comfort and protection properties.

## Anti-Bacterial/Anti-Fungal Fibres

Fibers treated with this type of finishes are co-polymer which can be added during polymerization and due to its fastness properties get improved. This fiber is available in various deniers for weaving and non-weaving fabrics. These fibres can be used in for garments, inner wear, bed sheets, pillow covers. These fibres are resistant to staphylococcus, salmonella and fungi like candida albicans.

The author Sivakumar et al. [13] in their research work have discussed various antimicrobial agents for imparting anti-microbial property. The solution of nanoparticles was applied on blends of polyester/cotton woven fabric with various concentration of Nano particles. The fabric was treated with finishes like antimicrobial and ultra-violet protective factor (upf) properties by using the culture like *Staphylococcus aureus, Klebsiella pneumonia and Escherichia coli*, it was notices that not only antimicrobial properties of the fabric was improved but it also showed ultra violet protection to the fabric for helping the skin getting tan due to Ultra violet radiation which not only improves soil release properties but also enhance self-cleaning ability.

The author discussed the synthesis of silver nano particles by using silver nitrates as a precursors which make the process ecofriendly. Water soluble photo initiator suggests here was trimethyl ammonium and methyl benzophenone chloride along with water as a solvent. Effective anti-microbial properties were observed on the treated fabric with long lasting effect.

In this research work the author El-Sheikh and Ibrahim [4] had very well thrown light on the methods of improving the durability of the antimicrobial property by photo cross-linking of silver nano particles in combination with regenerated cellulose membrane composites on cotton material. Applying the finish with N,N-Methylene di-acrylamide (MDA) with various concentration had proved to be effective antimicrobial activity on this fabric. It was found that antimicrobial activity was improved as per the concentration of MDA.

The author Bonaldi [2] discussed that many antimicrobial finishes can be developed by using ammonium compounds, aldehydes, minerals, organometallic and natural compounds to give this type of finish. Biocides can kill micro-organisms grown on the surface of the fabric and biostats retards the growth of micro-organisms. For protecting the flora of the skin most of the producers of anti-microbial agents prefer biostats instead of biocides.

It was well known that on the provision of favorable conditions growth of bacteria takes place. Synthetic fibres are more resistant towards micro-organisms as compared to natural fibres. The hydrophilic nature of the fibres makes the necessary growth of the micro-organism due to humid and warm environmental conditions which affects the person's skin. so by applying an antimicrobial finish to textile apparel not only prevents the growth but it also reduces the odor, colour loss and improves strength. The crude extract from asafoetida showed antimicrobial activity to a higher spectrum thus inhibiting respective fungi and bacteria. It has been found that asafoetida is a herb which was used as a preservative, and flavoring ingredients and medicinal values. This was used as a traditional medicine against the infection. The use of acetone, petroleum, ether and ethanol with methanol of asafoetida crude sample was subjected to screening for anti-microbial activity. The authors Shrivastava, et al. [11] have recommended that till now asafoetida was used for therapeutic and medicinal purposes but this can also be used with chemicals for applying the finishing effect on the fabric coming in direct contact to skin also reduces the effect of bacteria causing harm to the human being.

## Emf Finish

This type of finish is very much unknown because of it less usage and this helps to improve the life and quality if the individual by reducing the effect caused due to radioactive rays which are called electromagnetic radiation. The generation of this radiation takes place due to the combination of electronic and magnetic radiation and this liberates emf radiation. This produced emf rays are not harming suddenly at one impact, but it is harming the body slowly in its long run. Emf radiation is generated by the equipment's like mobile, TV Tower, electronic gadgets, scanner, printer, fax etc. This type of finishes is applied in fabrics like bedsheet, pillow cover, curtains, and blankets in hotels.

The author Ravindren et al. [10] in their research work had discussed that electromagnetic radiation generated by the electronic gadgets are creating a harmful effect on the living beings, so it is necessary to develop a finish on the fabric which will protect from the radiation. The author discussed the manufacturing of highly flexible composites by using a solution mixing technique which not only gives good mechanical property but it also shows good thermal properties. It was found that blending the materials together and using preferential distribution one can improve the conductivity of the electromagnetic radiation.so the making the composites with easy processing and imparting higher Emi shielding properties showed higher rate of absorbency of this radiation generated by electronic equipment's.

Electromagnetic radiation is harmful to the environment and humans so electromagnetic shielding effect is important which is generated by electrical and electronics equipment used in home appliances and industries. Nowadays the garments which we are using should have the desirable properties like flexibility, versatility, low mass and low cost. To prevent the effectiveness of radiation it is needed to limit the flow of emf radiation.

The author had discussed that shielding effect can be minimized in fabric by using shielding barriers like conductive material having di-electric constant along with high magnetic permeability. There are methods suggested for getting emf fabric by using metals in making the fabric but is it not flexible to produce such fabric and if we tried to produce costing of that fabric will be increased. Application of this antimicrobial finishes protect the textiles from the damage caused by the micro-organism along with electronic radiations.

Electromagnetic radiation generated by electronic equipment is harmful to a human being so a finished product is required to be developed which will absorb this radiation, this shielding effect should have a high absorption capacity and it should reduce the effect on the human body which us leading to harmful disease, many types of researches have been carried out by using nano-technology for getting shielding effect It has been observed that various organic, inorganic and nanoparticles combination has the ability to give the shielding effect of electromagnetic radiation generated by electronic equipment. Nowadays many researches have been carried out to generate soluble conductive polymers [6, 9].

The effect of low and high frequency electromagnetic radiation was studied by Karimi et.al. [7] shows that the exposure of this radiation leads to cause cancer, neurological, cardiovascular and reproductive disorders.

## Flame Retardant Finish

The flame retardant is a copolymer with a derivative of phosphonic acid and is made during polymerization. This gives the inbuild flame-retardant property to the fibres which can be used for several washes. The fiber must be used either 100 % single fiber or it should be blended with flame retardant viscose or acrylic fibres. Finishing is carried out of this fiber in the absence of a finishing agent otherwise it may get burnt during flammability can be applied in curtains, carpets and upholstery material, set covers, blankets etc. Many countries have issued the policy of using flame retardant fabric in public places. This specialty of the fabrics used in public places extinguishes itself when they get in contact with flame without generating smoke.

Researchers, Indi et al. [5], in a study shows about attaining flame retardancy by various methodologies like providing a heat sink which thermally decomposes through strong endothermic reactions like fusion or sublimation. The second method suggested by coating material with the insulation layer around the fibre by using boric acid and its hydrated salt below the pyrolysis point. Another method is of producing a pyrolysis reaction which produces less flammable volatile solution, and the last method was to prevent the combustion which interfere with free radical reaction for the provision of heating element required in flammability.

According to Papaspyrides et al. [8] flame retardant finish can be applied on a fabric by using either the fabric yarn having inherent property of flame retardant or by application of chemicals which are having flame retardancy properties. Many times, it is found that chemical finishes don't show higher flame retardancy as there are chances of getting washed out these finishes in the laundry. Inherently used flame retardants are nomex.

Flame retardant finish is required to be developed mostly in fabrics worn by children's and sleepwear carpets. All the flame-retardant finish should be able to produce char on the fibre after burning so that no toxic gases can be generated which can make breathing difficult of the persons in the surrounding. Most of the flame retardant is not successful because burning creates toxic nature of by products on burning. It is required to develop halogen free flame retardant now-a-days flame retardant chemistry is formed by using phosphorus, silicon and nitrogen-based compound. Many research are carried out focusing on green environment like enzymes and expendables graphite. Nowadays, sol gel layer, plasma and halogen free flame-retardant chemicals have been developed

The author had discussed the multifunctional finishes applied to fabric by using short processing steps and eco-friendly chemicals for maintaining ecology and functionality. In this research work the author Aslam et al. [1] had discussed that by using eco-friendly cross linkers like butane tetra carboxylic acid, zinc oxide nano particles, many properties like wrinkle recovery, antimicrobial, ultraviolet protection and antistatic properties can be improved. By imparting this crosslinker it was proved that washing fastness properties were improved up to 20 washing cycles. The Box-Behnken design was formulated by using various concentration levels of DSHP catalyst, BTCA cross linkers and ZnO as nano particles. (*BTCA-Butane-tetra carboxylic acid, UV-Ultraviolet, ZnO-zinc oxide, AgNPs-silver nanoparticles, NPs-nano particles).

The Singh et al. [12] had discussed the application of nanotechnology for the material having the wavelength ranging from 1 to 100 nm. Many properties like tensile strength, water-repellency, antimicrobial, helps in improvisation of surface structure, colour fastness and breathability by using Nano technology which not only improved the fabric structure, but it also showed the finish effect on the fabric for a greater number of washing cycles. Previously, it was believed that the main aim of chemical processing in textile industries is to remove the dirt and dust particles from textile materials but with the advancement in this finishing sector leads to enrichment of usefulness of textile materials.

## Conclusion

It has been found that according to the nature of human beings is deserving of comfort in their surrounding lifestyles and the very first thing coming in contact to a person is fabric and according to that, he had developed many finishes which give him all the comfortable properties for which he is deserving depending on the end use application. So, a multifunctional finish is needed to be developed to protect him from all microbial activity. Finishes are required to be developed to protect him from flames which comes into daily life contact in every household, many hotels and other places where fabric may catch fire very easily. The fire workers working in the field are required to be developed with a suit which will not catch fire easily and the time for fabric catching fire can be extended. Many chemicals and mechanical finishes are available which helps to derive the finish (Antimicrobial, Electromagnetic shielding and Flame-retardant finish) but it is also required to see that the finishing effect to stay on the fabric for longer time. This finish will also be helpful to the fire workers to protect them by sustaining the effect of flame retardancy for a longer duration. Electronic equipment generating radiation which is harmful and the finish is required to be developed which will absorb all this radiation and make a healthy environment in the household and surroundings.

## References

[1]  Aslam, S., Hussain, T., Ashraf, M., Tabassum, M., Rehman, A., Iqbal, K., et al. (2019). Multifunctional finishing of cotton fabric. *AUTEX Research Journal*, 19(2), 191–200.

[2]   Bonaldi, R. R. (2018). Functional finishes for high-performance apparel. In High-Performance Apparel, (pp. 129–156). Woodhead Publishing.

[3]   Cloud, R. M., Cao, W., & Song, G. (2013). Functional finishes to improve the comfort and protection of apparel. In Advances in the Dyeing and Finishing of Technical Textiles, (pp. 258–279). Woodhead Publishing.

[4]   El-Sheikh, M. A., & Ibrahim, (2014). One step photopolymerization of N, N-methylene di-acrylamide and photocuring of carboxymethyl starch-silver nanoparticles onto cotton fabrics for durable antibacterial finishing. *International Journal of Carbohydrate Chemistry*, 2014(1), 380296.

[5]   Indi, Y. M., Deshpande, R. H., & Pohane, A. W. (2014). Multifunctional finishing of textiles. *Asian Dyer*, 11(5), 44–50.

[6]   Kaplan, S., Deniz, O. G., Önger, M. E., Türkmen, A. P., Yurt, K. K., Aydın, I., et al. (2016). Electromagnetic field and brain development. *Journal of Chemical Neuroanatomy*, 75, 52–61.

[7]   Karimi, A., Ghadiri Moghaddam, F., & Valipour, M. (2020). Insights in the biology of extreme-ly low-frequency magnetic fields exposure on human health. *Molecular Biology Reports*, 47(7), 5621–5633.

[8]   Papaspyrides, C. D., Pavlidou, S., & Vouyiouka, (2009). Development of advanced textile ma-terials: natural fibre composites, anti-microbial, and flame-retardant fabrics. *Proceedings of the Institution of Mechanical Engineers, Part L: Journal of Materials: Design and Applications*, 223(2), 91–102.

[9]   Paul, R. (2015). Functional Finishes for Textiles: An Overview. In Functional Finishes for Tex-tiles, 156: 1–14. Cambridge: Woodhead Publishing.

[10]  Ravindren, R., Mondal, S., Nath, K., & Das, N. C. (2019). Investigation of electrical conduc-tivity and electromagnetic interference shielding effectiveness of preferentially distributed con-ductive filler in highly flexible polymer blends nanocomposites. *Composites Part A: Applied Science and Manufacturing*, 118, 75–89.

[11]  Shrivastava, V., Bhardwaj, U., Sharma, V., Mahajan, N., Sharma, V., & Shrivastava, G. (2012). Antimicrobial activities of asafoetida resin extracts (a potential Indian spice). *Journal of Phar-maceutical Research*, 5(10), 5022–5024.

[12]  Singh, A., Jahan, S., & Massey, S. (2019). Recent advances in chemical processing of natural and synthetic textiles." *International Journal of Communication Systems*, 7(2), 659–663.

[13]  Sivakumar, A., Murugan, R., & Periyasamy, S. (2016). Evaluation of multifunctional properties of polyester/cotton blend treated with unmodified and modified nano-TiO2 particles. *Materials Technology*, 31(5), 286–298.

# 18 Artificial intelligence and fashion industry

*Pranjali W. Chandurkar[a] and Tushar A. Shinde[b]*

SVKM's, Narsee Monjee Institute of Management Studies, Mukesh Patel School of Technology Management and Engineering (MPSTME), Centre for Textile Functions, Shirpur, Maharashtra, India

## Abstract

Now a day's AI going to become a part of every individual's life, it is not only transforming industrialism but changed the lifestyle also, customers especially the young generation, taking more technical advantages of this AI. The apparel and Fashion industry is one of the prominent sector who increase the priority of using AI tools. It accommodated almost all businesses, from sample designing to bulk production, from market publicity to customer support and lowers the possibility of mistakes. AI is the statistical analysis tool which makes some decisions based on massive amounts of data being generated. It helps to support and increase organizational activity, speed up market entry, and enhance customer service to prevent customers from being unhappy with the industry's items' size, color, and style. Consequently, the sector needs to embrace a customer-centric approach to effectively regulate industrial methods. With the use of AI chatbots, personalization, and trend forecasting, so generative AI has the potential to improve customer service, speed up time to market, and increase efficiency for fashion companies. AI is already assisting fashion brands of all sizes in promoting their products, improving sales, and improving customer satisfaction. The studied literature supports the complex concept of sustainability by highlighting effective customer happiness, accessible services, and responsible resource management—both now and in the future.

Keywords: Artificial intelligence, digital transformation, fashion industry, sustainable development, sustainable fashion

## Introduction

The apparel industry operates largely based on customer demand and encompasses various facets such as supply chain management, inventory control, demand-supply analysis, innovation, advertising, branding, and waste reduction. Artificial intelligence (AI) holds significant potential in identifying and addressing manual limitations within this industry, particularly concerning the volume of data required and the associated implementation costs [1]. AI systems are capable of analyzing consumer preferences, behavior, and purchasing patterns to uncover the key drivers behind fashion choices. These systems simulate human intelligence, enabling machines to think and act similarly to humans and perform complex tasks efficiently.

Recent technological advancements, such as virtual reality-based clothing and predictive analytics, are accelerating the evolution of the fashion industry. AI has emerged as a powerful tool in promoting sustainability within fashion, offering innovative solutions for reducing environmental impact [2]. The ongoing wave of digital transformation is reshaping industries worldwide, introducing new technologies that revolutionize traditional

[a]pranjali.chandurkar@nmims.edu, [b]tushar.shinde@nmims.edu

DOI: 10.1201/9781003716648-18

operational approaches [3]. Fashion companies are increasingly partnering with technology providers, investing in startups, and developing in-house tech capabilities to diversify revenue streams and minimize resource waste [4].

It is evident that technology has significantly influenced the textile and fashion sectors by enhancing efficiency, sustainability, and product innovation [5]. Despite persistent challenges, the integration of advanced technologies underscores the industry's potential to adapt to a rapidly changing world while addressing critical environmental and social issues.

AI can detect patterns in color trends, fabric preferences, style evolution, and regional fashion differences, allowing for remarkably accurate trend forecasting [6]. AI aims to replicate human cognition and perform tasks that typically require human intelligence [7].

AI-driven predictive analytics is being utilized to enhance inventory management. Overproduction and excess inventory, long-standing issues in the fashion industry, contribute significantly to environmental degradation. With predictive analytics, brands can better anticipate consumer demand, optimize production levels, and minimize surplus stock. Additionally, AI solutions provide real-time monitoring and analytics across the production process, helping brands detect inefficiencies and make informed decisions that promote resource conservation—especially in water and energy usage [8]. This demonstrates how AI is playing a vital role in fostering sustainability and operational efficiency in the fashion industry.

## Different Tools and Techniques of AI

**Machine learning (ML):** one of the very helpful techniques is used for collecting data and allows machines to learn automatically by using patterns and interferences rather than direct human guidance.

Rathore, [9] In addition to defining a set of rules and allowing the machine to learn by trial and error, machine learning techniques frequently train machines to reach a conclusion by providing them with numerous instances of correct results.

a)  **Neural networks**, a branch of machine learning, are composed of interconnected nodes organized in layers that process information simultaneously. These networks operate in parallel, allowing efficient data computation and node transfer. At their core, neural networks consist of three primary components that define their structure and functionality.

Hidden layers containing the synapse architecture and input layers containing data to be entered. The output layers that give the network's ultimate findings All things considered; neural networks suggest that thousands of millions of basic transformations can be connected to creating a statistical computer that can understand complex input-output correlations [10].

**Generative adversarial networks** (GANs) are an AI approach intended to increase unsupervised learning's effectiveness. GANs make use of two distinct neural networks: one produces results, while the other assesses how accurate these results are (Arus, 2022) [17]. In 2017, Amazon suggested using GANs in the fashion sector to develop AI fashion designers.

**Data mining** - AI is based on information. A good algorithm that learns from an enormous amount of data does, in fact, perform better than a fantastic algorithm that learns from little or no data. Data mining is the process of extracting valuable information from massive data sets in addition to data collecting. For example, social media data can be especially useful for the fashion business to understand consumer sentiment towards trends and goods [11].

## Application of AI in fashion industry

**AI in Fashion design:** By examining new patterns and swiftly combining this data into fresh design concepts, AI can also aid in the design process. This gives the industry greater reactivity and cuts down on the time needed to produce a new collection (Bharati, 1997) [18]. By analyzing trends in color, fabric, patterns, and cutting, as well as by producing visuals from descriptions or photos, AI can assist designers in producing new goods. By producing digital samples and carrying out fit testing, AI can also aid in streamlining the design process.

**Supply chain**: One of the fashion industry's most intricate and difficult features has been the supply chain. From identifying raw materials to managing inventories to ensuring on-time delivery, every stage of the process has the potential to be costly and inefficient. These procedures are now being streamlined and optimized by AI, which is completely changing the way the fashion business works. Logistics optimization, inventory control, and demand forecasting are all possible with intelligent algorithms. This lessens waste, overproduction, and makes businesses more sustainable. By using historical trends to forecast a brand's stock requirements, AI can help optimize the supply chain and prevent overproduction or stockouts. Additionally, supply chain logistics management can benefit from AI. For instance, AI systems can track and analyze shipping data to ensure that commodities are delivered as effectively as feasible [12]. This saves time and reduces carbon emissions, making the manufacturing cycle more sustainable.

**Personalized Shopping Experience:** AI may help consumers select the perfect outfit by providing styling advice, replying to questions about fit and size, and recommending popular fashion items. Chatbots and virtual assistants empowered by artificial intelligence can provide prompt, customized customer assistance. To give each customer a customized purchasing experience, AI systems may examine individual preferences and trends [13]. This special approach encourages consumers to purchase goods that better fit their tastes, which reduces return rates.

**Predicting trends and fashion forecasting:** This entails predicting trends using AI by using past performance data and current market analysis. Collect information from online plat forms like fashion shows, social media trends, past purchases and more are all included in the data. AI help to identify consumer preferences, upcoming fashion trends, and the most popular colors and styles of the upcoming season by leveraging enormous volumes of data. This is beneficial to manufacture for inventory management, waste reduction, and profitability boosts. Analytics for prediction.

**AI-powered chatbots and virtual assistants:** Customers can examine how clothing, accessories, and dressing senses would appear on them by using AI and augmented reality (AR) to create virtual fitting rooms. It lowers the number of returns and in-store clothing try-ons. By responding instantly and providing round-the-clock assistance, answering questions, making product recommendations, and mimicking the functions of a real shopping assistant, these AI technologies engage with customers and improve their overall experience.

**Fashion trends:** The AI analyses enormous volumes of data that are gathered from many different sources, including social media platforms, fashion blogs, online retail websites, and international fashion events. Numerous factors are examined, including color palettes, fabric choices, styles, and even local fashion tastes [14]. The Fashion Institute of Technology (FIT) and IBM are collaborating to use AI for fashion capabilities. These APIs used machine vision, deep learning, and natural language processing to help fashion brands improve customer experience.

**Customized recommendation:** On the basis of available data consumer choice analysis and preferences are set which help in to offer highly personalized recommendations. This increases customer interest and positive and fruitful conversion enhances customer satisfaction.

**Visual search technology:** If a consumer sees an outfit as per expectations and like then they can upload an image, specific clarity in choice then with help of AI will identify similar products from its database. This entails developing image recognition technology so that customers can search for fashion items using photos rather than language.

**Marketing campaigns and social listening:** Customer behavior and preferences are used by AI to generate customized email marketing campaigns. These may consist of product recommendations, exclusive deals, and more. AI tools examine social media sites to learn about consumer attitudes and viewpoints regarding a company or item. The brand can respond to public mood by amending its marketing approach with the aid of this information.

**Online trial platform and sustainable marketing:** By integrating computational intelligence (AI) and AR, clients may use their smartphones to technologically try on apparel or accessories [15]. One of the effective advertising tools help both buyer and supplier to show product reality virtually. Customers can have immersive experiences by virtually trying on garments, which also reduces and possibly eliminates unnecessary waste. Virtual tours of production sites can also be offered by firms using this technology, giving customers a vivid and memorable method to learn about their sustainable practices.

**Real-time monitoring:** AI makes it possible to analyze fashion websites and social media platforms in real time. Machine-learning (AI) systems can monitor hashtags, mentions, and interaction matrices to quickly identify which trends have gained traction.

**Examines consumer preferences:** AI investigates customer behavior, preferences, and buying patterns to identify factors that affect fashion choices. Using this data makes it easier to tailor marketing plans and product offerings to better match customer expectations [16].

**Market strategy and competitor analysis:** AI helps to decide certain targeted audience which are suitable to trending the fashion, according to different geographical, ethical, social and demographic condition to monitor market strategy by ensuring that what fashion products are suited to certain target audiences, this segmentation enables a more detailed grasp of regional trends (Z. X. Guo 2011) [19].

Some Popular AI tools are like The Fabricant, Style Sage, Tec packer, Vue.ai, Optitex

## Conclusion

The world of fashion is prepared to adopt artificial intelligence (AI)-based technology in the age of the Industrial Revolution. The technical expertise of experienced designers can be made more accessible to a larger audience by utilizing AI. AI technology is being used by young, tech-savvy consumers, such as those in generation, to express their uniqueness through custom designs in both online and offline settings. The establishment of a digital design model customized with fashion textile data making this research significant. AI seems to enable people with different backgrounds to make unique apparel without needing to know how to use design and editing software. This work is significant because it uses AI technology to implement the entire process, from textile design to production. Additionally, by connecting virtual and real clothing, AI-designed apparel may make it easier for people to express who they are.

## References

[1] Hossain, M. T., Shahid, M. A., Limon, M. G. M., Hossain, I., & Mahmud, N. (2024). Techniques, applications, and challenges in textiles for a sustainable future. *Journal of Open Innovation: Technology, Market, and Complexity*, 10, 100230.

[2] Giri, C., & Jain, S. (2017). A detailed review of artificial intelligence applied in the fashion and apparel industry. *IEEE Access*, 95376–95396.

[3] Fumi, A., Pepe, A., & Scarabotti, L. (2013). Massimiliano schiraldi fourier analysis for demand forecasting in a fashion company. *International Journal of Engineering Business Management, Special issues on Innovations in Fashion Industry.* 5, 1-10.

[4] Harison, E., & Koren, M. (2019). Identifying future demand in fashion goods. *Journal of Textile Science and Fashion Technology*, 3(3), 1–3. ISSN: 2641-192X, DOI: 10.33552/JTSFT.2019.03.000565.

[5] Chauhan, N., Yadav, N., & Arya, N. (2018). Applications of artificial neural network in textiles. *International Journal of Current Microbiology and Applied Sciences*, 7, 3134–3143. ISSN: 2319-7706.

[6] Smith, J. D. (2006). Evolution of sustainable fashion: an overview. *International Journal of Fashion Studies*, 1(1), 213–224.

[7] Johnson, H., & Williams, B. T. (2008). Impacts of fast fashion: what can we do? *European Journal of Marketing*, 42(2), 1–17.

[8] Chen, Y., & Zhao, X. (2011). The role of AI in fashion sustainability. *Advances in Artificial Intelligence*, 45(1), 32–43.

[9] Rathore, B. (2017). Exploring the intersection of fashion marketing in the metaverse leveraging artificial intelligence for consumer engagement and brand innovation. *International Journal of New Media Studies: International Peer Reviewed Scholarly Indexed Journal*, 4(2), 61–69.

[10] Jung, D. (2023). Development of customized textile design using AI technology. *Journal of the Korean Society of Clothing and Textiles*, 47(6), 1137–1156.

[11] Rathore, B. (2023). Integration of artificial intelligence & it's practices in apparel industry. *International Journal of New Media Studies (IJNMS)*, 10(1), 25–37. ISSN: 2394-4331.

[12] Acharya, A., Singh, S. K., Pereira, V., & Singh, P. (2018). Big data knowledge co-creation and decision making in fashion industry. *International Journal of Information Management*, 42, 90–101.

[13] Nayak, R. & Padhye, R. (2018). Artificial intelligence and its application in the apparel industry. In Automation in Garment Manufacturing Amsterdam, (pp. 109–138). The Netherlands: Elsevier.

[14] Rathore, R. S., Sangwan, S., & Kaiwartya, O. (2021). Green communication for next-generation wireless systems: optimization strategies, challenges, solutions, and future aspects. *Wireless Communications and Mobile Computing*, 2021, 1–38 .

[15] Khakurel, J., Penzenstadler, B., Porras, J., Knutas, A., & Zhang, W. (2018). The rise of artificial intelligence under the lens of sustainability. *Technologies*, 6(4), 100–106.

[16] Nishant, R., Kennedy, M., & Corbett, J. (2020). Artificial intelligence for sustainability: challenges, opportunities, and a research agenda. *International Journal of Information Management*, 53, 102104.

[17] Arus, K., & Disaya, C. (2022). Developing design approaches for tile pattern designs inspired by traditional textile patterns; Processes, 10(23), 2744–2762.

[18] Bharati, 1997 - change it toBharati Rathore (2019), Fashion Sustainability in the AI Era: Opportunities and Challenges in Marketing International Peer Reviewed/Refereed Multidisciplinary Journal (EIPRMJ), 8(2). ISSN: 2319-5045

[19] Z. X. Guo, W. K. Wong, S. Y. S. Leung, and M. Li (2011), Applications of artificial intelligence in the apparel industry: A review, Text. Res. J., 81(18), 1871–1892.

# 19 Sustainable synthesis of graphene oxide nanoparticles using green extract: characterization and textile applications, a review

*Poonia Poonam Prithvi Singh[1,a], Tasnim N. Shaikh[1,b] and Bharat Patel[2,c]*

[1]Department of Textile Engineering, Faculty of Technology and Engineering, The Maharaja Sayajirao University of Baroda, Gujarat, India

[2]Department of Textile Chemistry, Faculty of Technology and Engineering, The Maharaja Sayajirao University of Baroda, Gujarat, India

## Abstract

Graphene oxide (GO), a derived of graphene, is a two-dimensional material characterized by its exclusive structure improved with oxygen-containing functional groups. These functional groups give GO amazing properties such as high surface area, electronic conductivity, mechanical strength, and hydrophilic performance. Its flexibility arises from the ability to modify its chemical structure, supporting applications across diverse fields. GO finds extensive use in energy storage devices, water purification systems, biomedical engineering, and composite materials due to its excellent dispersibility in various solvents and compatibility with polymers. Moreover, its antibacterial properties for drug delivery further broaden its application scope. As an innovative material, graphene oxide continues to strength innovations in technology and sustainable development.

**Keywords:** Graphene oxide, green synthesis, nanotechnology, sustainability, textile composite

## Introduction

A composite material is known as the preparation of two or more ingredients that outcome in better properties than the original constituents. The two elements of composite always consist of a reinforcement and a matrix [5]. Reinforced matter acts as a functional group whereas matrix forms base ground for the composite [33]. Types of composites are usually defined on the basis of matrix. The major groups identified in this area are; i) Metal matrix composite, ii) Ceramic matrix composite, and iii) Polymer matrix composite [2]. Metal matrix composite (MMC) is made by distributing a reinforcing material into a metal matrix. Ceramic matrix composite (CMC) consists of ceramic fibres bounded in a ceramic matrix. Polymer matrix composite is also known as fibre reinforced plastics (FRP) in which the plastic (matrix) is reinforced with fibres (reinforcement) [33]. Nano composite textile is a widely raising category of FRP due to its excellent performance earned at a significantly reduced price in recent times [5]. In accordance, Nanotechnology has appeared as a

[a]poonampoonia2506@gmail.com, [b]t.n.shaikh-ted@msubaroda.ac.in, [c]b.h.patel-tchem@msubaroda.ac.in

DOI: 10.1201/9781003716648-19

transformative science, enabling matter at atomic and molecular scales to create materials with novel properties [16].

The graphene oxide (GO) has gathered attention due to its amazing mechanical, thermal, and electrical characteristics among nanomaterials [3]. It represents an oxidized derivative of graphene presenting oxygen-containing functional groups. Its hydrophilic nature, high surface area, and electronic properties make it a material of choice for a wide-range of applications, including textiles. The major strength lies in the GO's ability to form stable aqueous dispersions that allow direct incorporation into materials [8]. Table 19.1 shows in brief summarized comparison between the properties of graphene oxide on macro and nano level.

**Nano composite textiles:** It refers to composite fiber materials containing one or more nanoscale components [2]. This nanostructured component can be nanoparticle, nanotube, nanofiber etc. The most widely used nanoparticles in this area can be prepared either by nanoparticle synthesis or by processing nanomaterial into nanostructured particles [2]. Required nanoparticles can be synthesized either by chemical, physical, mechanical and biological method (Figure 19.1).

*Table 19.1* Comparative analysis of graphene oxide (GO) on macro and nano level.

| Property | Macro-level GO | Nano-level GO |
|---|---|---|
| Structure | Films, membranes, or powders with micrometer to millimeter thickness. | Single- or few-layer sheets with atomic thickness (~0.7–1.2 nm) and higher disclosure of individual sheets [8]. |
| Surface chemistry | Collective oxygen groups; hydrophilic but less reactive. | Rich in functional groups and offers more reactive surface areas [35]. |
| Mechanical properties | Moderate tensile strength (~10–40 MPa); Young's modulus ~1–20 GPa, is weakens due to inter sheet defects. | High intrinsic strength (~130 GPa for single sheets) [32]. |
| Electrical properties | Insulating or weakly conductive; conductivity limited by inter-sheet resistance. | Intrinsically insulating; better localized conductivity upon reduction shows better refurbishment [12]. |
| Optical properties | Strong UV absorption (~230 nm peak); minimal fluorescence. | UV absorption which displays fluorescence due to quantum confinement [27]. |
| Thermal properties | Stable up to ~200°C; low thermal conductivity due to inter-sheet scattering. | Poor thermal conductivity: localized heat transfer improves upon reduction [36]. |
| Hydrophilicity | Hydrophilic films; swells in water. | Highly hydrophilic and more dispersible in polar solvents due to higher surface area exposure [4]. |
| Surface area | Lower effective surface area (~50–150 m²/g) due to stacking. | Higher surface area (~200–800 m²/g after reduction) [12]. |

Source: Author

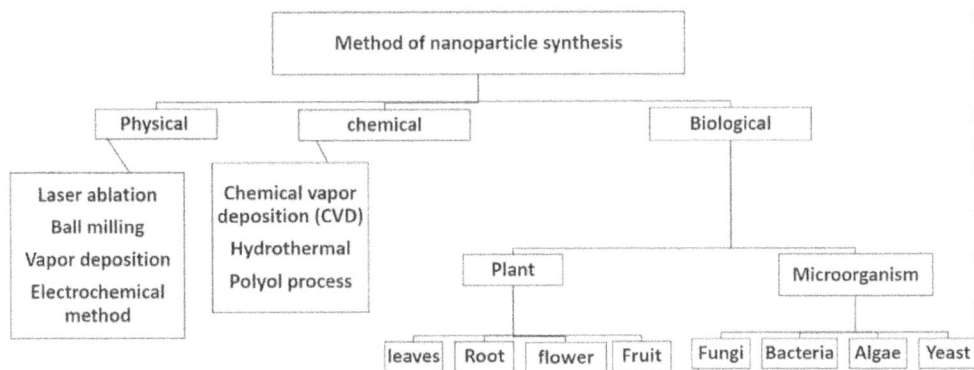

*Figure 19.1* Types of nanoparticles synthesis methods
Source: Author

## Literature Review

*Chemical synthesis of nanoparticles*

The chemical synthesis of GO nanoparticles, typically using Hummers' method, includes oxidizing graphite with potassium permanganate ($KMnO_4$) in concentrated sulfuric acid ($H_2SO_4$), followed by quenching with hydrogen peroxide ($H_2O_2$) [9]. This process yields GO with oxygen-functional groups, improving solubility and flexibility for applications [20]. However, it is restricted by the use of toxic reagents, group of hazardous waste, residual impurities, and structural defects that damage conductivity and strength [9].

**Physical synthesis of nanoparticles:** The physical synthesis of GO nanoparticles consist of physical methods like ball milling, high-energy laser beams or high pressure and temperature. In this approach the graphene is broken into nanoparticles with the help of high-energy and pressure [7]. This method does not use chemical agents, creating GO with fewer shortages and supporting its structural integrity. However, the process demands high energy, produces less quantities, and lacks oxygen-containing functional groups, which may assure solubility and functionalization. Also, maintaining uniform particle sizes can be challenging [7].

**Biological synthesis of nanoparticles:** In biological synthesis of GO nanoparticles method plant extracts, natural acids, or microorganisms are used as reducing and capping agents. Common constituents contain graphite as the precursor and natural agents like tea extracts, aloevera, or citric acid are used [18]. This method is environment-friendly and making GO biocompatible, which is suitable for use of biomedical applications. It shows limitations such as less production, limited scalability, and less control over the size and functionalization of the nanoparticles compared to chemical methods [18] (Figure 19.1).

**Plant-based synthesis:** Plant-based synthesis of GO is a new method which is innovative and eco-friendly to produce this high demanding GO material. This method uses biomass or plant materials as precursors, offering an alternative to conventional methods which depend on dangerous chemicals and high-energy demanding processes [18].

*Table 19.2* Summary of plant-based and microorganism GO synthesis research.

| Plant source | Nanoparticle size (nm) | Key features |
|---|---|---|
| Neem leaves (Azadirachta indica) | ~30–80 | Neem phytochemicals enhance stability and offer antibacterial properties Sharma, [1] |
| Aloevera (Aloe barbadensis) | ~40–90 | Aloe polysaccharides help in nanoparticle stabilization and biocompatibility [6] |
| Moringa leaves (Moringa oleifera) | ~50–120 | Moringa antioxidants enhance uniform size and functionalization [28] |
| Tulsi (Ocimum sanctum) | ~20–70 | Active phytochemicals confirm smaller size and uniform distribution [22]. |
| Eucalyptus leaves | ~40–100 | Flavonoids and terpenoids advance the reduction process and nanoparticle quality [34] |
| Ginger (Zingiber officinale) | ~30–60 | Bioactive compounds advance nanoparticle stability and functional properties [13]. |

Source: Author

*Table 19.3* Various microorganism based GO synthesis and their characteristics.

| Microorganism | Nanoparticle size (nm) | Key features |
|---|---|---|
| Bacteria (Escherichia coli) | ~20–50 | Enzymatic reduction makes stable nanoparticles with minimal agglomeration [10]. |
| Fungi (Aspergillus niger) | ~30–80 | Fungal metabolites act as reducing and capping agents, improving stability. [18]. |
| Yeast (Saccharomyces cerevisiae) | ~40–100 | Yeast cells facilitate uniform size and better biocompatibility [31]. |
| Algae (Chlorella vulgaris) | ~50–120 | Algal proteins and polysaccharides stabilize nanoparticles during synthesis [15]. |
| Actinomycetes (Streptomyces sp.) | ~30–60 | Produces highly stable and biofunctional nanoparticles [26]. |

Source: Author

According to Fardinpour, Taleghani and Zakerimehr [13] precursor material can be derived from various biomass options, such as agricultural water, carbonaceous enriched cellulose and starches received from the plant, fruit peels etc. The common resources, adopted by the various researchers till date with a brief mention about their outcomes, are abstracted in Table 19.2.

*Microorganism-based synthesis*
The major research under this criterion was related to the use of yeast, fungi, algae, bacteria mainly, as mentioned by Cobos et al. [10]. Their significance lies in the successful reduction and capping of nanoparticles by the microbial cells or say their secreted biomolecules.

Validating this eco-friendly pathway, Zhao et al. [37] have reported a sustainable GO nanoparticle synthesis by using *Escherichia coli* bacteria and *Aspergillus niger* fungi. These biosynthesized nanoparticles normally range from 20 to 120 nm in size and show biocompatibility, making them suitable for applications in drug delivery, bio-sensing, and environmental repair [37]. The outcome of various research conducted in this direction have been summarized in Table 19.3.

*Application of graphene oxide nanoparticles*
Regardless of synthesis technique considered the outputted Graphene oxide nanoparticles (GO NPs) embrace unique properties, such as high surface area, brilliant mechanical strength, and electrical conductivity than macro forms [18]. These have made them greater and multipurpose over usual macro GO in different fields. Some applications include:

*Drug delivery and biomedical applications*
**Cancer therapy**: For cancer treatment, graphene oxide nanoparticle is used to deliver chemotherapy drugs directly to tumor sites which help in reducing the side effects on the healthy tissues [11].

**Biosensors:** The high surface area and functionality properties of GO NPs help in sensing biological molecules, pathogens, and viruses. It provides high sensitivity. Because of the same features they can be used in medical diagnosis, such as imaging and the detection of disease biomarkers [27].

**Drug loading and release**: In drug delivery graphene oxide acts as an active carrier because of high surface area and its ability to form stable composites with drug molecules. This phenomenon was well elucidated by Itoo et al. [17], accordingly controlled drug release become possible due to inevitable coupling of the drugs with the respective functional groups of GO.

*Environmental remediation*
**Water treatment**: The GO NPs can effectively capture water contaminants like organic pollutants as well as heavy metals owing to their excellent adsorption capacity [19]. Due to this they can be successfully implemented to enhance functionality of the water filter. Anegbe, et al. [4] have suggested their sensible utilization in crafting filters to get rid of specific worried some toxins. It is indeed difficult to get separate oil and organic pollutants floating on the water surface and mainly arrived from the industrial discharge to the water bodies. The hydrophobic characteristics induced to the GO NPs treated filter materials, which has made them effective medium in the removal of these undesirable elements [4].

**Energy storage and conversion:** A lot of research has been done with GO NPs in this direction, and their reports admit a remarkable improvement in the performance of energy storage and conversion mediums like batteries, solar cells, super capacitors etc [30]. Mousavi et al. [24] have noted enhanced performance of lithium-ion and sodium-ion batteries by offering greater charge capacity and better cycle life. Similarly, Mahmoudi et al. [23] have found considerable improvement in the light absorption and electron transport efficiency of solar cell on making use of GO NPs as conductive layers. Whereas Li et al. [21] have validated high energy storage capacities and cycling stability of super- capacitors on GO NPs treatment.

**Electronics and sensors:** Jirickova et al. [18] have brought into limelight good sensitivity of GO NPs to various gases like ammonia, nitrogen dioxide etc., and suggested their suitability as gas sensor for better environmental safety. Going in agreement Murthy et al. [25] have also advocated their potential to sense a wide range of substances, gases and volatile organic compounds (VOCs) due to their large surface area and functionalization capability in chemical sensors. Looking at their excellent conductive properties, Esteghamat and Akhavan [12]   have used them successfully in the fabrication of transparent touch screens and sensors sort of flexible and electronic devices.

**Food packaging:** The GO NPs inherently possess antibacterial and antioxidant properties, and there by Rossa et al. [29] have utilized them as a green medium to extend shelf life of the packed foods by avoiding spoilage and contamination.

**Composite materials:** Fu et al. [14] have endorsed capabilities of GO NPs in terms of enhancing mechanical properties of composite materials on reinforcing them in polymer, made them tougher, lighter, and long-lasting. Their research outputs have pointed a new application horizon for GO NPs in industries like aerospace, automobile, and construction etc.

## Conclusion

The unique features of graphene oxide nanoparticles (GO NPs) have developed them as the most adaptable materials compared to commonly used macro arrangement. These have exclusively made them the material of the choice for the wide application domains starting from the basic human needs of water filtration to that of advanced medical science. Along with the evolution of the research this creditable medium will reach to the new height of end use application ranges in the future by covering up wide spectrum. It can be a key material for future technological advancement. Further one should be careful to discover this field of GO NPs with biological way rather than commonly acknowledged chemical and physical ways for the sake of environment as well as human health.

## References

[1] Akhtar, M. S., Jutt, D. S. R., Aslam, S., Nawaz, R., & Khan, M. (2024). Green synthesis of graphene oxide and magnetite nanoparticles and their arsenic removal efficiency from arsenic contaminated soil. *Scientifc Reports*, 14, 23094. https://doi.org/10.1038/s41598-024-73734-9.

[2] Al-Mutairi, N. H., Mehdi, A. H., & Kadhim, B. J. (2022). Nanocomposites materials definitations, types and some of their applications: a review. *European Journal of Research Development and Sustainability*, 3(2), 102–108.

[3] Altammar, K. A. (2023). A review on nanoparticles: characteristics, synthesis, applications, and challenges. *Frontiers in Microbiology*, 14, 1155622.

[4] Anegbe, B., Ifijen, I. H., Maliki, M., Uwidia, I. E., & Aigbodion, A. I. (2024). Graphene oxide synthesis and applications in emerging contaminant removal: a comprehensive review. *Environmental Sciences Europe*, 36(1), 15.

[5] Banea, M. D., & Da Silva, L. F. M. (2012). Adhesive joints in composite materials: a review. *Journal of Materaials Science*, 47(2), 11–29.

[6] Bhattacharya, G., Sas, S., Wadhwa, S., Mathur, A., McLaughlin, J., & Roy, S. S. (2017). Aloe vera assisted facile green synthesis of reduced graphene oxide for electrochemical and dye removal applications. *RSC Advances*, 7(43), 26680–26688.

[7] Caicedo, F. M. C., López, E. V., Agarwal, A., Drozd, V., Durygin, A., Hernandez, A. F., et al. (2020). Synthesis of graphene oxide from graphite by ball milling. *Diamond and Related Materials*, 109, 108064.

[8] Chouhan, A., Mungse, H., & Khatri, O. (2020). Surface chemistry of graphene and graphene oxide: a versatile route for their dispersion and tribological applications. *Advances in Colloid and Interface Science*, 283, 102215.

[9] Chugh, D., Viswamalya, V. S., & Das, B. (2021). Green synthesis of silver nanoparticles with algae and the importance of capping agents in the process. *Journal of Genetic Engineering and Biotechnology*, 19(1), 126.

[10] Cobos, M., De La Pinta, I., Quindos, G., Fernandez, M. J., & Fernandez, M. D. (2020). Graphene oxide–silver nanoparticle nanohybrids: synthesis, characterization, and antimicrobial properties. *Nanomaterials (Basel)*, 10(2), 376.

[11] Cui, G., Wu, J., Lin, J., Liu, W., Chen, P., Yu, M., et al. (2021). Graphene-based nanomaterials for breast cancer treatment: promising therapeutic strategies. *Journal of Nanobiotechnology*, 19, 1–30.

[12] Esteghamat, A., & Akhavan, O. (2023). Graphene as the ultra-transparent conductive layer in developing the nanotechnology-based flexible smart touchscreens. *Microelectronic Engineering*, 267, 111899.

[13] Fardinpour, P., Taleghani, H. G., & Zakerimehr, M. R. (2024). Facile green synthesis of graphene oxide/copper oxide nanocomposites using ginger essential oil and its enhanced antibacterial properties. *Materials Science and Engineering: B*, 300, 117100.

[14] Fu, X., Lin, J., Liang, Z., Yao, R., Wu, W., Fang, Z., et al. (2023). Graphene oxide as a promising nanofiller for polymer composite. *Surfaces and Interfaces*, 37, 102747.

[15] Hashemi, E., Giesy, J., Liang, Z., Akhavan, O., Tayefeh, A., Joupari, M., et al. (2024). Impacts of graphene oxide contamination on a food web: threats to somatic and reproductive health of organisms. *Ecotoxicology and Environmental Safety*, 285, 117032.

[16] Hulla, J., Sahu, S., & Hayes, A. (2015). Nanotechnology: history and future. *Human and Experimental Toxicology*, 34(12), 1318–1321.

[17] Itoo, A. M., Vemula, S. L., Gupta, M. T., Giram, M. V., Kumar, S. A., Ghosh, B., et al. (2022). Multifunctional graphene oxide nanoparticles for drug delivery in cancer. *Journal of Controlled Release*, 350, 26–59.

[18] Jirickova, A., Jankovsky, O., Sofer, Z., & Sedmidubsky, D. (2022). Synthesis and applications of graphene oxide. *Materials (Basel)*, 15(3), 920.

[19] Junaidi, N. F. D., Khalil, N. A., Jahari, A. F., Shaari, N. Z. K., & Shahruddin, M. Z. (2018). Effect of graphene oxide (GO) on the surface morphology & hydrophilicity of polyethersulfone (PES). *Material Science and Engineering*, 358, 012047. doi:10.1088/1757-899X/358/1/012047.

[20] Kwon, S., Lee, K. E., Lee, H., Koh, S. J., Ko, J. H., & Kim, Y. H. (2018). The effect of thickness and chemical reduction of graphene oxide on nanoscale friction. *The Journal of Physical Chemistry B*, 122(2), 543–547.

[21] Li, F., Jiang, X., Zhao, J., & Zhang, S. (2015). Graphene oxide: a promising nanomaterial for energy and environmental applications. *Nano Energy*, 16, 488–515.

[22] Mahata, S., Sahu, A., Shukla, P., Rai, A., Singh, M., & Rai, V. K. (2018). The novel and efficient reduction of graphene oxide using Ocimum sanctum L. leaf extract as an alternative renewable bio-resource. *New Journal of Chemistry*, 42(24), 19945–19952.

[23] Mahmoudi, T., Wang, Y., & Hahn, Y. B. (2018). Graphene and its derivatives for solar cells application. *Nano Energy*, 47, 51–65.

[24] Mousavi, S. M., Hashemi, S. A., Kalashgrani, M. Y., Gholami, A., Binazadeh, M., Chiang, W. H., et al. (2023). Recent advances in energy storage with graphene oxide for supercapacitor technology. *Sustainable Energy and Fuels*, 7(21), 5176–5197.

[25] Murthy, H. C. A., Kelele, K. G., Ravikumar, C. R., Nagaswarupa, H. P., Tadesse, A., & Desalegn, T. (2021). Graphene-supported nanomaterials as electrochemical sensors: a mini review. *Results in Chemistry*, 3, 100131.

[26] Nithyalakshmi, M., Siddharthan, N., & Balagurunathan, R. (2025). Fabrication of palladium nanoparticles and rGO-Pd nanocomposite by streptomyces maritimus: antimicrobial, antioxidant, and scalable applications. *Waste Biomass Valor.* 16, 17.

[27] Peña-Bahamonde, J., Nguyen, H. N., Fanourakis, S. K., & Rodrigues, D. F. (2018). Recent advances in graphene-based biosensor technology with applications in life sciences. *Journal of Nanobiotechnology*, 16(1), 75. DOI: 10.1186/s12951-018-0400-z.

[28] Perumalsamy, H., Balusamy, S. R., Sukweenadhi, J., Nag, S., & MubarakAli, D. (2024). A comprehensive review on Moringa oleifera nanoparticles: importance of polyphenols in nanoparticle synthesis, nanoparticle efficacy and their applications. *Journal of Nanobiotechnology*, 22(1), 71. doi: 10.1186/s12951-024-02332-8. PMID: 38373982.

[29] Rossa, V., Ferreira, L., Vasconcelos, S., Shimabukuro, E., & Madriaga, V. (2022). Nanocomposites based on the graphene family for food packaging: historical perspective, preparation methods, and properties. *RSC Advances*, 9(3), 374.

[30] Sang, M., Shin, H., Kim, K., & Yu, K. J. (2019). Electronic and thermal properties of graphene and recent advances in graphene based electronics applications. *Nanomaterials (Basel)*, 9(3), 374.

[31] Saurez-Diez, M., Porras, S., Laguna-Teno, F., Schaap, P. J., & Ramos, J. A. (2020). Toxicological response of the model fungus Saccharomyces cerevisiae to different concentrations of commercial graphene nanoplatelets. *Scientific Reports*, 10, 3232. https://doi.org/10.1038/s41598-020-60101-7.

[32] Shen, C., & Oyadiji, O. (2020). The processing and analysis of graphene and the strength enhancement effect of graphene-based filler materials: a review. *Materials Today Physics*, 15, 100257. https://doi.org/10.1016/j.mtphys.2020.100257.

[33] Strong, A. B. (2008). Fundamentals of Composites Manufacturing: Materials, Methods, and Applications, (2nd edn.), Society of Manufacturing Engineers.

[34] Wang, K., Liu, Y., Jin, X., & Chen, Z. (2019). Characterization of iron nanoparticles/reduced graphene oxide composites synthesized by one step eucalyptus leaf extract. *Environmental Pollution*, 250, 8–13.

[35] Wang, X., Bai, H., Yao, Z., Liu, A., & Shi, G. (2013). Functionalization of graphene oxide and its applications in nanocomposite. *Journal of Materials Science*, 48(11), 3966–3979.

[36] Zhang, S., Wang, H., Liu, J., & Bao, C. (2020). Measuring the specific surface area of monolayer graphene oxide in water. *Materials Letters*, 261(15), 127098. https://doi.org/10.1016/j.matlet.2019.127098.

[37] Zhao, H., Zhang, C., Wang, Y., Chen, W., & Alvarez, P. J. J. (2018). Self-damaging aerobic reduction of graphene oxide by escherichia coli: role of GO-mediated extracellular superoxide formation. *Environmental Science & Technology*, 52(21), 12783–12791.

# 20 Eco friendly finish: mosquito repellent fabric

*Tushar A. Shinde[1,a], Aishwarya S. Patil[2], Sachin M. Munde[3], Sandip P. Pati[4], Pranjali W. Chandurkar[1], Rajendra D. Parsi[1] and Vijay S. Shivankar[1]*

[1]Department of Centre for Textile Functions, SVKMS, NMIMS, MPSTME, Shirpur Campus, Maharashtra, India

[2]Department of Pharmacognosy, R. C. Patel Institute of Pharmaceutical Education & Research, Shirpur, Maharashtra, India

[3]Department of Chemistry, School of Science, Sandip University, Nashik, Maharashtra, India

[4]Department of Microbiology and Biotechnology, R. C. Patel Arts Commerce and Science College, Shirpur, Maharashtra, India

## Abstract

One of the important procedures in textiles that improves the fabric's functionality and performance is finishing. It has long been believed that good health is essential for people to live stress-free lives and to produce the finest results possible from any task. By offering the much-needed ability to keep mosquitoes away from the body. Mosquito-repellent fabrics are an innovative idea to advance in the textile apparel industry. In tropical regions in particular, these finished textiles product protect people from mosquito bites and may assurance against the various diseases like dengue, fever and malaria. This project was undertaking that uses of citronella oil and herbal extracts from tulsi and neem to create an environmentally friendly finished fabric that repels mosquitoes. A mosquito repellency activity test is used to assess the extracted chemicals' effectiveness after they are applied onto the fabric utilizing on pad-dry-cure and exhaust processes. It may provide the mosquito-repellent ability of the fabric by giving the treatment of chemicals like sequestering agent, wetting agent, and cross-linking agents were utilized. Followed by the substrate washing, drying and curing after that textile mosquito-repellent behaviour was examined.

**Keywords:** Citronella oil, cotton fabric, cross-linking agent, neem leaf, tulsi leaf, wetting agent, etc

## Introduction

A material or finishing technique used on skin, clothing, or other surfaces that keeps mosquitoes away is called a mosquito repellent [8]. Mosquitoee of the approximately 3000 mosquito species that cause fatal diseases are potentially dangerous and they are difficult to control. In various market products to control mosquitoes, but they can have negative effects on human health. Only female mosquitoes have the parts of the mouth needed for sucking blood [3]. They are to blame for illnesses including chikungunya, dengue, yellow fever, and malaria, among others [6]. The market is seeing an increase in demand for textiles with comfort, water repellent, crease resistance and mosquito repellent with another useful qualities. To create more aesthetically pleasing and highly functional value-added textiles, so textile scientists are looking into the potential uses of plant-based bioactive

[a]tushar.shinde@nmims.edu

DOI: 10.1201/9781003716648-20

compounds [10]. Plants with strong herbal qualities included tulsi and neem. It has utilized as raw constituents for necessary applications and is inexpensive and unprocessed. Global warming has caused mosquitoes to move from tropical to northern latitudes, which has resulted in a proliferation of mosquito-borne viral infection sources. Human health is impacted by numerous insects. Anyone can use this to stay far away from mosquitoes. The insect bites cause discomfort and sickness. Simple irritation, swelling, and pain are less severe side effects that can occasionally result from insect bites by mosquitoes [13]. Only a limited quantity of vaccination is available to treat these kinds of illnesses. Insects are repelled using various processes like spray, smoke, and chemical coils. The extensive usage of chemicals, this poses a risk to human health. Consequently, the creation of a workable natural repellent is required [5].

By infecting almost two million individuals with multiple fatal diseases, mosquito bites create a serious threat to public health. With an estimated 50–100 million cases each year, dengue was the major vector-borne illness that is spreading the fastest [7]. This mosquito has multiplied very fast and is becoming a global problem as it develops resistance to the various mosquito repellent products in the market. Numerous plants species generate a range of subordinate metabolites that are essential for protecting plants against insects and mosquitoes. Plants could serve as a substitute supply of insect repellents. Depending on the kind of activity they have, plant products can be employed as repellents to prevent mosquito bites or as insecticides to kill mosquito larvae or adults [2].

## Mosquito repellant plants

1. Citronella oil: Citronella oil is made up from plant leaves by the process of steam distillation process. Instead of destroying bugs, citronella oil repels them. It functions by covering off smells that insects find appealing. As a result, insects have trouble finding their food source. A common insect repellent is citronella oil. However, studies have shown that it may also aid in wound healing and have antifungal qualities [9].
2. Neem leaf: Traditionally, neem leaves and seeds have been utilized as a natural insect repellent. It has been discovered that the active components in neem possess repellent and insecticidal qualities [1]. Among the many compounds found in neem trees is sa-

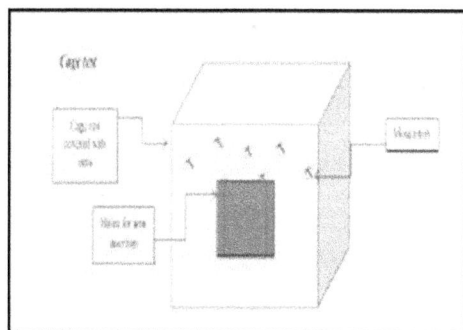

*Figure 20.1* Mosquito repellent cage [2]
Source: Author

line, which has a strong insect-repelling effect, particularly against mosquitoes. Natural dye or colour are not substantive, and it can be applied to the textile with the help of different mordants [11]. Other mixtures were obtained from neem leaves and seeds and applied naturally as a repellent for insects and insect repellents they worked in certain insect species [4]. This study"s goal is to determine how effective neem leaves were keeping mosquitoes away.

3. Tulsi leaf: The tulsi herb, often known as holy basil, can keep mosquitoes away. It has a unique clove-like scent which comes for their extreme eugenol contain. During the monsoon season, this plant is exceptionally good at eliminating mosquitoes and other insects, flies and bugs [12]

## Experimental Work

*Materials*

1. Material: As with the above experiments 100% cotton material is used with the forms of woven and knitted fabrics for this project. Apart from that the cotton sample we have utilised various natural ingredients like citronella oil, neem leaf, tulsi leaf. The processes taken for the experiment are pad-dry-cure and exhaustion method were used.
2. Fabric specification and chemicals:
3. Extraction process:
   i) Extraction process of neem leaf: The first step is to gather the fresh neem leaves from the plant. After placing the neem leaves on a plate, rinse them with fresh water. Give them around 20 minutes in boiling water. Put the leaves in a pan, grind them

*Table 20.1* Fabric specification and chemicals [14].

| Sr. No. | Types | Specification | Sr. No. | Chemical used |
|---------|-------|---------------|---------|---------------|
| 1. | Substrate | 100% Cotton (woven and knitted) | 1. | Sequestering agent |
| 2. | EPI/PPI | 85 / 55 | 2. | Wetting agent |
| 3. | Gram per square meter | 220 | 3. | BTCA (CRA) |

Source: Author

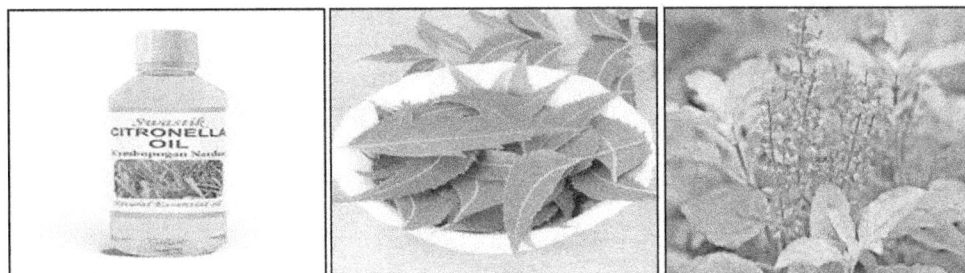

*Figure 20.2* a) Citronella oil b) Neem leaf c) Tulsi leaf [9]
Source: Author

in a mixer, and then put the mixture on low heat for around ten minutes. Pour the neem leaf mixture into the plate after chilling the mixture.

ii) Extraction process of tulsi leaf: Firstly, collect the fresh tulsi leaves from the plant and wash using fresh water. Take the leaves into a pan and grain them in mixer then place the mixture on gentle with hot water. Cold the mixture and pour the tulsi leaf mixture in the plate.

4. Application method:

Prepare the knitted and woven samples with weight of 5 grams of fabric sample with MLR ration 1:30. Take the 150 ml water and add the necessary chemicals like sequestering agent and cross-linking agents as per the standard calculations. Three separate pots of knitted and woven samples are heated to 80°C in a hot pan and treated with 4%, 6%, and 8% citronella oil. Twenty minutes later of heating, Samples are taken out of the hot plate. Three bars of pressure were applied to the samples to ensure that finishing chemicals penetrated the fabric's surface uniformly. Samples become dried using hot air woven at the temperature 90°C for 5 minutes and undergoes the curing process were done for 5 minutes at 120°C.

*Figure 20.3* Neem leaf extraction a) Fresh neem leaf (b) Wash with water (c) Crushing of neem leaf (d) Paste formation [4]
Source: Author

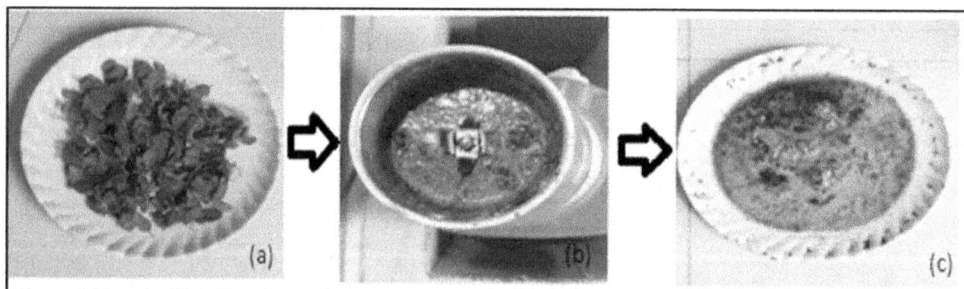

*Figure 20.4* Tulsi leaf extraction (a) Tulsi leaf (b) Grinding of leaf (c) Tulsi pastes
Source: Author

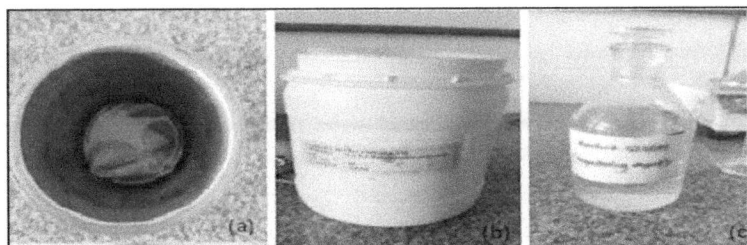

*Figure 20.5* Citronella oil treatment (a) Citronella oil pot (lemongrass) (b)
Source: Author

*Figure 20.6* Cage test for mosquitoes
Source: Author

5.  Cage test for evaluating mosquito repellency: The treated cloth with mosquito repellent can be evaluated in several ways. The most popular method is cage test.

    The setup of the experimentation at the bottom side of the cage [Figure 20.1] placed the treated sample. Each sample was left in the cage for 30 minutes so that the mosquitoes could contact it. After a certain time interval counts the mosquitoes that touched down on the fabric under the cage were noted. Since they settled where they sit initially, it did not travel outside the place. Some of the mosquitoes were repelled and some placed over the treated fabric was observed in that cage. After 30 minutes count and noted the quantise of mosquitoes in the cage where they died over the treated sample.

## Observation Table

*Mosquito repellency test before washing*

*Table 20.2* Repellency test before washing [14].

| Sr. No | Finishing agent | No. of mosquitoes exposed in cage | No. of mosquito escaped in cage | Mosquitoes landed on treated fabric | Mosquitoes repel from sample | Repellency (%) |
|---|---|---|---|---|---|---|
| 1 | Citronella oil | 15 | 14 | 2 | 12 | 93.33 |
| 2 | Neem leaf | 15 | 12 | 5 | 7 | 80 |
| 3 | Tulsi leaf | 15 | 10 | 8 | 2 | 66.67 |

Source: Author

### Repellency test: before washing

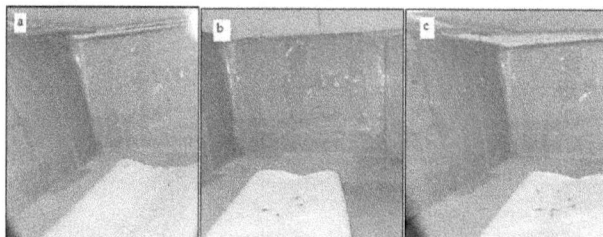

*Figure 20.7* Repellency test before washing (a) Citronella oil treated sample (b) Neem leaf treated sample (c) tulsi leaf treated sample
Source: Author

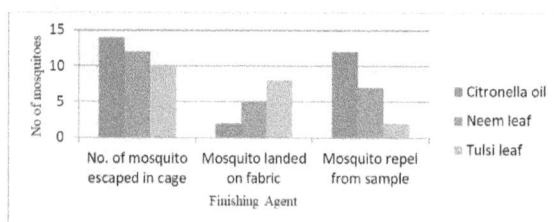

*Figure 20.8* Repellency test before washing
Source: Author

A test for mosquito repellency prior to washing yields gives better results. In comparison in Tulsi and neem leaves, citronella oil exhibits superior mosquito repellency in this test. However, the sample treated with neem leaves has a stronger mosquito-repelling effect than Tulsi, but not as well as the sample treated with citronella oil. Samples are treated with varying concentrations of citronella oil, neem leaf, and Tulsi leaf finishing agent; samples treated with 8% concentrations of citronella oil exhibit the best mosquito repellency effect. Compared to woven fabric, knitted cloth treated with citronella oil exhibits the best repellent results. These agents produce better results before washing, but the degree to which they deter mosquitoes after washing the samples reveals their impact.

### Repellency test: after washing

*Table 20.3* Repellency test: after washing [14].

| Sr. No | Finishing agent | No. of mosquitoes exposed in cage | No. of mosquito escaped in cage | Mosquitoes landed on treated fabric | Mosquitos repel from sample | Repellency |
|---|---|---|---|---|---|---|
| 1 | Citronella oil | 15 | 12 | 3 | 7 | 80% |
| 2 | Neem leaf | 15 | 10 | 6 | 4 | 66.67% |
| 3 | Tulsi leaf | 15 | 9 | 8 | 1 | 60% |

Source: Author

*Repellency test: after washing*

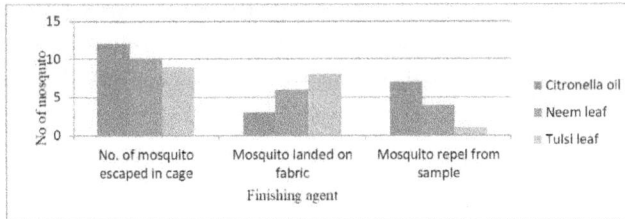

*Figure 20.9* Repellency test: after washing
Source: Author

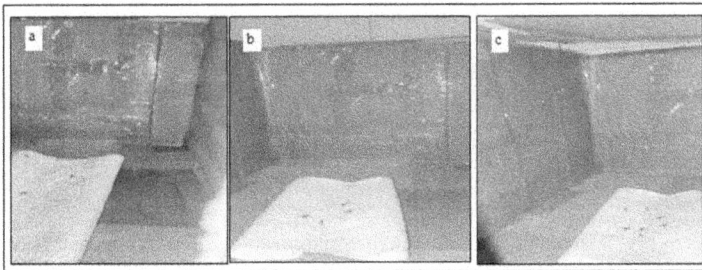

*Figure 20.10* Repellency test after washing (a) Citronella oil treated sample (b) Neem leaf treated sample (c) Tulsi leaf treated sample
Source: Author

The impact of insect (mosquito) repellent was significantly diminished after washing treatment. However, a single sample wash does not eliminate the effect. The tulsi leaf-treated sample's finish effect is eliminated after up to three washings. After three washings, the sample treated with neem leaves showed very little impact in keeping mosquitoes away. However, citronella oil repels mosquitoes and yields the best results for up to three washes. But the insect repellent decreases as increase the number of washings. Citronella oil works better to repel mosquitoes up to seven washes. In contrast to fabric samples treated with tulsi leaves and neem, citronella oil provides superior mosquito repellency for several washings.

## Conclusion

One of the main issues is the transmission of illnesses conveyed by mosquitoes. Textiles material serves as a physical block between human skin and blood-sucking mosquitoes to prevent the spread of illnesses to other people. The study was to determine the best applications of natural agents over the textile material that will resist or repel from fabric. The main focused was to compare the effectiveness of various finishing agents, such as citronella oil, neem leaf, and Tulsi leaf in terms of mosquito resistant agents. Based on the study, the Citronella oil repels mosquitoes an additional effectiveness than samples treated with Tulsi leaves and neem. It has been demonstrated via the use of these textiles that an effective textile fabric to treat with the mosquito repellent chemical exhibits the desirable qualities.

According to a test of mosquito repellency behaviour. It is also economical and good for the environment. Therefore, using natural insect repellents like citronella oil will work better. The higher the repellency percentages, the more mosquito repellents that need to be put to the cloth. In order to provide further research, it was advised that appropriate materials, a suitable repellent substance, and appropriate mosquito repellency test procedures be used.

# References

[1]   Alam, M. T., Karim, M. M., & Khan, S. N. (2009). Antibacterial activity of different organic extracts of achyranthes aspera and cassia alata. *Journal of Scientific Research*, 1(2), 393–398.

[2]   Anuar, A. A., & Yusof, N. (2016). Methods of imparting mosquito repellent agents and the assessing mosquito repellency on textile. *Fashion and Textiles*, 3, 1–14.

[3]   Gulrajani, M. L., Agarwal, A., & Lohia, C. (2007). Preparation of mosquito repellent fabrics. *Asian Dyer*, 5, 53–55.

[4]   Kamilu, B. S., Umar, A., Zubairu, A. Y., Egwuonwu, K. C., Umar, D. M. A., & Sani, M. (2024). Investigating the efficacy of neem leaves as mosquito repellent. *Global Academic Journal of Pharmacy and Drug Research*, 6, 2–18.

[5]   Katz, T. M., Miller, J. H., & Hebert, A. A. (2008). Insect repellents: historical perspectives and new developments. *Journal of the American Academy of Dermatology*, 58(5), 865–871.

[6]   Mia, R., Selim, M. D., Shamim, A. M., Chowdhury, M., Sultana, S., Armin, M., et al. (2019). Review on various types of pollution problem in textile dyeing & printing industries of Bangladesh and recommandation for mitigation. *Journal of Textile Engineering and Fashion Technology*, 5(4), 220–226.

[7]   Rehman, J. U., Ali, A., & Khan, I. A. (2014). Plant based products: use and development as repellents against mosquitoes: a review. *Fitoterapia*, 95, 65–74.

[8]   Sajib, M., Banna, B., & Mia, R. (2020). Mosquito repellent finishes on textile fabrics (woven & knit) by using different medicinal natural plants. *Journal of Textile Engineering and Fashion Technology*, 6, 164–167.

[9]   Sakulku, U., Nuchuchua, O., Uawongyart, N., Puttipipatkhachorn, S., Soottitantawat, A., & Ruktanonchai, U. (2009). Characterization and mosquito repellent activity of citronella oil nanoemulsion. *International Journal of Pharmaceutics*, 372(1-2), 105–111.

[10]  Shahid, M., & Mohammad, F. (2013). Perspectives for natural product based agents derived from industrial plants in textile applications–a review. *Journal of Cleaner Production*, 57, 2–18.

[11]  Shinde, T., Chaudhari, D., Patil, T., & Raichurkar, P. (2019). Development of natural dyes extracted from Catechu (kattha). *Chemical Processing*, 65(2), 40–44.

[12]  Singh, S., Mahour, K., & Prakash, S. (2009). Evaluation of mosquito repellent efficacy of Ocimum sanctum plant extract. *Journal of Herbal Medicine and Toxicology*, 3(1), 87–90.

[13]  Yi, H., Devkota, B. R., Yu, J., Oh, K., Kim, J., & Kim, H. (2014). Effects of global warming on mosquitoes & mosquito-borne diseases and the new strategies for mosquito control. *Entomological Research*, 44(6), 215–235.

[14]  Thite, Amol G., and M. Y. Gudiyawar. (2015). Development of microencapsulated eco-friendly mosquito repellent cotton finished fabric by natural repellent oils. *International Journal of Science Technology and Management.* 4.11: 166–174.

# 21 Random tests of milk sold by vendors in local market - pilot study

*Mahesh Vishwas Chaudhari[a], Krishna Pawar[b], Karan Patil[c], Nakul Chaudhari[d], Rajap Shiva Kumar[e], Vinodkumar[f] and Mayaram Rathod*

School of Agricultural Sciences and Technology, SVKM's Narsee Monjee Institute of Management Studies (NMIMS) Deemed-to-University, Shirpur, India

## Abstract

Milk is common food. It is also most vulnerable to adulteration which may lead to health problems to consumers. Majority of people in India prefer fresh loose milk on daily basis from local vendors. Though cooperative dairies check the milk for adulteration during procurement or before processing and packaging of milk, local sellers of loose milk may not follow this practice. Therefore, pilot study was carried out to detect commonly used adulterants in loose milk sold by vendors in local area. A total of one-hundred-twenty-five tests were performed to detect pond water, urea, hydrogen peroxide, sugar and starch/ cereal flour in milk. Presence of pond water and sugar was detected in milk. Further statistical analysis observed that the occurrence of sugar in the samples was not due to random chance, and therefore, it may be concluded that some factor is likely influencing presence of sugar in milk sold by local vendors. It is recommended that future large scale periodic testing will ensure healthy milk to all consumers.

**Keywords:** Adulteration, health, milk

## Introduction

"Milk has been known as nature's most complete food" Park, [10] and it is an important part of people's food regime. Fresh milk is the most vulnerable to adulteration and can cause serious health issues especially in infants [3, 14]. Minister of Ministry of Fisheries, Animal Husbandry and Dairying, Government of India on 21 March 2023 stated in Lok Sabha that "DAHD does not regulate the procurement and sale prices of milk in the country. Prices are decided by the cooperative and private dairies based on their cost of production and, by market forces, in general" (Department of Animal Husbandry and Dairying, GOI). The procurement is decided as percentage of milk fat and solid-not-fat (SNF) per litre of milk. Though cooperative dairies check the milk for adulteration during procurement or before processing and packaging of milk, local sellers of loose milk may not follow this practice. The households of rural and urban India prefer loose milk from local milk suppliers on daily basis.

The most common chemical adulterants like commercial urea, starch, flour, sugar, hydrogen peroxide, melamine, common salt, pond water, vegetable oil, etc are mixed in the milk

[a]mahesh.chaudhari@nmims.edu, [b]krishnapawar3000@gmail.com, [c]karandp2003@gmail.com, [d]nakulchaudhari9404@gmail.com, [e]rajapshivakumar@gmail.com, [f]vinod.rathod@nmims.edu

DOI: 10.1201/9781003716648-21

in unfair way to increase margin in income. For example, milk fat is used to prepare ghee and other value added milk products which fetch higher profit compared to milk therefore, milk fat is removed from milk and replaced by vegetable oil further detergents are added to emulsify and dissolve the oil in water giving a frothy solution, which is the desired characteristics of milk [13]. Starch, cane sugar, common salt, melamine and commercial urea are added to increase SNF in milk [2, 8, 11]. Hydrogen peroxide, Formalin, Salicylic acid, Benzoic acid are added due to preservative property of increasing the shelf life of the milk [12]. As per Domingo et al. [4] melamine, if ingested above safety level, can induce renal failure and death in infants. Hydrogen peroxide, detergent and starch in milk lead to gastro-intestinal complications as well as accumulation of starch in body may prove fatal for diabetic patients [13]. Additional urea in milk affects kidney [7].

Therefore, to evaluate hypothesis that loose milk is vulnerable to adulteration due to deficiencies in monitoring, unsanitary conditions and for monetary benefits, the present pilot study was planned to collect the milk sold by local sellers in Shirpur and test it in order to approximate the prevalence of milk adulteration in Shirpur.

## Literature Review

Yadav et al. [14] reviewed various milk adulterants as well as the purposes for mixing of milk with those adulterants, its health consequences, and different available adulterants detection techniques. Chugh and Kaur [3] reviewed the adulterants commonly added in milk as well as the various methods of qualitative detection adulterants in milk.

Latest studies to screen the milk samples for presence of adulterants in regions adjoining to Shirpur are shown in Table 21.1. Those studies indicated mixing of adulterants in milk available in local market.

Jawale et al. [6], Malpani et al. [9] and Admane et al. [1] tested the milk samples from local vendors from Parbhani, Akola and Bhandara districts in Maharashtra, respectively.

*Table 21.1* Recent studies for detection of adulterants in milk in nearby region.

| Sr. No. | Area | No. of Samples | Major Adulterants | Milk samples from | References |
|---------|------|----------------|-------------------|-------------------|------------|
| 1 | Parbhani sub-division | 468 | Detergents, Skim milk powder, Sucrose, Nitrate, Urea | Milk Vendor Collection centre | [6] |
| 2 | Nagpur tehsil | 100 | Sucrose, Sodium bicarbonate, Urea | Individual producer | [5] |
| 3 | Akola region | 16 | Water, Urea | • Milk vendors | [9] |
| 4 | Sakoli Town in Bhandara Distric | 80 | Water | Milk vendor (75%) Private dairy (50%) Hotel and restaurants (45%) | [1] |

Source: Author

All those studies found water and/or urea as common adulterant in tested milk samples. However, detergents, skim milk powder, sucrose and nitrate were also reported mixed in milk for economic benefits in unfair way.

## Methodology

The present pilot research was carried out over the period of six months between March, 2024 to November, 2024. Buffalo milk samples were collected randomly from local market in Shirpur town of Dhule district in Maharashtra state of India. Out of total twenty-five milk samples, 24 were from local milk sellers and 1 control sample was directly collected from buffalo farm. After collection all milk samples were immediately carried to School of Agricultural Sciences & Technology, Narsee Monjee Institute of Management Studies (NMIMS)– Deemed to be University, Shirpur campus, Dhule, Maharashtra, India for testing. Each milk sample was tested to detect presence of pond water, urea, hydrogen peroxide, sugar and starch/ cereal flour.

A Kit for Detection of Adulterants in milk (Large kit – LK1000) developed by the National Dairy Development Board's (NDDB), Anand, Gujarat was used in the present study to screen milk samples for adulteration. Each milk sample was tested as per the instructions laid by kit developers. For detection of urea as well as hydrogen peroxide in milk, each milk sample was mixed with respective reaction reagent provided by manufacturer. Further, change in colour of milk was observed, if any, for positive test results. For detection of mixing of pond water, test tube was rinsed with milk sample subsequently reaction reagent was added along the sides of test tube. The procedure was repeated for each milk sample under test. Detection of blue colour was observed for confirmation of presence of pond water in given milk sample, if any. Milk sample and Sugar Reagent was mixed in test tube and then placed in boiling water for 3-5 minutes followed by

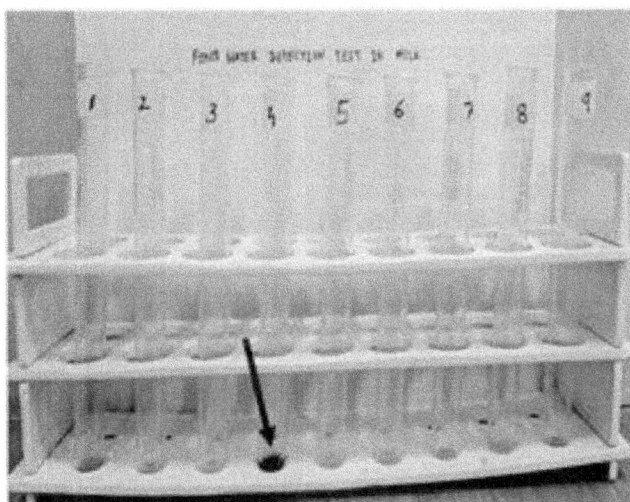

*Figure 21.1* Test to find pond water in milk. The arrow shows positive test result
Source: Author

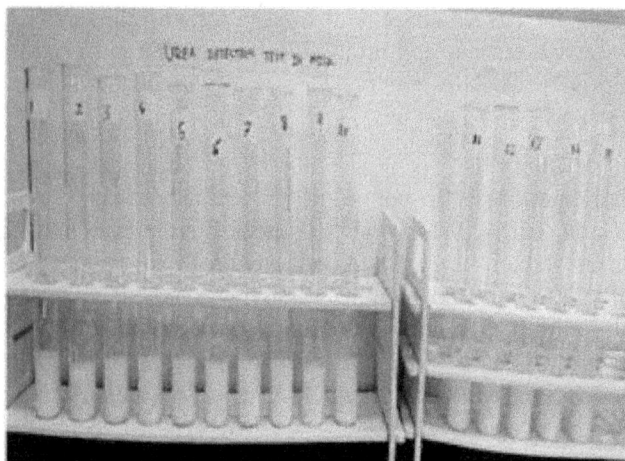

*Figure 21.2* Test to find urea in milk
Source: Author

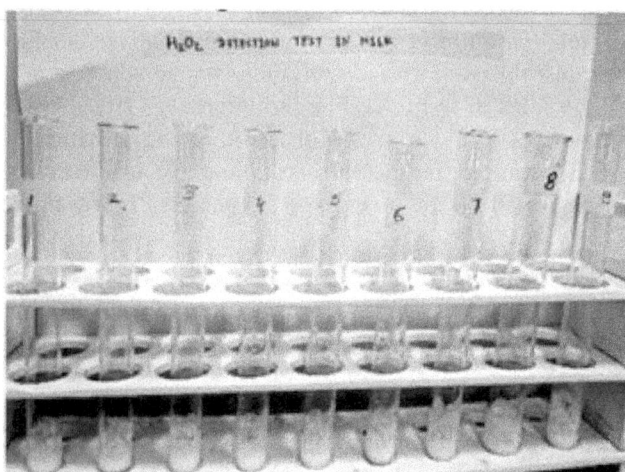

*Figure 21.3* Test to find hydrogen peroxide in milk
Source: Author

observation for change in colour of test to red for presence of sugar in milk sample. For starch/ cereal flour detection each milk sample was boiled for 5 minutes and cooled it. In next step few drops of Starch Reagent were added to the boiled milk in test tube to observe colour change to blue indicating presence of starch/ cereal flour, if any, in respective milk sample.

The qualitative test results were recorded and further analysed by binomial test for statistical significance.

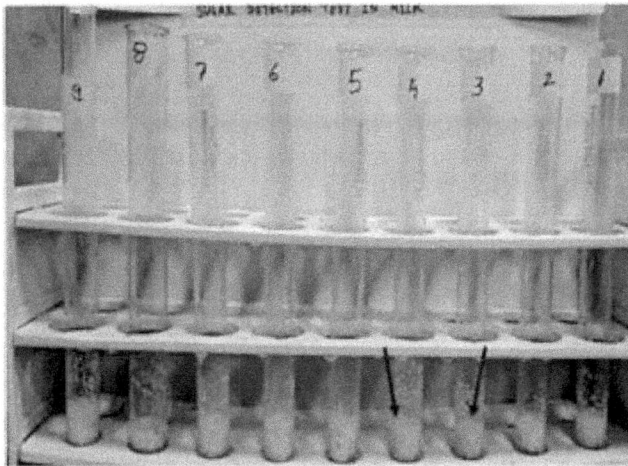

*Figure 21.4* Test to find sugar in milk. Arrow shows positive test results
Source: Author

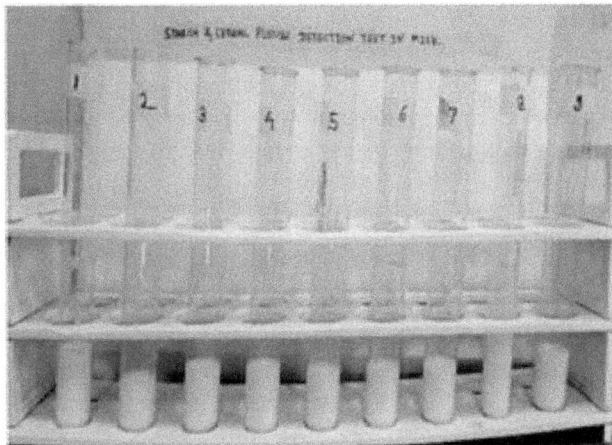

*Figure 21.5* Test to find starch/ cereal flour in milk
Source: Author

## Results

A total of 125 tests were performed to detect presence of pond water, urea, hydrogen peroxide, sugar and starch/ cereal flour milk samples which were collected randomly from local market. Test results are sown in Figures 21.1–21.5. The control milk sample was negative for all test results. As seen in Figure 21.1, occurrence of blue colour after test indicated presence of pond water milk. A total of two milk samples from local market indicated mixing of milk with pond water. In this study, tests to find urea, hydrogen peroxide and starch/ cereal flour in tested milk samples were found negative which indicated that those milk samples

*Table 21.2* Details of tests performed to find adulterants in milk.

| Milk Tested For | Present | Absent |
|---|---|---|
| Pond Water | 2 | 23 |
| Urea | 0 | 25 |
| Hydrogen Peroxide | 0 | 25 |
| Sugar | 4* | 21 |
| Starch/ Cereal flour | 0 | 25 |
| Total number of tests | 125 | |

*p<0.05
Source: Author

were devoid of adulteration with urea, hydrogen peroxide and starch/ cereal flour on the day of sample collection (Figures 21.2, 21.3 and 21.5). However, tests for detection of sugar in milk shown positive test results in four milk samples (Figure 21.4). Interestingly, one milk sample (sample number 4) was positive for presence of both pond water and sugar. The details of individual test results observed are shown in Table 21.2.

As shown in Table 21.2 a total of 125 tests for finding of adulterants in milk were performed. The presence of pond water and sugar was noticed in 2 and 4 number of milk samples, respectively. Further, binomial test was found statistically significant for presence of sugar in milk. It suggested that the chance of sugar finding in milk sold by vendors is not random. Similar results of adulteration of milk sold by local vendors were also reported by Jawale et al. [6], Jadhao et al. [5], Malpani et al. [9] and Admane et al. [1].

## Conclusion

Mixing of milk with adulterants by local vendors is now regularly observed by survey studies for detection of adulterants in milk. This pose serious health concern at present and in future also. Similarly, this pilot study showed sporadic incidence of milk adulteration in Shirpur and therefore future large scale periodic testing will ensure healthy milk to all consumers.

## Acknowledgements

All necessary facilities and funds were provided by SVKM's Narsee Monjee Institute of Management Studies (NMIMS) Deemed-to-University, Shirpur campus, India.

## References

[1]   Admane, M., Zinjarde, R. M., & Khupse, S. M. (2016). Quality of milk sold in sakoli town in bhandara district. *Advances in Life Sciences*, 5(21), 9824–9827.

[2]   Azad, T., & Ahmed, S. (2016). Common milk adulteration and their detection techniques. *Food Contamination*, 3, 22. https://doi.org/10.1186/s40550-016-0045-3.

[3] Chugh, R., & Kaur, G. (2022). A study on milk adulteration and methods of detection of various chemical adulterants qualitatively. In IOP Conference Series: Materials Science and Engineering (Vol. 1225, p. 012046). https://doi.org/10.1088/1757-899X/1225/1/012046.

[4] Domingo, E., Tirelli, A. A., Nunes, C. A., Guerreiro, M. C., & Pinto, S. M. (2014). Melamine detection in milk using vibrational spectroscopy and chemometrics analysis: a review. *Food Research International*, 60, 131–139. https://doi.org/10.1016/j.foodres.2013.11.006.

[5] Jadhao, R. J., Zinjarde, R. M., Mohale, D. D., & Gadekar, S. D. (2019). Studies on detection of adulteration of milk received from different sources in Nagpur tahsil. *Journal of Pharmacognosy and Phytochemistry*, 8(4), 2660–2662.

[6] Jawale, M., Chappalwar, A., & Devangare, A. (2022). Quality assessment of milk in supply chain of parbhani sub-division. *Indian Journal of Dairy Science*, 75(3), 248–254. https://doi.org/10.33785/IJDS.2022.v75i03.007.

[7] Kandpal, S. D., Srivastava, A. K., & Negi, K. S. (2012). Estimation of quality of raw milk (open & branded) by milk adulteration testing kit. *Indian Journal of Community Health*, 24(3), 188–192.

[8] Liu, Y., Todd, E. E., Zhang, Q., Shi, J. R., & Liu, X. J. (2012). Recent developments in the detection of melamine. *Journal of Zhejiang University Science B*, 13(7), 525–532. https://doi.org/10.1631/jzus.b1100389.

[9] Malpani, M. O., Rajput, P. R., Sohel, M., Pande, P. S., & Mane, V. D. (2018). Detection of food adulteration in milk and milk products collected randomly in akola region. *World Journal of Pharmaceutical Research*, 7(5), 1179–1185.

[10] Park, Y. W. (2009). Overview of bioactive components in milk and dairy products. In Park, Y. W. (Ed.), **Bioactive Components in Milk and Dairy Products**, (pp. 3–14). England: Wiley-Blackwell Publishers. https://doi.org/10.1002/9780813821504.ch1.

[11] Sharma, R., Rajput, Y. S., & Barui, A. K. N. L. N. (2012). Detection of Adulterants in Milk: A Laboratory Manual. Karnal, Haryana, India: National Dairy Research Institute.

[12] Singh, P., & Gandhi, N. (2015). Milk preservatives and adulterants: processing, regulatory, and safety issues. *Food Reviews International*, 31(3), 236–261. https://doi.org/10.1080/87559129.2014.994818.

[13] Singuluri, H., & Sukumaran, M. K. (2014). Milk adulteration in Hyderabad, India – a comparative study on the levels of different adulterants present in milk. *Journal of Chromatography and Separation Techniques*, 5, 212. https://doi.org/10.4172/2157-7064.1000212.

[14] Yadav, A. K., Gattupalli, M., Dashora, K., & Kumar, V. (2023). Key milk adulterants in india and their detection techniques: a review. *Food Analytical Methods*, 16, 499–514. https://doi.org/10.1007/s12161-022-02427-8.

# 22 Machine learning for sustainable agriculture

*Rajap Shiva Kumar[1,a], Krishna Chaitanya Tirunagaru[1,b], Nitin Misal[1,c], Kallanagouda Patil[2,d], Ashish Bankar[1,e], Mahesh Chaudhari[1,f], Indra Raj Singh[1,g] and Vinod Kumar Rathod[1,h]*

[1]School of Agricultural Sciences and Technology, SVKM'S Narsee Monjee Institute of Management Studies (NMIMS) Deemed-to-be University, Shirpur, Maharashtra, India

[2]Subject Matter Specialist(Argicultural Extension), ICAR-Krishi Vigyan Kendra, Gadag, Karnataka, India

## Abstract

In the current context of increased population, change in climate, loss in biodiversity and degradation of land, sustainable agriculture is necessary for steady supply of food. It places a solid emphasis on natural stewardship, resource productivity and farmer welfare. Precision agriculture is an important part in sustainable agriculture where it uses improved technologies like drones, machine learning (ML) algorithms, sensors and Global Positioning System (GPS) to improve the usage efficiency of water, nutrients and pesticides. By estimating crop water and nutrient prerequisites, machine learning models encourage data-driven decision-making. Moreover, ML-based yield forecast models combine information from numerous sources, counting soil, climate and satellite pictures, to more precisely anticipate yields and advise key farm planning. Through artificial intelligence (AI) driven remote sensing and computer vision, ML moreover revolutionizes the identification of pests and diseases, enabling early crop protection intervention. This procedure is fortified by the consolidation of drones, IoT-based sensors, and hyperspectral imaging. ML designs estimate soil characteristics and assess fertility for soil health management, advancing sustainable land-use practices. Big data analytics and data fusion from various sources, including sensors, satellites, drones, and weather stations, offer comprehensive insights into field conditions. These agricultural applications are powered by supervised, unsupervised, and reinforcement learning methods like decision trees, neural networks, support vector machines and random forests. Precision farming is improved, environmental effects are lessened, and economic viability is increased when machine learning and sustainable agriculture come together. A more resilient agricultural future is eventually fostered by ML's enhancement of productivity, resource efficiency, and sustainability through the use of predictive modelling and intelligent decision-support systems.

**Keywords:** Algorithm, machine learning, precision farming, sustainable agriculture

## Sustainable agriculture – overview

Agriculture's capacity to convey food and other materials to a developing worldwide population supports anthropological life and with it, all perspectives of human action. Climate alter, a high degree of biological diversity loss, land debasement caused by soil erosion, compactness, saline condition, pollution, fatigue and pollution of water resources, expanding

[a]rajapshivakumar@gmail.com, [b]krishna.tirunagaru@nmims.edu, [c]nitin.misal@nmims.edu, [d]kvpatil.1222@gmail.com, [e]Ashish.Bankar@nmims.edu, [f]mahesh.chaudhari@nmims.edu, [g]indra.singh@nmims.edu, [h]vinod.rathod@nmims.edu

DOI: 10.1201/9781003716648-22

expenses of production, an unfaltering diminish within the number of farms, poverty and so on causes country's population undermine farming capability to encounter needs of humans currently and within the near future [7]. Sustainable agriculture is required to address the issues. Sustainable agriculture is the term used to describe combined methods of crop and livestock production techniques with on farm applications. It will also satisfy human needs for fiber and food, improve environment and the natural reserve base on which agrarian economy is founded, increase the efficiency of utilization of non-renewable resources and agriculture based assets, incorporation through natural biological cycles and ensure the commercial sustainability of agriculture tasks, and increase the life quality of farmers and general population [22]. The high use of mineral fertilizer and other chemical inputs, the lack of advanced technology, the impact of change in climate, maintaining crop yield and land demand, dietary changes, increased food waste, distribution and access to food are some of the major obstacles that still stand in the way of achieving overall sustainability in agriculture [23]. Integration of technology, which can provide sustainable solutions for a range of issues, including waste management, transportation, agriculture, energy and water, can play a significant part in achieving development. Precision agriculture technology is revolutionizing the agricultural sector by boosting productivity, sustainability and efficiency [17]. These technologies use state-of-the-art methods such as GPS, IoT, drones, machine learning and data science to observe and cope with agricultural output with unparalleled accuracy [13]. By maximizing the usage of inputs like moisture, nutrients and pesticides, precision agriculture reduces waste, its ecological impact and encourages sustainable farming practices. In addition to increasing crop yields, this method enhances the long run health of ecosystem by decreasing pollution and safeguarding natural resources [11].

## Overview of machine learning in agriculture

IBM employee Arthur Samuels coined the term machine learning (ML) in 1959. The beauty of this area of research is that it aims to make computers capable of learning deprived of the requisite programming. This is one of the best exhilarating instruments ever seen. As the term implies, it raises processors' learning potential to parity with that of people. Machine learning is an area of artificial intelligence. The main objective of machine learning algorithms is to maximize task performance. Optimization is done by using examples or experience. Like human performance, ML increases with increased data volumes because it is a data-driven technology. The two processes that comprise the overall functisoning of machine learning systems are learning (used for training) and testing. A feature vector for learning is created by combining these features. This feature vector is utilized as a source and can be either binary numeric nominal or ordinal [10]. Machines can use training data to learn how to perform the task through experience during the learning phase. As soon as the learning performance reaches a suitable level, it stops. Therefore, the model generated in the training phase could be utilized for either grouping or forecasting categorization [21]. Fundamental understanding of artificial intelligence, that is machine learning, is key for intelligent data analytics and the creation of intelligent and automated applications related to that. From reinforcement to unsupervised, supervised semi-supervised and machine learning has a lot of algorithms. These processes include the generation of mathematic models to evaluate data trends for making predictions or decisions [24]. The models discover trends and enhance their accuracy over time through iterative analysis of historical data. As the model typically trains on a dataset, for finding relationships between output and input values. Supervised learning requires data to be labelled, while unsupervised learning applies unlabelled data to reveal underlying structures. Reinforcement learning guides individuals through incorporating interactions with the environment to achieve specific goals [2]. Such machine learning techniques for processing data, finding patterns and performing predictions or decisions autonomously include decision trees, neural networks, clustering algorithms and support vector machines. Large-scale, intelligent data analysis is also possible using deep learning, a subset of a broader family of machine learning algorithms [18].

Machine learning has several uses in the agricultural industry. The implementation of ML has dramatically changed the agricultural landscape in a variety of ways, increasing efficiency, productivity and sustainability [5]. According to Liakos et al. [8], these applications fall within the following categories: soil, water, and crop management, particularly in crop production. Currently this article specially kept a focus on ML applications related to sustainable agriculture *i.e.*, precision agriculture, yield prediction and yield modelling, pest and disease detection and soil health management. Figure 22.1.

## Applications of machine learning for sustainable agriculture

### Precision agriculture

By using contemporary technologies to increase crop output while lowering resource consumption, precision farming is transforming conventional agricultural systems. This data-driven strategy analyses and manages field variability using instruments such as drones, sensors, machine learning and GPS [9]. Precision farming helps farmers make site-specific, well-informed decisions by tracking variations in crop healthiness, composition of soil and moistness levels. In order to increase yield, improve efficiency, and support environmental sustainability, the main objective is to maximize the use of inputs including fertilizers, insecticides and water [3]. ML also aids in fertilizing more precisely and controlling water. Traditional methods for calculating the nitrogen nutrition index (NNI) rely on labour-intensive and economically expensive field measurements. Another approach integrates machine learning algorithms with unmanned aerial vehicles (UAVs) imagery. Qiu et al. [16] illustrated that six Rice-NNI estimation results using the ML algorithm show that the random Forest algorithm of coefficient of determination ($R^2$) and RMSE. The RMSE ranged from 0.03 to 0.07, with estimates from NNI being the highest at grain filling and early jointing stages.

### Yield prediction

Providing crop yield predictions is important for national and regional decision-makers and timely agricultural planning. To this end, ML algorithms are widely applied using information derived from fertilizer rates, genetic characteristics, environmental variables as well as land management techniques (Barbedo, 2019) [1]. A study conducted by Khanal et al. [5], observed that model predicted somewhat better corn income between predicted and observed corn yields, on a normal change of 1.48% (±8.85% standard deviation). The experimental corn yields ranged from 6.1 to 17.9 t ha$^{-1}$, and the anticipated corn yields stretched between 9.5 to 15.24 t ha$^{-1}$ and similar results indicated in the remote sensing processed images.

## Detection and control of diseases and pests

The intersection of remote sensing and AI vision technologies is breaking new ground in monitoring field crop health. Machine learning algorithms employ pattern recognition and classification methods based on multi-spectral data analysis and outlier detection for such diseases/stressors due to agriculture. Remote sensing also enables farmers to become a lot more proactive with investment management, maximizing output through identifying the crop health problem and solving them in real-time by the auspices of AI vision and machine learning [4]. The targeted application of pesticides made possible by AI and ML minimizes competition from weeds while also enhancing crop yield. In a field trial accompanied by Marquez [12], where AI guidance was issued to apply herbicide, the biomass of weeds was seen to be 40% lesser compared to a standard procedure for human spraying, even reduction in the herbicide application by 45.64%.

## Soil health and management

Machine learning has been applied for prediction of soil properties by integrating high-resolution geo-data with climate dynamics to predict crops and soil yield outcomes while recognizing the significance of soil health vis-a-vis agricultural productivity. This convergence with crop modelling through predictive models on soil fertility and crop yield using machine learning algorithms brings to light the holistic approach needed in agricultural research.

Along with this, satellite imagery and IoT-based soil sensors supplement the data by detailing soil conditions to make the projection more accurate, hence promoting sustainable farming practices [5]. In an experiment conducted by Khanal et al. [5] found that neural network model executed better in prediction of cation exchange capacity and soil organic matter have maximum $R^2$ and inferior RMSE, while Support Vector Machine model with

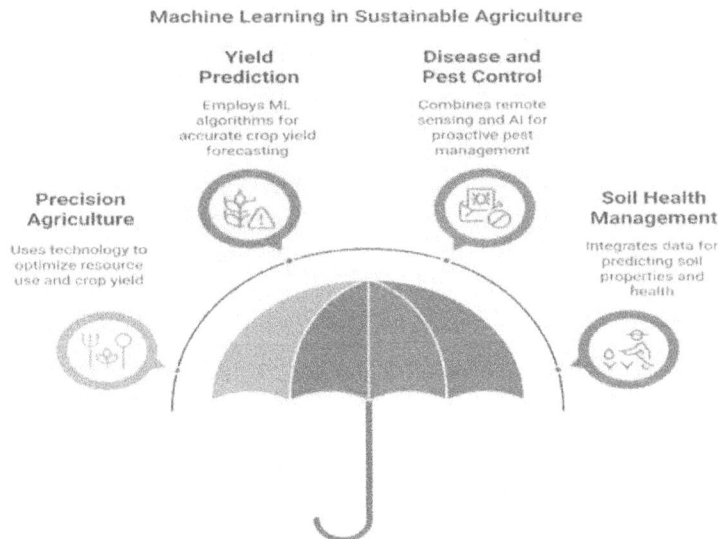

*Figure 22.1* Machine learning applications in agriculture
Source: Author

linear and radial kernel performance shown superior for extrapolation of Mg and K, respectively. Models for pH, cation exchange capacity, soil organic matter, K and Mg revealed $R^2$ in the range of 0.0–0.73, 0.17–0.78, 0.2–0.85, 0.0–0.56 and 0.0–0.55, correspondingly.

## Sources and techniques of data collection

Agriculture uses sensor innovation to accumulate data on field conditions in genuine time such as soil temperature, soil moisture and fertility levels. The comprehensive information required for precise decision-making in agrarian operations is given by wearable and ground-based sensors. Agriculturists may move forward in decision-making and enhance crop yields by keeping an eye on conditions within the field and altering their strategies appropriately. The wide-angle point of view given by satellite imagery and farther detecting permits for the observing of huge agrarian areas [15].

Drones are as of now fundamental instruments for accuracy agricultures broad airborne information collection because of their capacity to gather information and deliver high-quality imagery. Applying information mining procedures and machine learning calculations to tremendous amounts of farm information encourages the distinguishing proof of designs trend forecast and cultivating practice enhancement to boost sustainability and productivity [8].

## Machine learning algorithms used in agriculture

Machine learning procedures are revolutionizing farm practices through the provision of crop production estimates exact forecast and planning and the optimization of cultivating conditions based on verifiable information and future projections [19]. For occasion ML algorithms have been used to optimize fertilizer application amounts in order to balance expanding crop yield with diminishing natural impacts. Furthermore, ML is fundamental for keeping up soil fertility evaluating basic soil properties to illuminate crop rotation and management techniques assessing soil wellbeing and advancing vigorous crop yields [14]. A modern period of accuracy cultivating has been introduced in by the fruitful application of these strategies which has essentially moved forward agrarian management and efficiency. Kuradusenge et al. [6] highlighted how precisely ML models figure agricultural yields engaging farmers and other partners to form informed choices. To minimize harm and decrease reliance on chemical pesticides, convolutional neural systems (CNNs) have the potential to be utilized within the early location of plant infections. Tamayo-Vera et al. [20] summarized the application of different machine learning strategies in agriculture in a review paper. The following may be an outline of that summation.

*Table 22.1* Different ML techniques used for agricultural applications [20].

| Agricultural application | ML technique |
| --- | --- |
| Yield prediction | Extreme Gradient Boosting Naive Bayes, K-Nearest Neighbors, etc. |
| Detection of disease | CNN, ANN, GNN, etc. |
| Assessment of soil | Decision tree, random forest, Extreme Gradient Boosting etc. |

Source: Author

## Conclusion

Tending to worldwide issues counting resource consumption, biodiversity loss, and climate change requires sustainable farming. It empowers social well-being, natural conservation, and viable input utilization. Precision farming, abdicate forecast, insect control, and soil wellbeing management are all areas where machine learning (ML) is fundamental to the progression of sustainable cultivating. Drones, sensors, and AI-powered models are utilized in precision farming to maximize resource utilization, fertilization, and water system. Crop planning and asset allotment are upgraded by machine learning-driven yield forecast models. Moreover, ML underpins proactive management by progressing the distinguishing proof of pests and diseases with AI vision frameworks. IoT sensors and ML-based predictive models upgrade soil health monitoring, advancing sustainable soil management. When combined, these innovations revolutionize agriculture by making data-driven, naturally dependable, and profitable agricultural strategies possible.

## References

[1] Barbedo, J. G. A. (2019). Detection of nutrition deficiencies in plants using proximal images and machine learning: a review. *Computers and Electronics in Agriculture*, 162, 482–492.

[2] Dulac-Arnold, G., Levine, N., Mankowitz, D. J., Li, J., Paduraru, C., Gowal, S., et al. (2021). Challenges of real-world reinforcement learning: definitions, benchmarks and analysis. *Machine Learning*, 110(9), 2419–2468.

[3] Gawande, V., Saikanth, D. R. K., Sumithra, B. S., Aravind, S. A., Swamy, G. N., Chowdhury, M., et al. (2023). Potential of precision farming technologies for eco-friendly agriculture. *International Journal of Plant and Soil Science*, 35(19), 101–112.

[4] Heeb, L., Jenner, E., & Cock, M. J. (2019). Climate-smart pest management: building resilience of farms and landscapes to changing pest threats. *Journal of Pest Science*, 92(3), 951–969.

[5] Khanal, S., Fulton, J., Klopfenstein, A., Douridas, N., & Shearer, S. (2018). Integration of high resolution remotely sensed data and machine learning techniques for spatial prediction of soil properties and corn yield. *Computers and Electronics in Agriculture*, 153, 213–225.

[6] Kuradusenge, M., Hitimana, E., Hanyurwimfura, D., Rukundo, P., Mtonga, K., Mukasine, A., et al. (2023). Crop yield prediction using machine learning models: case of Irish potato and maize. *Agriculture*, 13(1), 225.

[7] Lal, R. (2008). Soils and sustainable agriculture - a review. *Agronomy for Sustainable Development*, 28, 57–64.

[8] Liakos, K. G., Busato, P., Moshou, D., Pearson, S., & Bochtis, D. (2018). Machine learning in agriculture: a review. *Sensors*, 18(8), 2674.

[9] Linaza, M. T., Posada, J., Bund, J., Eisert, P., Quartulli, M., Döllner, J., et al. (2021). Data-driven artificial intelligence applications for sustainable precision agriculture. *Agronomy*, 11(6), 1227.

[10] Lopez-Arevalo, I., Aldana-Bobadilla, E., Molina-Villegas, A., Galeana-Zapién, H., Muñiz-Sanchez, V., & Gausin-Valle, S. (2020). A memory-efficient encoding method for processing mixed-type data on machine learning. *Entropy*, 22(12), 1391.

[11] Majumder, D., Akhter, J., Mandal, A., Roy, R., Mondal, D., Bhatt, R., et al. (2021). Precision input management for minimizing and recycling of agricultural waste. *Input Use Efficiency for Food and Environmental Security*, 567–603. https://doi.org/10.1007/978-981-16-5199-1_19.

[12] Marquez, M.S.F.G. (2024). RGB and multispectral image analysis based on deep learning for real-time detection and control of weeds in cornfields (Doctoral dissertation, Centro De

Investigaciones En´ Optica A.C. Gobierno de Mexico Repository CIO. http://cio.repositorioin-stitucional.mx/jspui/handle/1002/1322.

[13] Mishra, S. (2022). Emerging Technologies—Principles and Applications in Precision Agriculture. In: Reddy, G.P.O., Raval, M.S., Adinarayana, J., Chaudhary, S. (eds) Data Science in Agriculture and Natural Resource Management. Studies in Big Data, vol 96. Springer, Singapore. https://doi.org/10.1007/978-981-16-5847-1_2.

[14] Mohamed, S. A., Metwaly, M. M., Metwalli, M. R., AbdelRahman, M. A., & Badreldin, N. (2023). Integrating active and passive remote sensing data for mapping soil salinity using machine learning and feature selection approaches in arid regions. *Remote Sensing*, 15(7), 1751.

[15] Nolde, M., Plank, S., & Riedlinger, T. (2020). An adaptive and extensible system for satellite-based, large scale burnt area monitoring in near-real time. *Remote Sensing*, 12(13), 2162.

[16] Qiu, Z., Ma, F., Li, Z., Xu, X., Ge, H., & Du, C. (2021). Estimation of nitrogen nutrition index in rice from UAV RGB images coupled with machine learning algorithms. *Computers and Electronics in Agriculture*, 189, 106421.

[17] Sarfraz, S., Ali, F., Hameed, A., Ahmad, Z., & Riaz, K. (2023). Sustainable agriculture through technological innovations. In Sustainable Agriculture in the Era of the OMICs Revolution, (pp. 223–239). Cham: Springer International Publishing.

[18] Sarker, I. H. (2021). Machine learning: algorithms, real-world applications and research directions. *SN Computer Science*, 2(3), 160.

[19] Sharma, R., Kamble, S. S., Gunasekaran, A., Kumar, V., & Kumar, A. (2020). A systematic literature review on machine learning applications for sustainable agriculture supply chain performance. *Computers and Operations Research*, 119, 104926.

[20] Tamayo-Vera, D., Wang, X., & Mesbah, M. (2024). A review of machine learning techniques in agroclimatic studies. *Agriculture*, 14(3), 481.

[21] Tripathi, P., Kumar, N., Rai, M., Shukla, P. K., & Verma, K. N. (2023). Applications of machine learning in agriculture. In Smart Village Infrastructure and Sustainable Rural Communities, (pp. 99—118). IGI Global.

[22] USDA National Agricultural Library, U.S. Department of Agriculture. Retrieved December 24, 2024, from https://www.nal.usda.gov/farms-and-agricultural-production-systems/sustainable-agriculture.

[23] Zerssa, G.W., Hailemariam, M. and Tadele, K.T. (2023). Improving the sustainability of agriculture: challenges and opportunities. In: Lousada, S.A.N. (eds) land-use management - recent advances, new perspectives and applications. DOI: 10.5772/intechopen.112857.

[24] Zhai, X., Yin, Y., Pellegrino, J. W., Haudek, K. C., & Shi, L. (2020). Applying machine learning in science assessment: a systematic review. *Studies in Science Education*, 56(1), 111–151.

# 23 A machine learning approach for crop recommendation for sustainable agriculture

*Varsha Nemade[1,a], Vishal Fegade[2], Deepti Barhate[1] and Suraj Patil[1]*

[1]Computer Science Department, Mukesh Patel School of Technology Management and Engineering, SVKM'S NMIMS Deemed to-be University, Shirpur, Maharashtra, India

[2]ASH Department, Mukesh Patel School of Technology Management and Engineering, SVKM'S NMIMS Deemed to-be University, Shirpur, Maharashtra, India

## Abstract

This study investigates crop recommendation by using machine learning algorithms for sustainable agriculture in varying conditions. The dataset includes parameters of soil and environment such as nitrogen (N), phosphorus (P), potassium (K), pH, temperature, humidity, and rainfall. These factors are analyzed through the application of machine learning models like decision tree, support vector machine, random forest, and K-nearest neighbor. It shows the development of comprehensive methodology that integrates soil and environmental data to provide the results and actions required to enhance yield of crop along with the reduction of the consumption of resources. It shows that random forest model has an impressive accuracy of 99.27%, establishing its efficacy in crop recommendation.

**Keywords:** Decision tree, K-nearest neighbor, random forest, support vector machine

## Introduction

In Global economy Agricultural forms are the backbone which ensures food security for human society. For Sustainable agriculture practices unpredictable climate changes and declining soil fertility are becoming the obstacle and becoming the significant threat in agriculture [5, 9]. Farmers are using the traditional crop selection processes which cannot predict actual soil characteristics and unpredictable weather conditions. There is always a complex inter relation between the crop requirement and soil and weather conditions [13]. This forces us to apply innovative solutions with the leverage of advanced technologies for better crop classification for enhanced crop yielding machine learning (ML) is a powerful tool for addressing the challenges by enabling data-driven decision making. ML algorithms analyse vast amount of data, it discovers the patterns and relationship that help to optimize agricultural practices crop classification has shown significant advancements through the application of machine learning, as it helps farmers select the most suitable crops for their soil and environmental conditions The environmental factors such as rainfall, temperature, and humidity alongside soil nutrients has shown enhance classification accuracy increased up to 15% in recent studies ensemble methods like Random Forest (RF) shows superior performance in diverse agricultural datasets [7]. This research builds on these advancements by implementing and comparing ML models—Decision Tree (DT), Support Vector Machine (SVM), RF, and K-nearest neighbor (KNN)—to classify crops using soil and environmental

[a]varsha.nemade@nmims.edu

DOI: 10.1201/9781003716648-23

data. With a focus on sustainability, this study aims to empower farmers to enhance yields while reducing resource consumption [16].

## Literature review

Various studies have shown that ML models optimize crop classification, resource allocation, and yield prediction, offering significant advantages over traditional methods. ML approach described for improving the agro based prediction for crop yield analysis. They recommend fertilizers on different soil and weather conditions and used RF and LR model for predicting crops prediction [3]. Performed analysis using different ML algorithms and perform analysis of different stages of crop cultivation using DL and ML models. This system enhances agricultural output using data – driven decision making in farm. They used 11 different algorithms. They focus on the problems faced by farmers like weed identification, soil compatibility, weather fluctuation, and crop selection. To minimize these problems, they proposed a novel recommendation system for crops based on meteorological data to suggest the most appropriate crops for a certain region [4]. ML models like SVM and RF to predict agricultural harvests from historical data. It also recommends appropriate fertilizers for specific crops through analytical analysis. They got 86.35% accuracy by using RF and 99.47% using SVM [1]. A novel crop recommendation model for helping farmers to select the right crops based on soil characteristics and seasonal conditions were proposed. They used different ML models like LR, KNN, NB, neural network (NN)and support vector classifier (SVC). These models are compared and validated using accuracy. Out of all the models NN shows the highest accuracy at 89.88%. The research shows the potential use of DL models in optimizing agricultural decision-making through the application of precise data-driven crop recommendations [14]. A model using a dataset of 28,242 instances with seven significant features was developed. The dataset consists of agricultural variables for determining the crop yield prediction like climatic conditions, rainfall rates and crop types. To improve the accuracy, they used different ensemble learning models and evaluating their performance. Out of the models evaluated, the AdaBoost regressor coupled with a DT showed the highest accuracy rate of 95.7%. This works shows the powerful use of ensemble learning and helps to increase accuracy and provide robust results, and this helps this helps farmers make data-driven, informed decisions [6]. Model developed for farming practices of maize, groundnut and Bengal gram in the Telangana state of India. They used various ML algorithms to estimate crop yield, and they got MAE with 468.16 and of 0.6087 cross validation score with RF regressor [12]. An in-depth study on the impact of rainfall patterns, soil conditions, and climate variations on agriculture using machine learning techniques was conducted. Their research aimed to enhance crop prediction by analyzing how these environmental factors influence plant growth. To achieve this, they implemented multiple ML models, including RF, SVC, DT and LR and they got accuracy 97%, 98% and 99% on LR, SVC, and DT respectively [15]. Different plant characteristics explored, like shape of the leaf, number of leaves, height, and biomass through explainable artificial intelligence. Their work facilitates improved crop management by identifying critical factors like water requirements and flowering times [8]. Oikonomidis et al. [11] explained about the crop choice in agriculture and present an intelligent crop suggestion system based on ML methods [11]. An overview of applying ML in crop management to attain smart and precise farming is described and they discussed different ML algorithms applied in crop forecasting, disease identification, and yield estimation, with the emphasis on improved decision-making and sustainability. The article also discusses challenges and future research gaps in applying [2].

## Methodology

Figure 23.1. describe the overall design of the proposed system used for crop classification using different environmental factors. Different classification algorithms and ensemble models were applied on the data. To perform this, the first step of this is data acquisition. The data then pre-processed, after that data divided into training and testing data. Hyper parameter tuning and cross validation is also applied on training data. Finally, each classifier evaluated on testing data.

### *Dataset and preprocessing*
The dataset includes parameters such as N, P, K, soil pH, humidity, temperature, and rainfall. It contains 2,200 instances derived from historical data and was sourced from the Kaggle platform [10]. The dataset encompasses 22 different crops. Preprocessing is applied to remove outliers and to handle missing values

### *ML models*
Various classification algorithms are applied to perform the recommendation of crops according to different soil and environmental conditions:

KNN: It calculates distances from labeled points and assigns a label to the new data point based on its nearest neighbors and classifies new points based on similarity with present data.

SVM: A classification method that does not require prior knowledge of data distribution. It uses hyperplanes to separate data points into classes.

DT: This technique classifies instances based on feature values, using splitting criteria like Gini Index or Information Gain. The leaf nodes represent the classification labels.

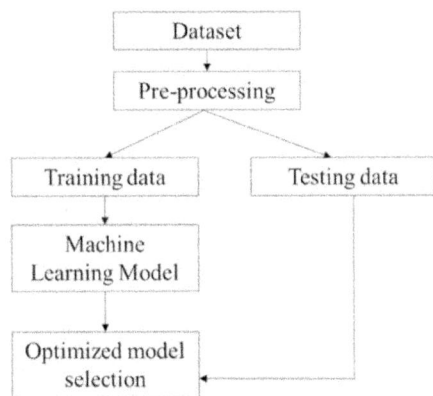

*Figure 23.1* Flow of proposed methodology
Source: Author

RF: This is an ensemble technique. It builds multiple decision trees on different samples of data. It aggregates the predictions of individual trees through majority voting for classification.

Hyper parameter tuning is performed to select the best parameter and also applied k-fold cross validation to get the robust result.

*Implementation*

All ML algorithms used in the work are implemented in Google Colab, utilizing a Jupyter Notebook environment. The implementation leverages the Scikit-learn library in Python, along with additional libraries such as NumPy, Pandas, and Matplotlib for data processing and visualization.

## Results and discussion

On the crop recommendation dataset different ML models are applied and their performance is measured by tuning the hyper parameters with five-fold cross validation and check

*Table 23.1* Comparison of ML models with hyper parameters.

| Algorithm | Hyper Parameters | Tuning | Result (%) |
|---|---|---|---|
| DT | Criterion | Criterion= gini | 98.54 |
| | Splitter | Splitter :best | |
| | | Criterion= gini | 96.00 |
| | | Splitter :random | |
| SVM | C | C:1,kernel:rbf | 98.06 |
| | Kernel | C:1,kernel:linear | 98.06 |
| | | C:10,kernel:rbf | 98.54 |
| | | C:10,kernel:linear | 97.93 |
| | | C:100,kernel:rbf | 98.54 |
| | | C:100,kernel:linear | 98.06 |
| | | C:1000,kernel:rbf | 98.54 |
| | | C:1000,kernel:linear | 98.06 |
| RF | n estimators | n estimators:1 | 94.24 |
| | | n_estimators:5 | 98.72 |
| | | n_estimators:10 | **99.27** |
| KNN | n_neighbors | n_neighbors:5 | 97.33 |
| | weights | weights':' uniform ' | |
| | | n_neighbors:5 | 97.51 |
| | | weights':'distance' | |
| | | n_neighbors:10 | 95.75 |
| | | weights':' uniform ' | |
| | | n_neighbors:10 | 96.84 |
| | | weights':'distance' | |
| | | n_neighbors:20 | 93.57 |
| | | weights':' uniform ' | |
| | | n_neighbors:20 | 95.27 |
| | | weights':'distance' | |
| | | n_neighbors:25 | 92.84 |
| | | weights':' uniform ' | |
| | | n_neighbors:25 | 94.66 |
| | | weights':'distance' | |

Source: Author

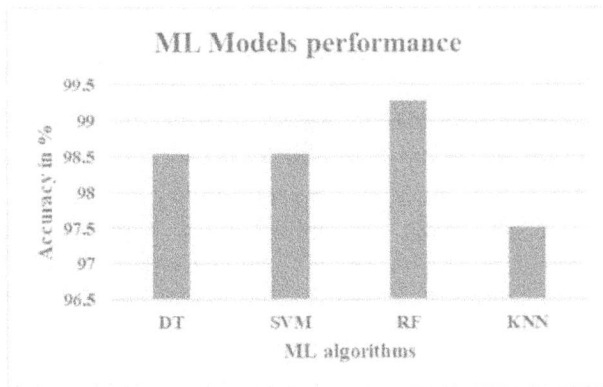

*Figure 23.2* ML models performance comparison
Source: Author

the results for different combinations of parameters. In this study, we evaluated the performance of various machine learning algorithms, including DT, SVM, RF and KNN under different hyper parameter configurations. Obtained results are shown in Table 23.1. The DT algorithm was evaluaTed using different values for the criterion and splitter hyper parameters, results shows that the "best" splitter provides effective performance compared to the "random" splitter when using the gini criterion. SVM was tested with different combinations of C values and kernel types. RBF kernel shows effective performance than linear kernel particularly for higher values of the regularization parameter C. The best configuration for SVM was found with C = 10, Kernel = rbf. Different values of n_estimators hyper parameter used for RF algorithm evaluation and n_estimators = 10 providing the best performance. The KNN algorithm was tested with different values for n_neighbors and weights. The results indicate that using the "distance" weight scheme consistently outperforms the "uniform" scheme. Additionally, smaller values of n_neighbors yield better performance compared to larger values, with the best configuration being n_neighbors = 5, Weights = distance.

To optimize the performance of ML model hyper parameter tuning performs an important role. Table 23.1 shows the results of all models with hyper parameter and Figure 23.2 shows the comparison of all models. Among all implemented algorithms RF with n_estimators = 10 achieved the highest accuracy of 99.27%, followed by DT with criterion = gini, splitter = best and SVM with C = 10, Kernel = rbf, both achieving 98.54%. KNN showed competitive performance, particularly with n_neighbors = 5, weights = distance, achieving 97.51% accuracy. These findings suggest that ensemble methods like RF can provide superior performance for classification tasks, while appropriate tuning of hyper parameters in SVM and KNN can also yield high accuracy. The study shows the importance of the N, P and K in crop selection. Farmers are able to: Avoid overuse of fertilizers, conserving cost and environmental burden. Predict water requirements of selected crops based on soil moisture levels and weather conditions, leading to improved irrigation control.

## Conclusion

This study demonstrates the potential of machine learning (ML) algorithms in enhancing sustainable agriculture by enabling accurate crop recommendations based on soil and environmental factors. By analysing key parameters such as as nitrogen, phosphorus, potassium, pH, temperature, humidity, and rainfall, using various ML algorithms. It shows that Random Forest model emerged as the most effective, achieving an impressive accuracy of 99.27%. The findings highlight the importance of integrating advanced data-driven approaches in agriculture to optimize resource use and improve crop yield. The proposed methodology offers a scalable and practical framework for supporting farmers in selecting the most suitable crops for their specific conditions. While study demonstrated the great accuracy in crop suggestion, there are some limitations that the model depends on climatic and soil factors, without considering economic constraints, market access, and farmers' availability of the crop. To enhance crop recommendation systems developed using ML to become more relevant and stronger in future, the development of models should be based on market patterns, cost-benefit, and budgetary constraints of farmers.

## References

[1] Bondre, D. A., & Mahagaonkar, S. (2019). Prediction of crop yield and fertilizer recommendation using machine learning algorithms. *International Journal of Engineering Applications and Science Technology*, 4(5), 371–376.

[2] Chaudhary, R. R., Bamane, K. D., Agrawal, H., Malathi, P., Gaikwad, A. S., & Patankar, A. J. (2024). A critical analysis of crop management using machine learning towards smart and precise farming. *Journal of Integrated Science and Technology*, 12(5), 809–809.

[3] Devan, K. P. K., Swetha, B., Sruthi, P. U., & Varshini, S. (2023). Crop yield prediction and fertilizer recommendation system using hybrid machine learning algorithms. In 2023 IEEE 12th International Conference on Communication Systems and Network Technologies (CSNT), (pp. 171–175). IEEE.

[4] Durai, S. K., & Shamili, M. D. (2022). Smart farming using machine learning and deep learning techniques. *Decision Analytics Journal*, 3, 100041.

[5] Hatuwal, B. K., Shakya, A., & Joshi, B. (2020). Plant leaf disease recognition using random forest, KNN, SVM and CNN. *Polibits*, 62, 13–19.

[6] Keerthana, M., Meghana, K. J., Pravallika, S., & Kavitha, M. (2021). An ensemble algorithm for crop yield prediction. In 2021 Third International Conference on Intelligent Communication Technologies and Virtual Mobile Networks (ICICV), (pp. 963–970). IEEE.

[7] Meenachi, L., Ramakrishnan, S., Sivaprakash, M., Thangaraj, C., & Sethupathy, S. (2022). Multi-class ensemble classification for crop recommendation. In 2022 International Conference on Inventive Computation Technologies (ICICT), (pp. 1319–1324). IEEE.

[8] Mostafa, S., Mondal, D., Panjvani, K., Kochian, L., & Stavness, I. (2023). Explainable deep learning in plant phenotyping. *Frontiers in Artificial Intelligence*, 6, 1203546.

[9] Muruganantham, P., Wibowo, S., Grandhi, S., Samrat, N. H., & Islam, N. (2022). A systematic literature review on crop yield prediction with deep learning and remote sensing. *Remote Sensing*, 14(9), 1990.

[10] Nalluri, V. (2023). Crop Recommendation Dataset. Kaggle. https://www.kaggle.com/datasets/varshitanalluri/crop-recommendation-dataset.

[11] Oikonomidis, A., Catal, C., & Kassahun, A. (2023). Deep learning for crop yield prediction: a systematic literature review. *New Zealand Journal of Crop and Horticultural Science*, 51(1), 1–26.

[12] Panigrahi, B., Kathala, K. C. R., & Sujatha, M. (2023). A machine learning-based comparative approach to predict the crop yield using supervised learning with regression models. *Procedia Computer Science*, **218**, 2684–2693.

[13] Petcu, M. A., Sobolevschi-David, M. I., Curea, S. C., & Moise, D. F. (2024). Integrating artificial intelligence in the sustainable development of agriculture: applications and challenges in the resource-based theory approach. *Electronics*, 13(23), 4580.

[14] Priyadharshini, A., Chakraborty, S., Kumar, A., & Pooniwala, O. R. (2021). Intelligent crop recommendation system using machine learning. In 2021 5th International Conference on Computing Methodologies and Communication (ICCMC), (pp. 843–848). IEEE.

[15] Shankar, P., Pareek, P., Patel, U., & Sen, C. (2022). Crops prediction based on environmental factors using machine learning algorithm. *Center for Development Economic Studies*, 9(11), 127–137.

[16] Rastogi, S. (2024). Comparative analysis of machine learning algorithms for crop variety prediction: performance metrics, data requirements, and methodological insight. *International Journal of Intelligent Systems and Applications in Engineering*, 12(22s), 1013.

# 24 Analyzing performance and growth trajectories of farmer producer organizations under SAMP India consortium: a comprehensive study of Gujarat state

*Om Maheshwari[1,a], Mohit Deshmukh[1,b] and Kallanagouda Patil[2,c]*

[1]School of Agricultural Sciences and Technology, SVKM's Narsee Monjee Institute of Management Studies (NMIMS) Deemed to be University, Shirpur, Maharastra, India

[2]Subject Matter Specialist (Agricultural Extension), ICAR-Krishi Vigyan Kendra, Gadag, Karnataka, India

## Abstract

This study is a survey of 77 business organizations (FPOs) operating in SAMP India FPCL Alliance, India Survey from the state of Gujarat, India. Through primary data collected through direct interactions with the staff of group business organization (CBBO) and FPO CEOs, the study examines the operational strategies, financial performance and institutional support systems that make FPOs successful. The study reveals significant differences in organizational growth where selected FPOs perform well. Key tips for successful FPOs include effective business partnerships, building trust through digital services, effective product design and packaging, reducing plant costs while strengthening business linkages, achieving success through private entrepreneurship and achieving success through collective efforts through SHGs to break gender stereotypes. Financial analysis shows that farmers in effective FPOs save an average of 15.2% and increase their income by up to 419%. This study demonstrates how effective CBBO support and marketing strategies can be in transforming agriculture into a sustainable business. By collecting case studies and analyzing performance data, this research provides insights into FPOs and stakeholders on development, economic integration, economic linkages and economic stability.

Keywords: Cluster-based business organization, farmer producer organizations, market linkages and sustainable enterprise, value chain integration

## Introduction

The Indian agricultural industry faces persistent challenges due to fragmented land ownership and limited market access of small and marginal farmers. With 85% of farmers engaged in marginal and small-scale businesses (Ministry of Agriculture and Farmers' Welfare, [3]), individual farmers face high costs, weak bargaining power and impacts on economic change [4, 6]. The farmer-centric model has emerged as a solution to these structural problems by promoting integration and integrating [7, 10. Each FPO will receive financial assistance of up to Rs 18 lakh for a period of three years. In addition, a provision has been made for matching equity grants up to Rs. 2,000 per farmer member of the FPO with a limit of Rs. 15.00 lakh per FPO and a credit guarantee facility up to Rs. 2 crore of project loans per FPO from eligible lending institutions to ensure institutional credit accessibility to FPOs [3].

[a]sayomm3@gmail.com, [b]deshmukhmohit567@gmail.com, [c]kvpatil.1222@gmail.com

DOI: 10.1201/9781003716648-24

The FPO ecosystem represents a transformative approach towards agricultural development, where farmers come together to achieve economies of scale and an enhanced market presence [1]. This change can take many forms, from integrating benefits and new digital services to creating specialized products and niche markets. Cluster-based business organizations (CBBOs), which form the core of this ecosystem, act as important institutional intermediaries and provide support to the development of FPOs [2]. CBBOs empower farmers, build capacity and connect businesses, creating a solid foundation for FPO growth [5]. They help FPOs implement various strategies such as reducing input costs through bulk purchasing, establishing strong business linkages and building sustainable business models. This organizational support is especially important in the early stages of FPO development when the organization is developing its operational and commercial capabilities [8]. Success stories from various FPOs show that this support can be combined with innovative methods such as SHG-based cooperatives and entrepreneurship to create good jobs. The key to evolution. Successful FPOs use various strategies to solve traditional agribusiness challenges, from digital innovation and unique packaging to cost optimization and gender-targeted campaigns. This study examines the effectiveness, efficiency and growth of FPOs under the SAMP India Alliance through a literature review and case study, focusing on the state of Gujarat. The benefits of joining an FPO are positive and significant; 9,983 more per year than non-members [9].

## Methodology

Our study focused on all 77 farmer producer organizations under SAMP India Consortium in Gujarat state. Over a 2-month period during our internship, we conducted interviews with 77 FPO CEOs and 5 CBBO regional heads using a standardized questionnaire. The survey was prepared to cover important aspects of FPO operations including registration details of FPO, geographical reach, shareholder demographics, financial performance, farmer savings on input costs, increase in income, Audit reports, profitability, and the nature of support received from CBBOs. The data collected was organized in Microsoft Excel and descriptive statistics were used to gather key points. Data was analyzed to identify trends in operational performance, economic benefits to farmers and impact of CBBO support on FPO development to evaluate FPOs in SAMP India Alliance by providing insight into their contribution to farmers' empowerment and sustainable agriculture.

## Results and Discussion

FPO registration trends from 2017 to 2024 are shown in Figure 24.1. The temporal distribution of FPO registrations showed a clear evolution in the formation pattern. Of the 77 FPOs, only 1.30% (1 FPO) were registered in 2017, followed by another 1.30% in 2020. A significant increase began in 2021, with 24.68% (19 FPOs) of the total registrations, followed by the peak year 2022 with 42.86% (33 FPOs). The momentum continued to 2023 with 28.57% (22 FPOs) of registrations, while early 2024 accounted for 1.30% (1 FPO) of the total. This pattern demonstrates the growing acceptance and implementation of the FPO model in recent years.

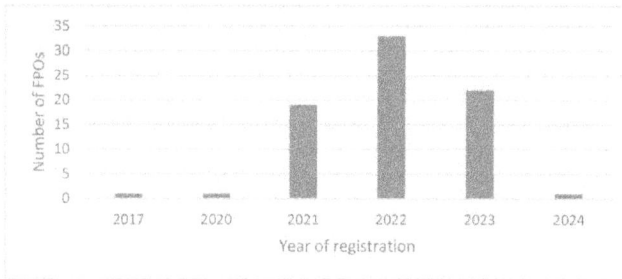

*Figure 24.1* Classification of FPOs based on year of registration
Source: Author

*Figure 24.2* Classification of FPO based of Turnover increase
Source: Author

Figure 24.2 shows the classification of FPO based on turnover. The analysis of business activities across 77 FPOs from 2022-23 to 2023-24 reveals diverse operational patterns. Notably, 36 FPOs (46.75%) marked their first financial year of operations in 2023-24, despite being registered in previous years. These organizations initiated substantial business activities, warranting formal audit reporting to tax authorities during this period. A significant portion of 29 FPOs (37.66%) demonstrated revenue growth compared to their 2022-23 performance, while three FPOs (3.90%) experienced revenue decline during the same period. Seven FPOs (9.09%) reported no business activity, indicating that their transaction volumes remained below the threshold, thus requiring formal audit reports for tax purposes. Only 2 FPOs (2.60%) reported losses in their first financial year of operations, suggesting relatively strong initial performance across the network.

Classifies the FPOs based on shareholder patterns are shown in Figure 24.3, The analysis of shareholder patterns reveals important implications for accessing government support schemes, particularly matching equity grants. While 49 FPOs (63.64%) maintain between 300–600 shareholders, and 17 FPOs (22.08%) have less than 300 shareholders, only 11 FPOs (14.29%) have over 600 shareholders. This distribution is particularly significant considering that FPOs can maximize benefits from the Matching Equity Grant scheme up to Rs. 15 lakhs by maintaining 750 shareholders (at Rs. 2000 per farmer member). The current distribution suggests that most FPOs have the potential to expand and optimize their access to this support scheme. Notably, the scheme requires at least 50% of shareholders to be small, marginal, or landless tenant farmers, with a preference for female farmers as shareholders.

*Figure 24.3* Classfication of FPOs based on number of shareholder
Source: Author

*Table 24.1* Turnover classification and growth analysis of FPOs (2022–23 to 2023–24).

| Low turnover | | Medium turnover | | High turnover | | Very high turnover | | No Business Activity | |
|---|---|---|---|---|---|---|---|---|---|
| 2022-23 | 2023-24 | 2022-23 | 2023-24 | 2022-23 | 2023-24 | 2022-23 | 2023-24 | 2022-23 | 2023-24 |
| 26 | 34 | 5 | 19 | 4 | 4 | 0 | 13 | 42 | 7 |

Source: Author

Table 24.1 shows turnover classification analysis of 77 FPOs reveals significant progress in business development under the CBBO guidance. FPOs are categorized by annual turnover: Low turnover (₹1-10 lakh), medium turnover (₹10–20 lakh), high turnover (₹20-30 lakh), and very high turnover (above ₹30 lakh). The year-over-year comparison shows a remarkable transformation: inactive FPOs decreased from 42 to 7, while FPOs achieving very high turnover increased from 0 to 13. This positive shift is particularly evident in the medium turnover category, which grew from 5 to 19 FPOs, indicating successful business development.

The significant reduction in inactive FPOs and the upward mobility across turnover categories illustrate the efficacy of the CBBO support mechanisms. The CBBOs by SAMP INDIA Consortium have assisted in the trajectory of growth with their skill and expertise in market linkages, capacity building, and business planning. They did not just activate the otherwise inactive FPOs but guided them toward higher revenue generation, thereby offering a sustainable model for FPO development and growth.

A detailed analysis of FPO operations showed encouraging performance metrics across different dimensions. The average profit is Rs. 47,103, which indicates that the business operations are viable. The participation of female shareholder's averages 19% across all FPOs, which indicates scope for improvement in gender inclusion. FPO membership has shown tangible economic benefits as farmers have experienced an average income increase of 17.7% and achieved an average savings of 15.2% through collective operations. The transition analysis indicates significant upward mobility in financial performance, as most

FPOs successfully move from lower to higher turnover categories. This is evidenced by the fact that FPOs with no business activity decreased significantly (from 42 to 5) and increased the medium and high turnover categories. The positive trend thus reflects the effectiveness of support mechanisms and business development strategies implemented across the FPO network.

**High-performing FPO case studies-**Among 77 FPOs, six organizations were the most successful through innovative business strategies and efficient use of resources. These success stories provide great insights for new FPOs.

### 1. Vaam Agro FPO
Good practice: Strategic turnaround through value chain integration
    Vaam Agro's journey began in 2019 in Vitthalapur block Mandal with great intentions but faced a potential loss of Rs. 21.56 lakh in their first year. However, the organization's leadership resolutely conducted an in-depth study of the market and farmers' needs, demonstrating that success in transitioning from agriculture is the foundation of agribusiness. The aim of to develop premium APRICA products, invest in identifying and classifying crops, and develop a wide range of spices, pulses, and grains. Their commitment to quality has led to partnerships with major retailers like ITC, Reliance Retail, and Flipkart. The results have been amazing; in just one year, they have turned a loss of Rs 21.56 crore into a profit of Rs 7.16 crore and increased their revenue by 351% in one year. Managing over 1,750 hectares of land and reaching out to over 6,750 customers, Vaam Agro is not only creating new jobs for over 1,000 of its farmer members but also enabling primarily rural people to compete effectively in the premium economy through good business and innovation.

### 2. Vijapur farmer producer corporate
Good practice: Building farmer trust through free digital services and competitive input shop. Vijapur FPC is in Vijapur blocks and covers producer farms in 25 villages. The success story of Vijapur FPC lies in its innovative approach to building trust and value. Its leaders acknowledge that farmers struggle with digital information and government services, resulting in significant time and financial losses. FPC has launched a free eKYC service to help farmers overcome bureaucratic hurdles and build trust in society. This feedback is the basis for future expansion. They have established a customer service center (CSC) model that has benefited 2,584 farmers through DBT products and services. Its stores offer an additional 10% discount to business owners, while government services save farmers $300–400 per application. The combination of digital innovation and tangible business results has led to phenomenal growth – transaction value has increased by 419% from Rs 15.18 crore in 2022–23 to Rs 78.79 crore in 2023–24. FPC's journey is the first time that trust in community investment has been integrated with sustainability. Value delivery creates a sustainable growth model that benefits the organization and its members.

### 3. Ranmal FPO
Good practice: Brand building and professional packaging excellence. Ranmal FPO's transformation began with a vision to promote agricultural products through products. Replicate the same for good customers. It is in Jamjodhpur district of Jamnagar. Starting with a small

business venture, they took a significant step by investing heavily in manufacturing and established 'NATRAM' as their brand name. Unlike many other FPOs that focus on retail, Ranmal chose to focus on wholesale and value addition. Their strategic focus on packaging and manufacturing has borne great fruit; from Rs 20.61 million in 2022–23 to Rs 114 million in 2023–24. The FPO has diversified its products under the brand name NATRAM, producing a variety of spice powders, pulses, ready-to-eat dry fruit kachori and groundnut oil. Their most notable success was setting up a joint venture in the state and working with FPOs in Kerala to regularly supply cumin and fennel seeds to the emerging markets of Delhi and Assam. Operating in 35 villages and 500 dealers, Ranmal FPO proves that TVEs can create quality products in the country with professional management and a wide range of interesting ideas.

## 4. Ranpur farmer producer company

Good practice: Reducing cultivation costs while strengthening market linkages-The Ranpur FPC revolutionized the traditional FPO model by placing farmer economics at the center of their strategy, located at Ranpur block district Botad covers. Recognizing that small farmers struggle with high input costs and market access, they developed a comprehensive support system. The FPC's innovative approach began with their agricultural input shop, which delivered substantial economic benefits through strategic cost optimization - offering 10–15% savings on input costs and facilitating access to subsidized seeds at 15–20% market rates. What sets the Ranpur FPC apart is their holistic approach to farmer support. Beyond the input shop, they initiated free form-filling services for various government schemes, saving farmers ₹300–400 per application. Their diversification into honeybee farming (managing 10 honeybee boxes) and successful acquisition of a ₹1.2 lakh subsidy for establishing a jeevamrut production plant demonstrated their commitment to innovation. Working across 20 villages with 504 shareholders, they've shown consistent growth from ₹2.63 lakh in 2022–23 to ₹10.49 lakh in 2023-24 turnover. Their future plans, including a peanut butter processing plant with potential export opportunities to the Dubai markets, showcase their ambition to continue creating value for their members through market expansion and value addition.

## 5. Krushi Dharatal FPC

Good practices: Success through niche market specialization

A small FPO called Krushi Dharatal FPC, located in Botad district, stands out with a unique vision of not competing with traditional horticulture in agriculture and has identified the right time. Focusing on the tea industry, they have built strong relationships with suppliers in Assam and have launched a special brand 'KD Tea' priced at Rs 300 per kg. This specialization reflects their understanding of the needs of the local market and the quality of the product, which is driving economic growth and value addition.

One of the most important of these is the launch of 'Kheti Nu Dava Khanu' grocery store in April 2023, which goes beyond selling produce to provide support to farmers. Combining specific recommendations with advice from agricultural experts on good agricultural practices, they have developed advice for 750 landowners, 85 of whom are women, across 20 villages. Their success in business integration and promotion proves that FPOs can create a competitive advantage by focusing on expertise and quality service.

**6. Meshvo Mahila Producer Company**
Good practice: Breaking the gender stereotype with SHG-based collective action.

Meshvo Mahila Producer Company is an innovative model of commercial farming based on women's cooperation. Formed in December 2022 in Bhiloda block of Aravalli district, the organization comprises women farmers from existing self-help groups (SHGs) and is a special model of women's economic empowerment in agriculture. This journey, starting with 1.355 million people, has shown the strength of focus and unity. The FPO has gained expertise in cattle feed production, including specialty crops like Makai bhardi, and a wide range of tea production. They have proved their financial management skills by successfully securing a loan of Rs 5 crore from Samunanti Financial Intermediaries and Services Limited.

The partnership with Reliance Group under the Svyam Shree project further validates their business model. It comprises 380 entrepreneurs, mostly ST (Schedule Group) women, across 20 villages, and Meshvo Mahila is proving that women-led businesses can overcome challenges.

**Key learning from FPOs**
It always strives to achieve social and economic support through collaboration and good business practices. VAAM AGRO stresses strategic change through value chain integration. Vijapur FPC demonstrates growth momentum through free digital services and competitive marketplaces that instill confidence among farmers. The success of Ranmal FPO epitomizes company marketing and packaging excellence. This has proved how plantation costs are reduced and a business link built up. It is a success result of a Krushi Dharatal FPC that comes from the skillful hand of a business implementer. Ultimately, Meshvo Mahila Produce Company shows how with self-help group unification comes the shattering of gender barriers to be brought about by producing successful women entrepreneurs. These findings are useful for understanding emerging FPOs and the different paths to corporate success.

**Role of CBBO services in FPO effectiveness**
While access to business professionals remains a challenge due to low compensation structures in the FPO ecosystem, new solutions have emerged from Samarth Agro, Mangalam Seeds Ltd., Kashvin Seeds Pvt, etc. CBBO is happening. Ltd. and Pashupati Cotspin Ltd. have formed the SAMP India Alliance of FPCL, which aims to increase efficiency by bringing together FPOs. The CBBO framework of the SAMP India Alliance has proven effective in the growth of FPOs through widespread support. CBBO supports the importance of FPO activities, including:

*   Initial exposure to farmers and organization formation
*   Capacity building and business planning support
*   Business linkages and effective business partnerships
*   Financial management and compliance Guidance

Support from the organization this alignment is particularly useful in helping FPOs overcome early operational challenges and develop sustainable business models.

**Key learnings from high-performing FPOs**

An analysis of the six case studies reveals crucial learning that contributes to FPO success. VAAM AGRO demonstrates the importance of strategic turnaround through value chain integration. Vijapur FPC showed how building farmers' trust through free digital services and competitive input shops can drive growth. Ranmal FPO's success highlights the significance of brand building and professional packaging excellence. Ranpur FPC proved the effectiveness of reducing cultivation costs while strengthening market linkages. Krushi Dharatal FPC demonstrated success through niche market specialization. Finally, the Meshvo Mahila Producer Company showed how breaking gender stereotypes through SHG-based collective action can create successful women-led enterprises. These findings provide valuable insights into emerging FPOs and highlight diverse pathways to organizational success.

**Role of CBBO support in FPO's success**

Government has well understood that they need private player in agriculture sector if they want to execute their schemes, this role has been appointed to various CBBOs through country for specialized focus over each FPO for at least initial years. Although accessing experienced corporate expertise remains a challenge due to limited remuneration structures in the FPO ecosystem, innovative solutions have emerged through CBBOs like Samarth Agro, Mangalam Seeds Ltd., Kashvin Seeds Pvt. Ltd., and Pashupati Cotspin Ltd., who have formed the SAMP INDIA Consortium of FPCL - a federation that enhances efficiency by collectivizing FPOs themselves. The CBBOs of the SAMP India Consortium was highly instrumental to the FPO with all-rounded supportive mechanisms. Generally, CBBOs provide many essential operations involving the FPOs. These include:

- Initial farmer mobilization and organization formation
- Capacity building and business planning support
- Market linkage development and value chain integration
- Financial management and compliance guidance

   This institutional support has been particularly effective in helping FPOs overcome early operational challenges and establish sustainable business models.

**Conclusion**

An overview of 77 FPOs under SAMP India demonstrates that FPO system is the correct way to modernize agriculture in country. The study demonstrates how effective CBBO support combined with innovative business strategies can create effective and efficient agricultural cooperatives. Key lessons learned from successful FPOs – including value integration, digital services, unique packaging, optimization, market expertise and gender integration – pave the way for new organizations. These trends and successes suggest that FPOs can achieve significant growth through focused and optimized strategies. The findings highlight the importance of local support in FPO development and suggest that with proper guidance and strategic planning, FPOs can increase farmers' income and employment. Future research should focus on long-term sustainability indicators and scaling strategies for successful FPO models.

## References

[1] Kumari, S., Bharti, N., & Tripathy, K. K. (2021). Strengthening agriculture value chain through collectives: comparative case analysis. *International Journal of Rural Management* 17(1_suppl), 40S–68S. https://doi.org/10.1177/0973005221991438.

[2] Ministry of Agriculture and Farmers Welfare. 2020. Formation and promotion of 10,000 farmer producer organizations (FPOs): Operational guidelines.Formation & Promotion of 10,000 FPOs Scheme Operational Guidelines in English.pdf

[3] Ministry of Agriculture and Farmers Welfare (2021). Farmer Producer Organization (FPO): Press release. New Delhi: Press Information Bureau.

[4] Onumah, G., Davis, J., Kleih, U., & Proctor, F. (2007). Empowering Smallholder Farmers in Markets: Changing Agricultural Marketing Systems and Innovative Responses by Producer Organizations. Washington, DC: World Bank.

[5] Prasad, C. S., Dutta, D., & Ravichandran, V. (2020). Issues in Policy Implementation: Insights from an E-Survey on Operational Guidelines for 10,000 FPOs. Working Paper 317. Anand: Institute of Rural Management.

[6] Rondot, P., & Collion, M. H. (2001). Agricultural Producer Organizations: Their Contribution to Rural Capacity Building and Poverty Reduction. Report of a Workshop, Washington, DC, June 28–30, 1999. Washington, DC: World Bank. http://documents.worldbank.org/curated/en/111471468740104722/pdf/multi0page.pdf.

[7] Shiferaw, B., Hellin, J., & Muricho, G. (2011). Improving market access and agricultural productivity growth in Africa: What role for producer organizations and collective action institutions? *Food Security*, 3, 475–489.

[8] Shivalingaiah, Y. N. (2020). Cluster-based business organizations—game changer in formation and promotion of FPOs. Doctoral dissertation, University of Agricultural Sciences, Bangalore.

[9] Singh, G., & Vatta, K. (2019). Assessing the economic impacts of farmer producer organizations: a case study in Gujarat, India. *Agricultural Economics Research Review*, 32(Conference Number), 139–148. https://doi.org/10.5958/0974-0279.2019.00023.5.

[10] Singh, G., Budhiraja, P., & Vatta, K. (2018). Sustainability of farmer producer organisations under agricultural value networks in India: a case of Punjab and Gujarat. *Indian Journal of Agricultural Economics*, 73(3), 70–85.

# 25 Revolutionizing financial analytics: the role of artificial intelligence in market prediction, customer retention, and churn modelling

*Bhavya Verma[1,a], Aryan Khandelwal[1,b], Pranay Nepalia[1,c], Aayushi Rajput[1,d], Aaditya Varshney[2,e], Kiran Salunke[2,f], Sugam Shivhare[2,g] and Vivekanand Bagal[2,h]*

[1]Department of Computer Science, SVKM's NMIMS, MPSTME, Shirpur, Dist. Dhule, Maharashtra, India

[2]Department of Computer Engineering, SVKM's NMIMS, MPSTME, Shirpur, Dist. Dhule, Maharashtra, India

## Abstract

In today's world, customer relationship management (CRM) analytics, real-time insights and predictions are empowered by artificial intelligence (AI) in the financial industry. This research investigates the implications of AI for financial datasets, market prediction, and customer retention at the same time concentrating on churn modelling. Machine learning prototypes, enabling AI-driven algorithms, can confirm difficult, non-linear patterns in both structured and unstructured financial data to improve credit scoring, risk assessment, and algorithmic trading. The use of alternate data sources combined with real-time updates in AI-based tools provides dynamic insights that optimize investment strategies and mitigate risks. The paper further discusses customer churn modelling in banking by examining a data set with 10,000 customers to find the most important predictors of churn. Machine learning models are used to analyze demographic, financial and behavioural factors to create an accurate classification framework. The result intends to bring illegitimate insights into financial institutions, refining customer safeguarding policies and implementing long-term development in an AI-driven monetary ecosystem.

Keywords: AI-driven risk assessment, credit scoring models, customer churn prediction, financial behaviour analysis, machine learning in finance

## Introduction

The development of artificial intelligence (AI) has been rapid, and it has brought positive changes in financial markets and institutions to improve decision-making, decreasing costs and risk management). Generative AI (GenAI) is this change that can produce complex outputs such as fraud detection insights and automated financial reports, which are very hard for traditional systems to replicate. This paper aims to establish that AI is still critical in finance and its application presents ongoing opportunities for innovation [3]. New innovations in AI such as ChatGPT and generative models have changed the way we create content, analyze data and converse with customers. The rapid adoption of ChatGPT indicates

[a]bhavyaverma435@gmail.com, [b]aryankhandelwal243@gmail.com, [c]nepaliapranay2000@gmail.com, [d]aayushirajput747@gmail.com, [e]aaditya.varshney@gmail.com, [f]kiran.salunke@nmims.edu, [g]sugam.shivhare@nmims.edu, [h]vivekanand.bagal@nmims.edu

DOI: 10.1201/9781003716648-25

the increasing importance of AI in various sectors, especially in finance where it improves customer interaction and operational processing. However, there are risks such as bias, data privacy, cyber threats and semi-transparency of decision making which requires strong governance frameworks [9]. In addition to automation, AI is also used in predictive modelling of historical and real-time data to forecast market trends, measure risks and optimize customer behaviour strategies. It facilitates algorithmic trading, portfolio management and financial risk assessments, and it facilitates the generation of artificial data and process automation [13]. With more than 95% of major banks adopting AI-based risk management, data quality, compliance, and ethics policy developments are emerging [10] AI-enabled churn modelling, which helps in customer retention by identifying potential churners and offering proactive interventions, is also becoming a reality [15]. It is therefore crucial to balance the innovation and governance of AI in finance to make it sustainable. Credit scoring and risk assessment form the backbone of any financial system. Such models are crucial in helping banks and other financial institutions determine the wealth status of individuals and businesses before they grant loans, issue credit cards, or provide other financial products. These systems have shifted from a purely traditional, rule-based approach to a data-driven one utilizing advanced artificial intelligence AI and machine learning ML algorithms. These tools have revolutionized how financial institutions evaluate credit risk, thereby dramatically affecting the lending environment [7, 17]. Table 25.1 illustrates the comparison between traditional and modern credit scoring models.

## Customary credit scoring models

The FICO score is a traditional credit scoring model that uses statistical techniques to predict the likelihood of default based on historical financial behaviour. The FICO model reviews

*Table 25.1* Comparison of traditional and modern credit scoring models.

| Model | Proposed model | Advantages | Drawbacks |
|---|---|---|---|
| **FICO Score** | Founded on credit history, payment behaviour, and credit mix. | Standardized, broadly acknowledged. | Restricted scope, eliminates real-time data. |
| **Decision Trees** | Breaches data into decision nodes to assess risk. | Easy to construe. | Susceptible to overfitting, subtle to noise. |
| **Random Forests** | Sums several DT for accuracy. | Diminishes overfitting, and high accuracy. | Computationally expensive, less interpretable. |
| **XGBoost** | Optimized gradient boosting model. | Fast, and handles sparse data well. | Involves careful tuning, computationally severe. |
| **AI-based Models** | Uses real-time, alternative data for assessment. | Dynamic, inclusive, and highly accurate. | Lacks transparency, and raises privacy concerns. |
| **Alternative Data Models** | Influences non-traditional data sources. | Profits those with limited credit history. | Regulatory and privacy challenges. |

Source: Author

five key factors: payment history (35%), amounts owed (30%), credit age (15%), new credit (10%), and credit mix (10%) to offer a standardized risk assessment tool. However, it has its restrictions; it does not incorporate real-time financial data like utility payments or rental history, thereby limiting its suitability for changing borrower profiles [1]. Logistic RRegression (LR) is also widely applied in credit risk modelling to quantify the probability of default (PD) based on historical data. Simple to use but fails to handle intricate financial activities and non-linear data relationships. However, conventional models have several major limitations, including limited data coverage, prejudice, fairness issues, and inflexibility in risk analysis [4]. In the future, advanced AI-based credit models may offer a more holistic and real-time risk assessment model.

**Contemporary credit scoring models:** Through accelerated insight, organizations and governments are able to improve services and fight fraud with the help of data analytics. They achieve efficiency, and healthcare organizations are better equipped to deliver patient care and cut costs. Future business success will be driven by innovations like IoT, blockchain, and data analytics. Borrowers' credit, income and employment history are analyzed by machine learning models for Decision Trees (DT) [12]. It refines DT to reduce variance and improve predictive accuracy on high-risk/low-risk loan classifying. GBMs and XGBoost improve accuracy by boosting and iteratively learning weak learners to model nonlinear credit risk dependencies [5, 2]. High-risk and low-risk borrowers are effectively identified by SVMs which are useful in determining the optimal separations in the multidimensional space for credit risk assessment [11].

**AI-Driven credit scoring models:** It uses real-time data to arrive at credit scoring from traditional models and therefore provides more accurate and dynamic credit analyses. Static models rely on historical behavior but AI looks at real-time financial transactions and therefore models that use fresh insights [16]. Such as social media activity, mobile or online usage, and transactions, enhance AI models which can be beneficial for people with limited credit history. However, the lack of transparency of deep learning, known as the black box effect, is an issue. SHAP and LIME techniques are proposed to enhance the interpretability to gain the AI decision-making trust of the stakeholders [8]. AI-based systems provide real-time credit ratings by constant tracking of the borrower's behaviour, and this provides the latest evaluations to the lenders. This is opposed to conventional models which are based on older financial information, hence making AI a game changer in credit risk analysis [6].

Despite advancements in AI and machine learning for credit scoring, several research gaps remain. A key issue is the interpretability of AI models, which can be addressed by developing better explainability techniques like SHAP and LIME to enhance transparency and trust. Additionally, the integration of alternative data raises privacy and ethical concerns, requiring research into frameworks that balance innovation with privacy protections and ethical considerations.

**Churn modelling and application in credit scoring:** Customer churn, the tendency of a customer to leave a financial institution, is one of the biggest challenges in the industry. Using machine learning and AI, predictive churn modelling is beneficial for banks to keep customers, decrease turnover, and increase profits. These models look at demographics, financial behaviour, accountancy activity, and service satisfaction to predict attrition. For example, customers with low balances, high levels of debt, or irregular payments are more likely to churn. Churn models traditional leverage neural networks, DT, and LR to determine behavioural trends and to quantify churn risk. Enhancement of the prediction accuracy is achieved through the application of NLP and deep learning in the analysis of unstructured data from social media and customer reviews. A case study of 10,000 bank customers is provided to show how AI-driven analytics can identify the key churn indicators that can be used for proactive retention tactics. It is important for financial institutions to maintain long-term customer relationships and business growth by predicting the insights with personalized interventions.

**Dataset overview:** This analysis is performed on the bank customer churn dataset made available by Kaggle, thus adhering to the ethical and privacy guidelines. The dataset does not reveal customer's personal identifiers but incorporates essential information in its structured format to support the churn prediction. The customer ID identifies each record while the row number is used to order the data. Although surname is provided, it is used as a reference rather than as a feature in the prediction model. Model training requires feature selection and demographic characteristics like Gender and Age can help in the understanding of the churn behavior. Tenure is a measure of how long a customer has been with the bank, while financial engagement variables such as Balance, NumOfProducts and HasCrCard give an overview of account activity. The IsActiveMember feature clearly differentiates between the active and inactive users and is therefore directly related to the churn probability. Also, EstimatedSalary can be used as an economic stability indicator. The exited variable is the target variable which classifies the customers as churned (1) and retained (0) to enable prediction for churn analysis and decision-making processes [14].

**Conceptual framework:** This study's conceptual framework as shown in Figure 25.1 classifies the key factors that cause customer to churn into three categories: demographic, financial, and behavioural factors. The model development process is divided into a clear pipeline, which starts with data collection and pre-processing, which involves inputting missing data, one-hot encoding of categorical variables, and standardization of numerical features. The feature selection keeps only the essential predictors, and the data is divided into 80-20 for training and testing purposes. For traditional credit scoring, LR is used because of its simplicity. At the same time, other machine learning models, including DT, gradient boosting (XGBoost) and SVM, improve predictive accuracy. An ensemble model based on VotingClassifier combines LR, Random Forest (RF) and XGBoost with soft voting for more accurate churn prediction. AI based dynamic scoring offers real time feedback to risk assessment. This framework improves credit assessment by incorporating non-traditional data sets (e.g. social media sites), thus enhancing financial inclusion while at the same time offering stable and data driven churn predictions that can be used to support decision making processes in financial institutions.

## Results

Figure 25.2 demonstrates the relationship between customer churn percentage and tenure by credit card ownership (HasCrCard: 0 or 1). Rate of churn is slightly higher for customers without a credit card (18.21%) than for those with one (16.80%) at tenure 7, indicating that financial features do affect retention. The overall Churn Percentage by Tenure is shown in Figure 25.3, with a decline through tenure 5, then a peak at tenure 8. This indicates that the customers in the middle are more stable than those who are new or long-time customers.

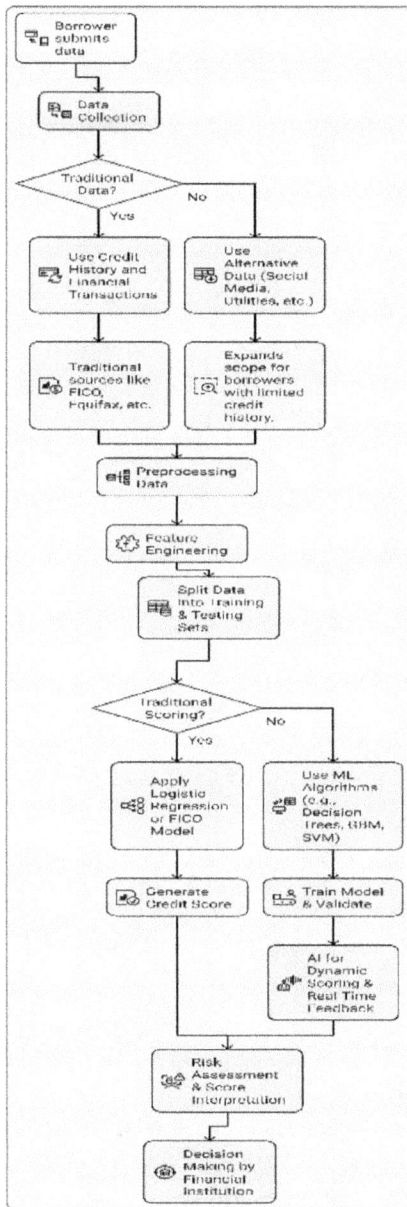

*Figure 25.1* Proposed model
Source: Author

These understandings are useful for enhancing AI-based churn prediction models that can enhance risk evaluation and credit scoring processes. Churn prediction is based on demographic and tenure-based insights, not on financial behaviour. Figure 25.3 shows churn trends by tenure: The highest initially at 24% then lowest at tenure 5 and then highest at

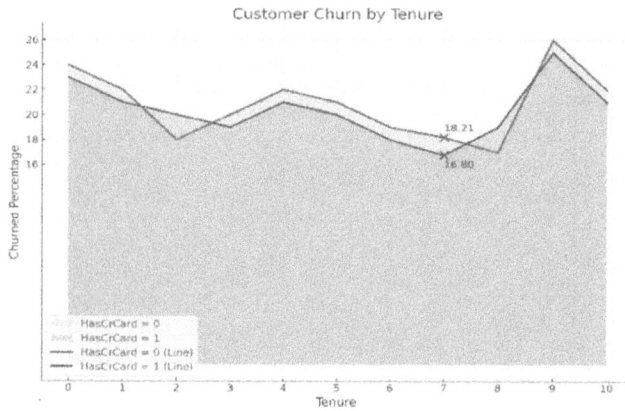

*Figure 25.2* Customer churn percentage and tenure
Source: Author

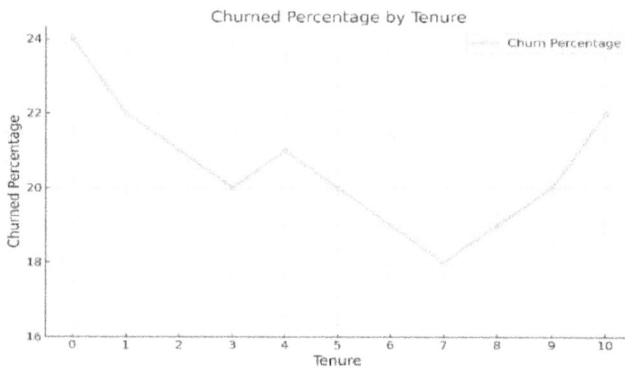

*Figure 25.3* Churn percentage by tenure
Source: Author

tenure 8, suggesting volatility at early and late tenure. This behaviour-based model helps to improve the churn predictions.

Figure 25.4 presents a credit score histogram with a concentration in the range of 600 – 800 and a sharp peak for highly creditworthy customers. The AI driven analytics improve the credit risk models, using the non-traditional data, the dynamic scoring and the personalized products, which accelerate the loan approvals and decrease the risk of default.

Figure 25.5 looks at customer activity, geography and balances. Germany has the highest mean balances while France and Spain have lower mean balances but significant variation in active vs. inactive customers. Regional strategies driven by AI can enhance customer retention, loyalty, and financial health.

The AI driven credit scoring improves loan evaluations, tenure-based retention and equitable decision making. It means risk assessment is better, customer loyalty is better encouraged, and the financially excluded such as those with sparse credit records are considered.

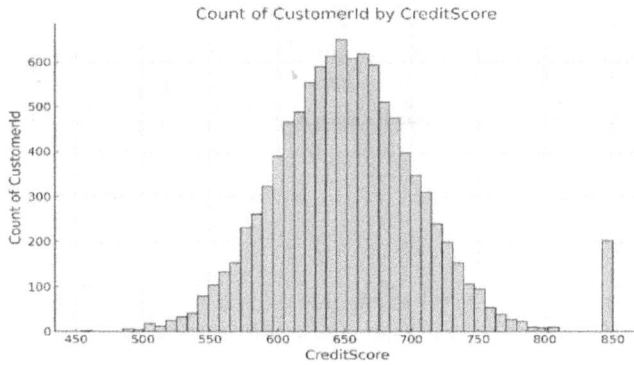

*Figure 25.4* Distribution of customer credit scores
Source: Author

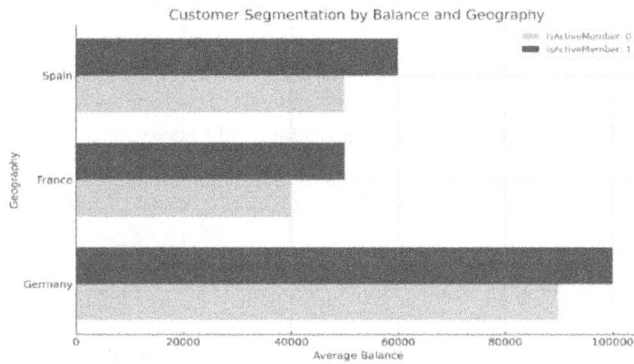

*Figure 25.5* Relationship between customer activities
Source: Author

In the analysis of traditional and modern scoring models, the proposed optimized RF model comes first with precision of 87%, which is 2.75% better than the RF model. After that, XGBoost and Ensemble models are close behind at 86%, exhibiting good predictive capability.

LR lags at 72%, having difficulty with the non-linearity. In general, tree-based models are more precise and are therefore suitable for classification tasks. The spike at a credit score of 850 indicates that it acted as a false roof rather than a real step at the end of the dataset. There is a sharp discontinuity at 850 there are no scores above it and the industry practices that indicate this is deliberate. They regard 850 as a high level of credibility and all top scorers are clustered in one category. It is also a structured limitation which is rather specific to credit rating systems than to some statistical anomaly.

## Future scope

Customer retention with AI-powered dynamic chatbots will continue to develop with NLP for easier conversation and XAI for the clarity of the process. In subsequent iterations, technology can be applied to the telecommunications, healthcare, and e-commerce sectors to improve the predictive analytics of consumer behaviour. The ability to integrate real-time learning mechanisms will allow the chatbots to grow dynamically, optimizing customer interaction management to make the retention methods more accurate and efficient in order to develop stronger relationships with the customers while upholding the principles of ethical AI and predictive modelling.

## Conclusion

The development of credit scoring and risk analysis has integrated the conventional statistical approaches and the new generation of AI and ML techniques. FICO scores and Logistic Regression are mostly used because they are easy to understand and implement, but they have limitations and restrictions regarding the availability of data. Decision Trees, Random Forest, and Gradient Boosting based AI-models are very effective at identifying patterns in data sets and making real-time risk assessments. New types of data such as data from social media or utility companies increase the availability of credit, allowing people without a traditional credit history to get credit. Future work needs to be done on the problems of black box AI, which can be unfair and non-transparent and which raise regulatory concerns. The use of the traditional approach combined with the new AI developments helps to maintain the effectiveness, fairness, and risk management of the credit ecosystem. These improvements are a contribution to the improvement of the assessment of credit worth to enhance access to financial services, minimize credit risks and define the future of financial decisions.

## References

[1]  Boukherouaa, E., & Shabsigh, G. (2023). Artificial intelligence and credit scoring: the road ahead. *Financial Services Review*, 27(2), 45–62.

[2]  Chen, T., & Guestrin, C. (2016). XGBoost: a scalable tree boosting system. In Proceedings of the 22nd ACM SIGKDD International Conference on Knowledge Discovery and Data Mining, (pp. 785–794). San Francisco, CA, USA.

[3]  Chlouverakis, K., and Ajay Rawal. (2025 ). How artificial intelligence is reshaping the financial services industry.EY CESA Financial Services 26 (2024).

[4]  Choi, H., Lee, K., & Song, M. (2023). Machine learning techniques for credit risk prediction. *Financial Risk and AI*, 5, 131–145.

[5]  Friedman, J. H. (2001). Greedy function approximation: a gradient boosting machine. *Annals of Statistics*, 29(5), 1189–1232.

[6]  Gupta, M., Verma, A., & Sharma, R. (2022). Real-time credit scoring using AI-driven transaction monitoring. *IEEE Transactions on Computational Social Systems*, 7(3), 423–432.

[7]  Liu, Z., Zhang, X., & Li, J. (2023). A comprehensive review of AI applications in credit scoring. *Journal of Financial Technology*, 12(4), 234–245.

[8]  Lundberg, S., & Lee, S.-I. (2017). A unified approach to interpreting model predictions. In Proceedings of Advances in Neural Information Processing Systems (NeurIPS), (pp. 4765–4774). Montreal, QC, Canada.

[9]  Luo, M., Liu, Y., & Hu, H. (2023). Artificial intelligence in finance: risks and opportunities. *Fintech Notes*, 2023(006), 1–12. Accessed August 2023. https://www.elibrary.imf.org.

[10] Mackintosh, J., & Quest, L. (2023 ). The Impact of AI in Financial Services. UK Finance and Oliver Wyman. November 22. Accessed November 22, 2023. https://www.ukfinance.org.uk/system/files/2023-11/The%20impact%20of%20AI%20in%20financial%20services.pdf.

[11] Pławiak, P., Abdar, M., & Acharya, U. R. (2019). Application of new deep genetic cascade ensemble of SVM classifiers to predict the Australian credit scoring. *Applied Soft Computing*, 84, 105740.

[12] Quinlan, J. R. (1986). Induction of decision trees. *Machine Learning*, 1(1), 81–106.

[13] Shabsigh, G., & Boukheroua, E. B. (2023). Generative artificial intelligence in finance: Risk considerations. International Monetary Fund, 2023. https://www.elibrary.imf.org.

[14] Sharma, K. D. (2025). Banking Churn Analysis & Modeling. Kaggle, May 2023. https://www.kaggle.com/code/kdsharma/banking-churn-analysis-modeling.

[15] Anita Edwards and Simon Lovegrove. (2025). UK Finance Report: Generative AI in Action: Opportunities & Risk Management in Financial Services. Regulation Tomorrow, January 28, 2025. https://www.regulationtomorrow.com/eu/uk finance report generative ai in action opportunities risk management in financial services/

[16] Wang, H., Chen, Y., & Lu, X. (2021). Leveraging alternative data sources for credit scoring: a machine learning approach. *IEEE Access*, 9, 51204–51214.

[17] Zhang, Y., Wang, S., & Xu, J. (2023). AI in credit risk assessment: a review of current approaches. *Journal of Finance and AI*, 8(1), 99–115.

# 26 An experimental investigation of a sliding track system for car chassis frames to reduce the severity of frontal impacts during collisions

*Sarode Pravin Laxmanrao[1,a] and Suryawanshi Sanjeev Damodar[2,b]*

[1]Department of Mechanical Engineering, R C Patel Institute of Technology, Shirpur, Maharashtra, India

[2]Department of Mechanical Engineering, S.S.V.P.'s B.S. Deore College of Engineering, Dhule, Maharashtra, India

## Abstract

Vehicle safety has emerged as a major concern, new technologies and strategies aimed at reducing both the incidence and severity of accidents via active and passive safety systems. Active safety systems aim to avoid collisions, whereas passive safety systems safeguard occupants after accidents by reducing impact forces and reducing injury risks. New Car Assessment Programs (NCAP) have been established to examine vehicle crash performance and issue ratings based on test results, thereby improving vehicle safety. This research focuses on the role of the vehicle chassis frame in occupant protection and highlights the need for further investigation into passive safety systems and chassis frame modifications to improve occupant safety. The innovative chassis frame developed in this study demonstrates substantial benefits, including a reduction in acceleration and a decrease in impact force on occupants Additionally, the time of impact is prolonged by approximately 3.5 to 5 times compared to conventional crash times. The seat assembly, mounted on a sliding frame, effectively keeps occupants away from the vehicle's rigid internal components by 0.018 to 0.140 meters during accidents. The design of this innovative chassis offers several societal benefits, including enhanced safety, improved impact absorption, technological innovation, and long-term cost savings. Notably, its structure is adaptable to both conventional internal combustion engine vehicles and new technology vehicles, such as electric vehicles. This adaptability underscores the potential for widespread implementation and contributes significantly to societal well-being by reducing casualties in vehicle accidents.

**Keywords:** Accidents, chassis, frame, injury, safety, vehicle

## Introduction

A vehicle traveling at high velocity possesses substantial kinetic energy. In the occurrence of an accident, this energy must be converted into an alternative form [47]. To avert accidents, brakes are engaged, transforming kinetic energy into thermal energy [8]. However, if the vehicle collides with a stiff surface or wall, the front section must be configured to dissipate this energy [2, 5]. Crumple zones are engineered into the front part of the car chassis to absorb and dissipate energy during a collision [27]. Crumple zones are intentionally positioned to distort upon impact, absorbing collision forces and safeguarding the occupants therein. Without these crumple zones and a well-designed chassis frame, the impact

[a]pravinsarodercpit@gmail.com, [b]sanjeevsuryawanshi1@gmail.com

DOI: 10.1201/9781003716648-26

of a collision could result in devastating consequences for the occupants of the vehicle [3]. Therefore, the design and construction of car chassis frames play a critical role in ensuring the safety of vehicle occupants in the event of an accident. to manage this energy absorption [10]. These zones collapse and deform upon a collision, causing metal components to bend and crumple, releasing energy. The goal of this design strategy is to lessen the severity of the deceleration experienced by prolonging the impact's length [4]. In the end, this reduces the force applied to the car's occupants, lowering the possibility of fatalities or major injuries. The chassis frame not only has crumple zones, but it also gives the car structural integrity and stability, which helps keep its shape and keeps people inside from being crushed in an accident.

*Enhancing vehicle safety through sliding track mechanism for improved impact management*

This study suggests developing a scaled model of vehicle chassis frame to mitigate impact severity [36]. The proposed design integrates sliding chassis frame, guided springs and solid dampers to effectively absorb impact energy and includes a locking mechanism alongside to minimize the repulsive forces generated during a collision, as stated by Newton's first law of motion [6]. This forward momentum can cause occupants to collide with structural components inside the vehicle, such as the steering wheel, windshield, and dashboard, leading to severe injuries. Even though crumple zones, airbags, and seat belts have been put in place, accidents still happen. To solve this problem, a new chassis frame has been created that is meant to make impacts last longer and keep people away from hitting the rigid parts inside the car [45].

The above diagram illustrates a comparative study between conventional and developed chassis frames in the context of vehicular accidents. The four figures within the diagram depict the following scenarios Figure 26.1(a): A conventional vehicle chassis frame,

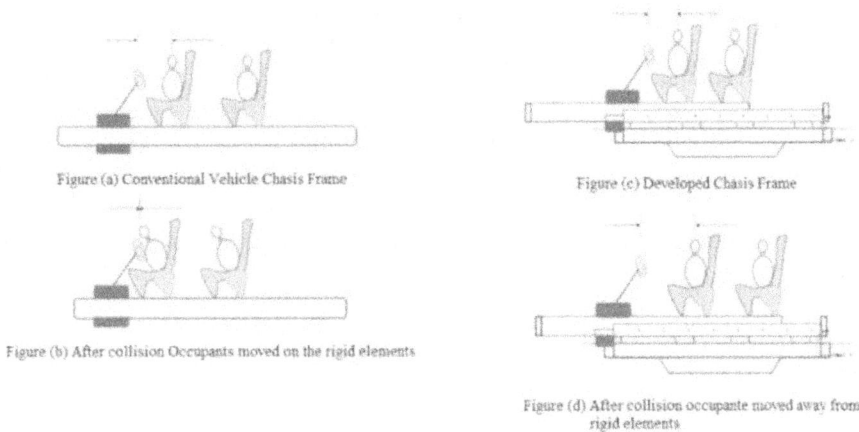

Figure (a) Conventional Vehicle Chasis Frame

Figure (b) After collision Occupants moved on the rigid elements

Figure (c) Developed Chasis Frame

Figure (d) After collision occupants moved away from rigid elements

*Figure 26.1* Comparison of fig a, b, c, d indicates the difference between conventional and developed chassis frame in case of accident
Source: Author

showcasing the typical arrangement of rigid elements and occupant positions. Figure 26.1(b): The same conventional chassis frame after a collision, highlighting how occupants are displaced and potentially impacted by rigid elements. Figure 26.1(c): A developed chassis frame, designed with enhanced safety features with sliding frame where occupant positioned on sliding frame Figure 26.1(d): The developed chassis frame after a similar collision, demonstrating how occupants are better protected and moved away from rigid elements. In the conventional chassis frame, occupants are likely to be displaced towards rigid elements, such as the dashboard or steering wheel, increasing the risk of severe injuries [29]. The developed chassis frame incorporates sliding frame with solid dampers that redirect or absorb impact energy, minimizing occupant displacement and reducing the likelihood of contact with potentially harmful structures [7].

*Research problem and objectives*
Approximately one-third of global road traffic fatalities involve passenger car occupants, with at least 56% of these fatalities resulting from frontal collisions [31]. Identifying critical injury zones is essential for regulators and automobile manufacturers to design safer vehicles [25]. The vehicle chassis plays a vital role in the overall structure of a vehicle [13]. To minimize the severity of accidents, it is essential to incorporate an impact energy-absorbing system within the chassis [50]. Modifying the structure of the vehicle chassis frame can help to achieve this objective, as it can reduce the impact's severity [23, 39]. By developing a vehicle chassis frame that can efficiently absorb impact energy, specifically for frontal impact. After the literature reviewed some of the objectives developed as follows as follows. Objectives: 1. The objective is to create a model of the vehicle chassis frame that will minimize the intensity of the frontal impact force on the occupant by creating a gap between the internal rigid barrier of the vehicle and the occupants in the event of a collision. 2. The objective is to develop a scaled model of the proposed chassis frame and establish an experimental setup to examine the results. 3. The objective is to conduct a numerical analysis of a designed model using sophisticated modelling and analysis software. Limitations and delimitations to conduct crash tests. Conducting crash tests at an institute level has several limitations, some of which include: Cost: Crash tests are often expensive and require a significant investment in equipment, materials, and personnel [20]. This can limit the ability of institutes to conduct regular or frequent tests. Space constraints: Crash tests require a large amount of space to set up and conduct, and many institutes may not have access to the necessary facilities [12]. Techniques used to overcome constrains. • Cost: To overcome the cost a small-scale model of Vehicle chassis frame (1:5) is developed to conduct experimental investigation. The length and width of the typical vehicle in the small category is used to derive the scale.

## Literature Review

*The role of chassis frames in vehicle dynamics*
The vehicle chassis plays a crucial role in crash safety by absorbing and distributing collision energy [13]. A well-designed chassis frame maintains the passenger compartment's integrity, reducing injury risks [38]. Recent advancements include using high-strength materials and computer-aided engineering to enhance chassis performance. The frontal

portion of the vehicle is designed to absorb kinetic energy during accidents [37]. Materials like aluminium and composites are increasingly used for their energy absorption capabilities [43]. Common injury sources in crashes include the door, roof, B-pillar, and steering assembly [15]. These components can cause severe injuries depending on the crash type and vehicle structure.

*Evaluating the effectiveness of current safety features*
It refers to the process of assessing how well existing safety features perform in real-world crash scenarios. Airbags, seat belts, and electronic stability control are evaluated for safety [29, 22]. This review will determine how successfully these safety features protect car occupants and prevent crash injuries. Crash tests and data analysis were used to evaluate safety measures in various crash scenarios [21]. Crash tests may involve frontal, side impact, rollover, and dummy tests for different vehicle occupant sizes and ages [14, 24]. The evaluation procedure considers crash speed and force, occupant injuries, and the effectiveness of safety measures like airbags and seat belts [16]. Safety features' performance and areas for improvement are assessed using this data.

*A critical analysis of current solution limitations and future research opportunities.*
Active and passive safety systems in vehicles receive varying levels of research attention, with passive systems being less explored [16]. Passive safety systems are crucial for mitigating collision effects by protecting occupants from vehicle components [44, 1]. Despite their importance, there is a shortage of research in enhancing passive systems, presenting an opportunity for advancement. Current safety features like airbags and seatbelts are insufficient to significantly reduce injury severity [26]. Developing innovative chassis designs, such as scaled frames with sliding mechanisms, could improve crashworthiness [48]. Addressing this research gap could lead to more comprehensive safety solutions and improved vehicle safety standards.

## Methodology

*Development of scaled model*
A 1:5 scaled model is created for experimentation. A small-scale model before a prototype is a cost-effective, safe, convenient, and accurate technique to test and verify a concept. Dimensional analysis and similitude can help engineers construct the full-scale prototype by confirming that the small-scale model's results are representative of the full-scale prototype's behaviour [32, 33]. These scaled models also have limitations like cost and Space which directly affect the ability to perform realistic, full-scale crash tests [35]. 1. Cost: Performing full-scale crash tests involves significant expenses related to equipment, materials, and personnel. 2. Space constraints: Crash tests require a substantial amount of space for setup and execution.

*Experimental setup*
The scaled model includes a chassis frame consisting of four main components: a base frame, a sliding frame, a solid damper, and a locking mechanism. An innovative chassis frame is constructed using a ladder-type design. The energy produced during accidents is

utilized to decrease the intensity of the impact by extending the duration of the collision, Witteman [50] specifically by expanding the length of the crumple zone [42]. Extending the duration of the accident decreases the force experienced by the occupants. A shorter deceleration pulse indicates a more severe crash, while a longer pulse corresponds to a less severe crash [41]. The crash pulse is represented as a time dependent curve of acceleration, and these parameters are recorded during crash tests [11]. The shape, duration, and peak acceleration of the crash pulse can be used to predict the severity of occupant injuries. The crashworthiness of a vehicle structure can also be analysed using crash pulse characteristics measured during crash tests [16]. Understanding the crash pulse allows for a direct correlation between energy variations during impact and the resulting occupant injuries [49]. The vehicle's crash pulse demonstrates a significant relationship with head and chest injuries sustained by occupants. By reducing the severity of crash pulses, the extent of occupant injuries can be minimized [41, 51]. The chassis frame is designed to lower the crash pulse's magnitude to a level that mitigates the risk of serious injury to occupants during a collision. Constraints in simulating frontal impact tests as per global norm of conducting crash test speed limits have been specified for all type for crash test [17] (Ambati et al., 2012a) [1]. As per Global New Car Assessment Program (GNCAP) the frontal impact test is typically conducted at a speed of 64 km/h (17.77 m/s) [17]. The Bharat New Car Assessment Program (BNCAP) is an Indian version of the New Car Assessment Program (NCAP). It is also recommending a speed of 64 km/h (17.77 m/s) for the frontal impact test (AIS197 2023). Undertaking such intricate crash tests involves significant complexity and expense. The formation of an impact with a velocity of 17.77 m/s, equivalent to 64 km/h, is not possible within a laboratory setting. A technique is employed to generate an effect utilizing a pendulum [46, 18]. A pendulum with a height of 16.09 meters is required to generate an impact of 17.77 m/s. The above-mentioned approach is not viable. Instead, a pendulum with a length of 2.68 meters and a bob mass of 21.6 kg is utilized for the purpose of experimentation. Performing full-scale crash tests with modern sensors and equipment demands extensive infrastructure and a well-established testing facility, making this approach impractical [19, 28]. Consequently, experiments are conducted using a scaled model of chassis frame, with

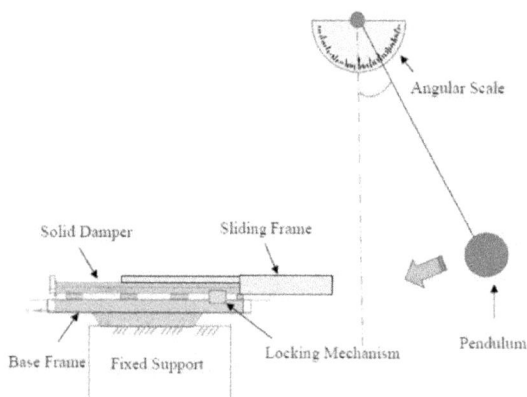

*Figure 26.2* Schematic diagram representing test set up for impact test
Source: Author

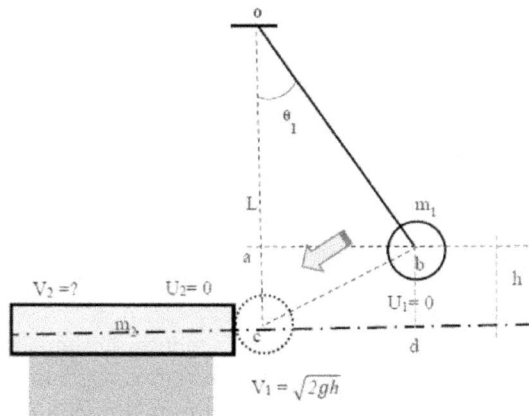

*Figure 26.3* Pendulum length in relation to maximum velocity
Source: Author

impact forces generated using a pendulum [40]. The thickness of the extruded rectangular hollow sections used in the scaled model varies between 1.6 mm and 2.0 mm, depending on the section, as determined by market availability.

The scaled model prototype is fabricated using arc welding, employing rectangular hot-formed structural steel pipes in accordance with IS 4923:1997 (IS 4923: 2009 2009). A scaled prototype of the fundamental chassis structure was developed and subjected to full frontal impact testing; a pendulum was employed to produce the impact force. Certain publications utilize an impact testing machine (ITM) to produce impact force for crash testing [9]. According to NCAP simulations, in most countries, a full-frontal crash impacts the vehicle at 56 kph (35 mph), while in some countries, GNCAP measures the impact test speed at 64 kph against a rigid wall to measure the deceleration pulse. In the present study, a series of impact forces are generated using a pendulum impact. By subjecting the pendulum to varying inclinations and releasing it, velocities and impact forces are achieved in the same direction. The experimental parameters include an inclination range spanning from 10 degrees to 60 degrees. The velocity of the pendulum's striking is determined through both analytical and experimental means. Analytical and experimental comparisons are made between displacement and change in velocity, Impulse, acceleration. The model of the chassis frame has been subjected to impact testing. The developed chassis frame consists of a base frame, sliding frame, solid damper, and locking mechanism. A crash test is conducted on the designed chassis frame using a dynamic pendulum with a weight of 21.6 kg and length 2.68 meters as shown in figure. The force of impact is generated by the dynamic pendulum. The initial positioning of the sliding frame of the chassis frame being examined is slightly forward over the base frame. When a collision occurs, the mobile frame undergoes a sliding motion through the tacks of the fixed base frame.

*Data collection and analysis methodology*
Data acquisition: In this study, key parameters like force, acceleration, and displacement arising from the impact of a pendulum on a chassis frame were investigated. To accurately

measure these parameters, a variety of sensors were employed. A Load Cell paired with an HX711 circuit was used to determine the impact force during crash tests, while a force resistive sensor (FRS) provided supplementary force measurements [34]. Displacement of the chassis frame due to impact was quantified using an ultrasonic sensor, which measured the distance the frame moved [6]. To capture the acceleration resulting from the pendulum's impact, an accelerometer sensor was utilized [34]. All sensor data were processed through an Arduino Uno board, ensuring precise and synchronized data collection throughout the experiments.

*Experimental evaluation of the sliding chassis frame for impact force reduction*

The auxiliary sliding frame mounted on the chassis frame is used to reduce the impact force and a solid damper sets return. The law of conservation of momentum is applied to estimate impact force and velocity [30, 37]. In the experiment, a pendulum's bob is released from 10° to 60° inclination to impact the sliding frame. The velocity of the sliding frame is determined by first calculating the bob's velocity. The experiment evaluates displacement, velocity, acceleration, and momentum for different release angles. The sliding frame's displacement is measured for each impact at various angles.

## Results

*Solid damper D0 experimental readings*

Main components of solid damper $D_0$ spring: A coiled metal spring, made of steel, forms the base of each device. It's compressed and exerting an upward force or apposite force. Metal inline rod: A rigid metal rod with base is passed through the spring and all cone structures. Conical sections: Multiple conical sections are stacked on top of each other, forming a tapered structure. These sections are made of soft materials, like aluminium.

Displacements of the sliding frame with damper $D_0$ were from 0.018m to 0.086 m as the pendulum was released from 10° to 60°. Compressed under impact, the cone into cone damper assembly reduced acceleration (13–91 m/s²) and force (268–1875 N). The crash scenarios will be compared with the fixed frame and these findings. Design of the damper severely limited impact forces and acceleration. The graph in Figure 26.7 compares the force on a fixed frame and a sliding frame ($D_0$) across inclination angles. Inclination (°) is on the x axis, and force (N) on y axis. The graph includes experimental and analysis results

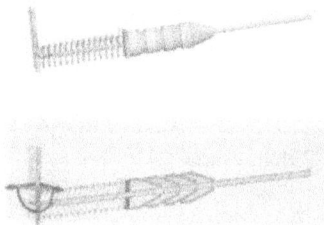

$D_0$- Damper Assembly

*Figure 26.4* Damper $D_0$ assembly
Source: Author

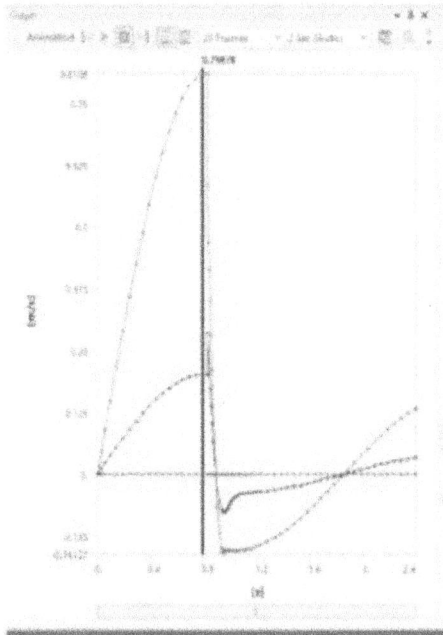

*Figure 26.5* Directional velocity for sliding frame with damper $D_0$ ($10^0$ impact)
Source: Author

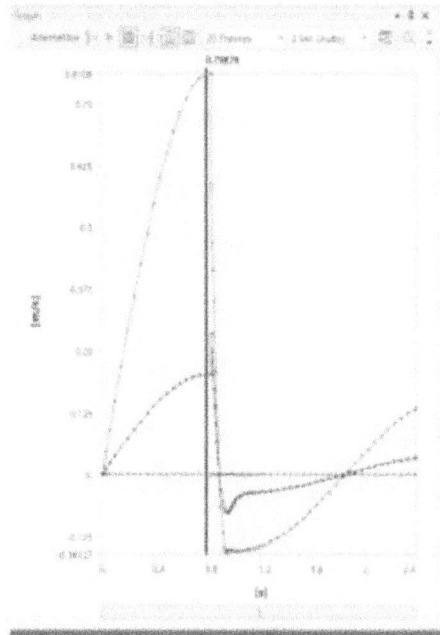

*Figure 26.6* Acceleration profile for sliding frame with damper $D_0$ ($10^0$ impact)
Source: Author

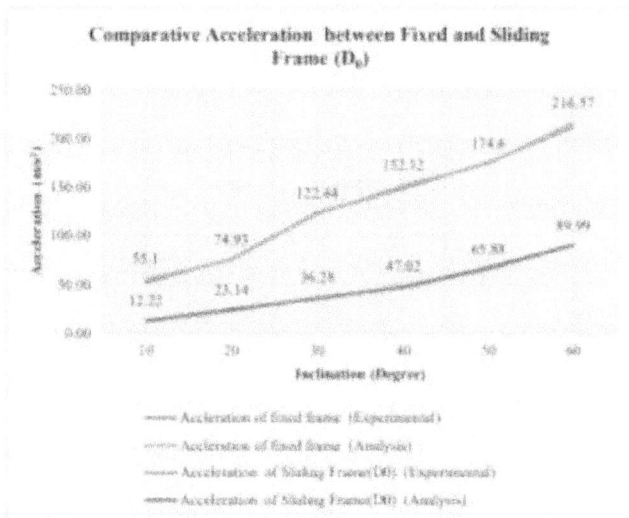

*Figure 26.7* Acceleration profile for sliding frame with damper D0 comparative with fixed frame (experimental +analysis)
Source: Author

on both frames and demonstrates that force increases with inclination. With the damper ($D_0$) the force exerted on the sliding frame will be lower because of the damper absorbing impact energy making the force lower.

*Solid damper D1 experimental readings*

Main components of solid damper $D_1$ are spring: A coiled metal spring, made of steel, forms the base of each device. It's compressed and exerting an upward force or apposite force. Metal inline rod: A rigid metal rod with base is passed through the spring and all cone structures. $D_1$- Damper assembly conical sections: Multiple conical sections are stacked on top of each other, forming a tapered structure. These sections are made of soft materials, like

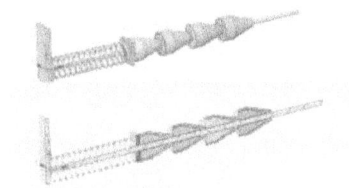

$D_1$- Damper Assembly

*Figure 26.8* Damper $D_1$ assembly
Source: Author

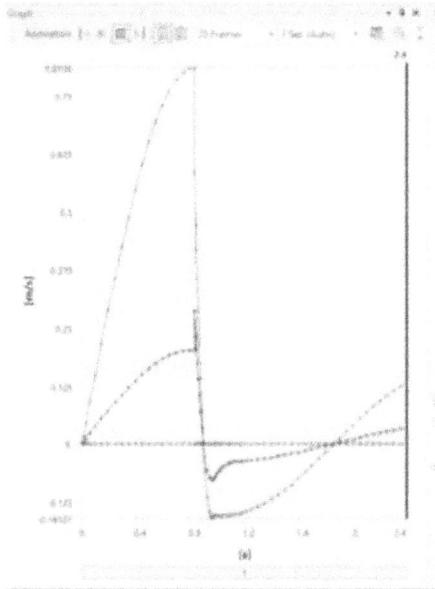

*Figure 26.9* Directional velocity for sliding frame with damper $D_1$ ($10^0$ impact)
Source: Author

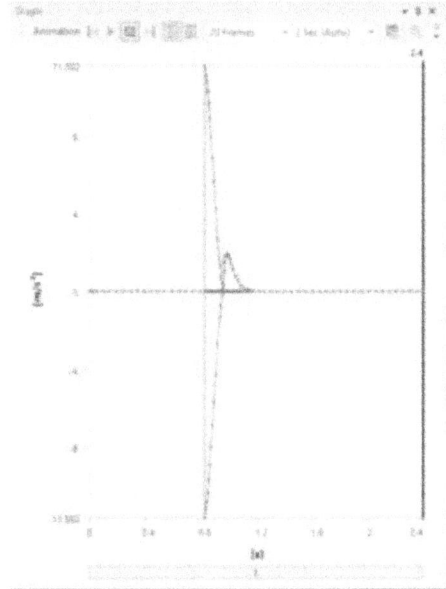

*Figure 26.10* Acceleration profile for sliding frame with damper $D_1$ ($10^0$ impact)
Source: Author

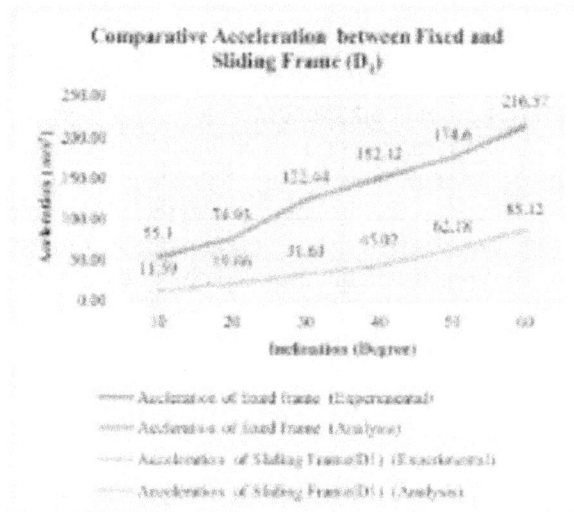

*Figure 26.11* Acceleration profile for sliding frame with damper D1 comparative with fixed frame (experimental +analysis)

Source: Author

aluminium. Inside rubber cone: Rubber cones are interspersed between the conical sections. The spring and conical sections and rubber cones work together to absorb and dissipate energy from impacts.

The displacement of the sliding frame with damper $D_1$ varied from 0.019 m to 0.092 m, depending on release angle of the pendulum from 10° to 60°. The compression under impact was achieved with this cone-into cone with rubber cone assembly i.e., compression of the assembly was obtained through impact, reducing acceleration (12–87 m/s²) and force (247–1732 N). The interpretations of crash scenarios based on these findings will be compared against the fixed frame. The impact forces and accelerations of the damper were well reduced by the design. The analysis of the sliding frame with damper $D_1$ was performed using the ANSYS rigid dynamics module. The results show that at a 10-degree inclination, the impact force is 234 N, with acceleration at 11 m/s² and displacement at 0.017 meters. At a 60° inclination, the impact force increases to 1724 N, with acceleration reaching 85 m/s² and displacement extending to 0.087 meters. The damper $D_1$ incorporates aluminium cones with an inner rubber cone, stacked with a coil spring. This design effectively absorbs impact energy through friction generated during the compression of the aluminium and rubber components, resulting in the observed reductions in both impact force and acceleration.

*Solid damper D2 experimental readings*

Main components of solid damper $D_2$ spring: A coiled metal spring, made of steel, forms the base of each device. It's compressed and exerting an upward force. Metal inline rod: A rigid metal rod with base is passed through the spring and all cone structures. Conical sections: Multiple conical sections are stacked on top of each other, forming a tapered structure. These sections are made of soft materials, like aluminium. $D_2$- Damper assembly 124

inside rubber cone: Rubber cones are interspersed with little extended length between the conical sections. The spring and conical sections and extended rubber cones work together to absorb and dissipate energy from impacts.

When the pendulum was let go at (10° to 60°) the sliding frame attached with damper $D_2$ showed displacements from 0.024m to 0.130m. Compression under impact was enabled by the cone into cone with extended rubber cone assembly which reduced acceleration (12–87 m/s²) and force (247–1732 N). The findings will be compared to the fixed frame in terms of the analysis of the crash scenarios. Design of the damper minimizes impact forces and acceleration to a large extent. The graph in Figure 26.15 compares the acceleration of a fixed frame and a sliding frame ($D_2$) across inclination angles. In the x-axis we have inclination (°), in the y axis acceleration (m/s²). Experimental and analysis results

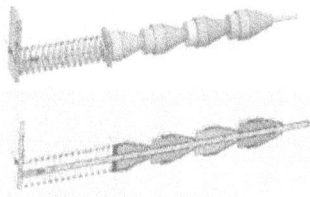

*Figure 26.12* Damper $D_2$ assembly
Source: Author

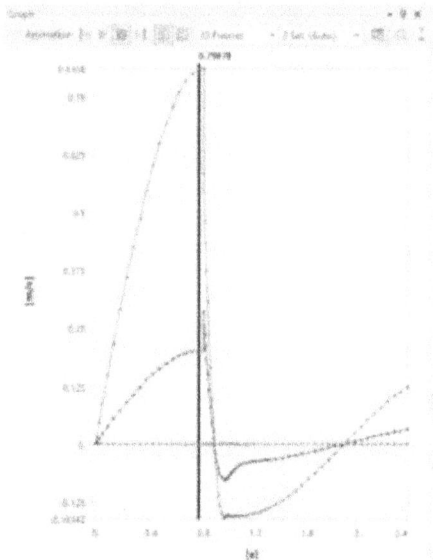

*Figure 26.13* Directional velocity for sliding frame with damper $D_2$ (10° impact)
Source: Author

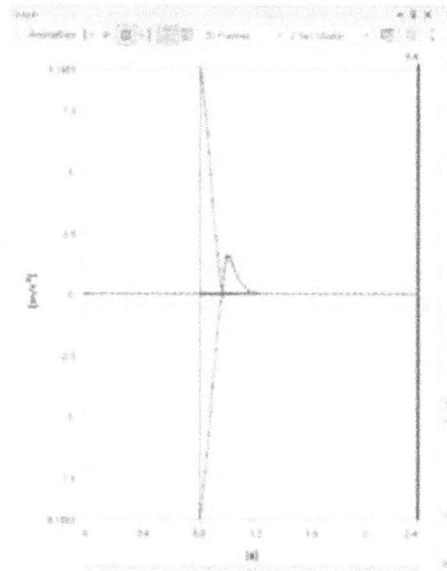

*Figure 26.14* Acceleration profile for sliding frame with damper $D_2$ (10⁰ impact)
Source: Author

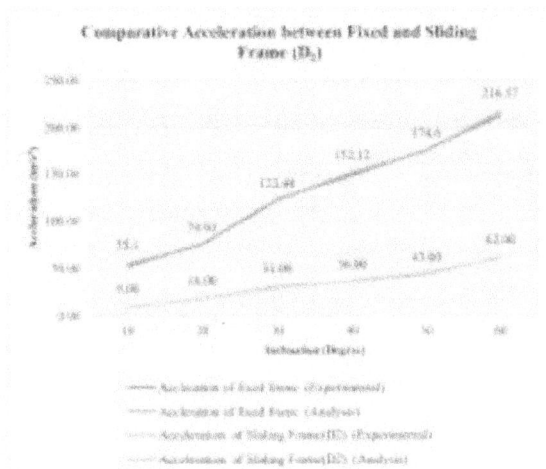

*Figure 26.15* Acceleration profile for sliding frame with damper D2 comparative with fixed frame (experimental +analysis)
Source: Author

for both frames are included, which indicates less acceleration in the sliding frame when damper $D_2$ is used. The damper takes up the impact energy to reduce the sliding frame's acceleration.

**Solid damper $D_3$ experimental readings**

Main components of solid damper $D_3$ **spring:** A coiled metal spring, made of steel, forms the base of each device. It's compressed and exerted an upward or opposite force. Metal inline rod: A metal rod with a fixed base is inserted through the cylindrical rubber stacks. Cylindrical rubber sections: A cylindrical structure is created by stacking many cylindrical sections vertically. These pieces are constructed from rubber with low density. $D_3$- Damper assembly intermediate rubber rings: High-density rubber rings are inserted between two low density rubber cylindrical pieces. These rubber components collaborate to effectively absorb and disperse energy resulting from impacts.

The displacement of the sliding frame equipped with damper $D_3$ under pendulum impact was recorded, ranging from 0.021 meters to 0.156 meters as the pendulum was released from inclinations of $10^0$ degrees to $60^0$ degrees. The rubber cylinders stack assembly of the damper effectively eased the movement of the sliding frame, enabling its compression under the impact load to a large extent. As the pendulum was released from 10°–60°, the pendulum accelerated from 11 to 53 m/s² and forced from 218 to 1022 N to the sliding frame with damper $D_3$ shows in Figure 26.19. Compression under impact was made possible using the damper which helped reduce acceleration and force to a significant extent. A comparison is then made with the fixed frame. Acceleration between fixed and sliding frames ($D_3$) is shown in the graph as a function of angle of inclination for the graph and x axis is the inclination (°) and the y axis is acceleration (m/s²). Experimental and analysis results are presented for both frames in the graph.

*Discussion of how the results impact the enhancement of car chassis frame design*
Results of the analysis indicate that sliding frames with dampers experiences much less damage in terms of the impact force, acceleration and displacement than fixed frame. Dampers $D_0$ and $D_1$ can reduce impact force and acceleration, $D_1$ is slightly more effective in force reduction. Damper $D_2$ has a balanced performance with good energy absorption at higher inclinations. Cylindrical rubber stacks within Damper $D_3$ enable maximum energy absorption and displacement, as well as the maximum force reduction and acceleration, especially at 60 degrees. On average, all dampers have a positive effect on sliding frame

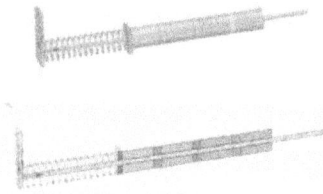

$D_3$- Damper Assembly

*Figure 26.16* Damper $D_3$ assembly
Source: Author

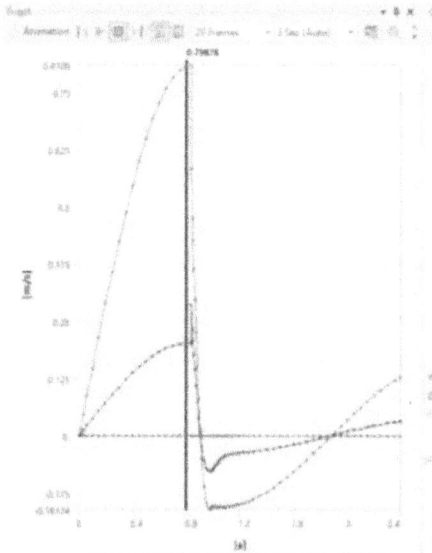

*Figure 26.17* Directional velocity for sliding frame with damper $D_3$ ($10^0$ impact)
Source: Author

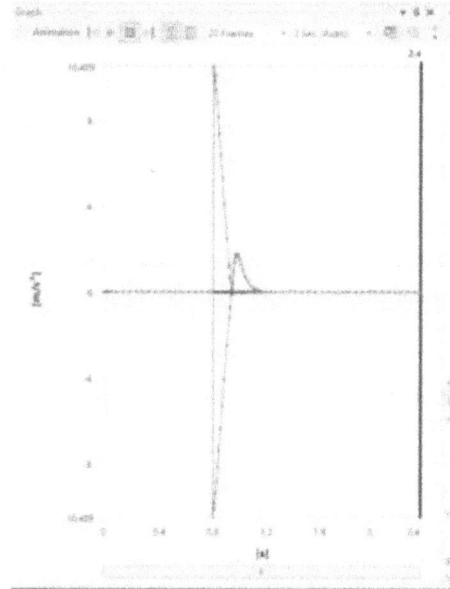

*Figure 26.18* Acceleration profile for sliding frame with damper $D_3$ ($10^0$ impact)
Source: Author

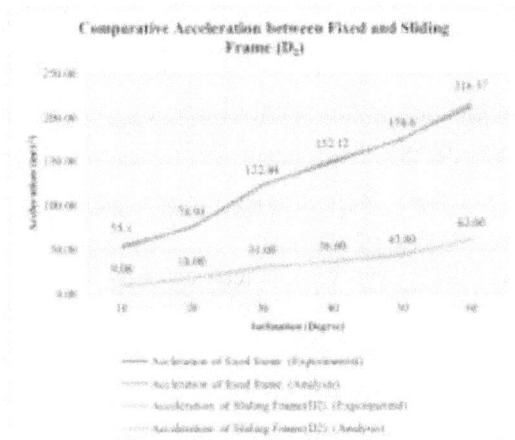

*Figure 26.19* Acceleration profile for sliding frame with damper D3 comparative with fixed frame (experimental +analysis)

Source: Author

performance, with damping $D_3$ showing the most promising in reducing the impact force and head acceleration.

## Discussion

In this study, the dynamic responses of a fixed frame and four sliding frames equipped with different dampers ($D_0$, $D_1$, $D_2$, and $D_3$) were evaluated, subjected to pendulum impacts at inclinations ranging from 10°–60°. The key parameters analysed include impact force, acceleration, and displacement. These parameters are critical for assessing the effectiveness of each damper system in mitigating the forces transmitted to the frame and improving the overall impact absorption capability.

## Conclusion

### Summary of the key findings from the study

The percentage of reduction in acceleration is about 58–78%. The percentage of reduction in impact force on occupants is 58–77%. Time of impact is prolonged by. Approximately 3.5–5 times more than conventional crash time: As the seat assembly is mounted on sliding frame. in an event of accidents, it keeps occupant away from inside rigid parts of vehicle by approximately .018 meters to 0.140 meters. The structure of this innovative chassis is so designed that it can be adopted by conventional (IC engine vehicles) as well as new technology vehicles (electric vehicles) as well

### Discussion of the importance of research for the field of automotive engineering

The innovative chassis frame developed in this research work offers substantial benefits to society by reducing casualties in vehicle accidents. Here are some ways in which it contributes to societal well-being.

**Enhanced safety:** The innovative chassis frame design enhances occupant safety by extending impact duration, reducing acceleration by 58–78%, and lowering impact forces by 58–77%.

**Impact absorption:** It incorporates solid dampers and a sliding frame to absorb and dissipate crash energy, minimizing injury risks by creating a crucial buffer zone between occupants and rigid vehicle components.

**Technological innovation:** This versatile design integrates seamlessly into both ICE and EVs, significantly improving vehicle safety.

**Long-term cost savings:** Additionally, it reduces long-term societal costs by lowering medical expenses, insurance claims, and emergency response burdens, ultimately contributing to overall road safety and well-being.

## References

[1]   Guide, A., & We, L. (1998). Objectives and experience of publishing crash-tests results in a european magazin. In Pageot, N. (Ed.), 16th International Conference on the Enhanced Safety of Vehicles, (pp. 2454–2461). Ontario Canada: Road Safety and Motor Vehicle Regulation Transport Canada. https://www-nrd.nhtsa.dot.gov/departments/esv/16th/.

[2]   Ambati, T., Srikanth, K. V. N. S., & Veeraraju, P. (2012a). Simulation of vehicular frontal crash-test. *International Journal of Applied Research in Mechanical Engineering*, 2(1), 262–267. https://doi.org/10.47893/ijarme.2012.1047.

[3]   Kullgren, A., Ydenius, A., & Tingvall, C. (1998). Frontal Impacts With Small Partial Overlap : Real Life Data From Crash Recorders. In Pageot, N. (Ed.), 16th International Conference on the Enhanced Safety of Vehicles, (pp. 259–265). Ontario Canada: Road Safety and Motor Vehicle Regulation Transport Canada. https://www-nrd.nhtsa.dot.gov/departments/esv/16th/.

[4]   Barrimi, M., Aalouane, R., Aarab, C., Hafidi, H., Baybay, H., Soughi, M., et al. (2013). The automotive body Vol-2 (system design). *Encephale*, 53, 485–503. http://dx.doi.org/10.1016/j.encep.2012.03.001.

[5]   Pipkorn, B., & Ericsson, M. (2011). Safety and vision impovements by expandable a-pillars. In 22th International Conference on the Enhanced Safety of Vehicles. Washington DC, USA: U.S. Department of Transportation National Highway Traffic Safety Administration (NHTSA). https://www-esv.nhtsa.dot.gov/Proceedings/22/isv7/main.htm.

[6]   Breed, D. S., & Summers, L. (2001). Development of an occupant position sensor system to improve frontal crash protection. In 17th International Conference on the Enhanced Safety of Vehicles. Amsterdam: U.S. Department of Transportation National Highway Traffic Safety Administration (NHTSA). https://www-nrd.nhtsa.dot.gov/departments/esv/17th/.

[7]   Brumbelow, M. L., & Zuby, D. S. (2009). Impacts and injury patterns in frontal crashes of vehicles with good ratings for frontal crash protection. In The 21st International Technical Conference on the Enhaced Safety of Vehicles (ESV), (pp. 1–13).

[8]   Chen, W. (2011). Thermal analysis on the cooling performance of a wet porous evaporative plate for building. *Energy Conversion and Management*, 52(5), 2217–2226. https://doi.org/10.1016/J.ENCONMAN.2010.12.029.

[9]   Cheruvu, K., & Deb, A. (2011). Crashworthiness of aluminium structures - an illustration through scaled model. *International Journal of Aerospace Innovations*, 3(3), 143–151. https://doi.org/10.1260/1757-2258.3.3.143.

[10]  Deb, A. (2010). Crashworthiness Design Issues for Lightweight Vehicles. Materials, Design and Manufacturing for Lightweight Vehicles. Woodhead Publishing Limited. https://doi.org/10.1533/9781845697822.2.332.

[11] Deb, A., & Naravane, A. (2006). An improved representation of vehicle incompatibility in frontal NCAP tests using a modified rigid barrier. *International Journal of Crashworthiness*, 11(1), 13–25. https://doi.org/10.1533/ijcr.2005.0380.

[12] Deb, A., Cheruvu, K. S., & Mahendrakumar, M. S. (2004). Energy-based criteria for crashworthiness design of aluminum intensive space frame vehicles. SAE Technical Papers. https://doi.org/10.4271/2004-01-1521.

[13] Radhakrishna, D. V., & Gurmukhdas, M. A. (2015). Experimental Investigation of a Inimitable Platform on Heavy Vehicle Chassis. *International Journal of Scientific & Engineering Research (IJSER)*, 6(6), June 2015, 680-686.

[14] Nohr, M., & Blume, K. H. (2009). Crash adaptive vehicle structures and components. In 21Th International Conference on the Enhanced Safety of Vehicles. Stuttgart, Germany: U.S. Department of Transportation National Highway Traffic Safety Administration (NHTSA). https://www-nrd.nhtsa.dot.gov/departments/esv/21st/.

[15] Grattan, E., & Clegg, N. G. (1973). Clinical causes of death in different categories of road user. Proceedings of the 1973 International Research Committee on Biokinetics of Impacts (IRCOBI) Conference, Amsterdam, The Netherlands, pp. 143–154. International Research Committee on Biokinetics of Impacts (IRCOBI).

[16] Eichberger, A., Wallner, D., Hirschberg, W., & Cresnik, R. (2009). A situation based method to adapt the vehicle restraint system in frontal crashes to the accident scenario. In 21th International Conference on the Enhanced Safety of Vehicles. Stuttgart , Germany: U.S. Department of Transportation National Highway Traffic Safety Administration (NHTSA). https://www-nrd.nhtsa.dot.gov/departments/esv/21st/.

[17] Euro NCAP (2015). Full width frontal impact testing protocol. Euro NCAP Testing Protocols 1.0.2 (April), 1–29. https://cdn.euroncap.com/media/20872/full-width-frontal-impact-test-protocol-v102.pdf.

[18] Gabauer, D. J., Kusano, K. D., Marzougui, D., Opiela, K., Hargrave, M., & Gabler, H. C. (2010). Pendulum testing as a means of assessing the crash performance of longitudinal barrier with minor damage. *International Journal of Impact Engineering*, 37(11), 1121–1137. https://doi.org/10.1016/j.ijimpeng.2010.03.003.

[19] Consolazio, G. R., Groetaers, M., & Innocent, D. (2016). Pendulum Impact Testing of Metallic, Non-Metallic, and Hybrid Sign Posts (FHWA/FL/13-4995-04, 276 pages). University of Florida, Department of Civil & Coastal Engineering. U.S. Department of Transportation, Federal Highway Administration.

[20] Lutter, G., Appel, H., Seeck, A., & Friedel, B. (1998). Philosopy and strategy of new car assessment program to rate crashworthiness. In Pageot, N. (Ed.), 16th International Conference on the Enhanced Safety of Vehicles, (pp. 2509–2517). Ontario Canada: Road Safety and Motor Vehicle Regulation Transport Canada. https://www-nrd.nhtsa.dot.gov/departments/esv/16th/.

[21] Johannsen, H., & Otte, D. (2015). Influence of impact type and restraint system triggering time on injury severity in frontal impact crashes. In 24th International Conference on the Enhanced Safety of Vehicles. Gothenburg, Sweden: U.S. Department of Transportation National Highway Traffic Safety Administration (NHTSA). https://www-esv.nhtsa.dot.gov/Proceedings/24/isv7/main.htm.

[22] Iraeus, J., & Lindquist, M. (2015). Pulse shape analysis and data reduction of real-life frontal crashes with modern passenger cars. *International Journal of Crashworthiness*, 20(6), 535–546. https://doi.org/10.1080/13588265.2015.1057005.

[23] Wang, J. T. (2005). An extendable and retractable bumper. In 19th International Conference on the Enhanced Safety of Vehicles. Washington DC, USA: U.S. Department of Transportation National Highway Traffic Safety Administration (NHTSA). www-nrd.nhtsa.dot.gov/departments/esv/19th/.

[24] Lenard, J., Hurley, B., & Hurley, P. (1998). The accuracy of CRASH3 for calculating collision severity in modern european cars. In Pageot, N. (Ed.), 16th International Conference on the Enhanced Safety of Vehicles, (pp. 1242–1249). Ontario Canada: Road Safety and Motor Vehicle Regulation Transport Canada. https://www-nrd.nhtsa.dot.gov/departments/esv/16th/.

[25] Jha, N., Srinivasa, D. K., Roy, G., & Jagdish, S. (2003). Injury Pattern among Road Traffic Accident Cases: A Study from South India. *Indian Journal of Community Medicine*, 28(2), 85–90. Indian Association of Preventive & Social Medicine (IAPSM).

[26] Langwieder, K., Hummel, T. A., & Anselm, D. (1998). The effect of airbags on injuries and accident costs. In Pageot, N. (Ed.), 16th International Conference on the Enhanced Safety of Vehicles, (pp. 338–358). Ontario Canada: Road Safety and Motor Vehicle Regulation Transport Canada. https://www-nrd.nhtsa.dot.gov/departments/esv/16th/.

[27] Lukoševičius, V., Juodvalkis, D., Keršys, A., & Makaras, R. (2023). Investigation of functionality of vehicle crumple zones recovered after a traffic accident. *Applied Sciences (Switzerland)*, 13(3), 1686. https://doi.org/10.3390/app13031686.

[28] Edwards, M., Happian-Smith, J., Davies, H., Byard, N., & Hobbs, A. (2001). The essential requirements for compatible cars in frontal collisions. In 17th International Conference on the Enhanced Safety of Vehicles. Amsterdam: U.S. Department of Transportation National Highway Traffic Safety Administration (NHTSA). https://www-nrd.nhtsa.dot.gov/departments/esv/17th/.

[29] Mohamed, A. A., Banerjee, A., & Banerjee, M. A. (1998). C) the fellowship of postgraduate medicine. *Postgraduate Medical Journal*, 74, 355–356. http://pmj.bmj.com/.

[30] Neades, J., & Smith, R. (2011). The determination of vehicle speeds from delta-V in two vehicle planar collisions. *Proceedings of the Institution of Mechanical Engineers, Part D: Journal of Automobile Engineering*, 225(1), 43–53. https://doi.org/10.1243/09544070JAUTO1462.

[31] Odero, W., Garner, P., & Zwi, A. (1997). Road traffic injuries in developing countries: A comprehensive review of epidemiological studies. Tropical Medicine & International Health, 2(5), 445–460. John Wiley & Sons, Ltd.

[32] Park, Y., Kim, B., & Ahn, C. (2020). Scaled experiment with dimensional analysis for vehicle lateral dynamics maneuver. In E. E. Carroll (Ed.), Proceedings of the FISITA 2020 World Congress (Lecture Notes in Mechanical Engineering, pp. 1288–1294). Springer, Cham.

[33] Poliey, M., & Alleyne, A. G. (2004). Dimensionless analysis of tire characteristics for vehicle dynamics studies. *Proceedings of the American Control Conference*, 4(January), 3411–3416. https://doi.org/10.23919/acc.2004.1384436.

[34] Ranadive, G., Deb, A., & Haorongbam, B. (2014). An assessment of load cell- and accelerometer-based responses in a simulated impact test. SAE Technical Papers, 1. https://doi.org/10.4271/2014-01-0198.

[35] Rezaeepazhand, J., Simitses, G. J., & Starnes, J. H. (1996). Design of scaled down models for predicting shell vibration response. *Journal of Sound and Vibration*, 195(2), 301–311. https://doi.org/10.1006/jsvi.1996.0423.

[36] Rezaeepazhand, J., & Simitses, G. J. (1996). Design of scaled down models for predicting shell vibration repsonse. *Journal of Sound and Vibration*, 195(2), 301–311. https://doi.org/10.1006/jsvi.1996.0423.

[37] Robinette, R. D., Fay, R. J., & Paulsen, R. E. (1994). Delta-V: basic concepts, computational methods, and misunderstandings. SAE Technical Papers, no. 41 2. https://doi.org/10.4271/940915.

[38] Rudd, R. W., Bean, J., Cuentas, C., Kahane, C. J., Mynatt, M., & Wiacek, C. (2009). A study of the factors affecting fatalities of air bag and belt-restrained occupants in frontal crashes. In 21th International Conference on the Enhanced Safety of Vehicles. Stuttgart, Germany: U.S. Department of Transportation National Highway Traffic Safety Administration (NHTSA). https://www-nrd.nhtsa.dot.gov/departments/esv/21st/.

[39] Sarode, P. L., & Suryawanshi, S. D. (2022). Evaluating frontal crash test of developed vehicle chassis frame structure to identify crashworthiness through scaled model for injury reduction. *Mathematical Statistician and Engineering Applications*, 71(3), 1991–2003.

[40] Schmitt, K. U., Muser, M. H., Thueler, H., & Bruegger, O. (2018). Crash-test dummy and pendulum impact tests of ice hockey boards: greater displacement does not reduce impact. *British Journal of Sports Medicine*, 52(1), 41–46. https://doi.org/10.1136/bjsports-2017-097735.

[41] Sequeira, G. J., & Brandmeier, T. (2020). Evaluation and characterization of crash-pulses for head-on collisions with varying overlap crash scenarios. *Transportation Research Procedia*, 48(2019), 1306–1315. https://doi.org/10.1016/j.trpro.2020.08.156.

[42] Sharpe, N., Vendrig, R., & Houtzager, K. (2001). Improved design for frontal protection. In 17th International Technical Conference on the Enhanced Safety of Vehicles, (pp. 1–10). http://www-nrd.nhtsa.dot.gov/pdf/esv/esv17/proceed/00137.pdf.

[43] Siva, N. J., Hari, B. U., & Student, P. G. (2013). Design and Structural Analysis of Heavy Vehicle Chassis Frame Made of Composite Material by Varying Reinforcement Angles of Layers. *International Journal of Advanced Engineering Research and Studies (IJAERS)*, 2(3), 10–13.

[44] Slik, G., & Vogel, G. (2007). Use of high efficient energy absorption foam in side impact padding. In 20th International Conference on the Enhanced Safety of Vehicles. Lyon, France: U.S. Department of Transportation, National Highway Traffic Safety Administration (NHTSA). http://www-nrd.nhtsa.dot.gov/pdf/nrd-01/esv/esv20/07-0185-W.pdf.

[45] Srinivas, G. R., Deb, A., & Chou, C. C. (2016). Lightweighting of an automotive front end structure considering frontal NCAP and pedestrian lower leg impact safety requirements. SAE Technical Papers, 2016-April (April). https://doi.org/10.4271/2016-01-1520.

[46] Veeresh, G., & Kori, M. (2021). IRJET- truck front structure pendulum impact as per AIS regulation. *IRJET- International Research Journal of Engineering and Technology*, 8(5), 3991–3998.

[47] Wang, D., Zhang, J., Wang, S., & Hu, L. (2022). Frontal Vehicular Crash Energy Management Using Analytical Model in Multiple Conditions. Sustainability, 14(24), 1–18. MDPI, Basel, Switzerland.

[48] Watanabe, T., Kuroda, I., Nakajima, T., & Masuda, M. (2019). Relationship between frontal car-to-car test result and vehicle crash compatibility evaluation in mobile progressive deformable barrier test. *Traffic Injury Prevention*, 20(sup1), S78–S83. https://doi.org/10.1080/15389588.2019.1597348.

[49] Witteman, W. J., & Kriens, R. F. C. (2001). The necessity of an adaptive vehicle structure deceleration pulses for different crash velocities. In 17th International Conference on the Enhanced Safety of Vehicles, no. Witteman: 1–10. https://www-nrd.nhtsa.dot.gov/departments/esv/17th/.

[50] Witteman, W. (2005). Adaptive frontal structure design to achieve optimal deceleration pulses. In 19th ESV Conference Proceedings, (pp. 1–8).

[51] Ydenius, A. (2010). Influence of crash pulse characteristics on injury risk in frontal impacts based on real-life crashes. *Traffic Injury Prevention*, 11(5), 526–534. https://doi.org/10.1080/15389588.2010.492053.

# 27 Leveraging big data analytics to build supply chain framework and its impact on UN sustainable development goals

*Praveen Kumar Loharkar[a] and Rajnish Katarne[b]*

Department of Artificial Intelligence and Machine learning, SVKM's NMIMS Mukesh Patel School of Technology Management and Engineering, Shirpur, Maharashtra, India

## Abstract

Supply chain management encompasses production, delivery, and distribution activities that pertain to goods and services. Large amount of data is generated at different levels of supply chain operations in the current era of automation and Industry 4.0. In this context, big data analytics (BDA) plays a significant role in drawing insights from the supply chain process data and in the identification of trends. This study aims to explore the literature to study the implications of big data analytics in the field of supply chain and its association with the sustainable development goals (SDGs) proposed by United Nations (UN).

In addition, a BDA application framework is proposed comprising of elements such as data cataloguing to capture relevant data, and applying descriptive, diagnostic, predictive, and prescriptive analytics using modern platforms for the attainment of organizational goals linked to the SDGs.

It is inferred through literature that the use of analytics would support informed decision-making and bring improvement in the overall performance. Furthermore, the integration of BDA into the operational process would ensure observance of commitments related to the environment, safety, and health of stakeholders. The proposed framework built based on earlier studies can be utilized by the organizations willing to introduce BDA into the supply chain domain-to monitor their contribution towards attaining SDGs.

**Keywords:** Big data, development, framework, supply chain, sustainability

## Introduction

Big data analytics (BDA) has emerged as a vital part of managing supply chains in various organizations to enhance their yield and efficiency [2]. Supply chain operations include the whole process of manufacturing, delivering, and distributing goods and services. Large amounts of data originate along the supply chain, be it inventory levels at different stages of operation, transportion metrics, production metrics, customer data, etc. The new advancements in the domain of BDA and tools have made it easier to analyse such vast amount of data that helps in the understanding of trends and insights. This further can be used to drive decisions and bring improvement within the overall supply chain performance [9]. There are a number of practical examples in the way companies use BDA for improving a range of operational performance criteria. For example, Amazon is using BDA to maintain inventory level estimates for demand and improvement of delivery routes to optimize its supply chain.

[a]ploharkar@gmail.com, [b]rajnish.katarne@nmims.edu

DOI: 10.1201/9781003716648-27

Similarly, Walmart monitors sales data, manages inventories, and improves its logistical processes in order to extend the supply chain efficiency [17].

In addition, BDA helps in enhancing the supply chain visibility quite significantly. Real-time data lets businesses keep track of the flow of items across the entire supply chain, identify bottlenecks and inefficiencies in it, and make immediate changes to quicken it up and make the supplies of goods to customers efficient [19].

The UN SDGs are now driving industry operations across the world. Approved by UN member states in 2015, these goals comprise of seventeen (17) objectives meant to realize sustainable development by 2030 [7]. The SDGs give importance to a fair and sustainable future for all people. By means of BDA applied in the SCM, productivity and efficiency can be raised, enabling the UN SDGs to be achieved [5]. These objectives span a broad spectrum in themes including gender equality, combating climate change, warranting sustainable consumption and production [4].

In this work, existing literature was reviewed with the purpose of finding answers to the following research questions.

- How is BDA helping in improving the efficacy of supply chains?
- How is a supply chain related to sustainable development goals?
- What are the main factors that influence the supply chain?

The aim was to build and propose a framework based on reviewed literature which would guide the data-driven sustainable supply chain practices.

## Literature review

The emergence of big data and BDA in the domain of SCM was explored by Jha et al. [9]. The work explored French and Indian economies to gain a comprehensive understanding from diverse perspectives. The study revealed crucial attributes that help organizations develop BDA capabilities. Internet of Things (IoT) is a thriving concept and has gotten very popular under the industry 4.0 paradigm. He et al. [8] carried out a study focused on IoT. It was observed that IoT-enabled BDA can transform resource acquisition and integration, industrial processes, transactions, and product development. In the similar context, a review of decision making in supply chain domain supported by IoT and BDA was carried out by Koot et al. [10]. The study found out that there are challenges such as live revisions in planning to accommodate the dynamic and stochastic characteristics of supply network.

Handling large datasets is important for applying BDA. In this context, Rao et al. [16] examined the difficulties in managing massive, unstructured data and provided a broad overview of a whole big data system. Li et al. [12] suggested data-driven SCM (DSCM) framework and demonstrated it with the hybrid vehicle's power split device. The framework is presently being used by a significant auto manufacturing company in Shanghai, and further case studies were estimated to be conducted verify its efficacy.

In the context of sustainability, The connection between SCM and the SDGs have been highlighted by Witkowski [18]. Emphasizing the relationship of several goals related to supply chain operations, the work shows how SCM uses BDA to increase production and efficiency. This paper underlined the need to implement innovative concepts in logistics and supply chains including "IoT," "Big Data," and "Industry 4.0". Subsequently, Magneto [13] did a study to examine the components of BDA and their relevance in sustainable SCM (SSCM) in manufacturing. Data processing, security, reporting, analytics, integration, and economics are mentioned as aspects of a successful BDA system. The study also mentioned the difficulties of integrating BDA into supply chains. The research developed a model for the interaction between BDA and SSCM and gave a probable checklist for managers to use in ensuring a successful BDA system.

Hassani et al. [7] summarized the potential value of Big Data in the attainment of each of the SDGs and identified obstacles that must be addressed, such as the high cost of the related technologies, the negligence of certain SDGs, and the emphasis on profit-generating aspects of development rather than addressing the negative consequences of unsustainable practices. The cost aspect was also discussed by Mondejar et al. [15]. Their research explored the various challenges, which primarily include the high cost of Big Data tools, the uneven attention paid to different SDGs, and the emphasis on profit-driven development, which ignores the negative consequences of unsustainable practices. The work further underlined the inter-relationship of the SDGs and the need to address all of them to establish a sustainable and impartial future for people and environment alike.

Martinez et al. [6] determined that climate change has substantial economic consequences. Thus, it requires strong collaboration between the public and commercial sectors to develop environmentally friendly industrial models. A framework on reduction of negative impact on environment by controlling factors related to transportation was proposed in the study on environmental sustainability using BDA approach [1].

In the context of Industry 4.0, Aravindaraj and Chinna [2] presented a review on interconnect between Industry 4.0 and managing warehouses to achieve SDGs. It has been stated that businesses stand to gain from Industry 4.0 in terms of increased monetary gains, enhanced sales and speed of production, heightened productivity and quality, along with the efficiency of firm's operations. Table 27.1 provides the summary of the literature reviewed in line with the identified research questions.

## Proposed Framework on using Big Data Analytics

In this section, the framework for applying BDA in supply chain and subsequent impact on attainment of SDGs has been presented. Figure 27.1 shows the block diagram of the framework.

## Data Cataloguing and Data Collection

In the domain of SCM, the following data is critical for analysis.

* Production service rate: This metric measures a supply chain's capacity to meet demand for goods and services. It is determined by dividing the number of units produced by the production time. Inventory turnover is another key metric, showing the speed at which stock is sold and refilled, computed by dividing the cost of goods sold by the mean stock on hand. Production time refers to the duration required to manufacture products or deliver services.

*Table 27.1* Summary of reviewed literature.

| Research question | Findings |
| --- | --- |
| How BDA is helping in improving the efficacy of supply chains? | It can help in optimizing supply chain operations by reducing the costs and improving the accuracy of forecasting. One can use predictive analytics, machine learning, and data analytics for this purpose. |
| How is a supply chain related to sustainable development goals? | An effective supply chain helps in environmental sustainability, social well-being, and economic progress which are the main components of the SDGs. |
| Main factors affecting supply chain performance | There are several factors that have an impact on the performance. A few of those are explained in the subsequent section. |

Source: Author

- Process performance indicators: Measures such as cycle time, lead time, and throughput time are frequently used to evaluate performance.
- Return on assets (ROA): This measures the supply chain's cost efficiency compared to assets invested and is calculated as net income divided by total assets.

This information can be utilized to make actionable insights into the better performance of the supply chains and assists in spotting the weak points.

## Big Data Analytics: Tools/Technologies to be used

Following are the prominent tools used in big data analytics.

- **Descriptive analytics**
  Descriptive analytics for SCM is essential as it provides a way of understanding business operations more comprehensively by analyzing data from a multitude of sources [9]. Using their business acumen, supply chain managers design interactive reports and dashboards offering analysis of their activities. Apart from tracking important indicators including production levels, inventory, and delivery times, the instruments can help managers derive trends in their data by means of pattern information. This helps supply chain managers to make better decisions and better knowledge of their activities.
- **Diagnostic analytics**
  Another important tool that can be used in SCM is diagnostic analytics. This analytics tool enables businesses to identify the root causes of accidents and issues. For instance, it can assist in determining the reasons why an inventory level was not as per the requirements, or a shipment was delayed. Supply chain managers may construct interactive dashboards and reports that offer insights into incident root causes using BI visualization tools.

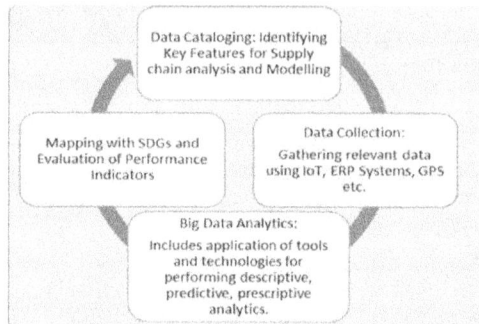

*Figure 27.1* Framework for implementing BDA in supply chain and measurement of SDG performance
Source: Author

- **Predictive analytics**

  Predictive analytics, helps businesses to forecast prospective outcomes and future trends [3, 17]. Predictive analytics may assist supply chain managers in forecasting demand, identifying interruptions, and streamlining operations by utilizing historical data and statistical models.

  Managers may create prediction models and spot trends and patterns in their data using statistical and machine learning methods from business intelligence (BI). This would help in making informed decisions.

- **Prescriptive analytics**

  Prescriptive analytics is an innovative SCM technology that goes beyond forecasting potential outcomes to suggest the optimal course of action. Supply chain managers may find the most effective methods to distribute resources, manage inventories, and optimize production schedules by integrating historical data, predictive analytics, and mathematical models [10, 14].

  Prescriptive analytics aids in optimizing the inventory levels. It can also suggest the ideal size of safety stock to reduce costs while assuring excellent service levels.

  Cloud computing, Python processing libraries like Pandas and Spark, and business intelligence (BI) tools such as Tableau, PowerBI, and Google Studio are some of the technologies that could be used to perform analytics as described above [11].

## Mapping with SDGs and Evaluation of Performance Indicators

This step involves linking the supply chain performance metrics with the relevant goals and measuring the impact. If the performance is below par, then improvement can be made in the existing supply chain. If required, the organization can restart the whole cycle beginning with the data cataloguing and data collection process.

## Conclusion

This study underlines the significance of BDA in SCM to enable businesses to work in a more efficient and productive way. This in turn would support the realization of the UN

SDGs. The review of existing literature establishes that organizations can contribute to a few important SDGs such as goal 9 ("Industry, Innovation, and Infrastructure"), goal 12 ("Responsible Consumption and Production"), and goal 13 ('Climate action") by introducing BDA in their supply chain operations.

The work also proposes a framework designed for BDA implementation in supply chain based on the limited literature review. It is identified that the major challenge in applying big data analytics is to ensure the right kind of data being captured and its relevance. Implementation of this framework would ensure sustainable practices in SCM and progress towards SDG attainment. One can extend this work by quantifying the effectiveness of the framework in various SCM applications.

## References

[1] Agrawal, R., Islam, N., Samadhiya, A., Shukla, V., Kumar, A., & Upadhyay, A. (2025). Paving the way to environmental sustainability: a systematic review to integrate big data analytics into high-stake decision forecasting. *Technological Forecasting and Social Change*, 214(May), 124060. https://doi.org/10.1016/j.techfore.2025.124060.

[2] Aravindaraj, K., & Chinna, P. R. (2022). A systematic literature review of integration of industry 4.0 and warehouse management to achieve sustainable development goals (SDGs). *Cleaner Logistics and Supply Chain*, 5(July), 100072. https://doi.org/10.1016/j.clscn.2022.100072.

[3] Biggio, L., & Kastanis, I. (2020). Prognostics and health management of industrial assets: current progress and road ahead. *Frontiers in Artificial Intelligence*, 3, 578613. Frontiers Media S.A. https://doi.org/10.3389/frai.2020.578613.

[4] Borges, F. M. M. G., Rampasso, I. S., Quelhas, O. L. G., Leal Filho, W., & Anholon, R. (2022). Addressing the UN SDGs in sustainability reports: an analysis of latin American oil and gas companies. *Environmental Challenges*, 7(April), 100515. https://doi.org/10.1016/j.envc.2022.100515.

[5] Chauhan, C., Kaur, P., Arrawatia, R., Ractham, P., & Dhir, A. (2022). Supply chain collaboration and sustainable development goals (SDGs). teamwork makes achieving SDGs dream work. *Journal of Business Research*, 147(April), 290–307. https://doi.org/10.1016/j.jbusres.2022.03.044.

[6] Martínez, J. M. G., Puertas, R., Martín, J. M. M., & Ribeiro-Soriano, D. (2022). Digitalization, innovation and environmental policies aimed at achieving sustainable production. *Sustainable Production and Consumption*, 32, 92–100. https://doi.org/10.1016/j.spc.2022.03.035.

[7] Hassani, H., Huang, X., Macfeely, S., & Entezarian, M. R. (2021). Big data and the united nations sustainable development goals (UN SDGs) at a glance. *Big Data and Cognitive Computing*, 5(3), 28. https://doi.org/10.3390/bdcc5030028.

[8] He, L., Xue, M., & Gu, B. (2020). Internet-of-things enabled supply chain planning and coordination with big data services: certain theoretic implications. *Journal of Management Science and Engineering*, 5(1), 1–22. https://doi.org/10.1016/j.jmse.2020.03.002.

[9] Jha, A. K., Agi, M. A. N., & Ngai, E. W. T. (2020). A note on big data analytics capability development in supply chain. *Decision Support Systems*, 138(March), 113382. https://doi.org/10.1016/j.dss.2020.113382.

[10] Koot, M., Mes, M. R. K., & Iacob, M. E. (2021). A systematic literature review of supply chain decision making supported by the internet of things and big data analytics. *Computers and Industrial Engineering*, 154(December 2020), 107076. https://doi.org/10.1016/j.cie.2020.107076.

[11] Lessmeier, C., Kimotho, J. K., Zimmer, D., & Sextro, W. (2016). Condition monitoring of bearing damage in electromechanical drive systems by using motor current signals of electric

motors: a benchmark data set for data-driven classification. In PHM Society European Conference, (Vol. 3, no. 1). https://doi.org/10.36001/phme.2016.v3i1.1577.

[12] Li, Q., & Liu, A. (2019). Big data driven supply chain management. *Procedia CIRP*, 81, 1089–1094. https://doi.org/10.1016/j.procir.2019.03.258.

[13] Mageto, J. (2021). Big data analytics in sustainable supply chain management: a. *Sustainability*, 13(7101), 1–22.

[14] Meissner, R., Rahn, A., & Wicke, K. (2021). Developing prescriptive maintenance strategies in the aviation industry based on a discrete-event simulation framework for post-prognostics decision making. *Reliability Engineering and System Safety*, 214(October), 107812. https://doi.org/10.1016/j.ress.2021.107812.

[15] Mondejar, M. E., Avtar, R., Diaz, H. L. B., Dubey, R. K., Esteban, H., Gómez-Morales, A., et al. (2021). Digitalization to achieve sustainable development goals: steps towards a smart green planet. *Science of the Total Environment*, 794(June), 148539. https://doi.org/10.1016/j.scitotenv.2021.148539.

[16] Rao, T. R., Mitra, P., Bhatt, R., & Goswami, A. (2019). The big data system, components, tools, and technologies: a survey. *Knowledge and Information Systems*, 60, 1165–1245. https://doi.org/10.1007/s10115-018-1248-0.

[17] Rozados, I. V., & Tjahjono, B. (2014). Big data analytics in supply chain management: trends and related research. In 6th International Conference on Operations and Supply Chain Management, (Vol. 1, no. 1, pp. 2013–2014). https://doi.org/10.13140/RG.2.1.4935.2563.

[18] Witkowski, K. (2017). Internet of things, big data, industry 4.0 - innovative solutions in logistics and supply chains management. *Procedia Engineering*, 182, 763–769. https://doi.org/10.1016/j.proeng.2017.03.197.

[19] Zahid, A., Leclaire, P., Hammadi, L., Roberta, C.-A., & El Ballouti, A. (2025). Exploring the potential of industry 4.0 in manufacturing and supply chain systems: insights and emerging trends from bibliometric analysis. *Supply Chain Analytics*, 10(June), 100108. https://doi.org/10.1016/j.sca.2025.100108.

# 28 Parametric optimization of maximum power point tracking for solar photovoltaic enabled electric vehicles

*Mayank Kothari[1,a], Ashish Mogra[2,b] and Pankaj Gulhane[2,c]*

[1]SVKM's NMIMS Mukesh Patel School of Technology Management and Engineering, Shirpur, India

[2]SVKM's NMIMS School of Technology Management and Engineering, Chandigarh, India

## Abstract

A photovoltaic (PV) model is proposed to improve the output efficiencies of PV systems. The optimized circuit is developed under a MATLAB/SIMULINK environment, enabling us to view power output values and current parameters depending on input parameters such as irradiance and temperature. This reference model is based on mathematical equations to compare the proposed optimized model. The Perturb & Observe (P&O) algorithm related to the maximum power point tracking (MPPT) method was employed in this base model. Comparisons between the base and the optimized model are achieved using MINITAB software. Various tools of MINITAB software are utilized in the proposed study, such as Taguchi Method, Regression analysis, and ANOVA. The actual power values gained from MATLAB were plotted against predicted power outputs obtained from the regression equation for both the base and the optimized circuits. These comparisons are presented through contour plots, bar charts, and Normal Probability plots. This comparison demonstrates that the suggested model outperforms the reference model in terms of efficiency and optimization. In Minitab analysis, it has been found that the p value is less than 0 for irradiance and temperature, which shows significant parameters for the analysis. The present research shows the significant impact on the photovoltaic model related to the automobile. In the future, heavy load analysis can affect their performance using the solar system.

**Keywords:** Maximum power point tracking, simulink, taguchi analysis

## Introduction

The transportation sector alone was responsible for over 28% of all greenhouse gas emissions in the United States in 2018. In the transportation sector, the major contributor was light-duty vehicles, which were powered by internal combustion engines and accounted for about 61 percent in terms of emissions. Also, there is uncertainty regarding oil reserves and for how long these reserves will be able to sustain the world's huge demand [8]. Conventional vehicles produce various hazardous gases which have serious implications for our health, the Air Quality Index (AQI), and the nature around us [6].

These modules are eminent factors for converting the Sun's solar energy into electrical energy [10]. These modules come in different shapes, sizes, and materials; these variations result in different efficiencies while producing energy. There are two types of PV panel arrangements, serial and parallel. In series arrangement, the current through each panel in

[a]Mayank.kothari@nmims.edu, [b]Ashish.Mogra@nmims.edu, [c]pankaj.gulhane@nmims.edu

DOI: 10.1201/9781003716648-28

a system is always equal. There are some main choices when it comes to which material to use while selecting a solar PV panel; mono-crystalline, poly-crystalline, and silicon [8]. These materials provide a user with different ranges of price, efficiency, and life cycle. So, there is no standard material to use, it all comes down to one's needs and applications when selecting the material for a solar PV panel. Maximum power output extraction from the system for system efficiency is the desired goal. At present, many literature reviews showcase MPPT techniques and point out their merits based on their performance, optimized parameters, cost-effectiveness, and adapting cost [2]. There are 22 MPPT techniques, each being unique, and bearing its advantages, disadvantages, and applicability [7, 13].

The task of solar cells is to convert sunlight to electricity, but the drawbacks associated with it are high initial cost and low conversion efficiency. Taguchi analysis is an organized statistical tool for analyzing experiments with different data sets [1]. It assists us to get the most optimized values which can be used in this system. This analysis method makes the experiment timeless by giving effective results. Signal Noise Ratio (S/N ratio) is a process used to minimize uncontrollable noise. The results are then analyzed using the ANOVA method, which helps to determine how much variation is found using different parameters. The main characteristics of the Taguchi Method can be summarized as Sonawane et al. [12]; Senthilkumar et al. [9]: Minimize loss function, Maximize signal-to-noise ratio, and optimized result. This paper obtains parametric output values, i.e., current and power outputs, from the base or reference model using MATLAB. A similar procedure is processed across the optimized model for the respective output values. These values are then fed to the MINITAB software, and various analyses such as Taguchi Analysis and Regression Analysis are performed on it. According to the analysis, the impedance of the PV modules drops as the irradiance rises. However, the impedance of the load essentially stays constant, which is consistent with the PV applications. Additionally, it was observed that warmer temperatures cause the module saturation current to rise, which lowers power output, and vice versa, which is also consistent with the PV application [5]. The newly created Puma optimiser (PO), which has never been used in this context before, is used in this research to present a novel method for extracting important parameters from the double diode model (DDM) of PV units. The main conclusions show clear distinctions between environmental and economic optimisation, which affect system performance and emphasise the necessity of a well-rounded strategy. Local factors including solar and grid signal volatility. It has been demonstrated that PV generation has a major impact on ideal system setups [11].

## System Modelling

*Table 28.1* List of terminologies and corresponding notations.

| Notation | Description | Notation | Description |
|---|---|---|---|
| $I_o$ | output current of photovoltaic | $V_{MP}$ | Maximum power point voltage |
| $V_o$ | output voltage of photovoltaic | G | Irradiance(W/m2) |
| $I_{SCS}$ | Under standard test conditions (STC) value of short circuit current | $I_{MP}$ | Maximum power point current |
| $I_{MPS}$ | At STC value of maximum power point current | T | Outdoor temperature (°C) |

| Notation | Description | Notation | Description |
|----------|-------------|----------|-------------|
| $V_{ocs}$ | At STC value of open circuit voltage | $T_C$ | Cell temperature (°C) |
| $G_S$ | At STC value of Irradiance | $I_{sc}$ | Short circuit current |
| $T_S$ | At STC value of Temperature (°C) | $w$ | Wind speed (m/s) |
| $V_{oc}$ | Open circuit voltage | | |

Source: Author

## Base Model

Power and current are the output parameters in the base model, whereas temperature and irradiance are the input parameters. The base model (Figure 28.1) helps us retrieve reference readings in realistic meteorological conditions. The mathematical model also helps us determine the various readings by changing the material of the PV Module [3]. The parameters undertaken are ambient, viz. Irradiance as 1000 W/m² and Temperature as 25°C (Figure 28.2) to compare them with the obtained readings of the optimized model.

A Pyranometer and a weather station are used to obtain incident global radiation on PV panels and outdoor temperature readings as input parameters to the model. Table 28.1 shows the details of terminologies and corresponding notations used in the mathematical model equations.

$$I_o = I_{sc} \cdot [1 - K_a \cdot (e^{\left(\frac{V_O}{K_b \cdot V_{OC}}\right)} - 1)] \tag{1}$$

Where,

$$K_a = \left(1 - \frac{I_{MP}}{I_{SC}}\right) \cdot e^{\left(\frac{-V_{MP}}{K_2 \cdot V_{OC}}\right)} \tag{2}$$

$$K_b = \left(\left(\frac{V_{MP}}{V_{OC}}\right) - 1\right) \Big/ \ln\left(1 - \left(\frac{I_{MP}}{I_{SC}}\right)\right) \tag{3}$$

It has been noted that various panel inputs cause the  and  coefficient values to fluctuate. Below are the changes in these temperature and irradiance characteristics.

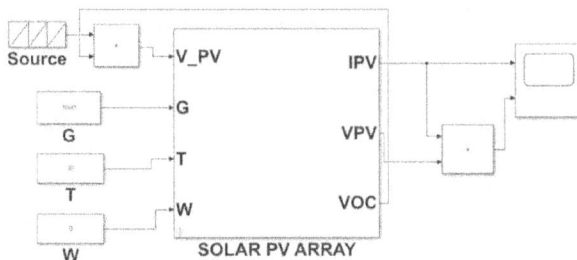

*Figure 28.1* Solar PV reference model
Source: Author

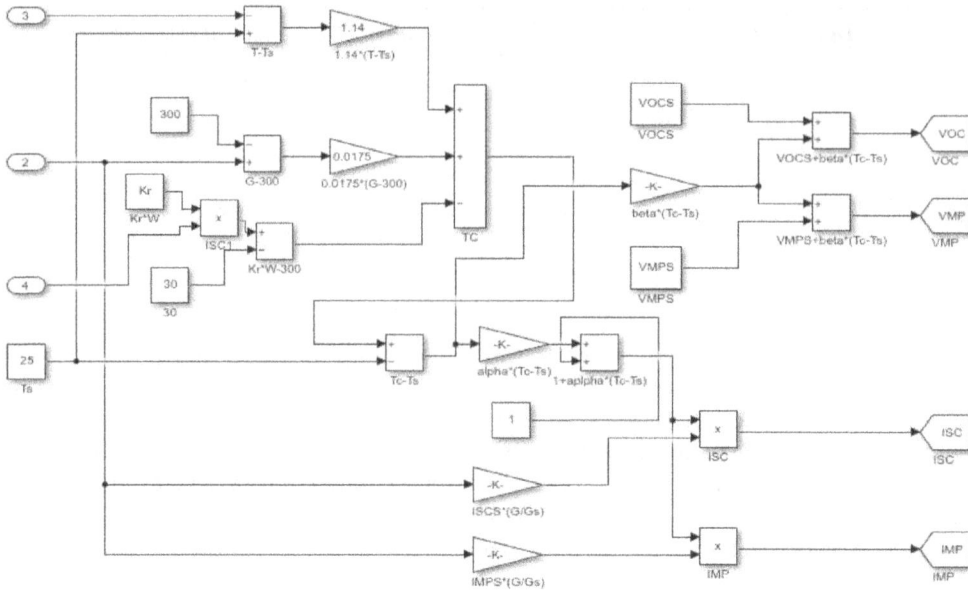

*Figure 28.2* PV panel subsystem block diagram
Source: Author

$$T_C = 1.14 \times (T - T_S) + 0.0175.(G - 300) + 30 \tag{4}$$

While interconnecting panel output and motor input, there were many variations in the power level, which led to a decrease in the health of the vehicle's electronic components. It is difficult to tap the most efficient combination of current and voltage values required to power an electric vehicle. Module characteristics, wind speed, and incident irradiance all have an impact on cell temperature. This parameter has less impact on system modelling. This parameter has a common connection between the static temperature and the outer temperature of the system.

## Methodology and Analysis

The method most frequently used to regulate the MPPT algorithm for PV modules is the Perturb & Observe (P&O) Algorithm. This method continuously compares the output power, voltage, and current to ascertain whether or not the system is operating at its maximum power point (MPP). First, measurements are made of the PV module's voltage and current. The product of these values gives us the power of the module. The algorithm then checks whether $\Delta P=0$ or not. If this condition is satisfied, then it is at MPP. If not, it checks whether $\Delta P>0$. If the status is satisfied, then it will check for $\Delta V>0$. The operational point is in the early half of the power-voltage relation if the condition is satisfied, and in the latter half if it is not.

The MPPT's job is to extract as much power as possible from the photovoltaic system and transfer it to the load (Figure 28.3). The buck-boost converter aids in increasing the voltage

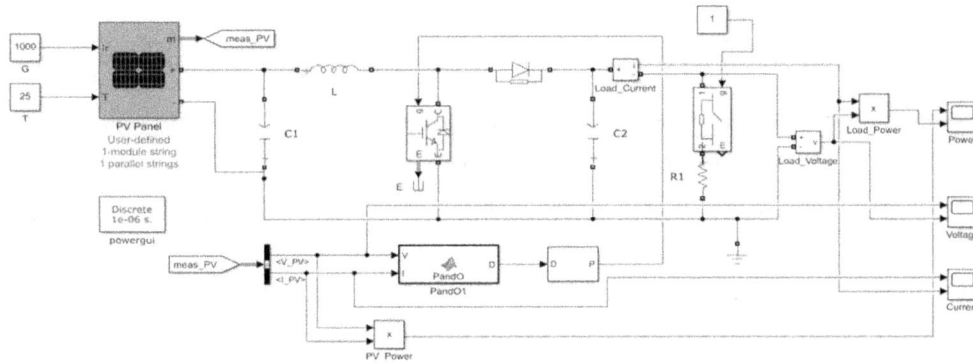

*Figure 28.3* Optimized model using MPPT
Source: Author

*Table 28.2* Array of inputs.

| Irradiance | Temperature |
| --- | --- |
| 250 | 20 |
| 250 | 25 |
| 250 | 30 |
| 400 | 20 |
| 400 | 25 |
| 400 | 30 |
| 1000 | 20 |
| 1000 | 25 |
| 1000 | 30 |

Source: Author

to the necessary level, which also increases the power. This helps us optimize the results with more output more efficiently. It also helps in reducing the high output needed to charge the batteries. Once the output is achieved, optimization, evaluation, and result analysis are performed to solidify the results.

The Taguchi method is a well-known and frequently used statistical and process optimization method, developed by Genichi Taguchi [4]. The objective of the S/N ratio is to improve the efficiency of power output. If the calculated value of S/N is small, it validates a more precise and accurate model. The Taguchi analysis consists of levels and arrays. In this case, the level is 3x3, hence an array of 9 combinations of irradiance (250, 400, 1000) and temperature (20, 25, 30) is formed as shown in Table 28.2. The combination with the highest power is better chosen for better-optimized results. The optimized model has the same set of input and output parameters. This optimization is enabled in the new model through buck & boost converters and P&O algorithm under the MPPT technology. The most preferable output parameters can be obtained for the values of irradiance above 950 W/m

*Table 28.3* Base and optimized model value.

| Input parameter values for base and Optimized Model | | Output parameter value | | |
|---|---|---|---|---|
| | | | Base Model | Optimized Model |
| Irradiance | 1000 | Current (in A) | 7.9 | 9.5 |
| Temperature | 25 | Power (in W) | 232 | 321 |

Source: Author

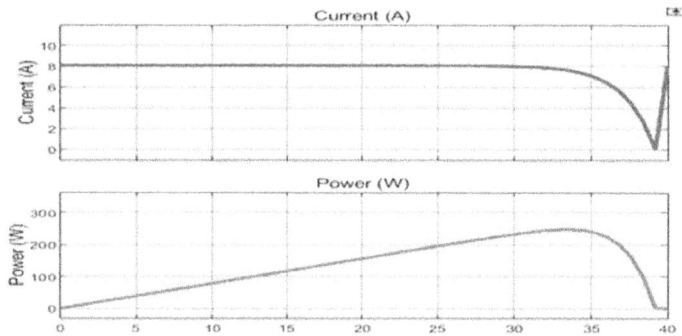

*Figure 28.4* Current & power graph (base model)
Source: Author

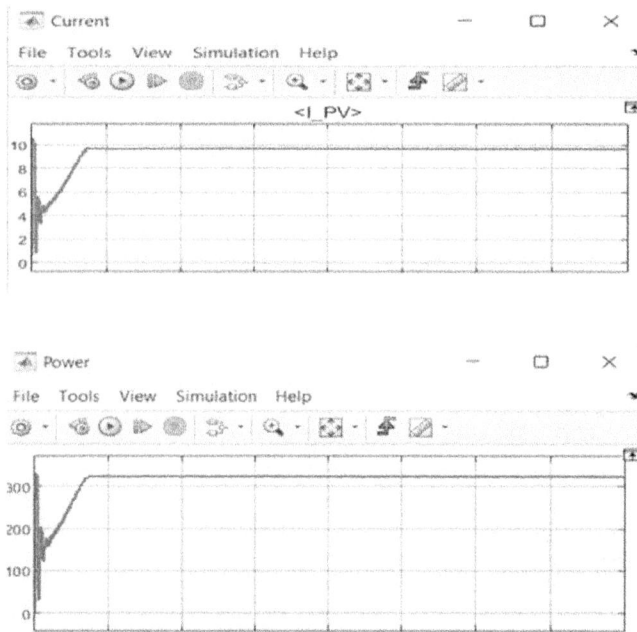

*Figure 28.5* Current & power graph (optimized model)
Source: Author

and temperature in the range between 25°C to 35°C. Figure 28.2. As shown in Table 28.3, the given irradiance and temperature viz. 1000 W/m2   and at 25°C the power output has increased from 232W to 321W.

## Results and Discussion

Considering the two input parameters, irradiance and temperature have obtained the outputs have been obtained in the form of power and current, shown in Figures 28.4 and 28.5. The base model depends on the mathematical modelling of the formulas, which are needed to find out the result values. These result values from the base model are ideal and do not involve variables that are usually found through real-life conditions. From the below contour chart, it is concluded that the most preferable values of power (>250 W) can be obtained when the values of temperature and irradiance are 30°C & 1000 W/m².

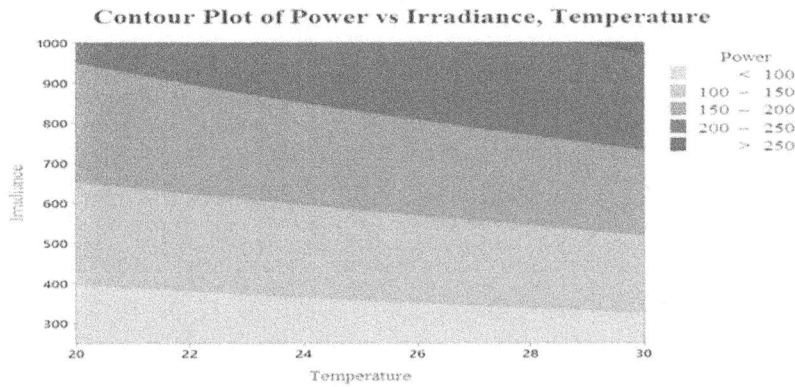

*Figure 28.6* Contour plot of power vs irradiance & temperature (base model)
Source: Author

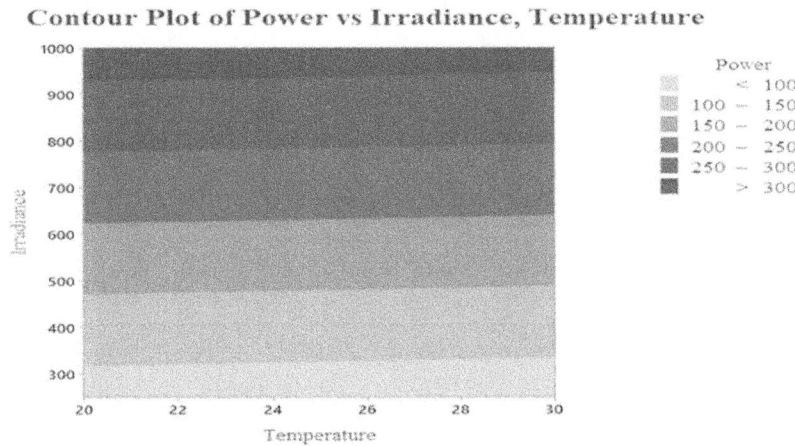

*Figure 28.7* Contour plot of power vs irradiance & temperature (optimized model)
Source: Author

The Shades in the contour plot shown in Figures 28.6 and 28.7 show a gradual increase in power output for different combinations of input data.

$$Power = 6.65 + 0.32841 \ Irradiance - 0.5667 \ Temperature \tag{5}$$

The power equation (5) is derived with the help of the regression analysis section of Minitab software. This equation helps in findings the predicted power shown in Figures. 28.8 and 28.9 to different input parameters by calculating the trends of output from an input in the given model.

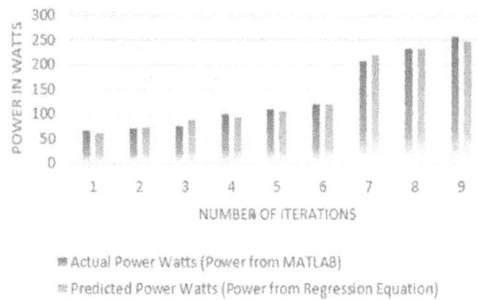

*Figure 28.8* Power comparison (Base Model)
Source: Author

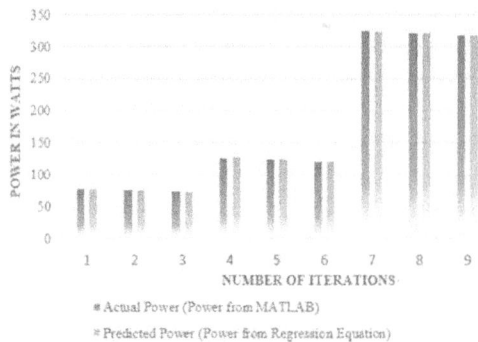

*Figure 28.9* Power comparison (optimized model)
Source: Author

*Table 28.4* Taguchi analysis (base model).

| Term | Coef | SE Coef | T-Value | P-Value | VIF |
|------|------|---------|---------|---------|-----|
| Constant | -43.4 | 18.8 | -2.30 | 0.061 | NA |
| Irradiance | 0.211 | 0.009 | 23.32 | 0.000 | 1.00 |
| Temperature | 2.620 | 0.717 | 3.65 | 0.011 | 1.00 |
| R-Sq | 98.93% | R-Sq(adjusted) | 98.58% | R-Sq(predicted) | 96.66% |

Source: Author

*Table 28.5* Taguchi analysis (optimized model).

| Term | Coef | SE Coef | T-Value | P-Value | VIF |
|------|------|---------|---------|---------|-----|
| Constant | 6.65 | 2.12 | 3.14 | 0.020 | NA |
| Irradiance | 0.328 | 0.001 | 323.56 | 0.000 | 1.00 |
| Temperature | -0.5667 | 0.0806 | -7.03 | 0.000 | 1.00 |
| R-Sq | 99.99% | R-Sq(adjusted) | 99.99% | R-Sq(predicted) | 99.98% |

Source: Author

**Base Model:** Power = (−43.4) + 0.21081 Irradiance + 2.620 Temperature     (6)

**Optimized Model:** Power = 6.65 + 0.32841 Irradiance - 0.5667 Temperature     (7)

Table 28.4 and 28.5 gives the detail parameter determined in Taguchi Analysis.

## Conclusion

The presented MATLAB/Simulink model suggests that Maximum Power Point Tracking (MPPT) utilization enhances the power and current output for a given area of the solar module. The outcomes are analysed the power and current values for basic as well as MPPT models of a solar PV array. It is observed that under the same conditions of irradiance and temperature, the current and power of the MPPT model always exceed when compared with the basic model. The use of Perturb and Observe algorithms while developing the MPPT ensures that the highest combinational values of voltage and current are captured. Thus, the power output from a MPPT enabled solar PV array under variable values of temperature and irradiance always comes out more, when compared to the basic model. The presented study is done under ideal conditions for both the solar PV array and the MPPT algorithm. In reality, factors such as sensor inaccuracies, delays in tracking, and environmental variations may affect the performance of the MPPT system. Future studies could explore the impact of these practical limitations on MPPT efficiency and investigate ways to mitigate these effects, such as through the use of advanced algorithms or improved hardware.

## References

[1] Araki, K., Ota, Y., & Yamaguchi, M. (2020). Measurement and modeling of 3D solar irradiance for vehicle-integrated photovoltaic. *Applied Sciences*, 10(3), 872.

[2] Ayaz, R., Nakir, I., & Tanrioven, M. (2014). An improved matlab-simulink model of PV module considering ambient conditions. *International Journal of Photoenergy*, 2014(1), 315893.

[3] Chowdhury, M. S. A., Al Mamun, K. A., & Rahman, A. M. (2016). Modelling and simulation of the power system of battery, solar and fuel cell powered hybrid electric vehicle. In 2016 3rd International Conference on Electrical Engineering and Information Communication Technology (ICEEICT), (pp. 1–6). IEEE.

[4] Dwivedi, A., & Das, D. (2015). Application of Taguchi philosophy for optimization of design parameters in a rectangular enclosure with triangular fin array. *Journal of the Institution of Engineers (India): Series C*, 96(4), 351–362.

[5]   Eze, V. H. U., Eze, M. C., Ugwu, S. A., Enyi, V. S., Okafor, W. O., Ogbonna, C. C., et al. (2025). Development of maximum power point tracking algorithm based on improved optimized adaptive differential conductance technique for renewable energy generation. *Heliyon*, 11(1), 1–17.

[6]   Kumar, A. V. P., Parimi, A. M., & Rao, K. U. (2015). Implementation of MPPT control using fuzzy logic in solar-wind hybrid power system. In 2015 IEEE International Conference on Signal Processing, Informatics, Communication and Energy Systems (SPICES), (pp. 1–5). IEEE.

[7]   Moyo, R. T., Tabakov, P. Y., & Moyo, S. (2021). Design and modeling of the ANFIS-based MPPT controller for a solar photovoltaic system. *Journal of Solar Energy Engineering*, 143(4), 041002.

[8]   Pathak, P. K., Yadav, A. K., & Alvi, P. A. (2020). Advanced solar MPPT techniques under uniform and non-uniform irradiance: a comprehensive review. *Journal of Solar Energy Engineering*, 142(4), 040801.

[9]   Senthilkumar, R., Nandhakumar, A. J. D., & Prabhu, S. (2013). Analysis of natural convective heat transfer of nano coated aluminium fins using Taguchi method. *Heat and Mass Transfer*, 49(1), 55–64.

[10]  Singh, S. P., Singh, P. P., Singh, S. N., & Tiwari, P. (2021). State of charge and health estimation of batteries for electric vehicles applications: key issues and challenges. *Global Energy Interconnection*, 4(2), 145–157.

[11]  Smajila, L., Trevisan, S., Golzar, F., Vaidya, K., & Guedez, R. (2025). Comparative analysis of techno-economic and techno-environmental approach to optimal sizing and dispatch of hybrid solar–battery systems. *Energy Conversion and Management: X*, 25, 100858.

[12]  Sonawane, P., Savakhande, V. B., Chewale, M. A., & Wanjari, R. A. (2018). Optimization of PID controller for automatic voltage regulator system using Taguchi method. In 2018 International Conference on Computer Communication and Informatics (ICCCI), (pp. 1–6). IEEE. https://doi.org/10.1109/ICCCI.2018.8441211.

[13]  Vasant, L. G., & Pawar, V. R. (2017). Optimization of solar-wind energy system power for battery charging using MPPT. In 2017 International Conference on Energy, Communication, Data Analytics and Soft Computing (ICECDS), (pp. 1308–1310). IEEE. https://doi.org/10.1109/ICECDS.2017.8389656.

# 29 Design and development of mopping robot

*Suresh Kurumbanshi[a] and Sachin Sonawane[b]*

Mukesh Patel School of Technology Management and Engineering, Shirpur, India

## Abstract

Cleaning robots are finding an increased usage in our homes. From vacuuming to mopping, these robots can do everything. In this paper, we have focused on the designing, functioning, and building of our mopping robot. Using the concerns of cleanliness which has been highlighted by the pandemic, we have aimed to build a low-cost mopping robot which uses Arduino as the controller along with a network of Infrared sensors and motors for sensing the obstacle in its path. There are a total of 4 motors in use, two for moving, two for cleaning, and a water pump for pumping the water. The whole robot is powered by a 12V Lithium-ion battery, equipped with an inbuilt battery charging circuit. The algorithm employed in this robot supports the path planning capabilities, hence reducing the interference of the user. The cleaning fluid given by the user is sprayed in the form of mist to clean the area and mops wipe it. We believe that cleaning robots can reduce the direct interaction of the user with the contaminant on the floor surface hence providing the potential to be used not only in homes but also in hospitals or other areas that require frequent cleaning. With the increased usage of robots in our daily life, cleaning robots are sure to see a boom in usage and development soon.

Keywords: Intelligent robotics, machine learning, mopping, path planning

## Introduction

The acceptance of robots in daily lives of humans has only seen a growth in the past decade. Now, they are not only the machines that work in sophisticated factories for industrial work but also in our homes. One such robot that has seen increased usage is the cleaning robot. Cleaning robots have come a long way, from human-controlled vacuum cleaners to autonomous systems which can map the room for effective cleaning. The cleaning robot industry only shows the potential to grow as history goes show, with some of the first prototypes being presented around 1991 [4].

A mopping robot is designed to clean the floor without wasting much water through the mist-spraying mechanism and it can be used as sanitation. Some products are already available in the market. iRobot launched its many variants is floor cleaning robot segment and one of its product Roomba which was widely accepted by customers for the last decades. An increase in demand [1]. iRobot has three main products in the market as follows: Roomba was launched in 2002, used for a dry vacuum cleaner with IR and RF technology Koselka [5] and with auto-charging mechanisms; Scooba that was launched in 2005, used for a wet washing of floor cleaner Jones [6] with IR technology along with virtual wall accessories Ziegler [3]; Braava was launched in 2006, used for floor mopping with IR technology with virtual wall accessories [7]. Samsung Electronics has launched the Samsung Jet Mop Cleaning Robot in 2020, used for mopping with the wall following technology, Dual Spin Technology and Automatic Water Dispenser [2].

[a]suresh.kurumbanshi@nmims.edu, [b]sachin.sonawane@nmims.edu

DOI: 10.1201/9781003716648-29

In our research work, we are focusing on making a mopping robot that overcomes the difficulties of vacuuming robots by using mist spray to clean or even sanitize the surface, depending on the cleaning solution given by the user. We aim to make it water-efficient and autonomous.

## Methodology

*Requirements*

It is important to have the right set of components to achieve our goals. Hence, we are using the following list of components (refer to Table 29.1) in our research work in Figure 29.1.

*Working*

We require our robot to be autonomous and efficient in cleaning. Hence, to achieve our goals, we have come up with a combination and sequence of various parts which can be represented by our block diagram Figure 29.1. The upper part of the block diagram is the battery charging system. We have included it in the robot assembly to avoid removing the battery for every time it needs to be charged. A voltage regulator has been added to provide the right voltage to the Arduino. There are three IR sensors that have been used to give the required inputs for the robot to be autonomous. These sensors help in the detection of obstacles and walls. Special care has been taken to avoid the detection of walls as obstacles so that the robot can clean along the boundary as well without running into it. These inputs are given to the Arduino.

*Table 29.1* List of components.

| Sr. no | Components | |
|---|---|---|
| | *Name of component* | *Required number* |
| 1. | Arduino Uno Rev3 | 1 |
| 2. | InfraRed sensors | 3 |
| 3. | L293D Motor Driver Module | 2 |
| 4. | 370 Diaphragm 3V-5V Self-Priming Small Micro Vacuum Pump | 1 |
| 5. | Adjustable brass Misting Nozzle Sprinkler Head | 1 |
| 6. | Dual Shaft Motor with 3V - 12V DC. | 4 |
| 7. | BC547 - NPN Transistor | 1 |
| 8. | 230V-12V 5A Step down transformer | 1 |
| 9. | BR1010 1000V 10A Full wave Bridge rectifier | 1 |
| 10. | LM7805 Voltage Regulator IC | 1 |
| 11. | 12V-2A Lithium-ion Rechargeable Battery Pack | 1 |
| 12. | Switch 15 x 21 mm | 1 |
| 13. | Cable 20-30-40cm 2.54mm 1pin Female to Male, Male to Male, Female to Female jumper wire | As per requirement |

Source: Author

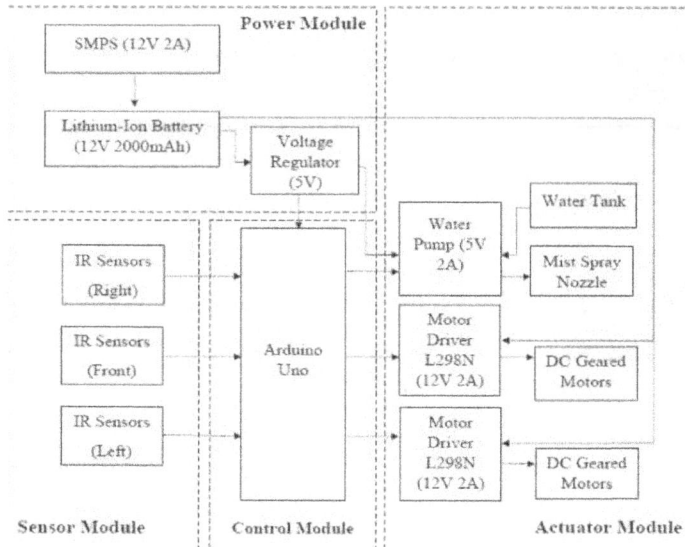

*Figure 29.1* Block diagram
Source: Author

In our research work, the Arduino is the central control system which processes the inputs from the IR sensors and controls the movement of robot through the motors, mopping action and the spraying of mist. The output from the Arduino is given to three components namely the water pump and two motor drivers. The water pump is used to pump the cleaning fluid in the water tank through the spraying nozzle at regular intervals. The Dual shaft motor is used to drive the wheels and well as the rotating mops placed in the front. The movement of robot and spraying process happens simultaneously.

*Mopping*
The mopping mechanism includes two rolling brushes. The brushes are connected to a DC geared motor. The mechanism is attached to the base of a robot with help of glue gun. The brush is used to clean the stains on the floor effectively.

*Water spraying*
Water spraying mechanism consists of a Vacuum pump Figure 29.2, Mist Nozzle Sprinkler Head Figure 29.3, pipes (Dia 4 mm). The motor is a self-priming motor, as it is self-primed when it starts. The inlet port of the motor is connected to the pipe and then to the water tank. The outlet port is connected through the pipe to the Mist nozzle for spraying purpose. Mist spray helps to reduce water usage. Spraying diameter can be controlled by revolving the nozzle outlet. The vacuum motor is connected to a 12V 2Ah Lithium-ion battery.

*Electronic circuitry*
There are IR sensor circuits, Arduino mega board circuits, Motor driver circuits and all these circuits are designed, analyzed and then implemented.

*Figure 29.2* Vacuum pump
Source: Author

*Figure 29.3* Nozzle head
Source: Author

*Figure 29.4* Motor driver
Source: Author

*Motor controllers*

The controller used is L293D Motor driver Figure 29.4. Which is a dual H-bridge motor driver integrated circuit, used for driving the motors in both directions i.e. forward direction and backward direction. The Motor driver take low current control signal and then amplifier signal to higher current signal. The amplified signal is used to drive the motors. It contains two H-bridge circuit, which can drive two DC motors simultaneously. The direction of the motor can be controlled by changing the input logic at pins 2&7 and 10&15. The pins 1&9 are motor speed control pins and must be high for a motor to start. The circuit is powered through a battery.

*Water pump controller*

The circuit used for controlling the vacuum motor consists of a transistor, relay and a resistance. Firstly, the voltage regulator is used to convert 14V DC to 5V DC which is to be used to run the motor. A transistor consists of two NP diodes connected back-to-back. It has three terminals i.e. emitter, base and collector. The working of a transistor is that it lets us control the flow of current through the collector to emitter channel by varying intensity of a small amount current flowing through the base. By looking at the beta value of the switching transistor we calculated the base current required and then the required resistance. The positive from the voltage regulator is connected to the Collector terminal and negative to the emitter terminal. We gave the control signal from Arduino to the base of a switching transistor (NPN) which drives a relay.

*CAD model*

The different views of our CAD model are presented top view Figure 29.5, front view Figure 29.6, isometric view Figure 29.7, side view Figure 29.8, and relay in Figiure 29.9. The CAD model gives a greater understanding of our robot.

## Results and Discussion

At first, all circuits are designed and tested. After optimization of values for Components, circuits were implemented on PCB. The observed values of our tested components are mentioned in Table 29.2.

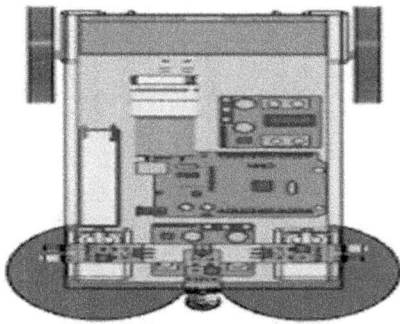

*Figure 29.5* Top view
Source: Author

*Figure 29.6* Front view
Source: Author

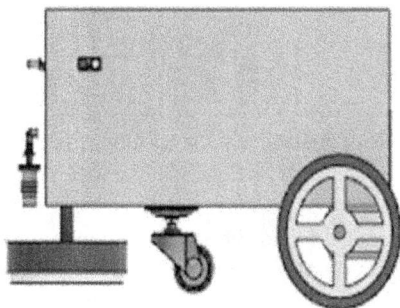

*Figure 29.7* Isometric view
Source: Author

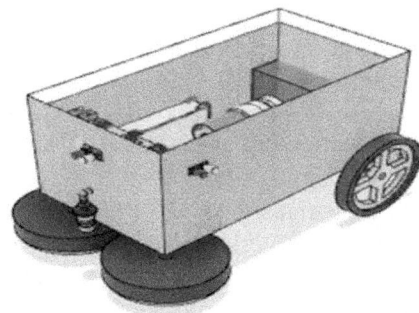

*Figure 29.8* Side view
Source: Author

*Figure 29.9* Relay
Source: Author

*Table 29.2* Observations.

| Sr. no. | Components | | |
|---------|------------|--|--|
| | *Component name* | *Input (each)* | *Output (each)* |
| 1. | Dual Shaft Motor with 3V - 12V DC. | Voltage:12 V Current: 40mA - 80mA | 60 RPM |
| 2. | InfraRed sensors | Voltage: 5 V Current: 20 mA | Range: 2 - 30 cm |
| 3. | Arduino Uno Rev3 | Voltage: 7V- 12 V | 14 digital I/O pins |

Source: Author

There is no need of priming the motor, as it is self-primed when it starts. The user needs to continuously check the water level of the tank as the motor should not run dry. If the motor is run dry, the heat generated may damage the insides of the motor. After that the user needs to just turn on the switch and the part of the user is done. To remove the excess work of replacing the battery every time in case of discharge, in the robot inbuilt battery charging circuit is placed. To charge it, the user just needs to connect it to the 230V supply.

From the experiment, it was observed that if the motor is continuously used, lots of water wastage occurs. Hence, to minimize that we controlled the motor operation with the Arduino. But the sourcing capacity of Arduino is 20mA max, which in not sufficient for driving the motor. For that, we gave the control signal from Arduino to the base of a switching transistor (NPN) which drives a relay as shown in Figure 29.9. The control signal is sent at a particular time gap. To regulate the current flow to the base we connected a resistance. For the operation of the motor 5V supply is needed for we used the voltage regulator (LM7805) to convert 12V to 5V and attached a heat sink to avoid the problem of heating. Table 29.3 represents the comparison of mopping robot features and their performance.

*Table 29.3* Comparison of mopping robot features and performance.

| Feature/Performance | This Paper | Recent Advancements (General Trends) |
| --- | --- | --- |
| Navigation/Path Planning | Uses IR sensors for obstacle detection, basic path planning. | Advanced algorithms (SLAM, LiDAR, camera-based navigation), machine learning for optimized paths, room mapping, zoning. |
| Cleaning Mechanism | Mist spraying, dual rotating mops. | Vibrating mops for better stain removal, dual spinning mops with varying pressure, automatic mop pad washing, steam cleaning. |
| Water Management | Mist spraying for water efficiency, manual water tank refilling. | Automatic water refilling/emptying, precise water dispensing, dirty water separation, water recycling. |
| Control System | Arduino Uno Rev3. | More powerful microcontrollers (ARM-based), integration with mobile apps, voice control, smart home integration. |
| Sensors | IR sensors for obstacle detection. | LiDAR, ultrasonic sensors, gyroscopes, accelerometers, cliff sensors, dirt detection sensors, cameras for visual navigation. |
| Power Source | 12V Lithium-ion battery with inbuilt charging circuit. | Higher capacity batteries for longer run times, fast charging, automatic docking and charging. |
| Autonomy | Autonomous operation based on IR sensor input. | Full autonomy with advanced mapping and path planning, zone cleaning, scheduled cleaning, adaptive cleaning based on dirt level. |
| Water Spraying | Mist spraying with adjustable nozzle. | Controlled spray patterns, adjustable spray intensity, detergent mixing, automatic spray activation. |
| Cost | Low-cost design using readily available components. | Wide range of costs, from budget-friendly to premium models with advanced features. |
| Cleaning Solution | User-defined cleaning fluid. | Integration with specific cleaning solutions, automatic detergent dosing, specialized cleaning modes. |
| Design Complexity | Relatively simple design with basic components. | More complex designs with advanced mechanical and electronic components, modular design for easy maintenance. |
| Connectivity | No wireless connectivity mentioned. | Wi-Fi, Bluetooth, app control, smart home integration. |
| Dirt Detection | Implicit obstacle avoidance, no specific dirt detection. | Optical dirt detection, particle sensors, AI-based dirt recognition. |

| Feature/Performance | This Paper | Recent Advancements (General Trends) |
|---|---|---|
| **User Interface** | On/off switch, no advanced interface. | Mobile app control, voice commands, touchscreens, LED indicators. |
| **Maintenance** | Manual cleaning of mops and water tank. | Automatic mop washing, self-emptying dustbins, easy component replacement. |

Source: Author

## Conclusion

Considering advancements in robotics, this research focuses on the crucial need for efficient and accurate path-planning algorithms in mopping robots. This paper proposes a cost-effective, Arduino-based mopping robot designed to enhance hygiene and efficiency, particularly in environments like hospitals. By employing mist spraying and basic autonomous path planning, the robot minimizes contamination risks and reduces labor demands. Its design prioritizes accessibility and consistent cleaning quality, effectively addressing key challenges in modern cleaning practices. This work underscores the potential of affordable robotics to improve overall cleaning standards and accessibility, providing a valuable tool to address heightened hygiene concerns, especially those highlighted by recent pandemics, and demonstrating its feasibility for widespread societal use.

## Acknowledgement

We would like to express our sincere gratitude to Siddhesh Dharmameher, Shashank Dand, and Pranisha Chaturvedi from SVKM's NMIMS, MPSTME, Shirpur Campus, for their significant contributions to the development of this work

## References

[1]   Prassler, E., Ritter, A., Schaeffer, C., and Fiorini, P. (2000). A Short History of Cleaning Robots. Autonomous Robots 9, 211–226. https://doi.org/10.1023/A:1008974515925.

[2]   Koselka, H., Wallach, B. A., and Gollaher, D. (2001). Autonomous floor mopping apparatus. U.S. Patent US6741054B2, filed May 2, 2001, and issued May 25, 2004.

[3]   Jones, J. L., Mack, N. E., Nugent, D. M., and Sandin, P. E. (2005). Autonomous floor-cleaning robot. U.S. Patent US6883201B2, filed January 3, 2002, and issued April 26, 2005.

[4]   Andrew, Z., Duane, G., John, M. C., Scott, P., Paul, S., Nancy, D., and Andrew, J. (2008). Autonomous surface cleaning robot for wet and dry cleaning. U.S. Patent US-7389156-B2, filed August 18, 2005, and issued June 17, 2008.

[5]   Michael, D., Philip, C. J., and Nikolai, R. 2014. System and method for autonomous mopping of a floor surface. U.S. Patent US8892251-B1, filed December 22, 2010, and issued November 18, 2014.

[6]   "Robot Vacuums and Mops." iRobot Corporation. iRobot®. Accessed July 22, 2025. https://www.irobot.com/.

[7]   "Jetbot Mop." Samsung. Accessed July 22, 2025. https://www.samsung.com/us/vacuums/#Jetbot-Mop/.

# 30 Beach litter detection and path optimization for autonomous cleaning drones using YOLOv8, tensorRT and ONNX

*Priyam Kuvadiya[a], Chirag Devgade[b], Sachin Sonawane[c] and Irbaaz Patel[d]*

Department of Artificial Intelligence and Machine Learning, SVKM's NMIMS, Mukesh Patel School of Technology Management and Engineering, Shirpur, Maharashtra, India

## Abstract

This work presents an innovative framework that combines computer vision, deep learning, and path optimization to enable autonomous drone-based litter collection on beaches. Utilizing YOLOv8L model, enhanced ArduPilotX and TensorRT. The system attains rapid and efficient object identification on NVIDIA GPUs. Aerial photography of high resolution obtained from drones subjected to pre-processing via normalization and augmentation for improving detection accuracy. Litter delineated with bounding boxes and centroid coordinates extracted as navigational waypoints for accurate drone maneuvering. A greedy pathfinding algorithm calculates the optimal route, significantly reducing the drone's travel distance to litter locations and thus maximizing operational efficiency. This framework enhances litter detection with a scalable and autonomous solution, addressing environmental concerns on a global scale. The optimized detection attains a mean Average Precision of 71.4% at 50% (mAP50), processing frames at about 70 frames per second (FPS) utilizing CUDA acceleration for real-time inference. Calculated trajectories are structured in JSON for ArduPilot, facilitating autonomous drone navigation.

Keywords: Beach litter detection, computer vision, hardware acceleration, path finding, YOLOv8L

## Introduction

Litter decomposition in marine coastal ecosystems is becoming a global issue affecting marine biodiversity, public health, tourism, and local economies. An estimated 8 million tons of plastic enter the ocean each year. NOAA studies show that plastics, being dominant pollutants of ecosystems and dangerous to marine life, constitute 90% of marine debris in certain parts of the world [9]. The manual cleaning efforts are inadequate in handling the problem. Even extensive operations address only 20% of littered areas in a single endeavor [1]. Therefore, researchers have focused on developing an automated system. The literature review below examines the current research on deep learning and UAVs for beach litter detection, emphasizing the shortcomings in present methodologies.

The issue of tiny item recognition in residential environments was tackled using a Faster R-CNN with Feature Pyramid Networks (FPN) and cross-entropy with focal loss [9]. With 8000 CCTV pictures, the accuracy was above 98%. This model's excessive dependence

[a]priyamkuvadiya19@gmail.com, [b]work.chiragdevgade@gmail.com, [c]sachin.sonawane@nmims.edu, [d]patelirbaazahmed@gmail.com

DOI: 10.1201/9781003716648-30

on a dataset restricts the applicability of models. The conditional random field (CRF) optimization for multi-level trash segmentation on RGBD pictures was also suggested by Wang et al. [12]. Using datasets like MJU-Waste and TACO, this work outperforms DeepLab [13]. However, it ignored the issues of light and size variations. To overcome the dataset's limitations, the "TU Delft Green Village" dataset for identifying floating debris in urban waterways was made available [8]. Their models, DenseNet121 and SqueezeNet, achieved accuracies of 91.7% and 89.6%, respectively. Accuracy diminished with unfamiliar litters. Trashbusters combining Yolov4 and DeepSORT for identifying the littering activity was introduced [7]. The system struck a compromise between speed and accuracy. However, high processing requirements obstructed its implementation. The optimized models were investigated, comparing YOLOv5x, Mask R-CNN, RetinaNet, and EfficientDet using their PlastOPol dataset [3]. Despite YOLOv5x attaining the best accuracy among the models, small things detection continued to pose difficulties. UAVs with YOLOv5 for beach litter detection, achieving a mean average precision (mAP) of 0.252 across several litter categories were used [11]. Their approach had challenges identifying tiny things. A CNN-based model for litter detection, employing transfer learning was proposed (Malik et al. 2023) [14]. Their method required high computational resources. A higher litter identification accuracy was attained using UAV images and neural networks [1]. Their methodology was deficient in pathfinding. YOLOv8 was tested for UAV-based power line inspection [2]. It attained an excellent accuracy of 83.8% at 243 FPS on GPU. They indicated diminished efficiency on CPU with a necessity for lightweight and efficient models. The progress of YOLO models was examined, specifically their appropriateness for edge devices in real-time applications [4, 5]. They emphasized the advancements in YOLOv10, including NMS-free training and large-kernel convolutions, which enhanced real-time performance. However, reconciling model complexity with detection accuracy in resource-limited settings continues to pose difficulties. The complete YOLO series, from YOLOv1 to YOLOv8 was examined, observing that although YOLOv8 showed considerable enhancements in speed and accuracy, it had difficulties with occlusions and clutter [6].

A significant deficiency in existing studies is the restricted emphasis on autonomous path optimization within drone-assisted litter-collecting systems. This proposal fills the research gap by designing an extensible, autonomous, and efficient framework to identify litter on beaches, utilizing advanced deep learning and a greedy pathfinding method to enhance drone navigation, minimizing travel duration. This work investigates a scalable system with high-performance computer vision and deep learning models for real-time, precise detection and localization of litter; develop an effective path optimization algorithm to minimize the drone travel distance, reducing energy consumption. This work proposed a drone-based solution for coastline litter detection and collection. The optimized YOLOv8L model with ONNX (Open Neural Network Exchange) and TensorRT empowers high-throughput litter detection on NVIDIA GPUs. The system processes high-resolution aerial imagery to identify miscellaneous wastes like plastics, metals, and organic debris. An advanced greedy pathfinding algorithm finds the shortest drone travel routes. These routes are encoded in JSON file and integrated with ArduPilot. The real-time performance of the system is preserved with CUDA-based acceleration.

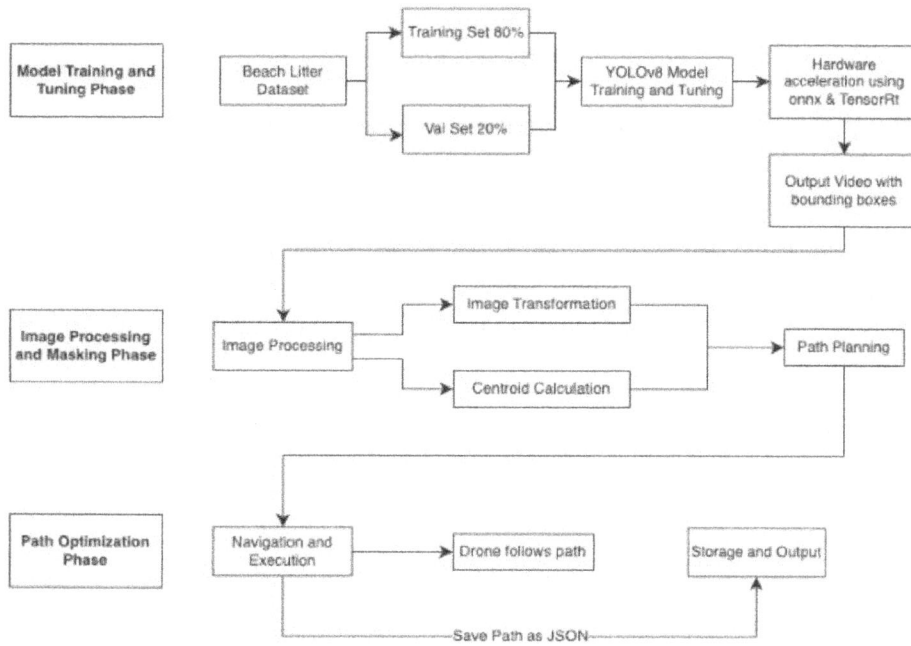

*Figure 30.1* Computational process flow
Source: Author

## Methodology

Figure 30.1 depicts the computational process flow of the proposed methodology. The process starts with dividing the image dataset into training (80%) and validation (20%). The YOLOv8L model, enhanced with ONNX and hardware acceleration, utilizes both datasets. The image processing transforms images to identify beach litter. The centroids of each detected object are calculated for path planning. Path planning uses centroids for navigation.

### Model training and optimization

The dataset used in this work consists of aerial images of the Saudi Arabian Red Sea coast captured by Martin et al. [10]. It comprises drone images with dimensions of 5472 × 3078, acquired at 10 meters altitude. The dataset categorizes litter, including plastic bottles, wrappers, and cans. Bounding boxes were added around litter objects in the images. The image annotations were stored as a text file. We used the computer vision annotation tool (CVAT) to classify different types of trash. This tool also specified x and y coordinates, width, and height. A detailed hyperparameter optimization of the YOLOv8L model (Figure 30.2) was performed on batching, learning rate, and dimensions. The performance was effective with 50 epochs and an input image of 640 pixels. The convergence of the model was based on an initial learning rate (lr0) of 0.001. To reduce the forgetting overtime factor, the lrf was controlled at 0.2, and a decay factor was added in training. It was found that SGD handles large datasets effectively. Afterward, the learning rate was halved as scheduled using the cosine schedule, providing smooth convergence without any sudden drops. A batch size of

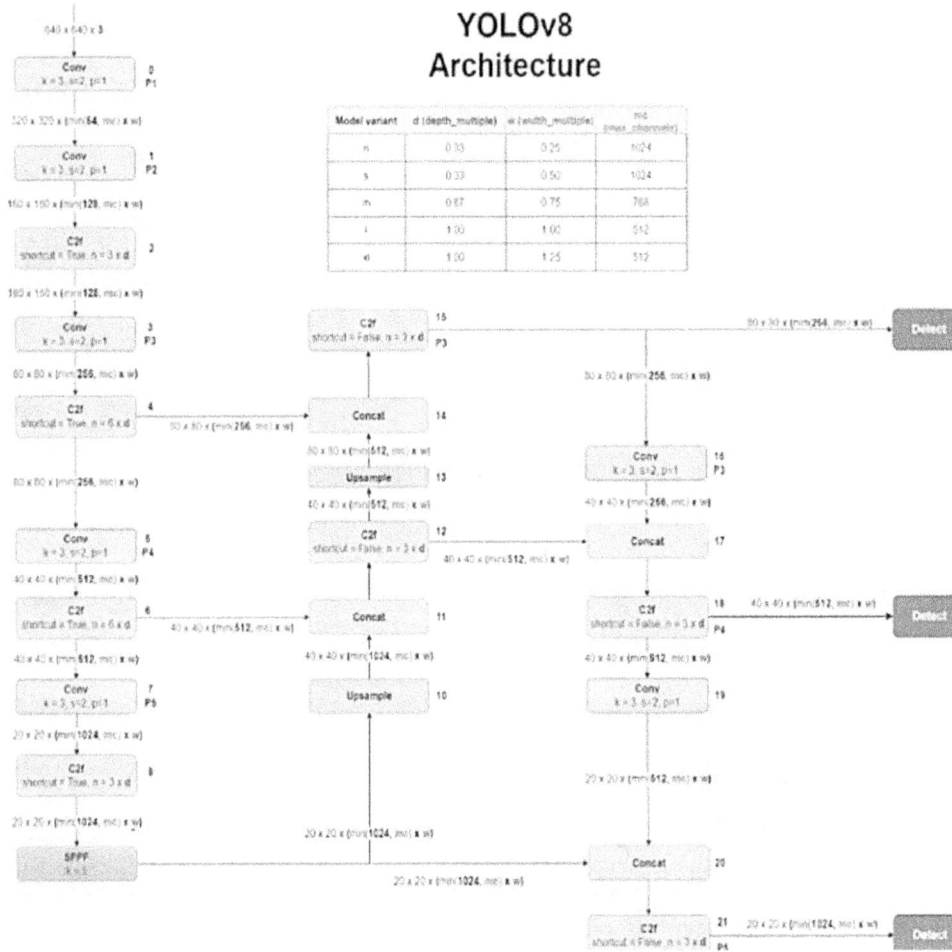

*Figure 30.2* Architecture of YOLOv8
(Courtesy: https://yolov8.org/yolov8-architecture-explained/).
Source: Author

16 was chosen to optimize the memory while ensuring consistent model updates. The set of data modifications allowed data transformation through flipping, scaling, and rotation and thus enhanced model robustness.

*Hardware acceleration*

The process was accelerated using ONNX and NVIDIA TensorRT. It converted the PyTorch file to ONNX format, a standard compatible with the TensorRT. ONNX enabled precision adjustment (FP16 or INT8) and a combination of layers. Having improved the processing time, TensorRT utilized the GPU-specific changes to accelerate FPS during inference. Figure 30.3 demonstrates the model's performance in detecting and bounding litter objects in real time.

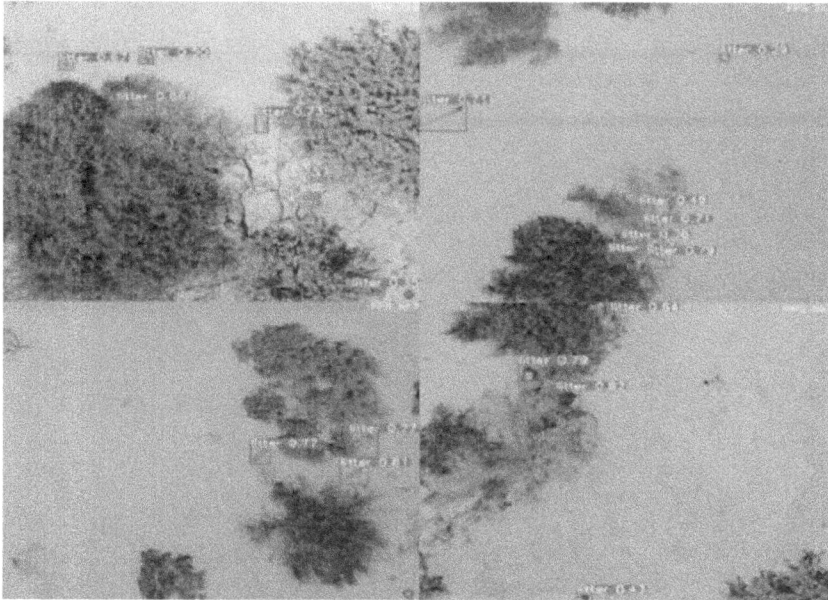

*Figure 30.3* Screenshots of the output video after testing
Source: Author

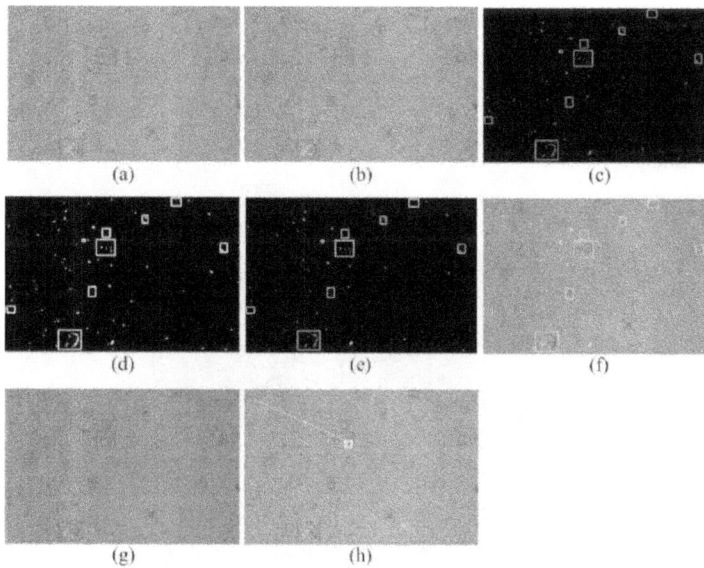

*Figure 30.4* (a) Original unprocessed aerial image, (b) Grayscale conversion, (c) Edge detection using canny algorithm, (d) Dilated image, (e) Eroded image, (f) Contours image depicts recognizable rubbish item outlines, (g) Image of centroid marks the centroids of filtered contours with small blue dots, (h) Annotated video frame
Source: Author

## *Image processing and path planning*

The OpenCV library was deployed for grayscale conversion, edge detection, dilation, erosion, and contour analyses. Figure 30.4 illustrates images from each operation. Greyscale images were processed with canny edge detection. Dilation and erosion enhanced object borders. The contours were filtered using a minimal area threshold, removing noise and unnecessary shapes. The x and y coordinates of the center are determined for each contour. The path planning in drone flying, navigating through unevenly distributed centroids. The greedy algorithm identified the nearest unvisited centroid as the subsequent destination. This approach includes selecting a location and calculating the Euclidean distance to each unexplored centroid. It continued until all the centroids were visited. The data was saved in JSON files.

```
{    "path": [              {            "
      latitude": 365,
      ": 198        },       ..."longitude
      "time taken seconds":
      0.00025391578674316406}
```

### Snippet of JSON file

The efficiency of the path planning algorithm was observed for the drone journey to the chosen centroids. To illustrate consecutive pathways and centroid locations, colored lines and markers (Figure 30.5) were used in the frame of the video. The following example explains the operation. Assume the starting or current position of the drone is (0,0), the target position is (7,6), and the possible moves are (0,1), (1,0), (1,1). The greedy algorithm calculates Euclidean distance for each move and chooses the shortest one, 7.81 for (1,1).

$$For\ (0,1): \sqrt{(7-0)^2 + (6-1)^2} = 8.60 \tag{1}$$

$$For\ (0,1): \sqrt{(7-1)^2 + (6-0)^2} = 8.49 \tag{2}$$

$$For\ (0,1): \sqrt{(7-1)^2 + (6-1)^2} = 7.81 \tag{3}$$

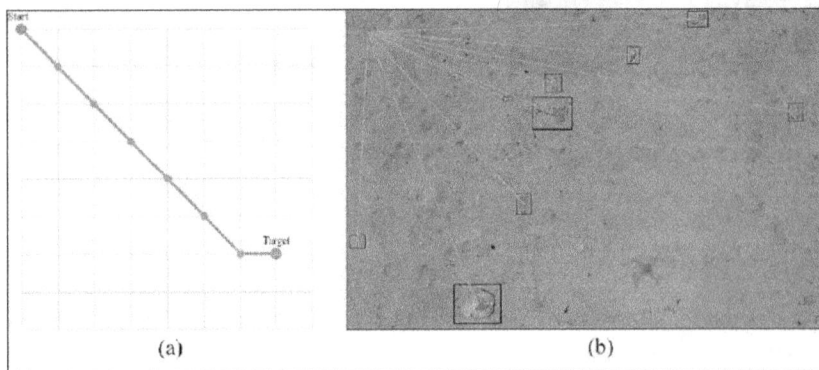

(a)  (b)

*Figure 30.5* (a) Path planning using greedy algorithm (b) Final annotated path frame for Ardupilot
Source: Author

The frame-by-frame analysis yields significant input images. The annotated images display the path of the drone. Each centroid in the path indicates the order of consecutive locations up to the destination, prioritizing navigation, with odd-numbered centroids denoting goals and even-numbered locations indicating returns to the origin. The annotated graphic assisted Ardupilot in adhering to the trajectory by offering distinct visual indicators for navigation.

## Results and Analysis

### Performance overview of YOLOv8l

When evaluating the impact of image size on model performance, Table 30.1 reveals that using a larger image size enhances several key metrics. With an image of 640 pixels, the model attains a mAP50 (mean average precision at a 50% intersection above the union threshold) of 0.53812, indicating that increased resolution aids the model in capturing finer information. The train/dfl_loss and val/dfl_loss are diminished, indicating superior model fitting. A precision of 0.82729 means a reduction in false positives. Table 30.2 explores how adjusting the number of training epochs impacts key model metrics. It compares mAP50, training and validation losses, recall, and precision over five epochs: 25, 50, 75, 100, and 200. The highest mAP50 of 0.53853 is achieved at 50 epochs alongside a lower val/dfl_loss (1.6782), better recall (0.43734), and similar precision. Table 30.3 demonstrates the effect of employing half_precision, transiting the model from 32 to 16-bit floating-point. It decreases memory consumption and accelerates GPUs computations, boosting mAP50 from 0.53853 to 0.58938 and recall from 0.43734 to 0.48571. The training and validation losses dropped from 1.3345 to 1.2184 and 1.6782 to 1.1957. Table 30.4 shows that applying hardware acceleration with ONNX and TensorRT FPS increases to 74.

Table 30.5 shows the impact of hyperparameter tuning on model performance over 50 epochs with hardware acceleration. It shows a significant improvement in mAP50 up to

*Table 30.1* Effect of image size on mAP50.

| Image size | Metrics/map50 | Train/Dfl_loss | Val/dfl_loss | Recall | Precision |
|---|---|---|---|---|---|
| 320 | 0.47519 | 1.9179 | 2.1423 | 0.41071 | 0.64972 |
| 640 | 0.53812 | 1.2373 | 1.2718 | 0.39286 | 0.82729 |

Source: Author

*Table 30.2* Effect of number of epochs on mAP50.

| Epochs | Metrics/map50 | Train/Dfl_loss | Val/dfl_loss | Recall | Precision |
|---|---|---|---|---|---|
| 25 | 0.46224 | 1.5986 | 3.0345 | 0.29494 | 0.67182 |
| 50 | 0.53853 | 1.3345 | 1.6782 | 0.43734 | 0.66319 |
| 75 | 0.51934 | 1.4112 | 1.5789 | 0.43816 | 0.69128 |
| 100 | 0.53812 | 1.2373 | 1.2718 | 0.39286 | 0.82729 |
| 200 | 0.53359 | 1.2504 | 1.8863 | 0.43571 | 0.67616 |

Source: Author

*Table 30.3* Effect of half precision parameter.

| Epochs | Metrics/map50 | Train/Dfl_loss | Val/dfl_loss | Recall | Precision |
|--------|---------------|----------------|--------------|--------|-----------|
| False | 0.53853 | 1.3345 | 1.6782 | 0.43734 | 0.66319 |
| True | 0.58938 | 1.2184 | 1.1957 | 0.48571 | 0.62353 |

Source: Author

*Table 30.4* Effect of hardware acceleration.

| Hardware acceleration | Metrics/map50 | Maximum FPS |
|-----------------------|---------------|-------------|
| Without acceleration | 0.58938 | 43 |
| With acceleration | 0.58513 | 74 |

Source: Author

*Table 30.5* Hyperparameter tuning with hardware acceleration.

| Parameters | Metrics/map50 | Maximum FPS |
|------------|---------------|-------------|
| Default Parameters | 0.58938 | 74 |
| Tuned Parameters | 0.71429 | 74 |

Source: Author

0.71429 with FPS 74. Configuring patience to 10 enables early ending, ceasing training if performance stagnates for 10 epochs. Switching to the stochastic gradient descent (SGD) optimizer helped reduce the risk of overfitting. An initial learning rate of 0.005 gave the model a stable start, while gradually lowering it by 0.2 in later stages enables fine-tuning. A high momentum of 0.95 improves learning stability. A 0.0005 weight decay regularized large weights. The training process utilized a 5-epoch warmup setting that gradually increased the learning rate. The data augmentation techniques incorporated in the process include color variations, scaling, translating, and flipping objects. The mix-up augmentation helped the model deal with occlusions and complex backgrounds.

Comparing these results with the results by Liu et al. [9] and Pfeiffer et al. [11], a Faster RCNN with high-resolution drone images was utilized to classify beach trash along Saudi Arabia's Red Sea. It achieved a mean sensitivity of 46.5% (up to 59.2% on higher-resolution images) and PPV of 63.8%, with ground truth measurements showing an 82% probability of detection for objects bigger than 2.5 cm by Liu et al. [9]. It was reported a mAP50-95 of 0.252 across all litter classes, with their best single-class performance reaching 0.674 [11]. The proposed model achieves a higher mAP50 of 0.58938 with half-precision training. This enhanced performance was achieved through multiple parameter optimization and floating-point precision reduction. The model exhibits precision at 0.82729. Our implementation achieved 74 FPS through hardware acceleration with ONNX and TensorRT, enabling real-time processing.

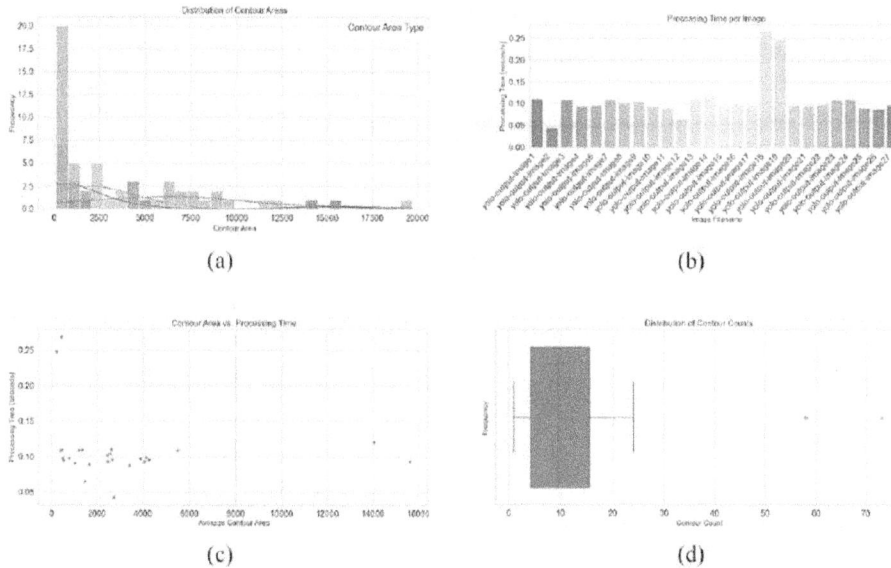

*Figure 30.6* (a) Final contour area distribution, (b) Time of processing per image, (c) Contour area vs processing time, (d) Contour count distribution
Source: Author

*Performance overview of image processing and path optimization*

The image processing block recorded every image with the total count, minimum, maximum, and average sizes of contours. The contours were outlined in the original image. These metrics were stored in a CSV file with a filename, number of contours, minimum, maximum, average contour area, total path distance, and processing time. Figure 30.6 depicts the visualizations implemented for this purpose.

The contour count bar chart shows contours in each image, pointing to the item density. In the histogram of contour area distribution, the distribution of areas is classified into lowest, highest, and average values, enabling the identification of trends or anomalies in item size. The bar chart on processing time per image was also plotted. Experimentation revealed that the path planning algorithm worked well with varying centroid spacing. The scatter plot depicts the correlation between average contour area and processing time. The box plot illustrates the distribution of contour counts, demonstrating the range and variability of images. The boxplot encapsulates item density by displaying the median, interquartile range, and probable outliers.

## Conclusion

This work focused on tackling the problem of coastal pollution by blending cutting-edge technology with a practical approach. The work achieves fast and better litter detection using the YOLOv8 model optimized through TensorRT. The combination of drone technology and image processing allows for extensive and efficient coverage of large beach areas, underscoring the effectiveness of this approach over labor-intensive cleanup methods. The work highlights a well-scale model. Utilizing hardware acceleration through CUDA and ONNX for model optimization allows the system to run with data loads, allowing drone autonomous and real-time operation with no interference. The path information it serves, in JSON format for ease of consumption by ArduPilot and other systems, speaks to the rigorous work that has brought this system to a state of practicality. This research points to more environmentally friendly and sustainable solutions having a good chance of being widely implemented.

## References

[1] Bak, S. H., Hwang, D. H., Kim, H. M., & Yoon, H. J. (2019). Detection and monitoring of beach litter using UAV image and deep neural network. In The International Archives of the Photogrammetry, Remote Sensing and Spatial Information Sciences, (Vol. XLII-3/W8, pp. 55–58). https://doi.org/10.5194/isprs-archives-XLII-3-W8-55-2019.

[2] Bellou, E., Pisica, I., & Banitsas, K. (2024). Aerial inspection of high-voltage power lines using YOLOv8 real-time object detector. *Energies*, 17(11), 2535. https://doi.org/10.3390/en17112535.

[3] Córdova, M., Pinto, A., Hellevik, C. C., Alaliyat, S. A. A., Hameed, I. A., Pedrini, H., et al. (2022). Litter detection with deep learning: a comparative study. *Sensors*, 22(2), 548. https://doi.org/10.3390/s22020548.

[4] Deng, J., Xuan, X., Wang, W., Li, Z., Yao, H., & Wang, Z. (2020). A review of research on object detection based on deep learning. *Journal of Physics: Conference Series*, 1684(1), 012028. https://doi.org/10.1088/1742-6596/1684/1/012028.

[5] Hussain, M. (2024). YOLOv5, YOLOv8, and YOLOv10: the go-to detectors for real-time vision. arXiv Preprint: arXiv:2402.67890. https://doi.org/10.48550/arXiv.2407.02988.

[6] Hussain, M. (2024). YOLOv1 to v8: unveiling each variant–a comprehensive review of YOLO. *IEEE Access*, 12, 42816–42833. https://doi.org/10.1109/ACCESS.2024.3378568.

[7] Jain, K., Juthani, M., Jain, J., & Nimkar, A. V. (2024). Trashbusters: deep learning approach for litter detection and tracking. arXiv Preprint: arXiv:2401.12345. https://doi.org/10.48550/arXiv.2404.07467.

[8] Jia, T., Vallendar, A. J., de Vries, R., Kapelan, Z., & Taormina, R. (2023). Advancing deep learning-based detection of floating litter using a novel open dataset. *Frontiers in Sec. Water and Artificial Intelligence*, 5, 1–12. https://doi.org/10.3389/frwa.2023.1298465.

[9] Liu, J., Pan, C., & Yan, W. Q. (2022). Litter detection from digital images using deep learning. *SN Computer Science*, 4(2), 134. https://doi.org/10.1007/s42979-022-01568-1.

[10] Martin, C., Zhang, Q., Zhai, D., Zhang, X., & Duarte, C. M. (2021). Drone images of sandy beaches and anthropogenic litter along the Saudi Arabian red sea (Vol. 1). *Data in Brief*, 35, 106954. https://doi.org/10.17632/gpdsntb3y6.1.

[11] Pfeiffer, R., Valentino, G., D'Amico, S., Piroddi, L., Galone, L., Calleja, S., et al. (2022). Use of UAVs and deep learning for beach litter monitoring. *Electronics*, 12(1), 198. https://doi.org/10.3390/electronics12010198.

[12] Wang, T., Cai, Y., Liang, L., & Ye, D. (2020). A multi-level approach to waste object segmentation. *Sensors*, 20(14), 3816. https://doi.org/10.3390/s20143816.

[13] YOLOv8 architecture explained. Accessed February 18, 2025, https://yolov8.org/yolov8-architecture-explained/.

[14] Malik, M., Chander Prabha, Punit Soni, et al. (2023). Machine Learning-Based Automatic Litter Detection and Classification Using Neural Networks in Smart Cities. *International Journal on Semantic Web and Information Systems*. 19(1), 1–20. https://doi.org/10.4018/IJSWIS.324105.

# 31 Blockchain integration with machine learning for supply chain management in industries: a survey

*Vanshika Gupta[a] and Aditya Bakshi[b]*

School of Technology Management and Engineering, Narsee Monjee Institute of Management Studies, Chandigarh, India

## Abstract

Supply chain (SC) is a collaboration of individuals, organisations, assets, tasks, and technology that are used in manufacturing and vending a merchandise. Everything ranging from the shifting of primal matters from the supplier to the producer to the destination to the customer is a part of SC. The SC can be disrupted and is at risk to deceit, cheating, and tampering even while using centralized supply chain management (SCM) systems. By making use of Blockchain technology there have been a lot of rises made in terms of decentralization, transparency,securecured solutions. By integrating blockchain with machine learning (ML) in the field of SC there are a lot of further advancements which can be unlocked. This paper delivers a detailed analysis of blockchain-based supply chain management by integrating ML. The paper discusses how blockchain and ML toarearegether be integrated to make the process of supply chain management more transparent, secure and decentralised for better results. Key topics are the introduction about what blockchain and ML are, the past work done in this field, and the future scope in this field which can further be explored and worked upon. Also, the paper provides a brief overview of other applications of Blockchain and ML when integrated together which have become a necessity in today's time.

Keywords: Blockchain, decentralization technology, ML, SC

## Introduction

As the world is moving towards globalization and the pace at which the technology is developing the complexity of global supply chain is also increasing, creating chaos and raising an urgent need for finding and innovating techniques to get rid of obstacles to address issues like lack of transparency, increasing number of fraudulent cases and security issues. Managed SCs are beneficial in the rise of organizations therefore, each organization tries to find and evolve technologies that help in the improvement of SCs [10].

There are a lot of challenges which make it difficult to manage these supply chains. The challenges range from the changing consumers' preferences and needs along with tough competition from the market. Factors like varied geographic locations, unreliable customer demands and needs along with rapid change in technologies coming up lead to difficulty in SC management. As the number of incidents increased and issues of product traceability along with accountability started emerging then there were demands of innovating a technology which could deal with these issues and provide a secure and reliable mechanism

[a]gupta.vanshika008@nmims.in, [b]addybakshi@gmail.com

DOI: 10.1201/9781003716648-31

for the SCM. The best-known technology found till date is blockchain technology (BT), which is the most promising technology along with the integration of ML which offers a transformative approach in dealing with the issues faced. BT is known for its decentralized and immutable ledger that is used in recording the transactions while ensuring transparency and security as it allows all the stakeholders to track and verify the transactions in real time without the need for depending on any intermediaries. ML complements this by helping in providing detailed and intelligent data analysis, useful and predictive insights which help the organizations in optimizing the processes [7].

The blockchain and ML together complement each other to address and solve these challenges which are faced while using the traditional SCM. Decentralization and transparency that uses the distributed ledger system to ensure that every transaction made in the chain is recorded immutably. Traditional SCMs lacks real time monitoring which led to inefficiencies in logistics, inventory management and demand forecasting. Blockchain helps in keeping track of real time transactions while ML uses this data for further analysis and inventory optimization. ML models which are highly used for this purpose are Long Short-Term Memory networks that accurately predict future demand thus optimizing the work. The parametric analysis of SC data using ML models aids in predictive maintenance of machinery, efficient resource allocation and better decision making for the suppliers and logistics providers [7].

Integration of blockchain and ML for SCM, while focusing on how these technologies can help in eradicating the problems of lack of transparency and fraud and chances of the success of supply chain management increase by a tremendous amount. Figure 31.1. shown below demonstrates the process of machine learning which is iterative in nature. Firstly, start with the collection of raw data and in pre-processing state the data is transformed into a structured format. The data is transformed several times. After thorough checks, a final model is selected for prediction to improve performance.

## Literature Review

The integration of Blockchain Technology and ML has surfaced as a very powerful tool which have gained utmost attention in the recent times in as all the industries are trying to

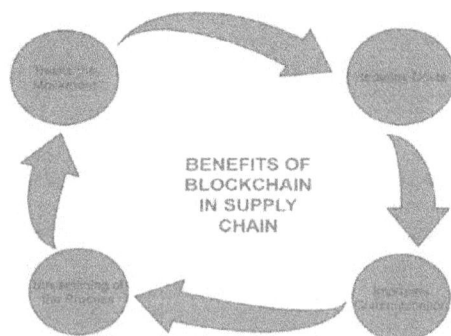

*Figure 31.1* Benefits of blockchain in supply chain
Source: Author

expand and revolutionize their businesses. This literature Review specifically marks and provides a deep insight into how the integration of these two very promising technologies enhances the transparency and traceability within the supply chains.

*Blockchain in supply chain*

Blockchain was first designed for cryptocurrencies basically like Bitcoin, but in recent years it has found immense applications in diverse fields [9]. The advantages of Blockchain in SC integration are addressing the issue of fraud and tempering to tackling inefficiencies in SCM and improving the decision-making process. Blockchain helps in the prevention of unauthorised and illegal changes by maintaining an immutable ledger of the transactions. This is made use particularly in pharmaceuticals, where regulatory compliance requires detailed tracking. This technology is revolutionizing the SCM by increasing transparency, security and efficiency [9].

*ML in supply chain*

The various research done in this field helped in finding out that the use of ML models in analysing complex datasets help in improving operational efficiency [12]. ML detects fraudulent transactions through anomaly detection algorithms, thereby reducing the risk of any financial and operational fraud. It predicts the supply-demand trends and also optimizes the warehouse management through time-series models, thus reducing and improving the supply chain efficiency. The usage of ML in SCM offers a wide range of advantages for the improvement of efficiency shown in Figure 31.2. ML learning algorithms not only enhance the productivity by automating decision making processes, leading to optimised resource allocation [12].

*Integration of blockchain and ML in supply chain*

This convergence of Blockchain and ML introduced several advanced methodologies which further improved efficiency in SCM thus leading to increased decision-making quality. The three key theoretical advancements have been explained in certain steps.

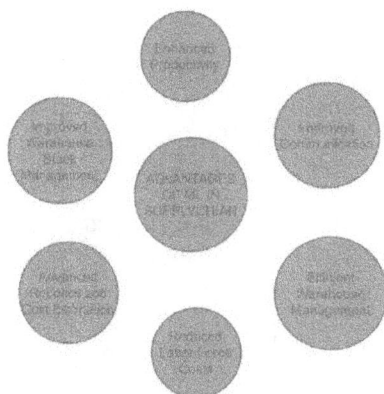

*Figure 31.2* Benefits of machine learning in supply chain
Source: Author

Smart Contraction Optimization: AI-enhanced smart contracts make use of ML models to automate and optimize the contract execution within the blockchain legered supply chains. These contracts are capable of dynamically adjusting to conditions on different basis like reducing processing latency. Federated learning (FL) in blockchain: A powerful tool which allows for ML training without compromising data privacy. This FL approach is particularly beneficial for SCM networks where the suppliers and manufacturers need to share their insights without the exposure of sensitive data [1].

*Table 31.1* Literature review of different state of art approaches.

| Name of author and year of publication | Methodology | Advantages | Disadvantages |
|---|---|---|---|
| [1] | System employs a fabric called Hyperledger Fabric to manage the drug SC, which ensures transparency. A ML module is used which makes use of N-gram and LightGBM that are coached on a UCI public drug Review dataset. | It enhances supply chain transparency, prevents counterfeit drugs, and also is used for offering tailored medication to the consumers. | The effectiveness of the system is limited by the small network size and also lacks real time implementation. |
| [10] | It starts with identifying critical factors that influence blockchain like competition pressure. After that the ML models assess the probability based on these factors. | This technique helps in offering a data driven framework that evaluates the blockchain adoption success rate. | It requires that the users should adjust the probability values manually. |
| [3] | Blockchain is used for ensuring data is not immutable and ML for helping in identifying patterns of fraudulent activities. | It improved fraud detection accuracy and also helped in real time monitoring. | Depends on high quality training data. |
| [16] | Blockchain technology was used to securely log sensor data collected from IOT devices. Machine Learning models were employed to predict potential risks. | It ensured that the system maintained the quality and traceability throughout the cold chain. | Highly costly to implement and also network scalability issues were faced. |

Source: Author

Explainable AI(XAI) in SCM: Traditional ML models used to often operate as black boxes which made it difficult for the holders to interpret the recommendations and predictions. By integration of XAI with blockchain, organisations are now capable of improving regulatory compliance, risk assessment and decision-making accuracy [9].

The use of blockchain in supply chain not only there will be improving security, openness, traceability and productivity [12]. In Table 31.1, literature review of different state of art approaches are presented.

## Proposed Model

In proposed model, collection of data from various chains has been presented. It starts with the collection of data from various supply chain sources and then integrating it into a blockchain.

Blockchain is used for ensuring the transparency of data along with maintaining its integrity. Blockchain technology can log sensor data along with the transaction details. After the data is put on the blockchain, the use of ML models is done to analyze the data. Techniques like supervised learning, neural networks and anomaly detection algorithms are used [15]. The diagram shown in Figure 31.3. illustrates the process of machine learning which is iterative in nature. Starts with the collection of raw data and in pre-processing state the data is transformed into a structured format. The data is transformed several times to ensure that it is suitable for training. Once the data is ready it is fed into the ML algorithms which apply various learning techniques on it.

The integration of Blockchain and ML in SCM usually follows a structured approach that enhances efficiency and security. The methodology begins with data collection from various sources and then storing of data in blockchain ledger and further processing it using ML algorithms. Anomaly detection techniques play a very crucial role in fraud prevention by identifying irregular patterns.

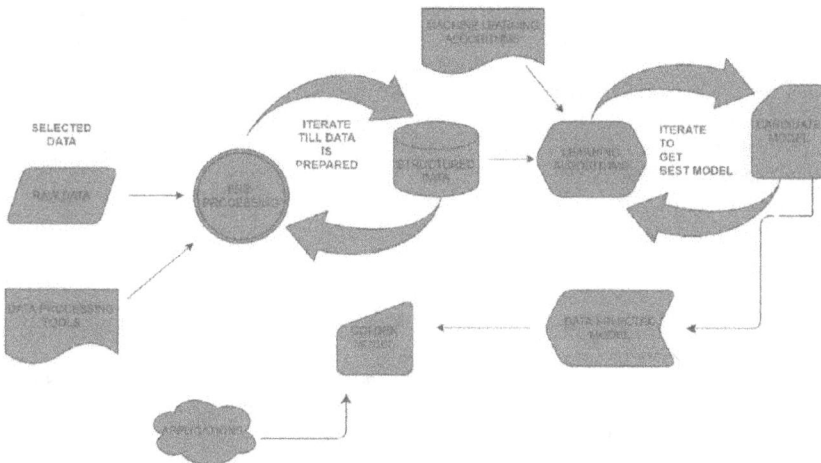

*Figure 31.3* Blockchain integration with machine learning
Source: Author

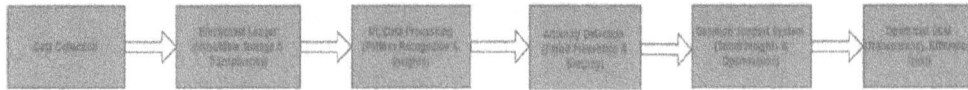

*Figure 31.4* Methodology flowchart
Source: Author

*Table 31.2* Applications of blockchain with machine learning.

| Name of author and year of publication | Description | Advantages | Disadvantages |
|---|---|---|---|
| [5] | The incorporation of blockchain and ML in **healthcare field addresses** several issues ranging from data security to personalized treatment. Blockchain provides transparent methods for storing data and ML helps in analysis. | They are very useful for data security, transparency and personalized medications | Few of the issues faced are scalability issues, Integration challenges and high implementation costs. |
| [8] | BT has robust security along with a distributed ledger system which helps in revolutionizing the **financial field by providing** transparency and integrity. Along with-it ML enhances detection of anomalies. | It increases the security of transactions, reduces false positive rates, enhances transparency. | There are challenges of scalability, high costs and vulnerability to attacks. |
| [6] | The collaboration of blockchain and ML in IoT improves the quality of service by taking into consideration the factors like reliability, scalability and security. Blockchain provides security and decentralized environment, and ML optimizes resource utilization. | It enhances security and better decision making along with resilience to failures. | It has high computational overhead; high energy consumption and implementation costs are also very high. |
| [14] | Integration of both the technologies in the education sector is very **beneficial as it helps in** managing, validating and analyzing student data in an **efficient manner.** | It ensures data security and authenticity and personalized learning along with improved recruitment process. | The implementation costs are very high, also the integration process is very complex. |

Source: Author

The process starts with the collection of data from multiple sources which are usually of two types of primary and secondary data types. The analytical framework is a mixed-method approach consisting of descriptive analysis to examine Blockchain and ML applications in SCM and predictive modelling analysing the efficiency of supply chain along with usage of blockchain simulation by using Hyperledger Fabric to evaluate real-time traceability. For blockchain framework the use of smart contract execution and node verification is done. Validation techniques such as cross-validation for ML models and cryptographic hashing for blockchain integrity assessment are used [15]. In Figure 31.4. detailed flowchart of integration of blockchain and ML is presented.

## Applications of Blockchain Using Machine Learning

In Table 31.2, various applications for integrating Blockchain with ML are presented.

## Future Scope

Blockchain and ML plays and holds a very important role in transforming a large number of industries and fields. The most promising field of application is data security and privacy. Blockchain's decentralized nature along with ML's ability to analyze and process large datasets helps in secured data sharing [13]. Industries like finance, healthcare and education gets benefitted by this integrated technology without any compromises with privacy [4].

Fraud detection and Cybersecurity also are one of the areas where integration of the two technologies can yield very fruitful results. Along with this other fields like supply chain, IoT and education sector can also benefit by making use of this integration as it helps in transparency, traceability and prediction of outcomes along with ensuring security and no compromises with the security [2]. Finance and climate action initiatives also benefit from this integration. Where the blockchain provides tokenized assess management and transparent carbon credit tracking the ML optimizes portfolio performance and optimizes strategies for reducing carbon footprints [11]. ML and Blockchain can be represented as a very transformative force with the potential to address some of the most challenges in the future.

## Conclusion

The integration of these technologies, namely blockchain and ML represents a very significant advancement not only in supply chain but also beyond that, hence promising to revolutionize many industries by increasing and enhancing transparency, efficiency and security. With the help of blockchain one can make immutable ledgers and use analytical powers of ML. Although there are challenges and hurdl es to overcome yet this is one of the most promising fields where the future research aims to focus on optimizing these technologies for exploring new applications to unlock full potential of this integration. This transformative force holds the promise of a more secure and rational future.

## Refernces

[1]   Abbas, K., Afaq, M., Ahmed Khan, T., & Song, W. C. (2020). A blockchain and machine learning-based drug supply chain management and recommendation system for smart pharmaceutical industry. *Electronics*, 9(5), 852. https://doi.org/10.3390/electronics9050852.

[2] Alshurideh, M. T., Hamadneh, S., Alzoubi, H. M., Al Kurdi, B., Nuseir, M. T., & Al Hamad, A. (2024). Empowering supply chain management system with machine learning and blockchain technology. In Cyber Security Impact on Digitalization and Business Intelligence: Big Cyber Security for Information Management: Opportunities and Challenges, (pp. 335–349). https://doi.org/10.1007/978-3-031-31801-6_21.

[3] Ashfaq, T., Khalid, R., Yahaya, A. S., Aslam, S., Azar, A. T., Alsafari, S., et al. (2022). A machine learning and blockchain based efficient fraud detection mechanism. *Sensors*, 22(19), 7162. https://doi.org/10.3390/s22197162.

[4] Chen, F., Wan, H., Cai, H., & Cheng, G. (2021). Machine learning in/for blockchain: Future and challenges. *Canadian Journal of Statistics*, 49(4), 1364–1382. https://doi.org/10.1002/cjs.11623.

[5] Cheng, A. S., Guan, Q., Su, Y., Zhou, P., & Zeng, Y. (2021). Integration of machine learning and blockchain technology in the healthcare field: a literature review and implications for cancer care. *Asia-Pacific Journal of Oncology Nursing*, 8(6), 720–724. https://doi.org/10.4103/apjon.apjon-2140.

[6] CheSuh, L. N., Fernández-Diaz, R. A., Alija-Perez, J. M., Benavides-Cuellar, C., & Alaiz-Moreton, H. (2024). Improve quality of service for the internet of things using blockchain & machine learning algorithms. *Internet of Things*, 26, 101123. https://doi.org/10.1016/j.iot.2024.101123.

[7] Chunduri, V., Raparthi, M., Yellu, R. R., Keshta, I., Byeon, H., Soni, M., et al. (2024). Blockchain-based secure optimized traceable scheme for smart and sustainable food supply chain. *Discover Sustainability*, 5(1), 101. https://doi.org/10.1007/s43621-024-00287-2.

[8] Dhanawat, V. (2022). Anomaly detection in financial transactions using machine learning and blockchain technology. *International Journal of Business Management and Visuals*, 5(1), 34–41. https://ijbmv.com/index.php/home/article/view/63.

[9] Jebamikyous, H., Li, M., Suhas, Y., & Kashef, R. (2023). Leveraging machine learning and blockchain in E-commerce and beyond: benefits, models, and application. *Discover Artificial Intelligence*, 3(1), 3. https://doi.org/10.1007/s44163-022-00046-0.

[10] Kamble, S. S., Gunasekaran, A., Kumar, V., Belhadi, A., & Foropon, C. (2021). A machine learning based approach for predicting blockchain adoption in supply Chain. *Technological Forecasting and Social Change*, 163, 120465. https://doi.org/10.1016/j.techfore.2020.120465.

[11] Kayikci, S., & Khoshgoftaar, T. M. (2024). Blockchain meets machine learning: a survey. *Journal of Big Data*, 11(1), 9. https://doi.org/10.1186/s40537-023-00852-y.

[12] Mahadevan, P., Choudhuri, S. S., Sundara Rajulu Navaneethakrishnan, D. A. A., & Jakhar, R. (2024). Blockchain and ai for engineering supply chain optimization and transparency. *Acta Scientiae*, 7(1), 691–705. https:// doi.org/10.17648/acta.scientiae.6389/1.

[13] Maheshwari, H., Chandra, U., Yadav, D., Gupta, A., & Kaur, R. (2023). Machine learning and blockchain: a promising future. In 2023 4th International Conference on Intelligent Engineering and Management (ICIEM), (pp. 1–6). IEEE. https://doi// 10.1109/ICIEM59379.2023.10166343.

[14] Shah, D., Patel, D., Adesara, J., Hingu, P., & Shah, M. (2021). Integrating machine learning and blockchain to develop a system to veto the forgeries and provide efficient results in education sector. *Visual Computing for Industry, Biomedicine, and Art*, 4, 1–13. https://doi.org/10.1186/s42492-021-00084-y.

[15] Verma, A. (2024). Integration of blockchain and artificial intelligence in supply chain management: a bibliometric & network analysis . IoT Based Recent Trends in Engineering and its Applications IBRTEA (2024):1–29.

[16] Zhang, P., Liu, X., Li, W., & Yu, X. (2021). Pharmaceutical cold chain management based on blockchain and deep learning. *Journal of Internet Technology*, 22(7), 1531–1542. https://doi// 10.53106/160792642021122207007.

# 32 Integrating blockchain implementation with artificial intelligence: a survey

*Nirupjit Kaur[a] and Aditya Bakshi[b]*

School of Technology Management and Engineering, Narsee Monjee Institute of Management Studies, Chandigarh, India

## Abstract

Blockchain technology and artificial intelligence (AI) are combined to revolutionize and cause a major impact that is always changing from time to time and leading to the creation of a number of practices and innovations in various industries. This article analyzes the evolution of blockchain and AI through the years, current research and applications and opportunities to be pursued in future are also discussed. The paper delves into the progress of the three phases in the domain, such as the first convergence that delves into basic ideas: increased attention that represents the features with various studies and experiments and mature integration period that highlights the state-of-the-art frameworks and real-world implementations. The combination not only provides the advantages of improved efficiency, data protection, automated decision-making and decentralized data access but also results in challenges of high cost, scalability and the regulatory issues in the industry.

Keywords: Artificial technology (AI), blockchain, data security

## Introduction

It's a result of the magnificent technological accomplishments of the 21st century, blockchain and artificial intelligence (AI) have proven to be two of the most radical discoveries in recent history. Blockchain technology has reformed the data management and security paradigms with the decentralized and immutable ledger while AI has increased the opportunities for automation and decision making. Their merging ensures not only automation but also trust and predictive analytics that help healthcare, finance, and energy Tyagi et al. [12] to solve essential issues related to operational security, privacy, and the integrity of the data [12]. This paper explores the historical development, uses, research gaps, recent developments, and benefits and drawbacks of merging blockchain technology with artificial intelligence in depth and detail.

## Scope of the Study

This is a study that covers all aspects of the merging of AI and blockchain, and it was made by the author (Figure 32.1). which is a survey. The core questions, such as use cases, advantages, limitations and future research directions, are defined. More precisely, it sheds light on: Security & Privacy Enhancements - AI-based systems which allow for the blockchain technology to be safe from frauds [9, 4].

[a]kaur.nirupjit019@nmims.in, [b]addybakshi@gmail.com

DOI: 10.1201/9781003716648-32

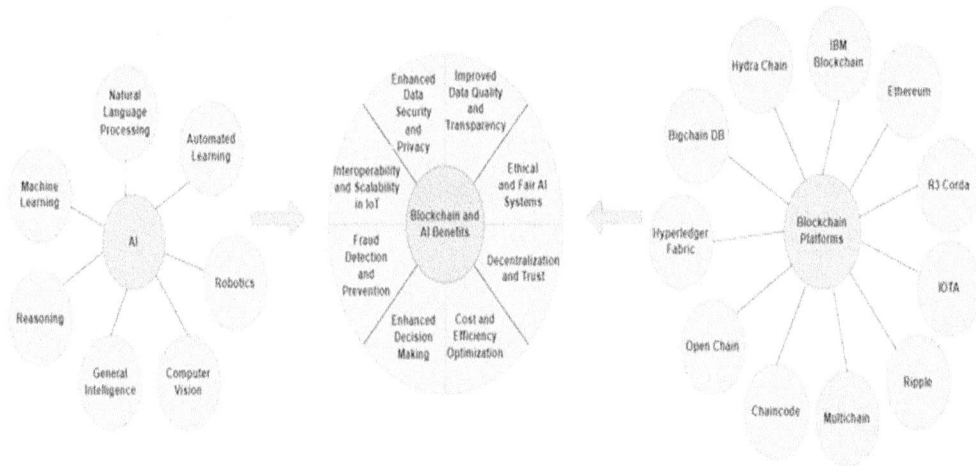

*Figure 32.1* Synergistic integration of blockchain and AI- key platforms and benefits
Source: Author

Scalability & Performance Optimisation - AI-based consensus mechanisms that also provide energy-efficient mining [12, 1]. Applications that are dedicated to the specific sectors of the economy, such as healthcare Wehbe et al. [15] and finance.

Regulatory & Ethical Considerations – Data privacy regulations and AI biases [11].

## Literature Review

The next part is about the inquiry that has been done so far on the merger of blockchain technology and artificial intelligence, theoretical frameworks, actual applications, and years' worth of implementations are included. Firstly, a theoretical convergence is given: the first between year 2016-2018 has been presented. The 1956 Dartmouth Conference was the birth of AI when the idea was introduced of construction and let computers/machines think for themselves just as the human brain does.

Blockchain technology was actually invented in 2008 with the publication of bitcoin [6]. Meanwhile, during this time, both the technologies were still in their early days, hence, were being looked at separately although some studies were being conducted to study the association between the two. The analyses made on blockchain technology included the most important attributes of such as transparency, decentralization, success and effectiveness in various areas such as supply chain management, government, voting, and AI were examined for its data-driven analytical capabilities. During this period, some implementations were designed to evaluate the benefits and the drawbacks of both the technologies together. Secondly, the research of the applications in those sectors of business, healthcare, smart contracts Brune [3] was also put under scrutiny through several experiments and varied topics for these applications by some of which included the real-world market. One major characteristic of this phase is the mature integration between technological and human sources in2022-present which was presented and was brought about by the change from theoretical frameworks to concepts of mental models to actual conditions and scenarios. This is the phase that signifies the simultaneous growth of both technologies and the discovery of their uses. Table 32.1 presents the comparison table with the author and year, methodology, advantages, and disadvantages presented.

*Table 32.1* Comparative analysis of blockchain-AI research studies.

| Ref no. | Author and year | Methodology | Advantages | Disadvantages |
|---------|-----------------|-------------|------------|---------------|
| [15] | (Wehbe et al., 2018) | CGM has been used to establish objectives, specify system needs, and suggest stakeholder and prototype testing in the healthcare industry. | Methodically maps complicated systems. Blockchain strengthens data security, reduces transaction costs. | Needs improvement, high costs, stakeholder reliance, and limited to the UAE. . |
| [12] | (Tyagi et al., 2020) | Feeding larger datasets through distributed ledger technologies providing better trained ML models. | Ensures data integrity, model reliability, reduced bias, transparency and driving innovation in energy and computing. | AI/ML processing is constrained by blockchain's internet speed and adoption is limited by its high complexity and integration costs. |
| [3] | (Brune, 2020) | Java EE supports enterprise systems, Groovy handles smart contracts, and PFA represents trained ML models. | AI allows intelligent decision making and automation in blockchain, reducing human intervention. Java EE and Groovy support enterprise scalability. | Requires real-world testing and may impact performance. |
| [6] | (Kumar et al., 2021) | Deep learning identifies cancer spots in lung CT scans, blockchain protects the movement of patient data between hospitals. | Helps in the early detection of cancer, medical data sharing and efficient resource use. | Healthcare integration is costly, time-consuming, and faces scalability and complexity challenges. |
| [16] | (Xie et al., 2021) | Wearables with AI capabilities track patients' vitals and activity in real time. | Real time monitoring of patients, secure handling of data and efficient chronic disease management. | Real-time data analysis is complex, costly, and raises privacy concerns. |

| Ref no. | Author and year | Methodology | Advantages | Disadvantages |
|---|---|---|---|---|
| [2] | (Alrubei et al., 2021) | A blockchain based architecture was designed to help distributed machine learning for DAI systems on IT devices. | Allows the integration of AI systems without **significantly affecting the** processing and power of IoT devices. | Faces issues in real-time response situations. Blockchain may introduce some energy overhead. |
| [17] | (Xuan and Ness, 2023) | Gathered information from two market segments to examine how **BT-AI influences** customer relationships and variations in value creation and business tactics. | AI-blockchain integration ensured security of data, privacy, personalized customer experiences and fostered partnerships. | Small sample limits market insights; adoption hindered by resistance, low digital literacy, and high resource needs. . |
| [9] | (Rane et al., 2023) | Examined the advantages of blockchain for **finance, audit effectiveness** and AI's role in detecting and predicting fraud. | Improved detection of fraud and its prevention, better regulatory compliance and enhanced transparency. | Lots of risk in security and attacks. |
| [7] | (Patel et al., 2024) | AI-driven based blockchain model has been presented. Here, encryption and its requiremets has been shown. | Automate processes with proper counterfeit mechanisms for maintaining privacy. | Latency in smart contracts has been increased. |
| [8] | (Qader and Cek, 2024) | Improved audit quality using PLS-SEM based Blockchain method. | Enhances transparency risk assessment and automation. | The cost implementation is very high. |
| [5] | (Hong and Xiao, 2024) | Investigating asset management, freight tracking and **efficiency using** blockchain-AI mechanism. | Improves forecasting with reduced waste and provides proper risk management. | Privacy and scalability issues. The cost is very high. |
| [14] | (Vashishth et al., 2024) | Resource allocation methods using AI techniques such as ML. | Good maintenance schedule with less outages for smart contracts. | Requires high privacy of data with greater interoperability. |

| Ref no. | Author and year | Methodology | Advantages | Disadvantages |
|---------|-----------------|-------------|------------|---------------|
| [10] | (Rustemi et al., 2024) | Expland blockchain secures credentials in identifying patterns of frauds. | Orgnaizational burden reduces and increases the processing speed. | Scaliabilty challenges i. both legal and ethical. |

Source: Author

## Comparative Analysis of Research on Blockchain-AI Integration

In examining blockchain-AI integration, various methodological approaches are used for different applications of blockchain and AI integration, such as: conceptual frameworks to evaluate healthcare applications as a goal-based modelling technique is suggested, experimental research is used in studies such as real-world datasets were used to apply machine learning on blockchain and survey-based research is used to examine blockchain-AI in auditing using PLS-SEM statistical modelling. In the examined works, the integration of Blockchain and AI varies, with a focus on security, scalability, regulation and optimisation. Out of the explored works, research focuses on extensive implementation, while a considerate amount of research highlights industry-specific uses like healthcare [16]. A few of the works focus on prevention of fraud and the security of IoT technology Alrubei et al. [2] and some of the works' emphasis on automation efficiency improvements Patel et al. [7], Vashishth et al. [14], exhibiting distinctions in security-goals. These differences in the various aspects of AI-Blockchain integration influence their implementation in various fields.

## Applications of blockchain using artificial intelligence

In Table 32.2, integrating blockchain application with AI is shown here.

## Discussion on the Applications

Blockchain-AI integration of the industries has made it possible to carry out data storage in such a way that the data is not open to alteration and with AI-driven cybersecurity,such tasks as the establishment of trust mechanisms and behavior learning systems can still be handled autonomously, and a lot more efficient that a human could do, at a much faster rate [6]. Although there are certain benefits and challenges associated with such a high-level integration, the consensus is that the benefits far outweigh the challenges. These applications include use cases in finance & banking, healthcare, education and industrial robotics; this technology in finance & banking supports regulation and also helps to leverage their compliance with the regulatory climate, thereby minimizing chances of fraud, but still subject to very costly regulations [17]; in health [17], it plays a crucial role in case of medical information and patient data, thus if HIPAA/GDPR is not present the only possibility is a breach and in such case all private information can be seen or stolen, in education, AI-automated verification through blockchain lowers credential fraud, but at the same time, there are issues related to the use of smart contracts in education sector that should be addressed, an example

*Table 32.2* Intergration blockchain applications with AI across various areas.

| Ref. No | Author and year | Description | Advantages | Disadvantages |
|---|---|---|---|---|
| [1] | (Al Shareef et al., 2024) | Renewable energy and decision-making integration based on 20 studies have been explained in this paper. | Privacy and security are enhanced with real time decision-making. | AI integration requires high energy to consume. |
| [13] | (Uddin et al., 2024) | Impact on communities and markets with metaverse and AI has been shown on paper. | User experience on integrating AI and blockchain is good. | Implementing metaverse gives high risks such as data breaches |
| [4] | (Fadi et al., 2022) | Paper focuses on cyber resilience and blockchain-AI security | Better privacy with high transaction rate. | Affect AI or data quality output when large system has been used. |

Source: Author

is the increased bureaucratic requirements for the record keeping which are also slower than the previous paper records, and in industrial robotics AI improves automation through which a significant amount of productivity can be realized. Still, the question of security has got to be asked and addressed [5]. At the same time, the situation can be changed and the positive sides of AI-Blockchain integration can be applied if certain actions are taken. The most simple way to do that is to be ready for the changes that are going to occur in the future and to make efforts in regard to them, not only to be obedient to the former algorithms; some of the necessary actions could be: introducing a consensus method for energy-saving, consent for the spread of data in the blockchain, employing a privacy-preserving AI technique, Future trends will be the combination of business and quantum processing.

## Future Work

Despite the expansion of blockchain and AI combination, scalability, energy efficiency and interoperability continue to be the chief issues. Exorbitant transaction costs, computational power consumption, and energy-intensive methodologies hamper the widespread use. The research is urgently required to implement consensus mechanisms that are of a lighter weight (e.g., layer-2 scaling) and the formation of AI algorithms that are most efficient for blockchain optimization [10]. The availability of cross-platform interoperability for blockchain-AI networks is a demand that can be met through the implementation of federated learning and the application of cross-chain AI models that will enable transactions to go further faster and cover more industrial areas. Additionally, negative public opinion towards the AI-Blockchain integration is partly related to ethical issues and regulation, which in turn lead to the GDPR/HIPAA compliance matter, the bias in AI along with the lack of decision-making transparency, etc [4]. While there have been many theoretical AI-related improvements, there are very few practical AI-blockchain applications used today. It may be the case that future research should concentrate on practical industry-scale applications in healthcare, finance, and education by not only ensuring compatibility with the respective infrastructures but also reducing the complexity and the costs. Real-life scenarios and pilot projects are some of the necessary steps for security, efficiency, and scalability verification apart from giving a future prospect of economic sustainability.

## Conclusion

Merging blockchain technology and AI in the healthcare, energy, wireless networks and security sectors has the potential to solve several problems, such as establishing data security, transparency, making better decisions and protecting privacy. On the other hand, the low energy use, data quality issues, challenges for integration, and the expensive part of computation are the major shortcomings. Additionally, the issue of scalability, interoperability, and ethical aspects would require more study in order that it can realize its full capacity.

## References

[1] Al Shareef, A. M., Seçkiner, S., Eid, B., & Abumeteir, H. (2024). Integration of blockchain with artificial intelligence technologies in the energy sector: a systematic review. *Frontiers in Energy Research*, 12, 1377950. https://doi.org/10.3389/fenrg.2024.1377950.

[2] Alrubei, S. M., Ball, E., & Rigelsford, J. M. (2021). The use of blockchain to support distributed AI implementation in IoT systems. *IEEE Internet of Things Journal*, 9(16), 14790–14802. https://doi.org/10.1109/JIOT.2021.3064176.

[3] Brune, P. (2020). Towards an enterprise-ready implementation of artificial intelligence-enabled, blockchain-based smart contracts. arXiv preprint arXiv: 2003. 09744. https://doi.org/10.48550/arXiv.2003.09744.

[4] Fadi, O., Karim, Z., & Mohammed, B. (2022). A survey on blockchain and artificial intelligence technologies for enhancing security and privacy in smart environments. *IEEE Access*, 10, 93168–93186. https://doi.org/10.1109/ACCESS.2022.3203568.

[5] Hong, Z., & Xiao, K. (2024). Digital economy structuring for sustainable development: the role of blockchain and artificial intelligence in improving supply chain and reducing negative environmental impacts. *Scientific Reports*, 14(1), 3912. https://doi.org/10.1038/s41598-024-53760-3.

[6] Kumar, R., Wang, W. Y., Kumar, J., Yang, T., Khan, A., Ali, W., et al. (2021). An integration of blockchain and AI for secure data sharing and detection of CT images for the hospitals. *Computerized Medical Imaging and Graphics*, 87, 101812. https://doi.org/10.1016/j.compmedimag.2020.101812.

[7] Patel, D., Sahu, C. K., & Rai, R. (2024). Security in modern manufacturing systems: integrating blockchain in artificial intelligence-assisted manufacturing. *International Journal of Production Research*, 62(3), 1041–1071. https://doi.org/10.1080/00207543.2023.2262050.

[8] Qader, K. S., & Cek, K. (2024). Influence of blockchain and artificial intelligence on audit quality: evidence from Turkey. *Heliyon*, 10, 9. https://doi.org/10.1016/j.heliyon.2024.e30166.

[9] Rane, N., Choudhary, S., & Rane, J. (2023). Blockchain and Artificial Intelligence (AI) integration for revolutionizing security and transparency in finance. 4644253 (2023). DOI: dx.doi.org/10.2139/ssrn.4644253

[10] Rustemi, A., Dalipi, F., Atanasovski, V., & Risteski, A. (2024). Enhancing academic credentials: the synergy of blockchain and artificial intelligence. In 2024 7th International Balkan Conference on Communications and Networking (BalkanCom), (pp. 206–211). IEEE. http://doi.org/10.1109/BalkanCom61808.2024.

[11] Tripathi, G., Ahad, M. A., & Casalino, G. (2023). A comprehensive review of blockchain technology: underlying principles and historical background with future challenges. *Decision Analytics Journal*, 9, 100344. https://doi.org/10.1016/j.dajour.2023.100344.

[12] Tyagi, A. K., Aswathy, S. U., & Abraham, A. (2020). Integrating blockchain technology and artificial intelligence: Synergies perspectives challenges and research directions. *Journal of Information Assurance and Security*, 15(5), 1554. ISSN 1554-1010.

[13] Uddin, M., Obaidat, M., Manickam, S., Laghari, S. U. A., Dandoush, A., Ullah, H., et al. (2024). Exploring the convergence of metaverse, blockchain, and AI: a comprehensive survey of enabling technologies, applications, challenges, and future directions. *Wiley Interdisciplinary Reviews: Data Mining and Knowledge Discovery*, 14(6), e1556. https://doi.org/10.1002/widm.1556.

[14] Vashishth, T. K., Sharma, V., Sharma, K. K., Kumar, B., Chaudhary, S., & Panwar, R. (2024). Intelligent resource allocation and optimization for industrial robotics using AI and blockchain. In AI and Blockchain Applications in Industrial Robotics, (pp. 82–110). https://doi.org/10.4018/979-8-3693-0659-8.ch004.

[15] Wehbe, Y., Al Zaabi, M., & Svetinovic, D. (2018). Blockchain AI framework for healthcare records management: constrained goal model. In 2018 26th Telecommunications forum (TELFOR), (pp. 420–425). IEEE. https://doi.org/10.1109/TELFOR.2018.8611900.

[16] Xie, Y., Lu, L., Gao, F., He, S., Zhao, H., Fang, Y., et al. (2021). Integration of artificial intelligence, blockchain, and wearable technology for chronic disease management: a new paradigm in smart healthcare. *Current Medical Science*, 41(6), 1123–1133. https://doi.org/10.1007/s11596-021-2485-0.

[17] Xuan, T. R., & Ness, S. (2023). Integration of blockchain and AI: exploring application in the digital business. *Journal of Engineering Research and Reports*, 25(8), 20–39. https://doi.org/10.9734/jerr/2023/v25i8955.

# 33 Harnessing IoT-enabled teaching strategies to enhance entrepreneurship education: evidence from STPE students in Andhra Pradesh

*Ashok Kumar Panigrahi[1,a], Narayana Maharana[2,b] and Suman Kalyan Chaudhury[3,c]*

[1]Mukesh Patel School of Technology Management and Engineering, NMIMS Deemed-to-be University, Shirpur, Maharashtra, India

[2]Department of Management Studies, GVP College of Engineering (A), Visakhapatnam, Andhra Pradesh, India

[3]Department of Business Administration, Berhampur University, Bhanja Bihar, Berhampur, Odisha, India

## Abstract

The convergence of digital technologies and education has opened new avenues for pedagogical innovation, particularly in cultivating skills critical for entrepreneurial success. This study examines the transformative potential of Internet of Things (IoT)-enabled teaching strategies in entrepreneurship education for science, technology, and professional education (STPE) students in Andhra Pradesh. A self-administered semi-structured questionnaire was used to collect data from 435 final-year engineering students by interview method and analysed to determine the efficacy of IoT-based teaching tools such as real-time data analytics, smart classroom environments, and linked gadgets in developing entrepreneurial skills. We observed that IoT methods significantly enhanced problem-solving, creativity, and decision-making skills among the students, though their impact on risk assessment abilities remains inconsistent compared to traditional methods. The study confirmed the role of IoT in providing a better learning experience that helps in filling the gap between classroom teaching with a cost-effective practical application while highlighting systemic challenges such as inadequate infrastructure, uneven digital literacy, and faculty readiness. The study contributes to the growing body of literature that focuses on the role of advanced digital transformation in the education sector and advocates for incorporating IoT into STPE curricula to equip future engineers with the skills needed to succeed in a rapidly changing business environment.

**Keywords**: Entrepreneurship education, innovation, Internet of Things, STPE

## Introduction

The education sector in India is undergoing a significant change due to rapid technological developments. Increased use of digital technologies like e-learning, MOOCs, Internet of Things (IoT), artificial intelligence (AI), etc., has been reshaping the modern education system, making it more interactive, customised, and data-driven (Kumar & Al-Besher, 2022 ; Mishra et al., 2020) [11,14,15]. The higher education sector has remained the sole facilitator of research, skill development, and student career building to make a thriving economy. In

[a]ashok.panigrahi@nmims.edu, [b]maharana.narayan@gmail.com, [c]sumankchaudhury72@gmail.com

DOI: 10.1201/9781003716648-33

recent times, the potential for IoT-enabled tools to enhance entrepreneurial skills in students has become an area of growing interest (Mishra et al., 2020; Sneesl et al., 2022) [15,16]. Entrepreneurship education traditionally focuses on theoretical learning in many higher educational institutions in India; until recently, with the help of innovative technologies, many primer institutions have emphasised experiential learning, where the students are encouraged to engage in real-world problem-solving activities with the help of technology [7] (Manhiça et al., 2022) [17]. IoT-enabled devices such as smartboards and interactive displays can allow students to brainstorm, create mind maps, and visually organise ideas (Srivastava et al., 2022) [18]. These devices help creative thinking by enabling real-time collaboration, where students can build innovative business ideas based on real-world data and scenarios. The core skills required by an entrepreneur like creativity, problem-solving, decision-making, and risk assessment, necessitate innovative teaching methods. IoT-enabled learning tools can assist in creating interactive learning environments that facilitate entrepreneurial skill development. However, despite the slow adoption of IoT in various educational domains, its effectiveness in developing entrepreneurial skills is not satisfactory. There is a need to assess how IoT tools influence students' ability to develop critical thinking and make better decisions by evaluating risks in business. Furthermore, it is also necessary to understand how the demographic differences due to gender, socio-economic background, and prior digital literacy level of the students affect their IoT-based learning abilities which is missing in the existing literature. Specifically, the study seeks to answer three critical questions-

- How do IoT tools influence the development of entrepreneurial skills like creativity, problem-solving, decision-making, and risk assessment?
- Does the inclusion of IoT devices contribute differently to entrepreneurial skills?
- What is the role of students' demographic characteristics in this learning process?

**Review of Literature**

The study is based on two important theories such as the constructivist learning theory [5] and technology acceptance models (TAM) propounded by Davis et al. [3] to explore the role of IoT in teaching and learning entrepreneurship skills. Jones (1995) [19] while working on constructivist learning theory, posits that "learning is most effective when students actively engage themselves to harness knowledge through hands-on experiences and interaction with their environment". TAM identifies two key factors "perceived ease of use" and "perceived usefulness" that influences the adoption of change, (Kolb, 1984) [20]. This particular theory is essential in understanding how technological changes can be adopted in entrepreneurship education. Additionally, it can be applied in this context to evaluate the acceptance and adoption of IoT by both students and faculties.

Negm [10] investigated how digital fluency impacts students' intentions to incorporate IoT into their distance learning experiences in higher education. Similarly, Alhasan et al. [1] claim undergraduate students' intentions to use IoT devices within smart classrooms have improved their engagement. As such, Shaqrah and Almars [12] posit that technology helps students understand complex phenomena, especially for the science students. Kumar & Al-Besher (2022) claim that e-learning systems have been developed to enhance higher education experience and increase student engagement. Furthermore, Din et al. (2023) [21]

also complimented by stating that IoT has been a key element in the evolution of the education system, optimising campus life by better managing classrooms, administration, energy consumption, security, and transportation.

Many researchers highlighted some barriers, such as high costs and the need for specialized equipment, which are the primary obstacles to the adoption of IoT in education [6] (Lubinga et al., 2023) [22]. The cost of IoT devices, sensors, and the necessary network infrastructure is not affordable for many educational institutions (Mozumder et al., 2023) [23]. Additionally, there are concerns about teacher readiness and the need for adequate professional development to ensure that the physical infrastructure is supported by learned instructors who can effectively integrate these technologies into their teaching methods [10]. Faculties are often reluctant to adopt new methods due to a lack of monetary reward for the additional effort (Sneesl et al., 2022) [16]. Another challenge lies in understanding the specific impact of IoT tools on the development of particular entrepreneurial skills (Mahto et al., 2018) [24]. While Kassab et al. [6] claim that the inclusion of technology in education has resulted in a better learning outcome, less attention has been paid to how these tools specifically influence entrepreneurial competencies such as creativity, risk assessment, and decision-making. IEE requires overall skills development beyond traditional academic learning [8]. The study of Fayolle and Gailly [4] suggests that IoT-enabled environments encourage creativity among the students to experiment with new ideas and iterate their business concepts in a simulated setting. Moreover, Maharana & Chaudhury [9], claim that experiential learning (EXL) helps improve creativity. Zhang & Liu [13], in their study, explored that the use of IoT in general business education can improve students' analytical and strategic thinking abilities.

## Methodology

The study uses a randomly selected sample of 435 STEM students from selected engineering colleges in Andhra Pradesh. The independent variables of the study IoT integrated entrepreneurship education (IEE) formulated as a single variable were measured using statements like "IoT tools provide better learning opportunities than classroom teachings", "IoT devices used along with theory classes make the class more engaging" and "IoT tools make the learning process more interactive", and "IoT tools used in the classroom helps better understand the complex concepts". TAM constructs include perceived usefulness (PU) and perceived ease of use (PEOU), and the dependent variables include entrepreneurial skills. These skills include 'creativity (CR)', 'risk assessment (RA)', 'problem-solving (PS)', and 'decision-making (DM)'. For the control variable, we have used the non-IoT-based factors responsible for entrepreneurial skill development discovered by prior studies [2] (Maharana, 2019) [25]. Factors like prior entrepreneurial experience, access to mentorship, and non-IoT-based EXL methods like fieldwork projects, apprenticeship, industrial visits, involvement in family business, etc., are selected as the control variable. Using descriptive statistics, regression model mediation and moderation analysis we analysed the data.

## Analysis

The demographic analysis presented in Table 33.1 provides an overview of the respondents' characteristics, revealing notable diversity in education, gender, socio-economic background, and exposure to IoT-based entrepreneurship teaching and education. The average years of education among the participants is approximately 16 years (SD = 1.08), suggesting a well-educated cohort of final-year engineering students. Male participants represent 58.9% of the sample, while females comprise 41.1%. The majority of students (54.7%) belong to the engineering and technology stream, followed by core science (25.3%) and professional subjects (20%). Many respondents lack a family business background (71.7%) or prior business exposure (78.4%), indicating limited entrepreneurial experience. However, 26.6% belong to business family background. Regarding socio-economic status, 41.6% belong to medium-income families, 35.4% from low-income families, and 23% from high-income families. Digital literacy levels show that most respondents have an average skill level (52.2%), and 31% possess high proficiency. When examining the use of IoT in teaching in the selected educational institution, we observed that 37.2% of institutes have very poor and 23.7% of institutes have moderate infrastructure, while only 17% report high integration, reflecting a significant gap in the adoption of IoT-enabled teaching methods across the sample.

*Table 33.1* Demographic profile (*N=435*).

| Variable | Categories | Frequency (Percentage) |
| --- | --- | --- |
| Years of education | Range (14-18 Years) | |
| gender (GEN) | Male | 256(58.9) |
| | Female | 179(41.1) |
| STEP Stream | Science | 110(25.3) |
| | Engineering | 238(54.7) |
| | Professional | 87(20.0) |
| Family business background (FBB) | Yes | 123(28.3) |
| | No | 312(71.7) |
| Prior business exposure | Yes | 94(21.6) |
| | No | 341(78.4) |
| Involvement in family business | Yes | 116(26.6) |
| | No | 319(73.4) |
| Socio-economic status (SES) | Low(<5L) | 154(35.4) |
| | Medium(5–10L) | 181(41.6) |
| | High(>10L) | 100(23.0) |
| Digital literacy level (DLL) | Poor | 73(16.8) |
| | Average | 227(52.2) |
| | High | 135(31.0) |
| Use of IoT in teaching | Poor | 162(37.2) |
| | Moderate | 103(23.7) |
| | Reasonable | 96(22.1) |
| | High | 74(17.0) |

Source: Author

*Table 33.2* Multiple regression analysis of independent variables and control variables on entrepreneurial skills.

| Independent-variable | CR *β(t)* | RA *β(t)* | PS *β(t)* | DM *β(t)* |
|---|---|---|---|---|
| IEE | 0.485(6.929*) | 0.452(5.573*) | 0.523(7.341*) | 0.504(6.109*) |
| EXL | 0.352(5.677*) | 0.283(3.975*) | 0.322(5.194*) | 0.303(4.262*) |
| PDL | 0.185(3.491*) | 0.223(4.330*) | 0.255(4.999*) | 0.202(3.877*) |
| GEN | 0.054(1.317) | 0.026(0.619) | 0.064(1.488) | 0.075(1.786**) |
| SES | 0.121(1.743) | 0.107(2.019**) | 0.151(2.961*) | 0.145(2.772*) |
| EB | 0.107(1.754) | 0.125(1.978**) | 0.117(1.896) | 0.131(2.148**) |
| FBB | 0.085(1.667) | 0.114(2.227**) | 0.095(1.854) | 0.105(2.059**) |

Note: *IEE: IoT in Entrepreneurship education, EXL: Non-IoT-based experiential learning, PDL: Prior digital literacy, GEN: Gender, SES: Socio-economic status, EB: Educational background, FBB: Family business background.*
Source: Author

*Table 33.3* ANOVA for gender differences in entrepreneurial skills.

| Skill | F | Sig. | Post-Hoc |
|---|---|---|---|
| CR | 2.351 | 0.101 | - |
| RA | 1.563 | 0.213 | - |
| PS | 3.656 | 0.053** | 0.033** |
| DM | 4.128 | 0.042** | 0.028** |

Source: Author

The findings given in Table 33.2 highlight that IEE significantly enhances students' CR, PS, RA, and dm skills, reinforcing the effectiveness of digital tools in fostering entrepreneurial abilities. EXL also plays a crucial role in skill development, complementing IoT-enabled methods. Additionally, PDL positively influences all entrepreneurial skills, underscoring the importance of equipping students with digital competencies. SES emerges as a key factor in shaping RA PS and DM abilities, while FBB contributes to RA and DM. Gender does not significantly affect entrepreneurial skill outcomes except DM, whereas EB moderately influences RA and DM abilities among the students.

Table 33.3 presents the results of the analysis examining whether there are significant gender differences in the development of entrepreneurial skills. No significant differences were found in creativity (F = 2.351, p = 0.101) or risk assessment (F = 1.563, p = 0.213). However, problem-solving (F = 3.656, p = 0.035) and decision-making (F = 4.12, p = 0.042) showed significant gender-based differences, with males potentially excelling in decision-making. These results suggest gender may influence certain entrepreneurial skills, warranting further investigation.

Data presented in Table 33.4 shows how prior digital literacy moderates the relationship between IoT in IEE and dependent entrepreneurial skills. The interaction term IEE × PDL indicates that prior digital literacy significantly moderates the relationship between IoT in IEE and entrepreneurial skills. This suggests that learners with higher digital literacy benefit more from IoT-based education in developing creativity, risk assessment, problem-solving, and decision-making skills. The significant positive interaction suggests that digital literacy amplifies the positive impact of IoT tools on these skills.

Table 33.5 presents the mediation analysis results where we have verified the mediation effect of the variable non-IoT-based EXL in the relationship between IEE and entrepreneurial skills. It can be observed that non-Iot-based EXL partially mediates the relationship between IoT in entrepreneurship education (IEE) and entrepreneurial skills. This confirms that while IoT education directly impacts all four entrepreneurial skills, the effect is strengthened through the enhancement provided by EXL activities, which are non-IoT based. The mediation effect supports the idea that IoT tools and non-IoT EXL help further improve entrepreneurial skills.

*Table 33.4* Moderation analysis for prior digital literacy (PDL).

| Variables | CR | RA | PS | DM |
|---|---|---|---|---|
| IEE | 0.45** | 0.42** | 0.50** | 0.48** |
| PDL | 0.18** | 0.15* | 0.17** | 0.14* |
| IEE × PDL | 0.09* | 0.08 | 0.11** | 0.10* |

*Significance Levels: \*\*p < 0.001; \*p < 0.05*
Source: Author

*Table 33.5* Mediation analysis for non-IoT-based learning impact.

| Variables | CR | RA | PS | DM |
|---|---|---|---|---|
| EXL | 0.35** | 0.30** | 0.32** | 0.28** |
| IEE | 0.52** | 0.45** | 0.48** | 0.50** |
| EXL → IEE | 0.40** | 0.38** | 0.41** | 0.39** |
| Mediation indirect effect (IE) | 0.18** | 0.15** | 0.17** | 0.16** |

*Significance levels: \*\*p < 0.001; \*p < 0.05*
Source: Author

*Table 33.6* Interaction effects of socio-economic status (SES) and IoT tools.

| Variables | CR | RA | PS | DM |
|---|---|---|---|---|
| IEE | 0.48** | 0.45** | 0.52** | 0.50** |
| SES | 0.23** | 0.20** | 0.25** | 0.21** |
| IEE × SES | 0.12* | 0.10* | 0.14** | 0.13* |

*Significance Levels: \*\*p < 0.001; \*p < 0.05*
Source: Author

Table 33.6 shows the moderation effect of the demographic variable socio-economic status, which indicates that it significantly moderates the impact of IoT tools on entrepreneurial skill development. The results suggest that learners from higher SES backgrounds may experience more significant benefits from IoT-enhanced education than those from lower SES backgrounds. This may be because higher SES enables students to have better educational opportunities and admission to premier institutes. However, the impact of academic performance to get into premier institutions cannot be ignored, but here, interaction suggests that while IoT tools are effective for all learners, their effect is maximised for those with higher socio-economic advantages, potentially due to access to better resources and support systems by joining premier institutes.

## Implications and Suggestions

The findings demonstrate the effectiveness of the use of IoT devices while teaching entrepreneurship in higher education institutions for better developing entrepreneurial skills. Furthermore, recognising the differences in impact across distinct IoT products will help instructors choose the most effective resources for focused skill development. To remove various teaching and learning-related inefficiencies, proper training programmes should be organised for the instructors. Moreover, it is suggested that industrial collaboration, along with technology use, could further strengthen the learning experience of the students. The gender discrepancies indicated that educational programs should include personalised techniques to offer equitable skill development chances for both genders.

## Conclusion

The study confirms that Internet of Things (IoT)-based teaching methods significantly contribute to developing four entrepreneurial skills, that are creativity, risk assessment, problem-solving, and decision-making. When effectively implemented, these findings support the notion that integrating technology into education can bridge the gap between traditional teaching methods and the dynamic demands of IEE in the changing business scenario. It also highlights that using IoT along with non-IoT based teaching methods further improves entrepreneurial skills. Thus, educational institutions providing such facilities could explore this aspect in the students and offer specialised training to develop entrepreneurial intent. The favourable influence of demographic factors like socio-economic status and digital proficiency emphasises the need for targeted educational strategies.

## Limitations and Scope

The sample is restricted to engineering students in Andhra Pradesh, limiting the generalizability of the findings. Data reliance on student responses may introduce bias, despite controlling for socio-economic status and prior digital literacy. Additional factors like individual motivation or external learning resources may also influence results. Future research should expand the sample to diverse educational institutions, including business schools and polytechnics, to enhance demographic representation. Comparative studies and experimental or longitudinal designs could further explore the long-term impact of IoT-based learning on entrepreneurial skill development.

# References

[1]  Alhasan, A., Hussein, M. H., Audah, L., Al-Sharaa, A., Ibrahim, I., & Mahmoud, M. A. (2023). A case study to examine undergraduate students' intention to use internet of things (IoT) services in the smart classroom. *Education and Information Technologies*, 28(8), 10459–10482.

[2]  Bergmann, H., Hundt, C., & Sternberg, R. (2016). What makes student entrepreneurs? on the relevance (and irrelevance) of the university and the regional context for student start-Ups. *Small Business Economics*, 47(1), 53–76. https://doi.org/10.1007/s11187-016-9700-6.IDEAS/RePEc.

[3]  Davis, F. D., Bagozzi, R. P., & Warshaw, P. R. (1989). User acceptance of computer technology: a comparison of two theoretical models. *Management Science*, 35(8), 982–1003.

[4]  Fayolle, A., & Gailly, B. (2008). From craft to science: teaching models and learning processes in entrepreneurship education. *Journal of European Industrial Training*, 32(7), 569–593.

[5]  Hein, G. E. (1991). Constructivist learning theory. *Institute for Inquiry*. Available at:/Http://Www. Exploratorium. Edu/Ifi/Resources/Constructivistlearning. HtmlS.

[6]  Kassab, M., DeFranco, J., & Laplante, P. (2020). A systematic literature review on internet of things in education: benefits and challenges. *Journal of Computer Assisted Learning*, 36(2), 115–127.

[7]  Liu, M., Gorgievski, M. J., Zwaga, J., & Paas, F. (2023). How entrepreneurship program characteristics foster students' study engagement and entrepreneurial career intentions: a longitudinal study. *Learning and Individual Differences*, 101, 102249.

[8]  Maharana, N. (2020). Entrepreneurial lessons from the Bhagavad Gita. *PURUSHARTHA: A Journal of Management, Ethics and Spirituality*, 13(2), 74–86.

[9]  Maharana, N., & Chaudhury, S. K. (2022). Entrepreneurship education and entrepreneurial intent: a comparative study of the private and government university students. *IIM Ranchi Journal of Management Studies*, 1(2), 191–208.

[10]  Negm, E. (2023). Intention to use internet of things (IoT) in higher education online learning–the effect of technology readiness. *Higher Education, Skills and Work-Based Learning*, 13(1), 53–65.

[11]  Popchev, I., Orozova, D., & Stoyanov, S. (2019). IoT and big data analytics in e-learning. In 2019 Big Data, Knowledge and Control Systems Engineering (BdKCSE), (pp. 1–5).

[12]  Shaqrah, A., & Almars, A. (2022). Examining the internet of educational things adoption using an extended unified theory of acceptance and use of technology. *Internet of Things*, 19, 100558.

[13]  Zhang, H., & Liu, X. (2021). Teaching system of undergraduate entrepreneurship education under the background of internet of things. *Mobile Information Systems*, 2021(1), 4298724

[14]  Kumar, K., and A. Al-Besher. (2022). IoT Enabled E-Learning System for Higher Education. Measurement: Sensors 24: 100480.

[15]  Mishra, A. S., J. Karthikeyan, B. Barman, and R. P. Veettil. (2020). Review on IoT in Enhancing Efficiency among Higher Education Institutions. *Journal of Critical Reviews*. 7(1), 567–570.

[16]  Sneesl, R., Y. Y. Jusoh, M. A. Jabar, and S. Abdullah. (2022). Revising Technology Adoption Factors for IoT-Based Smart Campuses: A Systematic Review. *Sustainability (Switzerland)*. 14(8), 4840. https://doi.org/10.3390/su14084840

[17]  Manhiça, R., A. Santos, and J. Cravino. (2022). The Impact of Artificial Intelligence on a Learning Management System in a Higher Education Context: A Position Paper. *International Conference on Technology and Innovation in Learning, Teaching and Education*: 454–460.

[18]  Srivastava, A., S. Singh, and L. Sapra. (2022). A Review Paper on Emerging Trends of E-Learning in India. *Journal of Algebraic Statistics*. 13(2), 1281–1286.

[19]  Jones, A. (1995). Constructivist Learning Theories and IT. *Information Technology and Society*: 249–265.

[20] Kolb, D. A. (1984). Experiential Learning: Experience as the Source of Learning and Development. FT Press. https://doi.org/10.1016/B978-0-7506-7223-8.50017-4

[21] Din, I. U., K. A. Awan, A. Almogren, and J. J. P. C. Rodrigues. (2023). Swarmtrust: A Swarm Optimization-Based Approach to Enhance Trustworthiness in Smart Homes. *Physical Communication.* 58: 102064.

[22] Lubinga, S., T. C. Maramura, and T. Masiya. (2023). The Fourth Industrial Revolution Adoption: Challenges in South African Higher Education Institutions. *Journal of Culture and Values in Education.* 6(2), 1–17. https://doi.org/10.46303/jcve.2023.5

[23] Mozumder, M. A. I., A. Athar, T. P. T. Armand, M. M. Sheeraz, S. M. I. Uddin, and H.-C. Kim. (2023). Technological Roadmap of the Future Trend of Metaverse Based on IoT, Blockchain, and AI Techniques in Metaverse Education. *25th International Conference on Advanced Communication Technology (ICACT)*: 1414–1423.

[24] Mahto, R. V., W. McDowell, S. Sen, and S. Ahluwalia. (2018). Internet of Things (IoT) and Entrepreneurship Education: Opportunities and Challenges. *Annals of Entrepreneurship Education and Pedagogy–*2018: 162–186.

[25] Maharana, N. (2019). Entrepreneurial Attitude of Independent Business Owner and Franchisee. PhD diss., Department of Business Administration.

# 34 English language learning in the digital age: analyzing the role of technology in reducing educational disparities in India

*Abhijeet Dawle[1,a] and Amol Dapkekar[2,b]*

[1]SVKM's NMIMS, MPSTME, Shirpur, Dhule, Maharashtra, India

[2]Thakur College of Engineering and Technology, Mumbai, Maharashtra, India

## Abstract

This study is mainly interested in indicating the changeable influences of technology on English language learning in India and highlights educational inequalities in urban and rural places. By referring to the existing articles and case studies, the paper tackles infrastructural challenges and gaps in digital literacy while mirroring the successful cases that promote equal education. On the one hand, English can be understood as the language of the global community. This can lead to increased opportunities in the job market and social mobility which would underline the importance of every individual having equal access to language teaching resources. The essential question is how low-priced applications, websites, and interactive multimedia may be used to bridge the gap between the haves and the have-nots including those students living in remote areas, those lacking qualified teachers, or those with socioeconomic needs. However, issues, such as inconsistency in access, ignorance of the existence of the digital divide, and poor development of infrastructure, are still of prime importance. Hence, the paper prescribes guidelines for the legislatures to introduce programs that would strengthen the sustainable introduction of technology to English language teaching and enrich the education of Indian learners, consequently, diminishing the disparities in English language learning in India. This paper uses the National Education Policy (NEP) 2020, Digital India, and EdTech initiatives, as focal points. This, in turn, amplifies inclusivity providing equal education to every individual and ensuring that no one is left behind in digital inclusivity when it comes to English language learning. It focuses on the effects of adaptive learning through AI and digital literacy programs supported by the government. These solutions are then evaluated using some quantitative evaluation metrics like precision, recall, and F1-Score. The paper analyses possible policy interventions and public-private partnerships to promote tech-based language education.

**Keywords:** Digital literacy, digital tools, edtech platforms, english language learning, inclusive education, mobile technology, multilingual education, technology-driven learning

## Introduction

### Background

English is significant internationally and can help students accomplish their educational and career goals in India. On the contrary, many rural populations and underprivileged communities face difficulties in getting access to proper English education. Technology now has the power to fill in the gap by providing easily and cheaply accessible ways for students

[a]abhijeet.dawle@nmims.edu, [b]amoldspeaks@gmail.com

DOI: 10.1201/9781003716648-34

to learn English. Because of smartphones and better internet, students can now, in places where transportation is a problem, access digital platforms to personalise their learning, practice with real-life materials and connect with native speakers online. These tools make the learning process more exciting and fruitful for students to achieve their goals. By using technology intelligently, we will be in a position where every individual has a level playing field in terms of learning English and reaping the beautiful opportunities that come with it. The Digital India initiative and public-private partnerships have strengthened digital literacy, but gaps persist [1].

## Importance of English in India

English is one of the most demanded skills in a multinational company. English communication reaches every Indian every day so that we can talk and share knowledge at least by understanding each other across the language gap. The need for English in India is like a bridge for economic mobility. Digital tools and multilingual education are recognised in the National Education Policy (NEP) 2020 to reduce linguistic barriers. The argument for including regional language in NEP is to save the mother tongue, it is impossible to ignore English for more opportunities in the world. The possibilities of these advancements, on the other hand, are through AI-enabled adaptive learning and government-led efforts that have made attainment possible but for sustainable progress [3]. Adaptive learning platforms using artificial intelligence (AI) facilitate customized coaching and overcome hurdles with the learner at his pace.

## Research objectives

- To analyse how technology influences English language learning in India.
- To examine how digital tools reduce educational inequalities.
- To identify barriers and opportunities in implementing technology-driven language education.

## Literature Review

### Technology and language learning

Technological advances have reshaped language learning everywhere. Zeng [9] states that "technology has acted as a central element of English language learning by giving learners the instruments with which to apply language skills independently, making learning more personalized and accessible" (p. 86). This educational reform has equipped students with the newfound ability to focus on their preferred ways of study, applications that teach them, resources that require them to practice and tools that stimulate their abilities to listen, speak, read, and write. Along these lines, Roozafzai [5], in another study, states that "digitalization in language learning contexts has given rise to smarter and more flexible platforms that essentially adapt to the different needs of learners" (p. 140). Technology enhances personalised learning. AI-powered platforms such as Duolingo and Hello English adjust lessons based on learner progress. These systems adapt to the learner's performance by utilizing AI, giving precise feedback and creating personalised lessons that deal with the strengths and weaknesses of the learners, thus making learning a more efficient and fascinating process.

*Challenges in the Indian context*

Rapid transition of digital tools in language learning is seen in urban and semi-urban areas however; rural regions still have a long way to go. Digital language labs are stated by Bhasin [1], "to offer a dynamic and participatory module for learning English but its use is limited in rural/remote and underprivileged regions (p. 1). Nearly all of this is infrastructure-related (low power, poor internet, etc.), which limits technology-based learning solutions from being implemented. Government programs like PM eVidya and Diksha aim to address these issues if implemented effectively focusing on the basic internet amenities. Policies such as BharatNet seek to improve internet penetration, which is crucial for expanding access [6].

*The role of informal learning tools*

Democratizing access to language learning: Informal digital learning, mobile apps and online tools have had a meaningful impact on the accessibility of language education. Lee [3] states that "informal digital learning offers learners more control over their language acquisition process, empowering them to learn at their own pace" (p. 156). The different platforms like Duolingo, Babbel and YouTube Tutorials offer variety in terms of taste and standards of skills. These platforms provide interactive games and quizzes along with real-time forums that make learning fun and less scary. Additionally, they frequently have multimedia - videos, audio clips and interactive dialogues to develop listening & speaking skills. Also, different from other tools it helps to track progress, focusing on points learners want to work on like vocabulary or grammar. It also supports the learners in tracking progress, focusing on areas of improvement. While cost-effective, these tools require structured integration with formal education [8]. The desirability of these tools is furthered by their cost and accessibility, especially in regions where formal language learning resources are scarce or very expensive.

## Methodology

*Case studies*

The insights from the EdTech platforms like Byju's, Duolingo and Hello English are used widely in India for English language learning purposes. Such platforms were evaluated based on their accessibility, features, and effectiveness in addressing educational disparities. The UNESCO report [7] assesses various EdTech platforms assessing their instructional methods and game-based components in language learning. The use of mobile applications in the case of Duolingo and Hello English is also examined to understand the importance of these applications and identify the support for their English learning and explore their motivation levels [2]. Various other case studies and comparative analyses are done to explore the effectiveness of AI-driven language learning tools.

*Review of recent research papers & data analysis*

Following the review of case studies, concerned research papers were evaluated that would provide trends and challenges from literature as well as the best practices. Previous research, which consisted of the literature on formal digital learning, digital language laboratories, and the role of AI in language learning, was reviewed. Performance metrics such as precision, recall, and F1-Score were used to assess AI-driven tools. They were also compared

*Table 34.1* Comparison of digital learning tools [9].

| Feature | Duolingo | Hello English | Byju's |
|---|---|---|---|
| AI Adaptivity | Yes | Yes | Yes |
| Regional support | Limited | High | Moderate |
| Gamification | High | Medium | Low |
| Cost | Free/Paid | Free/Paid | Paid |

Source: Author

with traditional language learning methods (Table 34.3) [10]. Table 34.1 provides a comparison of digital learning tools such as Duolingo, Hello English and Byju's with its AI adaptivity and other features.

Duolingo is best suited for casual learners who prefer a fun, gamified experience and global language options. Hello English excels for users looking to learn regional languages, especially those from India, with moderate gamification and free content. Byju's is ideal for those seeking a structured, academic-oriented learning experience, with personalized content at a premium price.

## Results and Discussion

### *Accessibility and inclusivity*
The urban areas have many platforms available whereas rural places have very limited or sometimes no access to affordable devices. Sinha [6]    asserts, "The use of modern technology in Indian educational institutions has led to a far more accessible mode of learning for students residing in the remotest areas" (p. 19). Urban learners are getting top-notch learning, whereas Rural Schools deal with occasional internet and shared devices making it unequal learning for all. Programs like BharatNet and Digital India Rehm & Uszkoreit, [4] are enhancing digital access. Digital India is a national mission of the Government to make IT and internet access available to all so that eventually India might emerge as a 'digitally empowered' country. BharatNet is another mega project to build a high-speed broadband network across India so that rural areas can get connected to the internet. With the carefully curated goal of bridging this gap and enhancing educational opportunities for all students, increasing internet connectivity in rural communities from government programs such as Digital India and BharatNet is a crucial first step.

### *The role of mobile technology*
Smartphones serve as the primary medium for digital learning. Platforms like Hello English and WhatsApp-based learning groups have enhanced accessibility [3]. The increase in the use of smartphones by students has enabled the easy availability of internet resources and mobile applications for educational materials. Using Hello English mobile app provides facilities for education in urban and rural both sides on platforms like mobile apps that carry interactive classes as well as language learning resources. Also, WhatsApp-based learning groups are popular in which teachers and students can schedule time directly over cell phones- share resources and discuss live. These platforms have revolutionized the

accessibility to students learning in their usual conditions, at their own pace without hiring costly or substantial physical infrastructure-controlled equipment.

### Challenges in implementation
While technology might have the power to change how language education should be delivered, implementation has a fair number of challenges as well.

### Infrastructure
The availability of good and fast internet is a big bottleneck, particularly in underprivileged rural and remote areas. In addition to this, there is little electricity available, digital devices cannot be used. The lack of this infrastructure sets out the barriers to scale for a lot of digital language learning projects.

### Digital literacy
Many teachers in rural schools are not trained to integrate technology into their teaching practices effectively. Similarly, students with limited exposure to digital devices may struggle to navigate language learning platforms, reducing the potential impact of these tools.

### Content localization
India's linguistic diversity necessitates the availability of content in regional languages, but the current offerings are insufficient. Zeng [11] highlights that "digital technology has empowered learners to break free from traditional learning constraints, fostering agency and enabling more autonomous language development" (p. 118). However, these constraints persist in contexts where the above challenges remain unaddressed.

### Government and corporate initiatives
NEP 2020 promotes digital inclusion in education by encouraging the integration of technology to enhance learning accessibility. Several initiatives have successfully leveraged digital tools to enhance language learning in India, particularly among marginalized groups. For example, Pratham, a non-governmental organization, has implemented digital learning programs that provide tablets preloaded with educational content to underprivileged students. These initiatives have demonstrated measurable improvements in language proficiency and overall academic performance.

Zadorozhnyy and Yu [8] emphasize the importance of such tools in teacher education, stating that "informal digital learning tools have empowered English teachers to enhance their teaching effectiveness" (p. 270). Following are the Government and Corporate initiatives with their impact on supporting digital literacy.

PMeVidya initiative aims to provide schools with digital content. This effort intends to deliver education not only wide but also reach out to all students irrespective of their geography by using different mediums like radio programming, and online and TV-based learning. Diksha offers a range of digital tools and training courses, along with resources to enhance teaching practice. It enhances the quality of teachers who are all set in education and improves teacher's competency. These programs help educate children from low-income communities by enhancing internet broadband and decreasing the digital gap in education.

*Table 34.2* Government and corporate initiatives supporting digital literacy [8].

| Initiative | Organization | Impact |
|---|---|---|
| Digital India | Government | Broadband access expansion |
| PM eVidya | Government | Digital content for schools |
| Diksha | Government | Teacher training resources |
| Infosys Digital Learning (Springboard) | Infosys | Free digital courses |
| TCS iON | TCS | Online learning solutions |

Source: Author

*Table 34.3* Performance metrics comparison [8].

| Metric | AI-Based Learning | Traditional Methods |
|---|---|---|
| Precision | 89% | 75% |
| Recall | 85% | 70% |
| F1-Score | 87% | 72% |

Source: Author

The platforms of Infosys and TCS provide free learning resources to learn on your way and courses that are meant for digital literacy, as well as education-centric skill development. The efforts of the government with that of the private sector are going to drive India's digital education agenda- after all, it is the only way more teachers and students will soon have access to such state-of-the-art resources and ultimately enable the nation to accomplish its long-term educational development (Table 34.2) goals.

**Model performance analysis**

The effectiveness of digital learning tools was measured using precision (89%), recall (85%), and F1-score (87%). A comparison with traditional classroom-based learning showed improved retention rates [8].

A comparison of AI-based learning vs. traditional Methods shows that AI systems have better results than traditional approaches on all three main metrics: Precision, Recall and F1-Score. In short, AI-based learning is competent in both degrees of accuracy and cover, so much better than the traditional methods.

**Conclusion**

The digital tools in India may be the key to an inclusive and effective education system that caters to the varied needs of learners across regions using its diverse languages of instruction. With flexible learning, engaged content and expert paths, these tools on a mobile platform empower multilingual access to high-quality resources for students who would otherwise be left behind. In many rural areas, poor internet connectivity, unreliable electricity, and the lack of affordable devices restrict access to these transformative technologies. Even where access is available, the lack of teacher training and the limited availability of regionally localized content hinders the effective integration of digital tools into the learning process. These challenges have to be dealt with holistically. The training of teachers must also increase digital literacy so that they can learn to use technology in their teaching.

Public-private partnerships must work together. For example, initiatives such as Digital India can partner with private-sector EdTech innovations to develop scalable models of digital learning. Devices and affordable data subsidies will help to fill the socio-economic inequalities ensuring that no one is left behind. Technology is shifting the landscape in Indian education as far as English language instruction is concerned. EdTech platforms, enterprise initiatives and government initiatives have the potential to bridge some educational gaps. Indian technology is changing the world via English language education and paving new learning avenues by bridging differential access to quality education. In addition to corporate donations from companies like Infosys and TCS, programs such as Digital India, PM eVidya and Diksha are also helping increase broadband adoption, teachers' training and digital information access. Thus, India is set to lead the way in making a digitally inclusive and accessible language education system.

## References

[1]  Bhasin, K. (2012). Learning english as a second language & role of digital language lab. *International Journal of Scientific Research*, 3(4), 1–2. https://doi.org/10.15373/22778179/apr2014/182.

[2]  Hidayati, T., & Diana, S. (2019). Students' motivation to learn english using mobile applications: the case of duolingo and hello english. *JEELS (Journal of English Education and Linguistics Studies)*, 6(2), 189–212.

[3]  Lee, J. S. (2020). The role of informal digital learning of english and a high-stakes english test on perceptions of english as an international language. *Australasian Journal of Educational Technology*, 36(2), 155–168. https://doi.org/10.14742/ajet.5319.

[4]  Rehm, G., & Uszkoreit, H. (2012). The English Language in the Digital Age. Springer Science & Business Media.

[5]  Roozafzai, Z. S. (2024). Teaching english as a foreign language and smarter learning environments in the new age of digital transformation. *Educational Challenges*, 29(1), 135–158. https://doi.org/10.34142/2709-7986.2024.29.1.10.

[6]  Sinha, K. K. (2022). Role of modern technology in teaching and learning the english language in indian educational institutions. *Indonesian Journal of English Language Studies (IJELS)*, 8(2), 19–30. https://doi.org/10.24071/ijels.v8i2.4713.

[7]  UNESCO (2023). Global Education Monitoring Report 2023: Technology in Education – A Tool on Whose Terms? Paris: UNESCO.

[8]  Zadorozhnyy, A., & Yu, B. (2023). Preservice english language teachers and informal digital learning of english (IDLE) in Kazakhstan. *Language Learning and Leisure*, 66, 269–290. https://doi.org/10.1515/9783110752441-012.

[9]  Zeng, S. (2018). Understanding language learners' (Non) use of digital technology. In English Learning in the Digital Age, (pp. 167–184). https://doi.org/10.1007/978-981-13-2499-4_8.

[10]  Zeng, S. (2018). The trends of english learning-related use of technology: the role of technology. In English Learning in the Digital Age, (pp. 85–116). https://doi.org/10.1007/978-981-13-2499-4_5.

[11]  Zeng, S. (2018). 'Breaking away' with digital technology: the role of agency. In English Learning in the Digital Age, (pp. 117–137). https://doi.org/10.1007/978-981-13-2499-4_6.

# 35 Transforming education through cloud technologies: a review of accessibility challenges and solutions

*Mayank Sohani[a] and Upendra Verma[b]*

Computer Department, Mukesh Patel School of Technology Management and Engineering, Shirpur, NMIMS Deemed-to-be University, Maharashtra, India

## Abstract

Cloud-based solutions have emerged as key instruments for transforming education worldwide. As cloud computing technology keeps growing, more institutions offer courses through these means for their teaching and learning process. The scalability, flexibility, and affordability of this technology ensure that more people can access it to achieve education. This paper discusses how these cloud-based platforms are shaping the future of education, based on their advantages and challenges, and the implications on the development of an interactive, personalized, and collaborative learning environment. The introduction of cloud-based solutions is creating a revolution in education across the globe in newer and exciting ways. Increasingly, cloud computing technologies offer alternatives to the way in which businesses and students learn. This research endeavors to explore the transformative essence of cloud platforms towards shaping the future of education, throwing light on their merits and demerits along with implications in making learning interactive, personalized and collaborative. Finally, the impact of cloud computing may change the dimensions of education in terms of its wide adoption.

Keywords: Cloud computing, cloud-based solutions, flexible and cost-effective solutions, next-generation education, scalable

## Introduction

Cloud computing has redefined how learning content and resources interrelated with students, teachers, and institutions. There are many impacts of cloud computing on education but foremost is its role in lessening the digital divide- the gap between those having access to modern digital technologies and those who do not have. Low-cost, scalable access through cloud-based platforms such as Google Classroom, Microsoft Teams, and Moodle provides remote students in underserved regions opportunities to have the same rich quality learning experiences as any student attending a well-endowed school as per ITU's report on global connectivity and examples such as Project Loon and Google for Education to demonstrate the impact of cloud solutions [2, 22].

The use of cloud technologies in education faces many challenges, despite significant advantages. Most of the challenges have been observed especially in low-income and rural areas. The most pressing challenge has been internet connectivity. Internet connections are usually poor and unreliable in most areas, preventing access to these learning tools by students located in underprivileged areas and therefore, making them ineffective [5, 19].

[a]sohanimayank@gmail.com, [b]upendra4567@gmail.com

DOI: 10.1201/9781003716648-35

Moreover, there are issues of data privacy and security that become critical issues with the pervasive use of cloud technologies in educational settings. With more students' data being stored and processed online, concerns on the safety and privacy of personal information have become front-line issues [15]. This literature review synthesizes multiple studies that explore the role of cloud computing in enhancing educational accessibility and equity, focusing on both the opportunities and challenges that come with its adoption [20].

**Cloud computing and educational accessibility-** Cloud computing is considered one of the catalysts that make education more accessible. It offers scalable, remote, and cost-effective solutions to educational institutions and learners alike. Cloud platforms may democratize access to educational resources by overcoming traditional barriers imposed by infrastructure, especially in remote and underserved areas. Cloud-based LMS has democratized the access to educative resources such that curriculum content has reached the learners in the rural and underserved areas and is allowing them to interact with their instructors [14].

**Cloud Technologies for Personalized Learning** -Besides, cloud computing is also one significant advantage for customized learning. Additionally, via cloud-based platforms, information can be collected in real-time and student progress and performance always tracked. Timely adjustments in the curriculum, feedback, and pedagogies can then be made by the teacher while teaching; this autonomy will enhance the entire education process [6].

**Challenges in Connectivity and Infrastructure-** Clouds hold promise; however, various challenges prevent broader access to these technologies. One among these is the digital divide, i.e., the gap between urban and rural areas and between rich and poor communities with regard to internet access and technological infrastructure. Unreliable internet connectivity in rural areas is a hindrance to the development of educational tools based on cloud learning [19].

**Data privacy and security concerns-** The use of cloud-based technologies in education raises great concerns for data privacy and security. Storing sensitive data on cloud server computing poses serious risks against student data protected under such computation, given increased data breaches and cyberattacks. To combat these risks, they hold that educational institutions should implement appropriate security measures in works with legislatures such as GDPR [8, 9].

**Teacher training and pedagogical integration-** Many teachers lack digital literacy and pedagogical knowledge needed to implement cloud-based tools in the classroom. Even where teachers have familiarity with the tools, it can be hard for them to adopt them, so they fit into their teaching practices. To handle this, professional development programs are designed to equip teachers with the skills and knowledge for their utilization in cloud technology [1, 17].

**The role of cloud computing in lifelong learning-** Cloud technologies have also given rise to MOOCs, through which free or highly affordable education is made accessible to learners worldwide. These cloud-supported MOOCs transform the conventional model of higher education through quality education available to everyone on earth; therefore, promoting educational equity [13].

**Literature review: cloud computing opportunities and challenges in educational systems-** The global education sector is increasingly adopting cloud tools while the opportunities presented by these technologies are immense. Yet the challenges to face are huge, such as digital equity, privacy, and infrastructural inadequacies. This section examines cloud technologies on transforming education while addressing the challenges that need to be overcome for equitable access and quality education for all [7].

## Opportunities

**Increased accessibility to educational resources-** Another important advantage is that cloud computing enhances access to educational resources and materials for the less fortunate or dispossessed sections of the population. In cloud computing, students can access their learning materials online at anytime, anywhere, and on any device enabled for the internet [14].

**Personalized and adaptive learning-** Cloud technologies are driving and pulling toward personalized learning, which tailors the educational experience to individual student needs, learning styles, and pace. Adaptive learning systems that run on cloud-based platforms can analyze student performance in real-time and alter the curriculum. Learning platforms like DreamBox hand Knewton cater to every student's learning pace by providing customized paths for students to develop mastery in content [11, 24].

**Collaboration and interactive learning-** Cloud computing enables more collaboration and interaction in the confines of the classroom. Students may collaborate, in real time, on their shared documents, projects, and presentations using such tools, namely Google Docs, Microsoft OneDrive, and LMS collaborative spaces. It is in such an environment that the differing time zones allow students and teachers to communicate with one another, regardless of place, in real time to thereby make the learning process all-encompassing and immersive [8, 18].

**Cost-effectiveness and scalability-** Cloud computing provides cost-effective solutions that greatly minimize the costs associated with conventional educational methods. Moreover, cloud solutions often entail the pay-per-use model which will cut down the expenses on education by not having to buy expensive software licenses, textbooks, and equipment [14].

**Support for lifelong learning-** Cloud computing supports lifelong learning. Cloud technologies give adult learners the flexibility to develop themselves with continuous access to education as the need for constant professional development continues to be on the rise. Such platforms- supported by cloud computing-including Coursera, edX, and Udemy, allow students to take free or paid MOOC offerings at their own times [13]. Other platforms support micro-credentials and certifications which are steadily recognized on the job market, allowing the individual to upskill or reskill throughout the course of their careers. Therefore, cloud technologies are key enabling factors to access continuous learning [4].

## Challenges

**Digital divide and connectivity issues-** One of the main factors influencing equality in the use of cloud-enabled technologies in education is still unequal internet access, especially in rural and low-income areas. Additionally, contend that a lack of access to suitable infrastructure exacerbates educational disparities in rural places [10, 19]. Disparities in access to digital devices are also represented by the digital divide. Increasing infrastructure expenditures, providing subsidies for digital devices, and assisting with community digital literacy projects are a few potential approaches [21].

**Data privacy and security concerns**- Educational institutions are fundamentally changing the way they operate as a result of the transition to cloud-computing based solutions. In a recent study, incidents of data breach, unauthorized access, and cybercrimes against educational institutions when their data is stored in the third-party server, and they found out that the risk of data breach or unauthorized access may be higher than normal [23]. The problem of data ownership for students has also been criticized. The main priority of education institutions is to provide maximum security and privacy for the data of students while adhering to the GDPR and FERPA regulations in USA [8].

**Teacher training and pedagogical integration**- The successful application of cloud computing in the teaching world depends on the preparation of the teacher. In most cases, the majority of teachers out there have a major problem with digital literacy based on OECD's global finding and do not have the pedagogical knowledge to make cloud-based platforms work effectively in their classrooms [12]. Professional development programs not only on technical skills but pedagogical approaches that will work best with cloud technologies. Educators should be able to use cloud-based resources to develop student-centered learning that promotes interactivity, and the development of critical thinking among the learners in these institutions [3, 16].

**Technical support and maintenance**- Sustaining technical services and support for cloud technology are essential, which is a very challenging task, especially for educational institutions with limited funding. In spite of the fact that cloud-based solutions generally avoid the requirement for physical infrastructure, schools remain in need of reliable IT support for the continued running of cloud services, uptime, and troubleshooting [6, 17].

**Existing educational cloud-based systems**- This comparative discussion of tools and methods for using cloud technologies to transform education, as far as accessibility, equity, and personalized learning is concerned, is presented. Comparison comprises commonly employed cloud-based tools and approaches that are being discussed in regard to features, benefits, drawbacks, and match to learning objectives [7].

## Key observations from comparative analysis

**Access to resources:** That is, cloud technology, such as LMS and cloud storage (e.g., Google Drive, Dropbox) offers strong solutions for aggregation of educational resources as well as for easy access and sharing of resources across devices and geographical limits.

The learning tools created by MOOCs are freely available and appear to be particularly beneficial to students in so-called low-resource settings [13].

**Personalized learning:** Adaptive learning platforms like Knewton and DreamBox present personalized learning paths that make content more engaging and accessible according to individual student progress [24].

The use of AI-powered educational tools (AI tutors, chatbots) provides highly personalized learning, continuously adapting to student responses and feedback, thus ensuring equity in learning [15].

**Collaboration:** Cloud-based collaborative technologies such as Google Docs and Microsoft OneDrive facilitate real-time collaboration and make peer-to-peer learning and teamwork more practical, even when participants are geographically dispersed [17].

Examples of virtual classrooms that offer synchronous, real-time instruction, overcoming geographic distance and promoting the expansion of campus-based virtual learning include Zoom and Google Meet.

**Inclusivity and equity:** Cloud-based platforms must reach students with disabilities. That is only possible by including assistive technologies—like screen readers or speech recognition applications—in the framework. Such resources should be significant for promoting just access to education and helping these groups in marginalized and deprived areas [5].

**Challenges and limitations:** The availability of Cloud-based platforms does not overcome connectivity issues as well as issues about the privacy of data. Lack of internet, specifically in rural and poor communities, has been one reason to point out inadequacies of cloud-based solutions. Secondly, there are issues to do with privacy and security over third-party servers used in the storage of confidential information regarding educational details [8, 23].

Implementation of these technologies demands significant training for teachers in their use. Professional development for incorporating cloud tools in pedagogy is something that often comes up as a topic [1, 20].

## Emerging trends and future directions of cloud-based educational systems

The potential of cloud-based educational tools and technologies is enormous, from increased accessibility and personalization to the global issue of educational equity. However, in the future, it is essential to consider the needs and opportunities for cloud technologies in education, particularly with respect to technological advancement, changes in learning environments, and the need for more inclusive and personalized education [2].

## Conclusion

Cloud computing is opening great opportunities for changing the face of education through improved accessibility, personalization of learning experiences, collaborative approaches, and cost-effective solutions. However, educators, policymakers, and institutions need to address some of the most important challenges that arise with cloud technologies, including digital divide, data privacy, teacher training, and technical support. In this regard, cloud technologies can be an important tool in building a more equitable and accessible global education system.

However, challenges such as data security, digital literacy, and infrastructural deficiencies would need to be overcome if cloud technologies are to be taken to their best potential.

## References

[1]   Al-Emran, M., & Teo, T. (2020). Do knowledge acquisition and knowledge sharing really affect e-learning adoption? an empirical study. *Education and Information Technologies*, 25(3), 1983–1998. https://doi.org/10.1007/s10639-019-10062-w.

[2]   Ali, A. (2022). An overview of cloud computing for the advancement of the e-learning process. *Journal of Theoretical and Applied Information Technology*, 100(03), 847–855. https://www.jatit.org/volumes/Vol100No3/22Vol100No3.pdf.

[3]  Akram, F., & Kumar, R. (2020). Analysis of collaborative and convenient e-learning on cloud computing. In Proceedings of International Conferences on Smart Electronics and Communication (ICOSEC), (pp. 805–808). DOI: 10.1109/ICOSEC49089.2020.9215239.

[4]  Agrawal, S. (2021). A survey on recent applications of cloud computing in education: COVID-19 perspective. *Journal of Physics: Conference Series*, 1828(1), 012076. DOI: 10.1088/1742-6596/1828/1/012076.

[5]  Castillo, N. M., Adam, T., & Haßler, B. (2022). 4. Improving the impact of educational technologies on learning within low-income contexts. In Learning, Marginalization, and Improving the Quality of Education in Low-income Countries, (Vol. 113). DOI: 10.11647/obp.0256.04.

[6]  Cheng, C.-H., & Liu, W. X. (2017). An appraisal model based on a synthetic feature selection approach for students' academic achievement. *Symmetry*, 9(11), 282. https://doi.org/10.3390/sym9110282.

[7]  Eljak, H., Osman, A., Saeed, F., & Hashem, I. A. T. (2024). E-learning-based cloud computing environment: a systematic review, challenges, and opportunities. *IEEE Access*, 12, 7329–7355. DOI: 10.1109/ACCESS.2023.3339250.

[8]  Jamison, S. G. (2019). Creating a national data privacy law for the United States. *Cybaris®, an Intellectual Property Law Review*, 10, 1. https://open.mitchellhamline.edu/cybaris/vol10/iss1/2.

[9]  Jose, G. S. S., & Christopher, C. S. (2019). Secure cloud data storage approach in e-learning systems. *Cluster Computing*, 22(S5), 12857–12862. DOI: 10.1007/s10586-018-1785-z.

[10]  Khan, H. U., Ali, F., & Nazir, S. (2022). Systematic analysis of software development in cloud computing perceptions. *Journal of Software: Evolution and Process*, 1–26. https://doi.org/10.1002/smr.2485.

[11]  Khan, M. A., & Salah, K. (2020). Cloud adoption for e-learning: Survey and future challenges. *Education and Information Technologies*, 25, 1417–1438. https://doi.org/10.1007/s10639-019-10021-5.

[12]  Li, C. (2022). The education cloud platform for digital resources with block chain under intelligent learning environment. *Creative Education*, 13, 599–608. DOI: 10.4236/ce.2022.132036.

[13]  Liu, B., Xing, W., Zeng, Y., & Wu, Y. (2021). Quantifying the influence of achievement emotions for student learning in MOOCs. *Journal of Educational Computing Research*, 59(3), 429–452. https://doi.org/10.1177/0735633120967318.

[14]  Nayar, K. B., & Kumar, V. (2018). Cost benefit analysis of cloud computing in education. *International Journal of Business Information Systems*, 27(2), 205–221. https://doi.org/10.1504/IJBIS.2018.089112.

[15]  Nguyen, A., Ngo, H. N., Hong, Y., Dang, B., & Nguyen, B. P. T. (2023). Ethical principles for artificial intelligence in education. *Education and Information Technologies*, 28, 4221–4241. https://doi.org/10.1007/s10639-022-11316-w.

[16]  Rahhali, M., Oughdir, L., Jedidi, Y., Lahmadi, Y., & Khattabi, M. Z. E. (2022). E-learning recommendation system based on cloud computing. In Proceedings of 6th International Conference Wireless Technologies, Embedded, Intelligent System, Cham, Switzerland: Springer, (pp. 89–99). doi: 10.1007/978-981-33-6893-4_9.

[17]  Sawant, S. (2021). Online collaborative learning tools and types: their key role in managing classrooms without walls. In Human-Computer Interaction and Technology Integration in Modern Society, (pp. 12–41). DOI: 10.4018/978-1-7998-5849-2.ch002.

[18]  Shukur, B. S., Ghani, M. K. A., & Burhasnuddin, M. (2019). A cloud computing framework for higher education institutes in developing countries (CCF_HEI_DC). In Intelligent and Interactive Computing. Cham, Switzerland, (pp. 397–409). DOI: 10.1007/978-981-13-6031-2_24.

[19]  Showalter, D., Hartman, S. L., Johnson, J., & Klein, B. (2019). Why Rural Matters 2018-2019: The Time is Now. A Report of the Rural School and Community Trust. Rural School and Community Trust. https://eric.ed.gov/?id=ED604580.

[20] Thavi, R., Jhaveri, R., Narwane, V., Gardas, B., & Jafari Navimipour, N. (2024). Role of cloud computing technology in the education sector. *Journal of Engineering, Design and Technology*, 22(1), 182–213. DOI: 10.1108/JEDT-08-2021-0417.

[21] Wu, W., & Plakhtii, A. (2021). E-learning based on cloud computing. *International Journal of Emerging Technologies in Learning (iJET)*, 16(10), 4–17. Kassel, Germany: International Journal of Emerging Technology in Learning. DOI: https://doi.org/10.3991/ijet.v16i10.18579.

[22] Zhang, G., Li, J., & Hao, L. (2015). Cloud Computing and its application in big data processing of distance higher education. *International Journal of Emerging Technologies in Learning (iJET)*, 10(8), 55–58. DOI: 10.3991/ijet.v10i8.5280.

[23] Zhu, J. J., Tuo, L., You, Y., Fei, Q., & Thomson, M. (2024). A preemptive and curative solution to mitigate data breaches: corporate social responsibility as a double layer of protection. *Journal of Marketing Research*, 61(4), 778–801. https://doi.org/10.1177/00222437231218969.

[24] Sahu, T. N., Sen, N., & Maity, S. (2024). Revisiting, Reframing and Recovering Learning Loss: An Arched Impression on Primary Education During Covid Epoch. *Education and Urban Society*, 57(3), 217–244. https://doi.org/10.1177/00131245241293141

# 36 Object detection using YOLOv8 with custom dataset preparation

*Sahil Mehta[a], Kshamta Mathur[b], Sakshi Godse[c] and Rashmi Patel[d]*

Mukesh Patel School of Technology Management and Engineering, (MPSTME), Shri Vile Parle Kelavani Mandal's Narsee Monjee Institute of Management Studies, Mumbai, Maharashtra, India

## Abstract

Object detection is essential in many applications, such as safety systems and surveillance. The goal of this project is to apply the state-of-the-art object recognition model YOLOv8 to a specific dataset designed for emergency collision avoidance systems. To meet YOLOv8's format requirements, the dataset was hand labelled and cleaned up, capturing things such as vehicles, people walking, and obstacles in an array of different scenarios. Additional data and methods of transfer learning were used in order to enhance the model's performance. Experiments show that the model has a mean average precision (mAP), which is of [0.43], indicating that it is precise and efficient. The real-time detection capabilities of the device may lead to its usage in comprehensive safety frameworks. Additional studies will look at more improvements and adapt the principle to edge devices for better real-time processing.

**Keywords:** Bounding box, data augmentation, data preprocessing, dataset splitting (train/test/validation), image labelling, object classes

## Introduction

The application of artificial intelligence (AI) in the automotive industry resulted in significant improvements in safety systems. The term "real-accident identification" is an essential element of automobile safety since it may avert further harm while immediately contacting rescue workers. The objective of this project is to build an accident detection system that examines and identifies accidents utilizing video input and artificially intelligent (AI) models, especially YOLOv8, convolutional neural networks (CNN), Random Forest (RF), and Logistic Regression (LR). Using the YOLOv8 model to identify objects in real time, critical features such as rapid movements, collisions, and other irregularities that lead to an accident have been recognized by the system. After detection proof, the CNN, RF, and LR models further examine data to classify and assess the likelihood of an accident, improving the system's accuracy and responsiveness. The main focus of this project is to give a tool that has video-based accident detection that can quickly detect occurrence and provide quick alerts in a short duration [1, 5]. In place of present sensors, it moves towards a sensor-based approach, promoting vehicle security by providing accurate accident detection using computer vision and ML techniques [7]. The crucial model that emerged in this study is YOLO. YOLO is used for real-world environment detection, allowing the car to process

[a]sahilmehta0502@gmail.com, [b]kshamta.mathur@nmims.edu, [c]sakshisgodse05@gmail.com, [d]rashmi.patel@nmims.edu

DOI: 10.1201/9781003716648-36

a single frame in a forward pass and make quick decisions [1, 3]. Object detection plays a critical role in self-driving cars as it enables quick responses based on real-time environmental data [1, 4]. The most recent advanced developments in identifying objects in a specific area of computer vision have been smoothly integrated into YOLOv5, YOLOv7, and YOLOv8, and their procedures are explained in this paper [1]. The brief description gives the overall fundamental significance of detecting objects, fitting completely within the main body of the research. The clarification of object detection adds importance within diverse contexts, such as vehicle recognition across different scales and environments, emphasizing its multiple uses [3]. Using a customized dataset for YOLOv8 training, the study has executed efficient real-time detection and analysis of diverse road users. The algorithm also provides multi-object detection, which optimizes computational resources, ensuring accuracy in complex traffic scenarios, contributing to the safety and reliability of autonomous vehicles [5]. As artificial intelligence and computer vision dynamically evolve, the proposed YOLOv8 detection model highlights the ability to specialize in object detection and underscores the importance of exploring new fields of detection [1, 8]. The use of transfer learning and integration of data from multiple weather datasets was suggested to improve YOLOv8-based object detection in adverse weather conditions. For identifying key objects on roads in inclement weather, two free datasets—ACDC and DAWN—were combined. Training weights were collected from the dataset and merged versions and subsets were created based on features [7]. For the identification of PPE worn by employees, the Safety Helmet and Vest (SHEL5K) and Color Helmet and Vest (CHV) datasets, which contain 5,000 images, were used. These datasets include eight object classifications, such as goggles, vests, and helmets. Following the dataset's division into training, testing, and validation subsets, various YOLOv8 models were assessed using measures like mAP50, precision, and recall. Notably, YOLOv8x and YOLOv8l excelled in PPE detection, particularly in recognizing person and vest categories [2]. To minimize the spatial information sparsity caused by downsampling and increase the effectiveness of feature extraction, the model incorporates the Receptive Field Convolutional Block Attention Module (RFCBAM) into the backbone network. Additionally, a novel neck architecture called the Balanced Spatial and Semantic Information Fusion Pyramid Network (BSSI-FPN) was developed for multi-scale feature fusion [9]. The Insulator Defect Image Dataset (IDID), representing power line insulators, contains a large class depicting undamaged insulators and two relatively small classes depicting different types of damaged insulators [4]. The integration of YOLOv8 for object, person, and weapon detection with audio analysis, alongside distance estimation and email notifications, marks a substantial leap in security surveillance technology, offering swift threat detection and coordinated responses [6]. A YOLOv8-based underwater object detection framework was designed to address challenges posed by the underwater environment, including noise, blur, color distortion, and illumination variation [10]. The dataset used was initially small, but data augmentation techniques and an increase in the number of training images improved their robustness. The YOLOv8s model was trained for 75 epochs, resulting in a 23% increase in mAP@0.5. The experiment evaluated the accuracy improvement achieved by training the modified dataset using the bag-of-freebies technique [11]. The development of object detection methods and the benefits of deep learning-based approaches over traditional methods have been widely studied. In intelligent transportation systems, applications such as vehicle identification, localization, tracking, and counting within traffic scenarios have gained substantial traction [1, 5]. Initially, the model differentiates motorcycle riders who are wearing safety helmets from those who are not. Riders without helmets are marked, and their number plates are processed using Optical Character Recognition (OCR) [2]. The utilization of 3D vision techniques in the automation of logistical operations has also been studied. Deep learning models such as YOLOv8 and Roboflow-trained object and keypoint detection models have been used to create a 3D vision system. The method includes outcome analysis, deep learning-based model building, and data collection and annotation [8].

## Proposed Work

### Objective of the work
1.   Train YOLOv8 on a custom dataset.
2.   Detect specific objects from videos and images.
3.   Evaluate the model's performance on new data.

### Detailed problem statement
This research aims to provide a precise object detection method for a unique dataset by leveraging YOLOv8, a new platform for real-time object recognition. The aim is to develop a model capable of effectively tracking and recognizing items in pictures and videos while attaining remarkable speed and accuracy

### Software requirements
Google Colab is used for code. It is a well-liked IDE among developers due to its exceptional debugging features, lightning-fast performance, applicability for machine-learning applications, and ease of use. Like Google Sheets or Docs, many people can work on the same notebook at once.

### System implementation
Using a pre-trained YOLO v8 model, the developed system analyses video input from wearable devices to continually track and identify occurrences. This identifying system enables real-time distinction between drivers, passengers, and hazardous accident conditions. These detections are frequently reviewed by the system to assess the likelihood of an accident. Upon cleaning and manufacturing, the data is used to train different types of machine learning models. The application selects its most accurate model and uses it to forecast future incidents. Training modifies the model's parameters to improve performance and produce accurate predictions. In order bring notice to those designated items, labelled boxes and boxes featuring the terms "car," "person," or accident.

## Experimentation and Results

Real-time recognition of objects using a YOLOv8 model was used, with the emphasis on automobiles, pedestrians, and potential crash events. A broad variety of photos and videos collected via public databases were employed to train the model. Techniques for data augmentation were used to improve the model's ability for generalization. The trained YOLOv8 model was employed to create a system that continuously analyzes footage from connected

*Figure 36.1* Car detection with bounding box value
Source: Author

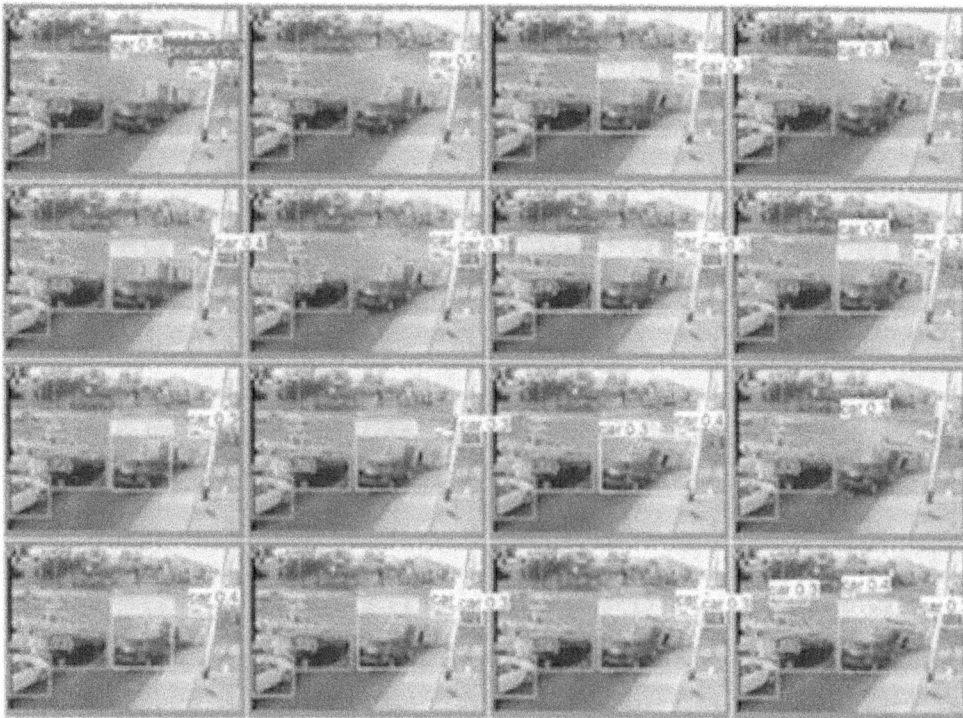

*Figure 36.2* Accident frame object detection
Source: Author

devices. As shown in Figure 36.1, the YOLOv8 model successfully detects vehicles in a given video frame using bounding boxes. Real-time monitoring of the environment has been rendered possible by the use of frames and tags to indicate saw objects (Figure 36.2). The system's performance has been assessed using metrics like precision, recall, and mAP. According to the results, the simulator was able to precisely pinpoint objects of interest even under challenging conditions. Figure 36.3 displays the F1-Confidence curve, illustrates how the model's F1-score varies with various confidence thresholds. The precision of

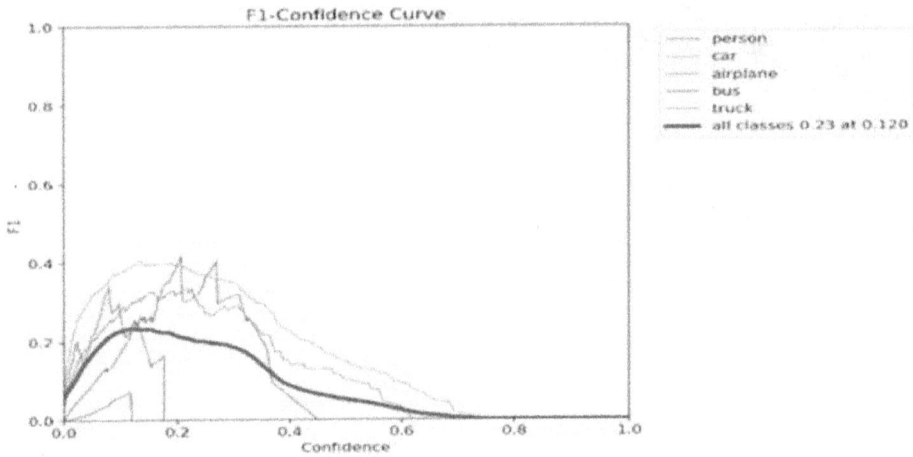

*Figure 36.3* F1-Condfidence curve
Source: Author

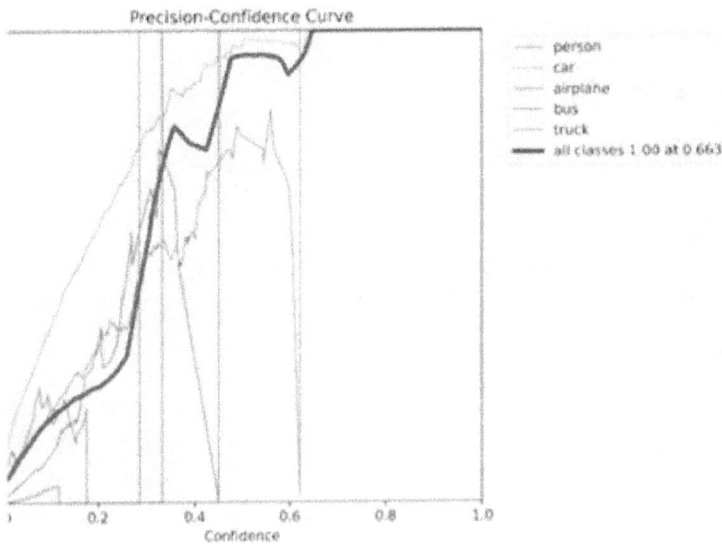

*Figure 36.4* F1-Precision confidence curve
Source: Author

the YOLOv8 model fluctuates with confidence scores, as depicted by the precision-confidence curve in Figure 36.4.

*Data collection and pre-processing*
Starting with data collection which is the first process in this project and undoubtedly the most important one. The dataset obtained from Kaggle which is video and image files which

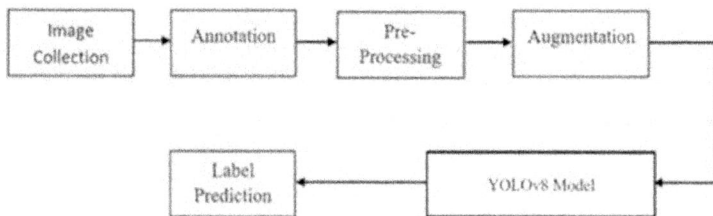

*Figure 36.5* Yolov8 based accident detection system flow
Source: Author

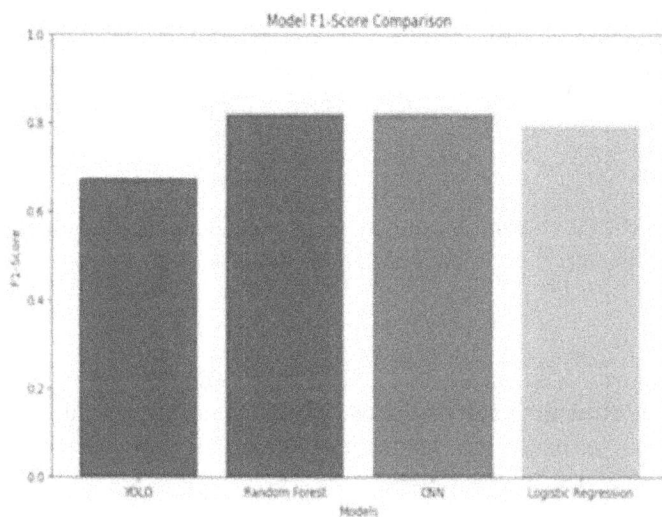

*Figure 36.6* Bar chart: Object detection model performance
Source: Author

```
Classification Report:
              precision    recall  f1-score   support

           0       0.95      0.95      0.95     60253
           1       0.94      0.94      0.94     52565

    accuracy                           0.95    112818
   macro avg       0.95      0.95      0.95    112818
weighted avg       0.95      0.95      0.95    112818


Confusion Matrix:

Confusion Matrix :
[[57123  3130]
 [ 3011 49554]]
```

*Figure 36.7* Classification report of the algorithm
Source: Author

are used to detect accidents. The video files are unlabelled. The images files are labelled with objects like person, car, and motorcycleaccidentsaccidentsaccidentsaccidentslabelled files are used to develop accident detection model (Figure 36.5). Then these video files were converted to frames. Then each frame has its own label which is used for detection of objects.

*Model training and evaluation*

Figure 36.6 displays a bar graph that contrasts the F1-Score of four various machine learning models: CNN, RF, LR, and Yolo. The various models appear on the horizontal axis, and the F1-score, which varies between 0 to 1, is shown on the vertical axis. The RF model surpasses the other three models based on F1 score, based on the chart. classification report and a confusion matrix appear in the supplied graphic in Figure 36.7. The classification report's high precision, recall, and F1-Scores for both classes (0 and 1) exhibit excellent performance in determining both positive and negative cases. The model's entire accuracy of 0.95 demonstrates its effectiveness. The misreading provides solid evidence for this conclusion.

## Conclusion

Successfully prepared and trained YOLOv8 on a custom dataset. Achieved real-time object detection. Future scope: Deploy the model for real-world applications.

## Future Scope

**Edge device deployment:** Optimize YOLOv8 for deployment on edge devices to enhance real-time processing capabilities. **Real-time alert systems:** Implement an automated alert system integrated with emergency response services for immediate action upon accident detection.

## References

[1]   Afrin, Z., Tabassum, F., Kibria, H. B., Imam, M. R., & Hasan, M. R. (2023). YOLOv8 based object detection for self-driving cars. In 2023 26th International Conference on Computer and Information Technology (ICCIT), (pp. 1—6). IEEE.

[2]   Barlybayev, A., Amangeldy, N., Kurmetbek, B., Krak, I., Razakhova, B., Tursynova, N., et al. (2024). Personal protective equipment detection using YOLOv8 architecture on object detection benchmark datasets: a comparative study. *Cogent Engineering*, 11(1), 2333209.

[3]   Ganesan, M., Chokkalingam, B., & Kandhasamy, S. (2024). Implementation of different road user detection with custom dataset using deep learning algorithm for autonomous vehicle. In 2024 IEEE 4th International Conference on Sustainable Energy and Future Electric Transportation (SEFET), (pp. 1–7). IEEE.

[4]   Goudah, A. A., Jarofka, M., El-Habrouk, M., Schramm, D., & Dessouky, Y. G. (2023). Object detection in inland vessels using combined trained and pretrained models of YOLO8. *Advances in Computing & Engineering*, 3(2), 64–73.

[5]   Gupta, H. S., Sameer, M., & Ahmad, G. (2023). Real-time vehicle detection using yolov8 and data augmentation approach. In 2023 IEEE Fifth International Conference on Advances in Electronics, Computers and Communications (ICAECC), (pp. 1–6). IEEE.

[6] Jyothsna, V., Alle, C., Kurnutala, R., Ganesh, K. N., KushalKarthik, K. R., & Pydala, B. (2024). YOLOv8-based person detection, distance monitoring, speech alerts, and weapon identification with email notifications. In 2024 International Conference on Expert Clouds and Applications (ICOECA), (pp. 288–296). IEEE.

[7] Kumar, D., & Muhammad, N. (2023). Object detection in adverse weather for autonomous driving through data merging and YOLOv8. *Sensors*, 23(20), 8471.

[8] Li, Y., Li, Q., Pan, J., Zhou, Y., Zhu, H., Wei, H., et al. (2024). SOD-YOLO: small-object-detection algorithm based on improved YOLOv8 for UAV images. *Remote Sensing*, 16(16), 3057.

[9] Safaldin, M., Zaghden, N., & Mejdoub, M. (2024). An Improved YOLOv8 to Detect Moving Objects. IEEE Access. 1–1. 10.1109/ACCESS.2024.3393835.

[10] Thakur, A., Dubey, A. K., Vashisth, R., Tomar, I., & Chauhan, S. (2023). An Improved Underwater Object Detection based on YOLOv8 Segmentation. Preprint. DOI:10.13140/RG.2.2.14007.53925

[11] Tomaszewski, M., & Osuchowski, J. (2020). Effectiveness of Data Resampling in Mitigating Class Imbalance for Object Detection. In 3rd International Workshop on Information Technologies: Theoretical and Applied Problems (ITTAP-2023) (CEUR Workshop Proceedings, Vol. 3628, ISSN 1613-0073). Ternopil, Ukraine.

For Product Safety Concerns and Information please contact our EU
representative GPSR@taylorandfrancis.com
Taylor & Francis Verlag GmbH, Kaufingerstraße 24, 80331 München, Germany